FRENCH GRAMMAR

THE EASY WAY

Fabienne-Sophie Chauderlot, Ph.D
California Polytechnic State University

BARRON'S

ABOUT THE AUTHOR

Fabienne-Sophie Chauderlot has taught all courses of French language and philosophy for twenty years at California Polytechnic State University, Wayne State University, the University of Puerto Rico, the University of California San Diego and Riverside, Mesa Community College, and San Diego State. Professor Chauderlot has received various awards for her excellence in teaching.

Dr. Chauderlot earned an M.A. (Maîtrise) in American Literature at the Université des Lettres et Sciences Humaines as well as an MBA (D.E.S.S.) at the Institut d'Administration des Entreprises in Aix-en-Provence, while she lived in France and was also studying philosophy. She then earned an M.A. in French, and a Ph.D. in Critical Theory from the University of California, San Diego. Her academic expertise is in Eighteenth Century literature and Enlightenment philosophy, Twentieth Century post-structuralist literary critique and philosophy, as well as Women's Studies.

© Copyright 2004 by Barron's Educational Series, Inc.

All inquiries should be addressed to:
Barron's Educational Series, Inc.
250 Wireless Boulevard
Hauppauge, New York 11788
www.barronseduc.com

Library of Congress Catalog Card No.: 2003052486

ISBN-13: 978-0-7641-2435-8
ISBN-10: 0-7641-2435-8

Library of Congress Cataloging-in-Publication Data
Chauderlot, Fabienne S.
    French grammar the easy way / Fabienne S. Chauderlot.
        p.   cm.—(Easy way)
    Includes index.
    ISBN 0-7641-2435-8
        1. French language—Grammar.   2. French language—
    Textbooks for foreign speakers—English.   I. Title.   II. Series.
PC2112.C43 2004
448.2′421–dc21

                                                        2003052486

PRINTED IN THE UNITED STATES OF AMERICA
9 8 7 6 5 4 3 2

CONTENTS

PREFACE

So you have decided to learn a foreign language? Congratulations! It opens unlimited opportunities to discover new things, rethink old ones, and meet different people. You will become more interested in your part of the world and more appealing to the rest of it.

If you think about it, learning a language is not something new to you; you have already done it. Remember when all you could say was "areu-areu" (that's how French babies talk) and when you looked at Dr. Seuss' books, all you could see were spots on a page? Reading and looking at French texts may feel the same way at times, but there is a difference—you are older, your life is more complicated, and your head is full of all kinds of information. You can no longer dedicate all your energy to learn, as we say in French, the "b—a—ba" of communication. And in terms of French grammar, there is a lot of data. If you had nothing else to do, like when you were a child, you could learn through repetition. Or you can try also to rely on what you have acquired since childhood: logical thinking.

FRENCH GRAMMAR THE EASY WAY was written with you in mind: young adults who have a lot of energy and dedication, many things to do, but not as much time as they wished to dedicate to each one of them. So my postulate is that, instead of relying on memory, practice, and immersion, as you could when you were a child, what would be helpful is a solid understanding of the mechanisms of the French language. Although they sometimes feel like it, rules were not invented to torture kids. Rules generally have a good reason for being. Once you can see it, it will make so much sense that learning them will become a smooth and painless process.

I propose, therefore, that we follow the French philosopher Descartes' approach: to "demolish everything completely and start again right from the foundations." Let us begin with a clean slate (*tabula rasa*, as they call it in Latin): temporarily set aside what you have memorized so far and embark on a journey of understanding.

This book divides the grammar rules in as many parts as possible and takes you from the simplest point to the most complex as methodically as Descartes recommended in his famous *Discourse on the Method*. Eventually you will have reviewed the system that any language forms, in its entirety. You will develop a control of the language based on an analytical presentation of all its components and an illustrated presentation of their interaction. This is guaranteed to support your understanding, help your memorizing, and facilitate your own sentences, recreating and making all efforts as enjoyable as empowering.

For example, you will not be asked to remember that "the past participle agrees with the direct object if the **passé composé** is conjugated with the auxiliary verb *avoir*, and the direct object is placed before the past participle, but the past participle agrees with the subject if it is conjugated with *être*"—first, because this rule that generations of French and foreign students have learned for decades is simply not true; second, because no one can remember that kind of convoluted language these days, and they should not have to: we simply have too much to do and too little time for this "et patati et patata" (*blah-blah-blah*). So what this book will show you is what agreement means, how the **passé** composé is formed, what it has in common with the participe **passé** (can you guess?), why this verb form should agree with anything in the first place, and why it should also be very selective about when and with what it agrees. Past participles, like moods and many other French words or concepts, are very picky. However, when you understand why they should be so, remembering when to make them agree with the direct object complement (regardless of the auxiliary verb), or how to use them altogether, will be very easy.

My wager is that, if the reasons for the rules are explained to you and you are shown how they participate in the progressive generation of meaning, it will not be a problem if you forget them. You will be able to logically reconstruct the rule by putting together the pieces of the puzzle that you do remember and filling in the blanks deductively.

No learning is ever easy—French grammar, roller-blading, desktop publishing, or making *choux à la crème* (cream puffs)—whatever the object of knowledge, the process is always slow and demanding. But this method makes learning or reviewing French grammar a lot easier and quite a lot of fun.

Complementary explanations and practice activities can be found on-line at:
http://www.alariviera.com/FrenchGrammarPractice

Acknowledgments

This book is the result of years of reciprocal teaching to and learning from all my students from San Diego State, Mesa College, the University of California at San Diego and at Riverside, the University of Puerto Rico, Wayne State University, California Polytechnic State University, and the students from across the United States who trusted me with their vacations and embarked on my Wayne au Soleil and À la Riviera study abroad programs. Teaching is not a job; it is a vocation, and, thanks to you all, it has never stopped being my passion.

Thank you also to these professors who taught me about learning and teaching and living *not* the easy way: Jean-Paul Eyrard, Danièle Guéraud, Hélène Christol, Nadia Rigaud, William A. O'Brien, Luce Giard, James Watson, Eve Bannet, Jacques Derrida, Don Spinelli, Louise Jefferson, Linda Bomstad, Paul Miklowitz, Judy Saltzman.

And a special *Salut les Copains*, to Nandita, Kenneth, John, and Jeff, and Indra, and Dan, and Caroline, and Melissa, and Jim; and to the first students I will never forget, James, Valérie, Olin, Fraser. If you ever pick up this book, may this bring you warm memories of our youth.

All my tenderness to my little "sisters," Heather and Naomi; their learning French allowed me to meet one of the kindest women ever. This is in Memory of my American mother Connie Frakes.

My love to my friends, Brigitte, Jessica, and Papy Pascal.

All my gratitude goes to Edward P. Ross, for his patient support, precious encouragement, and unalterable genuine and rare kindness. And "miaou!" to our Tofa, Vanille, Fripouille, and Cléa, whose constant sitting, walking over the keyboard, standing, lying on my books, cleaning, scratching my notes, and purring on my desk made long hours of looking at a screen not the easiest but the most joyful way of writing a grammar book.

Merci encore, et encore, et toujours à mes parents,
Georgia et Michel,
et à ma yaya Sophie,
avec tout mon amour,
San Luis Obispo, Californie, le 11 Août 2003

Chapter 1

PRELIMINARY CONCEPTS

Words
Basic Notions

Présentation	Overview
La Langue	Language is composed of an endless number of combinations of words organized together in sentences according to grammatical rules.
Les Mots La Nature La Fonction	Words have a: • **Nature: what a word is by itself, prior to being inserted in a sentence** Nature of Words in the nominal group: Noun - Article - Adjective - Pronoun Nature of Words in the verbal group: Verbs - Adverbs Nature of Words linking words and groups: Preposition - Conjunction • **Function: what the word does in the context of the sentence** Ex: Function of a Noun: Subject or Complement.
Les Catégories de Verbes	There are 3 categories of verbs: • **General Verbs:** express actions, can be used by themselves or in combinations. • **Auxiliary Verbs:** can be used by themselves or to help form compound tenses. • **Modal Verbs:** can be used by themselves or in combination with other verbs to express a wider range of meaning.
Les Caractéristiques du Verbe	Verbs have 3 characteristics needed to choose the right form of their conjugation: 1. **Person** = the subject: who does the action, 2. **Tense** = the time: when is the action performed, 3. **Mood** = the concreteness: how real the action is.
Les Personnes	There are 6 persons that rule over the right form of their conjugation: • **3 Persons singular designating 1 being or object** = 1st, 2nd, 3rd person singular, • **3 Persons plural designating 2+ beings or objects** = 1st, 2nd, 3rd person plural. • **The 2nd person plural - Vous - also designates a single but important person.**

Les Temps	There are 2 types of tenses to designate past, present, and future actions: • **Simple tenses** = formed with 1 element: the stem of the verb + an ending, • **Compound tenses** = combines 2 components: an auxiliary + the past participle. There are different sets of endings to identify each tense.
Les Modes	There are 5 types of moods to specify if the action is real, potential, or only virtual: • **Infinitive mood** = the action is only virtual, not performed yet, • **Indicative mood** = the action is real, performed in the past, present, or future, • **Imperative mood** = a command has been given, but the action is not performed yet, • **Conditional mood** = the action depends upon another one to be performed first, • **Subjunctive mood** = the action depends on someone else's decision. Each mood includes some of the various tenses.
La Phrase = Une Structure	A sentence is first an underlying structure pre-organizing meaning, then a series of juxtaposed words chosen to express an infinite number of situations.
	The basic French structure is: Nominal Group Subject + Verbal Group + Nominal Group Complement

Les Deux Types de Phrases	The two types of sentences are:
	• **Simple Sentence**
	Composed of 1 clause - that is only one conjugated verb, thus 1 clause: called Independent clause,
	• **Compound Sentence**
	Composed of 2 or more clauses - that is 2 or more conjugated verbs.
	Possible combinations are:
	  1. 2 or more independent clauses coordinated
	  2. 1 Principal and 1 or more conjunctive subordinate clauses
	  3. 1 Principal and 1 or more relative subordinate clauses
	  4. 1 Principal and subordinate clauses both conjunctive and relative

La Proposition	A clause is made of 1 conjugated verb. Other elements (subject, complements...) are possible but not mandatory to form a clause. There are as many clauses as there are Conjugated Verbs (CV): Ex: 2 CV = 2 clauses; 6 CV = 6 clauses

Mots de Jonction	Linking words are:
	• **Conjunctions**
	  1. of Coordination: Mais, ou, et, donc, or, ni, car (*But, or, and, in fact, therefore, neither, for*)
	  2. of Subordination: [...] que, comme, si, quand (*that, as, if, when*)
	• **Relative pronouns**
	  1. Simple: Qui, que, dont, où (*Who, whom/that, whose, where*)
	  2. Compound: Lequel..., Auquel..., Duquel... (*Which/whom, to which/whom, of which/whom*)

Conjonctions de Coordination	• **Conjunctions of Coordination link:** 2 or n **Independent coordinated Clauses**
Conjonctions de Subordination	• **Conjunctions of Subordination link:** 1 Principal Clause + **Conjunctive Subordinate Clause(s)**
Pronom Relatif	• **Relative Pronouns link:** 1 Principal Clause + **Relative Subordinate Clause(s)**
La Proposition Principale	**The Principal Clause** can form a sentence—start with a capital letter, end with a period—and still make sense by itself, without any other clause.
La Proposition Subordonnée	**The subordinate clause** cannot be used by itself if it is separated from the principal clause. Without the principal, the words that remain do not form a correct or meaningful sentence on their own, which is why they are subordinate to the other clause, that is principal.
L'Alphabet Phonétique Basic Phonetic Symbols	A particular alphabet has been designed to translate sounds into standard signs. It is important to know it since the beauty of the sound may lead to variations in grammatical rules.

Sounds

Phonetics

Pronunciation

At first glance, French grammar has little to do with phonetics. The former imposes rules on the behavior of words. The latter tracks patterns in pronunciation and provides a series of symbols to represent the most common sounds.

Verification

In French, however, phonetics and pronunciation are strangely connected because grammar sometimes bends its rules to allow the language to sound better. Remember: aesthetics is always important.

Having a basic understanding of French sounds, then, and keeping them in memory while reading about grammar, will help you understand certain grammatical exceptions. When it is the case, we will indicate the phonetic phenomenon that explains the exception.

The sounds [ø] and [ɛ̃] are very difficult to pronounce one after the other (see chart, below). Try it and you will see how hard it is on your mouth. Moreover they sound ugly. The **e** is thus dropped and is replaced by an apostrophe, which allows the **d** sound to flow into the vowel more easily, as in:

une part *de un* gateau (**a piece of cake**) becomes une part *d'un* gateau

TABLE OF SYMBOLS
(Basic French Phonetic Alphabet Symbols)

Voyelles (Vowels)	Example	Consonnes (Consonants)	Example
[i]	ici, lit, il, dimanche	[p]	papier, pas, parapluie
[e]	bébé, télévision, et	[b]	bébé, bar, babar
[ɛ]	belle, paix, vrai	[t]	tentative, tétu, toi
[a]	papa, chat, car	[d]	Dordogne, dedans, dix
[y]	tu, vu, bureau, bus	[k]	coquille, crabe, kilo
[ø]	peu, deux, dangereux	[g]	gorille, guillotine, Guy
[œ]	peur, heure, couleur	[f]	face, fille, affaires
[u]	tout, vous, cours	[v]	vive, évasé, vingt
[o]	trop, cadeau, beaux	[s]	salle, saucisse, sucre
[ɔ]	donne, or, alors	[z]	zodiaque, zoo, zut!
[ə]	le, petit, devoir	[ʃ]	chiche, chaine, mache
[ɛ̃]	un	[ʒ]	gitan, sage, à, jeun
[ã]	dans, quand, jambe	[l]	les, lola, Lancelot
[õ]	bon, thon, allons	[r]	rare, areu-areu!, reine
Semivoyelles		[m]	marmite, moi, mime
[j]	yeux	[n]	nonne, Anne, ni . . . ni
[ɥ]	lui	[ñ]	vigne, campagne
[w]	loué	[ŋ]	parking, marketing

Chapter 2

THE NATURE OF NOUNS

The Nature of Nouns

A noun is a word that designates
- a person
- an animal
- a concrete object
- an abstract notion
- an action
- a place

Nouns can be classified according to different characteristics of the person or thing they designate.

CLASSIFICATION OF NOUNS: OVERVIEW		
	Nom Propres (Proper Nouns)	**Noms Communs (Common Nouns)**
Animate	Human	
	Philippe Les Fournier M. Chatelet	Mon ami *(My friend)* Une famille *(A family)* Le philosophe *(The philosopher)*
	Animals	
	Tofa, Vanille, Fripouille, Cléa Ussia Titi	Mes chattes *(My cats)* Ma chienne *(My dog)* Le canari *(The canary)*
Inanimate	La France, Les États-Unis Un Monet Des Cartier	Des pays *(Countries)* Un tableau *(A painting)* Des bijoux *(Jewels)*

> **NOTE** The distinction between animate and inanimate nouns is the key factor when choosing a personal pronoun to replace them.
>
> Je pense souvent **à** mon père—Je pense souvent **à lui**.
> (*I often think about my father—I often think about him.*)
>
> Je pense souvent **à** mon enfance—J'**y** pense.
> (*I often think about my childhood—I often think about it.*)

Nouns are simple to learn but to be used correctly, you need to pay attention to three factors:

1. The gender of the noun—**le genre**
2. The number of the noun, and if it is plural how to form this plural—**le nombre**
3. The function of the noun—**la fonction**

Gender

There are only two genders in French: the feminine and the masculine. But the masculine third person singular of a pronoun is also used to designate neuter or impersonal objects or people as in **on dit** (*they say*), **c'est normal** (*that's normal*), **il était une fois** (*once upon a time*).

> **TIP BOX**
> Always learn a noun with its article. When wondering, "what's the French word for table?" do not say "table," but instead say *LA table*.

Certain categories of nouns are mostly feminine or masculine. Chances are, though, they all have at least one exception. Use the following groups only as guidelines in case you cannot verify the gender in a dictionary.

Generally Feminine Nouns

- *Êtres femelles (Female Workers, Animals, Beings)*

     la boulangère, une chienne, la fillette, une épouse . . . *(the baker, a dog, the little girl, a wife)*

Exception! Feminine forms that did not exist in the past:

     la professeur, la pompière, la mairesse *(the teacher, the fireman, the mayor)*

Today, numerous professions are now feminized:

> la ministre, la pilote, la doctoresse, etc. *(the minister, the pilot, the doctor)*

- *Pays, Fleuves, et fruits en -e (Countries, Rivers, Fruit Ending in "-e")*

> La France, la Seine, la cerise, la rose . . .

Exception! le Mexique, le Rhône

- *Commerces (Shops and Trades)*

> la boulangerie, la peinture, la physique, la géographie *(bakery, painting, physics, geography)*

Exception! Le garage

- *Noms en -tion/-té/-ense (Nouns Ending in -tion/-té/-ense)*

> -tion: la récréation
> -té: Liberté-Égalité-Fraternité
> -ense/anse or -ence/ance: une élégance, la conscience
> -e + double consonant + e: la messe, la pelle, la mallette, la flemme
> *(mass, shovel, attaché case, laziness)*

Exception! le pâté, le silence, le squelette *(pâté, silence, skeleton)*

- *Noms abstraits en -eur (Abstract Nouns Ending in -eur)*

> La paleur, la chaleur, la peur, la largeur, la couleur, la douceur *(paleness, heat, fear, width, color, softness)*

Exception! le bonheur *(happiness)*

Generally Masculine Nouns

- *Êtres mâles (Male Workers, Animals, Beings)*

> le boulanger, le docteur, un lion, un garçon, le mari *(butcher, doctor, lion, boy, husband)*

Exceptions! Many animals have a feminine noun that designates both male and female creatures:

> la souris, la baleine, la girafe *(mouse, whale, giraffe)*

- *Calendrier (Days, Months, Seasons of the Year)*

  le lundi, un avril, le printemps *(Monday, April, spring)*

- *Langues (Languages)*

  le Français, le Japonais, le Suédois, le Swahéli *(French, Japanese, Swedish, Swahili)*

- *Arbres et buissons (Trees and Shrubs)*

  le chêne, le roseau, le pommier, le palmier *(oak, reed, apple tree, palm tree)*

- *Pays, fleuves, et fruits (Countries, Rivers, and Fruit not ending in -e)*

  le Maroc, le Portugal, le Gabon, le Brésil, le Mississippi, le Nil *(Marocco, Portugal, Gabon, Brazil, the Mississippi, the Nile)*

  le citron, l'avocat, le raisin *(lemon, lawyer/avocado, grape)*

Exception! le Mexique, le Rhône, le gingembre *(Mexico, the Rhone, ginger)*

- *Mots anglais (Most English Imported Nouns)*

  le baseball, le marketing, le shopping, le web, le surfer, le pull

Exception! une interview

- *Mots utilisés comme noms (Most Other Parts of Speech Used as Nouns)*

  le déjeuner, le bleu, un oui ou un non, le vrai ou le faux *(lunch, blue, a yes or a no, true or false)*

Exception! Adjectives and participles may be both: **le passant—la passante, le nouveau—la nouvelle, le jeté—la jetée** *(the passerby, the new boy in school, the news, the throw, the pier)*

- *Noms en -sme / -ment / -eau (Nouns Ending in -sme / -ment / -eau)*

  -asme/-isme: le sarcasme, le pessimisme, le socialisme, le marasme *(sarcasm, pessimism, socialism, depression)*

  -eau: le bateau, le chapeau, le sceau *(boat, hat, seal)*

  -ment: le gouvernement, le désarmement, un sentiment *(government, disarmament, feeling)*

Exception! la peau, la jument *(skin, mare)*

Think of and list other exceptions to these categories.

_____

_____

_____

Feminine and Masculine Nouns

Certain nouns are used in both genders and may have different meanings. Here are a few examples:

Mots au Masculin	Mots au Féminin
le crêpe (*fabric*)	**la crêpe** (*French pancake*)
le faux (*forgery*)	**la faux** (*a scythe*)
le mémoire (*a reminder note, a souvenir book*)	**la mémoire** (*memory*)
le mort (*the dead*)	**la mort** (*death*)
le moule (*the mold*)	**la moule** (*a mussel*)
le mode (*mood, method*)	**la mode** (*fashion*)
le somme (*a nap*)	**la somme** (*the total*)
le tour (*a trick*)	**la tour** (*the tower*)
le poste (*a TV or radio set*)	**la poste** (*the post office*)
le vase (*a vase*)	**la vase** (*silt*)

NOTE Although foreigners often associate an ending in **e** as a sign of the feminine, this is not valid for nouns. **E** is the most commonly used letter in French, which is why there are many more **e** tiles in the French Scrabble game than in the English one.

le collège, le musée, le spectacle, un article, le frère, un arbre, le livre, le ministre, le rêve, un poème (***college, museum, show, article, brother, tree, book, minister, dream, poem***)

Number

> **NOTE** Although the use of the singular and plural is quite similar in French and in English, there are some cases in which they differ: French tends to use the singular then.
>
> **On Sundays,** I used to eat a croissant.
> > **Le dimanche,** je mangeais un croissant.
>
> I see a lot of men with hats on their head**s**.
> > Je vois beaucoup d'hommes qui ont **un chapeau** sur **la tête**.
>
> *In the first example, the singular is always used for neuter or generic cases, as in "every Sunday" without particular distinction.*
> > *In the second example, the French language prioritizes logical reasoning—there might be a lot of men but they have only one head and can therefore wear only one hat. This is what "Men with hats on their heads" evokes to a French speaker:*
>
>

Simple Nouns

Contrary to gender, one can always use a singular noun in the plural, or vice versa. A few points are worth noting:

- There is no noun in French that cannot be used in the plural, but certain nouns cannot be used in the singular.

  > les ténèbres, les obsèques, les fiançailles, les moeurs *(darkness, the funeral, the engagement, customs)*

- A few nouns have a different meaning according to their number.

  > le ciseau *(a plane)*, les ciseaux *(scissors)*

- Certain nouns have the same meaning both in the singular and in the plural.

    le pantalon, les pantalons *(pants)*

- Certain nouns are pronounced differently in the singular and in the plural.

DIFFERENCES IN PRONUNCIATION			
Singulier—Singular		**Pluriel—Plural**	
Un boeuf	ɛ̃ βŒf	Des boeufs	de βø
Un oeuf	ɛ̃ nŒf	Des oeufs	de zø
Un os	ɛ̃ nɔs	Des os	de zo
(ox, egg, bone)			

- Certain nouns change completely in the plural.

    un oeil—des yeux, de l'ail—des aulx *(an eye, garlic)*

IMPORTANT!

The general rule is that most nouns go from singular to plural by adding an *S*.

But there are more particular cases, summarized in the following table.

Formation of the Plural	Examples	Some Exceptions
Addition of an s **to most endings**	les livres les amis les départements les poissons les peurs les zoos	
(books, friends, departments, fish, fears, zoos)		
Addition of an s **to nouns ending in -ou**	les trous les clous	les choux, hiboux, genoux, cailloux, bijoux, joujoux, poux
(holes, nails)		

Formation of the Plural	Examples	Some Exceptions
Addition of an x to nouns ending in -eu -au -eau	les feux les neveux les tuyaux les chapeaux les oiseaux	les bleus, les pneus les landaus
(lights, nephews, pipes, hats, birds, bruises, tires, baby carriages)		
Replacement of -al **by** -aux	les journaux les chevaux	les bals, les chacals, les festivals, les carnavals
(newspapers, horses, balls, jackals, festivals, carnivals)		
Addition of an s to nouns ending in -ail	les détails	les travaux, les émaus, les coraux
(details, works, enamels, corals)		
No change to words ending in -s; -x; -z	les fils les prix les nez	
(sons/threads, prices, noses)		

TIP BOX

Since final consonants are rarely pronounced in French, the only way to know that a noun is in the plural in a conversation is by paying attention to the article that accompanies it.

With the indefinite article **un** it is easy since the plural form is very different: **des**.

But with the definite article **le**, if it is not articulated properly, people may understand it as the plural **les**. Therefore, always be careful to pronounce **le** as [lə] (as in **devenir**) and not [le] (as in **été**).

Compound Nouns

A compound noun is a noun made up of two hyphenated elements. Although the rules to create words in general are much stricter in French than in English, there are different ways of forming compound nouns. Here are some guidelines for each composition but the plural often depends on the meaning intended for the compound word.

Noun Composed of:	Formation of Plural	Some Exceptions
Noun + Noun Adjective + Noun Adjective + Adjective Both words are added plural indicators	des oiseaux-mouches les belles-mères	des timbres-poste[1] les années-lumière[1] les grand-mères[3] les demi-journées[3]
(hummingbirds, mothers-in-law, stamps, light-years, grandmothers, half days)		
Noun + Preposition + Noun First noun only is added a plural indicator	Des arcs-en-ciel[1]	des tête-à-tête les pot-au-feu
(rainbows, face to face, stews)		
Verb + Noun Noun only is added a plural indicator Or Both words remain singular	des tire-bouchons[2] des abat-jour	
(corkscrews, lampshades)		
Verb + Verb No plural indicator	Des garde-manger[2]	
(food pantries)		
Foreign words Plural indicator on the second noun	des snack-bars[4] des tee-shirts des pull-overs des week-ends	

The reasons to modify or conserve either, both, or none of the words can be as follows:

- Factual

[1]Even if there are many rainbows, there is still only one sky. All the stamps are used for the mail in general. These years relate to light as a measuring unit.

- Grammatical

[2]Verbs have specific markers when they are conjugated with a plural subject. The **s** ending does not apply to them.

- Etymological or Arbitrary

[3]The adjective **grand** does not vary in front of a feminine noun: la grand-mère—les grand-mères; la grand-route—les grand-routes. But it does agree with masculine words: mes grands-oncles!
Demi never changes: un demi-frère, une demi-sœur, des demi-heures, les demi-points.

- Logical

[4]Since these words are foreign, it is difficult for the French to know what they are originally: a noun + a noun or a verb + a verb or an adverb + a noun, etc. So they all are treated in the same way, by adding an **s** at the end, which is the most common way of marking the plural in French anyway.

> **IMPORTANT!**
> Do not try to deduce logically the gender of a noun; learn it as part of the noun itself.
>   In case of doubt about the plural of a noun, use the previous categories as guidelines but verify its formation in your dictionary.

Practice What You Learned

Exercises are rated according to four levels of difficulty:

- Beginner easy [*]
- Beginner challenging [**]
- Intermediate [***]
- Advanced [****]

1. Find all the common and proper nouns in this advertisement. Identify the proper nouns. [*]

Déclinez la mayonnaise

Aïoli: à une mayonnaise (2 jaunes d'œufs, 1 c. à s. de moutarde, sel, huile d'olive), incorporez 4 gousses d'ail pelées et pilées.

Cocktail: incorporez 2 cuil. à soupe de ketchup, 1 trait de cognac, 2 traits de Worcestershire sauce et quelques gouttes de Tabasco.

Verdurette: incorporez 2 cuillerées à soupe de fines herbes (persil, cerfeuil, estragon, ciboulette) mélangées et finement ciselées.

2. Add their article **un** or **une** to the following nouns. Refer to the rules that apply to certain groups of words. [*]

____ garçon, ____ dame, ____ garage, ____ homme, ____ lionne, ____ pharmacienne, ____ étudiante, ____ musicienne, ____ assiette, ____ fourchette, ____ chienne, ____ monsieur, ____ téléphone, ____ bicyclette, ____ fromage, ____ télévision, ____ sculpture, ____ téléscope, ____ nuage, ____ baguette, ____ image, ____ balance, ____ bâtiment, ____ voiture, ____ bateau, ____ aventure.

3. Put the articles, nouns, and adjectives in the plural: [*]

A. Un cheveu blond _____

B. Un caillou bleu _____

C. Un bureau spacieux _____

D. Un monsieur poli _____

E. Un noyau dur _____

F. Un cours intéressant _____

4. Put the following sentences in the plural: [**]

A. L'homme est un animal spécial. _____

B. Le saphir est un bijou merveilleux. _____

C. Le chien est un animal amical. _____

D. Le chou est un légume indigeste. _____

E. Le zèbre est un cheval sauvage. _____

F. J'ai un marteau et un clou. _____

5. Insert the definite articles in front of all the nouns and rewrite them in the feminine or masculine, singular or plural, according to gender and context of the story. [***]

Pour le confort de nos clients, dans tous les modèles Citroën comme la **C3 Pluriel**

(vitre) _____

(chauffage) _____

(carrosserie) _____

(pneu) _____

(siège) _____

(transmission) _____

(frein) _____

sont de qualité exceptionnelle

Dans (modèle) _____ _____de haut de gamme, comme (cabriolet) _____ _____ C3 Pluriel, (contrôle) _____ _____de (vitesse) _____ _____est électronique et (frein) _____ _____anti-dérapants. Ne craignez plus (pluie) _____ _____, (neige) _____ _____ou (orages!) _____ _____ et en Citroën appréciez (paysage) _____ _____!

Chapter 3

ARTICLES

The Nature and Function of Articles

Gender and Number

Articles not only make the gender and number attributes visible for the nouns they accompany, they also add information to it. In many ways, they are comparable to and behave like adjectives: They agree with the gender and number of the noun.

Specificity

Articles determine how specific the object is that the noun designates.

To correspond to the noun, there are specific feminine and masculine, singular and plural forms of articles. They can all also be classified in three different categories.

THE THREE CATEGORIES OF ARTICLES			
Category	Number	Gender	
		Masculine	Feminine
Definite	Singular	LE / L'	LA / L'
	Plural	LES	
Indefinite	Singular	UN	UNE
	Plural	DES	
Partitive	Singular	DU / DE L'	DE LA / DE L'
	Plural	DES	

> **NOTE** The partitive articles result from the combination of the preposition DE and the definite articles. DE is one of the two most commonly used prepositions in French along with À. This combination DE + article to designate a part of something is logical since DE is used to indicate the origin, where something comes from, of the word to which it relates.

All nouns can be used with any category of articles. Your choice among them will give a particular value to the noun.

The Use of Articles

Definite Articles

DEFINITE ARTICLES		
Gender	Masculine	Féminine
Number		
Singular	Le / L'	La / L'
Plural	Les	

In general, a noun with a definite article refers to something well known, already mentioned in a discussion or a written text, or specified by another element in the sentence.

- Definite articles accompany nouns that represent beings or things considered as known:

    J'ai visité **la** cathédrale. (*I visited the cathedral.*)

- Definite articles are necessary when the noun is modified by another noun or a clause:

    J'ai visité **le** magnifique musée de Picasso. (*I visited the magnificent Picasso museum.*)

    J'ai visité **le** musée qui est à Antibes. (*I visited the museum that is in Antibes.*)

- Definite articles accompany general or abstract nouns:

    J'aime **les** animaux et j'adore **les** chats. (*I love animals and I adore cats.*)

    La liberté est la chose la plus précieuse pour tout être humain. (*Freedom is the most precious thing for any human being.*)

- Definite articles are used with body parts (instead of the possessive adjective):

  Levez **la** main pour poser une question. *(Raise your hand to ask a question.)*

  Il a un chapeau rouge sur **la** tête. *(He has a red hat on his head.)*

  Il se lave **les** dents et tire **la** langue! *(He brushes his teeth and sticks out his tongue!)*

- Definite articles are used with proper nouns, titles, and languages:

  Les Grimaldi sont une famille célèbre à Monaco et dans le monde. *(The Grimaldis are a famous family in Monaco and worldwide.)*

  Le Général de Gaulle était un héros de la deuxième guerre mondiale. *(General de Gaulle was a hero of the second world war.)*

  Le français n'est pas plus difficile que **l'**anglais. *(French is not any more difficult than English.)*

- Definite articles are used with daily meals, weekdays, dates, seasons, holidays, and regions:

  Le poète Jacques Prévert a écrit: "Je hais **le** dimanche." *(The poet Jacques Prévert wrote "I hate Sundays.")*

  Je mange une banane pour **le** petit déjeuner. *(I eat a banana for breakfast.)*

  Mon anniversaire est **le** 11 août; mon signe est **le** Lion. *(My birthday is on August 11; my sign is Leo.)*

  J'aime toutes les saisons sauf **l'**automne et **l'**hiver alors . . . j'habite **la** Californie du sud. *(I like all seasons except autumn and winter, so I live in southern California.)*

  le 14 juillet, **la** Noêl, **la** Toussaint, **le** 11 novembre, etc. *(July 14, Christmas, All Saints Day, November 11.)*

(THINK!) Do you know why the dates mentioned above are French holidays and can you list other ones?

- _____ - _____ - _____

- _____ - _____ - _____

- _____ - _____ - _____

- Definite articles are used with subjects, sports, topics, and games in general:

    > **le** capitalisme, **les** maths, **le** tennis, **les** scandales financiers, **les** échecs, **la** grammaire française rendue facile *(capitalism, math, tennis, financial scandals, chess, French grammar made easy)*

    > **La** pêche était le loisir préféré de mon père Michel. *(Fishing was my father's favorite hobby.)*

TIP BOX
Most nouns that are not used with an article in English will require an article in French. In most cases it will be a definite article, unless "some" could replace the absence of the article in English. When I write in English and am in doubt, I suppress the article I would use in French and leave the word as is. When in doubt, insert a definite article where there is none in English:

> *(Children are cute.)* = Les enfants sont mignons.

> *(Martha wants children (= some children).)* Marthe veut des enfants.

Indefinite Articles

INDEFINITE ARTICLES		
Gender	Masculine	Féminine
Number		
Singular	Un	Une
Plural	Des	

In general, nouns are used with indefinite articles when there is no specific knowledge of the person or object designated.

- Indefinite articles are used when objects or people are considered less by themselves than as one element of a class:

    Marc a encore acheté **une** raquette. *(Marc bought a racket again.)*

    C'est **un** prof de tennis. *(He is a tennis instructor.)*

    Il a toujours **des** balles dans sa voiture. *(He always has balls in his car.)*

- Indefinite articles may be used in the plural to indicate a vague quantity:

    Céline a vu **des** lions pendant son voyage au Kénya. *(Celine saw lions during her trip to Kenya.)*

    Jean-Philippe a couru pendant **des** heures. *(Jean-Philippe ran for hours.)*

    Des pompiers de New York sont venus à Paris. *(Firemen from New York came to Paris.)*

Because of this quantity aspect, there is much similarity between the use of an indefinite article that may mean "one" in the singular or "a few, a lot" in the plural and the partitive articles that always mean "some."

Partitive Articles

PARTITIVE ARTICLES		
Gender	Masculine	Féminine
Number		
Singular	Du / De l'	De la / De l'
Plural	Des	

As their name indicates, partitive articles accompany nouns that refer to a part or piece taken from a larger whole. In general:

- Partitive articles are used when the noun designates a certain quantity of a product that does not constitute an object in itself:

  Elle mange **du** chocolat. *(She eats chocolate.)*

  Roger fait **du** pain meilleur que celui de notre boulanger. *(Roger makes better bread than our baker.)*

- Partitive articles are used when the noun designates a part of an identifiable whole:

  Sophie a mangé **du** gâteau et bu **du** thé.—*implied: a piece of the cake that is in the fridge and some tea. (Sophie ate some cake and drank tea.)*

  Karine a choisi **des** pêches très mûres.—*implied: among the pile in the store. (Karine chose very ripe peaches.)*

  Des pompiers de New York sont venus à Paris.—*implied: a group among all the September 11 New York firefighters came to Paris. (Some firefighters from New York came to Paris.)*

Remarkable Facts about Articles

As shown previously, articles are very simple to use once you remember to make them agree in gender and number with the noun and evaluate the level of specificity of that noun. There are nevertheless a few gray areas that should make you STOP and THINK.

Elision and Apostrophe

Le—La	Become l' in front of words beginning with a vowel or mute "h". This is simply due to the fact that it is difficult to pronounce two consecutive vowels and it is considered an ugly sound. Try to pronounce them out loud and see how much easier and more harmonious the second is! ~~Le événement~~: [~~la e~~ ven m⁻a][le ven m⁻a] ~~La année~~: [~~la a~~ ne] [la ne] l'événement, l'hôpital, l'année, l'histoire *(the event, the hospital, the year, the story)*

Du / De la vs. De

Du De la	Since the partitive articles are composed with the preposition **de**, **du** and **de la** can be both: • a partitive article: Tu veux **de la** soupe au pistou—some. *(Do you want some pesto soup?)* • the preposition **de** simply followed by the definite article: Diderot parle **de la** philosophie de Rousseau—of the. *(Diderot speaks of Rousseau's philosophy.)*
Du/De la vs. De	Adverbs of quantities are followed by the preposition de + noun (without an article). Pas de is a quantity adverb (simply, the quantity is 0) as in un peu de, beaucoup de, assez de. **This is why partitive articles are not used in the negative sentences that express a null quantity (but they can be used in other negative sentences).** Le bébé boit du lait. Le bébé ne boit pas du lait. *(This means that the baby does not drink any of the milk that you are presenting her. This translates: The baby does not drink any of the milk.)* Le bébé ne boit pas de lait. *(This means that this baby drinks a quantity of milk equal to 0. This translates: The baby does not drink any milk.)* Le bébé boit beaucoup de lait. *(The baby drinks a lot of milk.)*

De vs. Du / De la

De vs. Du/ De la	The previous explanation does not mean that there cannot be sentences like the following:
	Je ne veux pas **du** lait.—pas **de le** lait que tu as acheté le mois dernier.
	But in this case, **du** is the contraction of the preposition **de** and the definite article **le**, because this milk is a specific one. This does not mean that I want 0 milk. It means *I do not want any of this milk* (that you bought last month).

Omission of the Article

NO Indefinite Article	The indefinite article is omitted in French while it would be used in English:
	• when the nominal group is in apposition (set between commas):
	Mon directeur de thèse, homme aussi mystérieux que brillant, s'appelle William Arctander. *(My dissertation director, a man as mysterious as he is brilliant, is named William Arctander.)*
	• after a noun or personal pronoun + **être** + a profession (**not after c'est**):
	[Fabienne] Elle **est professeur**. **C'est un** professeur. (*[Fabienne] She is a professor*.)
	[Edward] Il **est ingénieur**, directeur de Acrocat Software. **C'est un** ingénieur. *(Edward is an engineer, the director of Acrocat LLC.)*
	• after the preposition **sans**:
	À vaincre **sans** effort, on triomphe **sans** gloire. *(Winning without effort leads to triumph without glory.)*

Practice What You Learned

Exercises are rated according to four levels of difficulty:

- Beginner easy [*]
- Beginner challenging [**]
- Intermediate [***]
- Advanced [****]

1. Find all the definite articles used in the *Ratatouille Niçoise* recipe below. There are 13 of them. Be careful, an article accompanies a noun; it cannot therefore precede a verb. [*]

R E C E T T E

La ratatouille
"La ratatouia nissarda"

Temps de préparation:
30 mn / cuisson 45 mn
Saison:
été-automne, de juillet à octobre

Pour 8 personnes

Ingrediénts
0,600 kg de poivrons rouges & jaunes
1,200 kg de courgettes beurre longues
1,200 kg d'aubergines
0,400 kg d'oignons blancs ou paille
1,200 kg de tomates bien mûres
0,030 kg d'ail (soit 5 gousses)
10 feuilles de basilic
0,25 l d'huile d'olive
1 bouquet garni : thym, laurier,
queues de persil plat, feuilles de céleri
sel fin et poivre du moulin

Éplucher les gousses d'ail, les oignons. Préparer les légumes : couper les extrémités des courgettes, aubergines, égrainer les poivrons ; les laver ; les couper en dès de 2 à 3 cm de côté.
Faire chauffer l'huile d'olive dans une poêle et y faire rissoler (dorer) successivement les légumes séparément, les égoutter dans une passoire, les verser dans une cocotte.
Monder et épépiner les tomates, les concasser et les rajouter aux légumes. Ajouter l'assaisonnement : sel, poivre du moulin, le bouquet garni et les gousses d'ail écrasées.
Couvrir la préparation de papier sulfurisé et du couvercle. Laisser mijoter 40 à 45 minutes de préférence au four (thermostat 4 à 5).
En fin de cuisson, avant de servir, rajouter le basilic haché.

2. Complete the sentences in the following paragraph with the appropriate definite, indefinite, or partitive **article. Justify your answers.** [**]

A. D'après _____ portrait robot de _____police: _____

B. _____suspect aurait _____yeux bleus: _____

C. et _____pantalon vert: _____

D. Il est sorti de _____bagarre avec _____oeil au beurre noir: _____

E. et _____ menton tuméfié: _____

F. Le pistolet lui a échappé _____mains: _____

G. Le policier a réagi sans _____violence: _____

H. et avec _____calme de tout professionnel: _____

3. Complete the sentences in the following paragraph with the missing definite, indefinite, or contracted articles when appropriate. [**]

A. _____appartement de Samira est _____appartement superbe.

B. _____éclairage _____séjour est vert et celui de _____chambre bleuté.

C. Au milieu _____salon, il y a _____podium avec _____coussins de toutes _____couleurs.

D. _____ plafond de _____salle de bains est peint avec _____étoiles argentées comme _____ciel d'hiver.

E. _____lit où dorment _____invités est couvert d' _____ tissu en soie grise sans _____ motif, mais il y a _____ palmiers verts et gris sur _____ tapisserie derrière _____ lit.

F. C'est _____ chambre marocaine et très exotique!

4. In the following sentences explain the use of the preposition, the contraction, or the article. [***]

Example:

Je ne veux pas **de** fromage: preposition **de** after a quantity adverb (**pas de**)

A. J'adore les gâteaux ___au___ chocolat: _____

B. Veux-tu ___du___ gâteau au chocolat: _____

C. Elle ne lit jamais ___de___ magazines: _____

D. Céline ne veut pas ___de la___ crème que tu utilises: _____

E. C'est une spécialité ___du___ chef: _____

F. La pâte ___de la___ tarte est légère mais croustillante: _____

G. Donne-moi un morceau ___de la___ tarte: _____

Chapter 4

LINKING WORDS—PREPOSITIONS

Introduction

Prepositions establish relationships between the words in a sentence. The preposition indicates which type of relationship exists between which words. Although they are small, simple words and have English counterparts, their use can be tricky.

Because the number of relationships between words is almost endless, the prepositions are flexible and may have slightly different meanings depending on their context.

Types of Prepositions

Most prepositions can be grouped according to the type of information they allow. They can be followed by a noun (a nominal group or a pronoun) or a verb.

Date

- Dates are expressed in a different order in French:

    jour—mois—année (*Day—Month—Year*)

    11/08/60 (Eleventh of August 1960)

    2/12/30 (Second of December 1930)

    22/3/1926 (March 22, 1926)

    28/12/1901 (December 28, 1901)

- Names of months are not capitalized.

- To express a date use: **Nous sommes le** or **On est le** ... :

    Aujourd'hui, **nous sommes le** 5 octobre 2002. (*Today is October 5, 2002.*)

    On est le 25 décembre; c'est Noël! (*Today is December 25; it's Christmas!*)

- The definite article **LE** precedes a date or the day:

    San Luis Obispo, **le** 5 octobre 2002 (*San Luis Obispo, October 5, 2002*)

> Nous sommes **le** dimanche 5 octobre et il fait très chaud en Californie. *(Today is Sunday, October 5, and it is very hot in California.)*

- Months are used with the preposition **EN**:

> Halloween est **en** octobre, la Saint Valentin **en** février et les grandes vacances **en** juillet. *(Halloween is in October, Valentine's Day in February, and summer vacations in July.)*

- Seasons are all masculine but **AU** is used in front of a consonant and **EN** in front of a vowel or aspirated H:

> Nous sommes **au** printemps. *(It is spring.)*

> Nous sommes **en** été, **en** automne, **en** hiver. *(It is summer, fall, winter.)*

- Years are used with **EN**, centuries with **AU**:

> Nous sommes **en** 2002. (This is 2002.)

> La révolution française était en 1789, **au** dix-huitième siècle. *(The French revolution was in 1789, in the eighteenth century.)*

 Make a list of all the English prepositions you can think of.

_____

_____

Location

Prepositions indicative of location can be composed of one word, or a word and the preposition DE. They are used in the same way as in English. The principal prepositions are:

- *among*   PARMI
- *at the back of*   AU FOND **DE**
- *behind*   DERRIÈRE
- *below*   AU-DESSOUS **DE**
- *between*   ENTRE
- *close to*   PRÈS **DE**
- *far from*   LOIN **DE**
- *in*   DANS
- *in front of*   DEVANT
- *next to*   À COTÉ **DE**
- *on*   SUR
- *over*   AU-DESSUS **DE**
- *over—above*   AU-DESSUS **DE**
- *under*   SOUS

Circumstances

OVERVIEW OF PRINCIPAL PREPOSITIONS	
Le temps (*Time*)	à, avant, après, dès, depuis, jusqu'à, pendant, vers, entre, pour (*at, before, after, as soon as, since, until, while, towards, between, for*)
Le lieu (*Location*)	à, de, dans, à l'intérieur de, sur, entre, sous, au-dessus de, au-dessous de, près de, loin de, devant, derrière, à côté de, hors de, auprès de, contre, en face de, parmi, vers, en, chez (*at, from, in, inside, on, between, under, over, below, near, far, in front of, behind, next to, outside, close to, against, facing, among, toward, in, at the home of*)
Le moyen (*Means*)	avec, par, grâce à, au moyen de (*with, by, thanks to, using*)
La cause (*Cause*)	à cause de, en raison de, vu, par suite de, étant donné, sous prétexte, selon (*because of, due to, considering, consequently to, given that, under the pretext, according to*)
Le but (*Goal*)	pour, afin de, en vue de, dans l'intention de, de façon à, de manière à, dans le but de (*for, in order to, with . . . in mind, intending to, so as, in such a way that, with the objective of*)
La condition (*Condition*)	selon, à condition de, dans le cas de, à moins de, à part, hormis / sauf (*depending, with the condition that, in the case that, unless, apart, except*)

IMPORTANT!

The same words can be used as prepositions or as conjunctions.
As prepositions they are followed by a NOUN.
    As conjunctions, they are followed by QUE and a complete clause.

Il travaille POUR le PLAISIR.
(*He works for the pleasure of it.*)

Il travaille **pour QUE ses parents se reposent.**
(*He works for his parents to rest.*)

Je ferai un picnic AVANT les
PLUIES. (*I'll organize a picnic
before the rainy season.*)

Je ferai un picnic **avant QU'il ne pleuve.**
(*I'll organize a picnic before it rains.*)

Refer to the section on **Compound Sentences** *in Chapter 15*

Prepositions and Nouns

In general, nouns following a preposition tend to add information about the object of or the circumstances surrounding the action.

> Vers 7 heures, Marie se levait de son lit, allait dans la salle de bain en pyjama, se brossait les dents avec du dentifrice liquide à la fraise et se réveillait enfin grâce à sa douche. Pendant ce temps-là, de son côté, son petit ami Vincent lui préparait du café par gentillesse, mettait du beurre sur ses tartines de pain et de la confiture ou du fromage selon son humeur. (*Around 7, Marie would get **out of** bed, go **to the** bathroom **in** her pajamas, brush her teeth **with** strawberry-flavored liquid toothpaste, and she'd finally wake up **under** the shower. **In** the meantime, **on** his side, her boyfriend Vincent would kindly make coffee **for** her, put butter **on** her bread slices and jam or cheese, **depending on** his mood.)*

In particular, certain prepositions are used to describe the situation of the action in space and time.

Space—Origin or Position: From—To—In

Town	**DE**	Giancarlo arrive de Rome ce soir.
	À	Jacques vit à Paris. Georgia va à Cannes. Ton frère se trouve à New York.
(Giancarlo arrives from Rome tonight.) (Jacques lives in Paris.) (Georgia goes to Cannes.) (Your brother is in New York.)		
Feminine Countries and States or the Six Continents	**DE**	Le meilleur chocolat vient de Suisse.
	EN	Fab est née en France; elle travaille en Californie. La France est en Europe. Rio est en Amérique. Tokyo est située en Asie. Les kangourous vivent en Australie. La Polynésie française est en Océanie. Le Sahara est en Afrique.
(The best chocolate comes from Switzerland.) (Fab was born in France; she works in California.) (France is in Europe.) (Rio is in South America.) (Tokyo is located in Asia.) (Kangaroos live in Australia.) (French Polynesia is in Oceania.) (The Sahara desert is in Africa.)		
Masculine Singular Countries and States Starting with a Vowel	**EN**	En Iran, Oregon, Angola, Israël

Masculine Countries and States	**DU** **DES** **D'**	Le café du Brésil est célèbre. L'ambassade du Maroc est ouverte toute la journée. Le pétrole des Émirats Arabes est un atout. *Note: The final **e** of **de** is maintained in front of countries starting with an aspirated "**h**" that is not mute.* *Serguei vient de Hongrie.* *Marika part de Hollande.*
	AU— **AUX**	Certaines capitales aux États-Unis sont: Austin au Texas Sante Fe au Nouveau Mexique Lansing au Michigan Cheyenne au Wyoming Memphis au Tennessee
(Brazilian coffee is famous.) (The Morrocan embassy is open all day.) (The oil from the Arab Emirates is an advantage.) (Sergei comes from Hungary.) (Marika leaves from Holland.)		
Masculine Singular/Plural Regions or Specific Location in States	**DANS** **LE—** **LES**	On fait du fromage dans le Cantal. Mes valises ont atterri dans l'Ohio, moi dans le New Jersey! Il y a des alpacas dans les Andes.
(Some cheese is made in Cantal.) (My suitcases landed in Ohio; I landed in New Jersey!) (There are alpacas in the Andes.)		

Time—Duration: For—Since—In—Ago

Four principal prepositions—depuis, pendant, pour, en—are used to translate the various aspects of duration. Somewhat equivalent English counterparts are: for—since—in—ago.

Space **(Origin)** *Since* *For* *Ago*	**DEPUIS** Now	The action or situation started a while ago and is still current. The origin can be a date or a number of days, years, etc. • Je suis professeur depuis 15 ans. (***I have been a professor for 15 years.***) • David vit aux États-Unis depuis 1985. (***David has been living in the USA since 1985.***) • Raïssa est partie depuis trois jours. (***Raïssa left three days ago.***)
Time **(Duration)** *During* *For*	**PENDANT**	The action has lasted, is lasting, or will last for a certain amount of or reference to time. • Adèle a dormi pendant l'après-midi. (***Adèle slept during the afternoon.***) • Guy lit pendant deux heures le soir. (***Guy reads for two hours at night.***) • Boris ira en Russie pendant l'été. (***Boris will go to Russia during the summer.***)

Future Duration *During* *For*	**POUR** [diagram: box labeled "Now" with arrow pointing to bracketed arrow →]	This is an estimated duration of an action or situation that will take place in the future. It can start from now on or be contemplated for later in the future. • Fabrice part à Cannes pour cinq semaines. (***Fabrice is going to Cannes for five weeks.***) • Nadia va prendre des cours pour trois mois. (***Nadia will take classes for three months.***)
Performance *In*	**EN** [diagram: bracketed dashed arrow ------→]	**En** indicates how long the action takes. • Arthur court 10 kms en 30 minutes. (***Arthur runs three miles in 30 minutes.***) • Peggy a appris le français en six mois. (***Peggy learned French in six months.***)

NOTE DEPUIS can be replaced by "Il y a ... que" or "ça fait ... que" at the beginning of a duration expressed in numbers:

Il y a deux heures **que** Joachim et Nathan jouent au foot. (*Joachim and Nathan have been playing soccer for two hours.*)

Ça fait un mois **que** Béatrice a son permis de conduire. (*Béatrice got her driver's license a month ago.*)

TIP BOX

Since both **pendant** (for a present, a past, and a future action) and **pour** can express the **duration** of an action but **pour** concerns only **future** actions, it is safer to **always use** pendant—even though the English equivalent of **pendant** means **for** as well as **during**. In this case, **pour (for)**, the instinctive translation, is much less frequent and even dangerous.

RIGHT: J'ai travaillé **pendant** une semaine. Je travaillerai **pendant** une semaine. (*I worked for a week. I will work for a week.*)

WRONG: J'ai travaillé pour une semaine. —Je travaillerai **pour** une semaine.

Time or Space Indication

A series of prepositions can be used to convey a situation that is encountered both in time and in space. The principal ones are used very frequently and should be memorized.

À **(At, To)**	**A point in space or in time** Nous sommes **à** l'université, **au** troisième étage. (*We are at the university, on the third floor.*) Laure arrive **à** huit heures. (*Laure gets to class at eight o'clock.*)
De . . . à **(From . . . to)**	**A distance from one point in space or time to another** Il y a 800 kms **de** Paris **à** Marseille. (*There are 800 kms from Paris to Marseille.*) Cela prend **de** 8 **à** 9 heures de conduite en voiture. (*It takes 8 to 9 hours of driving by car.*)
Jusqu'à **(Until)**	**A limit ahead in space or time** Ce bus va **jusqu'à** la Place de la Concorde. (*This bus goes all the way to the Place de la Concorde.*) En France l'école est obligatoire **jusqu'à** 18 ans. (*In France, school is mandatory until 18.*)
À partir de **(From)**	**A point of departure in space or time** Il y a toujours des encombrements **à partir de** Lyon. (*There are always traffic jams after Lyon.*) Il y a toujours des encombrements **à partir de** 18 heures. (*There are always traffic jams from 6 o'clock on.*)
Environ **Vers** **(Around)** **(About)**	**An approximate distance or duration** Cannes est à **environ** 10 kms d'Antibes. (*Cannes is about 6 miles from Antibes.*) Cela prend **environ** un quart d'heure l'hiver mais plus d'une heure l'été! (*It takes about 15 minutes in winter but over an hour in summer!*) La gare est **vers** la plage. (*The train station is in the direction of the beach.*) Nous y arriverons **vers** midi. (*We will get there around noon.*)
Entre **Parmi** **(Between)** **(Among)**	**A place between either two or more elements** Deux est **entre** un et trois. (*Two is between one and three.*) Je fais **entre** trois et quatre heures d'aérobic par semaine. (*I do between three and four hours of aerobic exercise a week.*) Il y a un espion **parmi** nous! (*There is a spy among us!*) Je réserve quelques minutes pour méditer **parmi** toutes mes heures de travail. (*I put aside a few minutes among hours of work to meditate.*)

Combinations [Verbs and Prepositions] + Verb

In French, verbs can be linked to another verb in three different ways.

> **NOTE** When two general verbs follow each other, the first one is conjugated and the second one is always in the infinitive (with or without a preposition).

1. **Verbe + Infinitif** (Verb + Infinitive).
   Most conjugated verbs can be followed by an infinitive:

   > J'aime nager. Tu penses sortir. Elle va partir. (*I like to swim. You think about going out. She is going to leave.*)

2. **Verbe + À** (Verb + À).
   Some conjugated verbs need À before the following verb in the infinitive:

   > Octave s'apprête **à** changer sa voiture. (*Octave is getting ready to change his car.*)

TIP BOX

The preposition À generally indicates a movement of the subject **towArd** something Ahead.

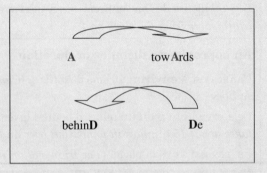

The preposition DE generally indicates something happening from an origin that is **behinD** the subject.

In case you do not have access to a dictionary to verify which preposition is needed with a particular verb, remember these opposite directions to guess—but this is not a rule. Different prepositions may change the context of the action:

> Jouer à—to play a sport: Elle joue au foot. (*She plays soccer.*)

> Jouer de—to play an instrument: Elle joue aussi du piano. (*She also plays piano.*)

---

3. **Verbe + De** (Verb + **De**).
   Some conjugated verbs need **DE** before the following verb in the infinitive:

> Kenneth essaie **de** parler en français. (*Kenneth tries to speak in French.*)

Principal Verbs Directly Followed by an Infinitive

Fill in the translation of the following verbs. You will find the solutions before the exercise section at the end of this chapter.

<table>
<tr><td colspan="8" align="center">IMPORTANT!
Note that the use of prepositions does not translate literally:

• Some verbs that take a preposition in English may not do so in French.
• Some verbs that do not take a preposition in English may require one in French.
• Some verbs that take a preposition in English and in French may not use the same one.</td></tr>
</table>

adorer	aimer	aller	compter	croire	descendre	désirer	détester
devoir	écouter	entendre	entrer	envoyer	espérer	faillir	faire
falloir	laisser	monter	oser	paraître	partir	penser	pouvoir
préférer	prétendre	se rappeler	regarder	rentrer	savoir	sembler	sentir
sortir	souhaiter	valoir mieux	venir	voir	vouloir		

Nina **adore mariner** les bananes dans l'Armagnac. (*Nina loves to marinate bananas in Armagnac.*)

Viviane **va laver** ma valise délavée. (*Viviane will wash my suitcase.*)

Pierrette **pense parvenir** à Paris sans problème. (*Pierrette thinks she will get to Paris without a problem.*)

Victoire **veut vendre** sa voiture à Victor. (*Victoire wants to sell her car to Victor.*)

Principal Verbs Followed by *À* and the Infinitive

 Fill in the translation of the following verbs; you will find the solutions before the exercise section at the end of this chapter. Note the difference in prepositions used for many verbs.

aider à	**s'amuser** à	**apprendre** à	**s'apprêter** à	**arriver** à
s'attendre à	**avoir** à	**chercher** à	**commencer** à	**consentir** à
consister à	**continuer** à	**se décider** à	**demander** à	**encourager** à
enseigner à	**forcer** à	**s'habituer** à	**hésiter** à	**s'intéresser** à
inviter à	**se mettre** à	**obliger** à	**parvenir** à	**passer du temps** à
penser à	**persister** à	**pousser** à	**préparer** à	**renoncer** à
rester à	**réussir** à	**servir** à	**songer** à	**tenir** à

Anne et Aline **ont à annoncer** qui a gagné la Palme d'Or. (*Anne and Aline have to announce who won the Palme d'Or*—the highest award at the French Festival of Film in Cannes.)

Cecile **se décide à danser** la salsa. (*Cecile decides to dance salsa.*)

Patrice ne **pense** pas **à payer** ses impôts. (*Patrice does not think about paying his taxes.*)

Henri **hésite à traduire** toutes ces phrases en français. (*Henri hesitates to translate all these sentences in French.*)

Principal Verbs Followed by *DE* and the Infinitive

 Fill in the translation of the following verbs. You will find the solutions before the exercise section at the end of this chapter.

s'agir de	avoir peur de	cesser de	continuer de	craindre de
décider de	demander de	se dépêcher de	essayer de	finir de
garantir de	jouir de	manquer de	se méfier de	offrir de
persuader de	prier de	promettre de	refuser de	regretter de
remercier de	se servir de	se souvenir de	tâcher de	venir de

Il **s'agit d'**apprendre ces verbes et leur préposition. (*The point is to learn these verbs and their prepositions.*)

Denis **demande de** partir vers dix heures ce soir. (*Denis is asking to leave around 10 o'clock tonight.*)

Olga **a oublié de** finir son courrier. (*Olga forgot to finish her mail.*)

Je **tâcherai d'**envoyer un cadeau aux mariés. (*I will try to send a present to the newlyweds.*)

Combinations [Verbs and Prepositions] + Nouns

Verbs can also need a preposition when they are followed by a noun that complements them. As we have seen earlier in this chapter, there are numerous prepositions that can be used according to the type of information we wish to provide.

Verbs that need to be used with **à** or **de** are particularly important since their construction will determine how to choose the appropriate personal pronoun.

 Fill in the translation of the following verbs; you will find the solutions before the exercise section at the end of this chapter. Note the difference in prepositions used for many verbs or even the absence of the preposition altogether in English.

Principal Verbs Followed by *À* + Noun of Person/Thing

une personne—quelqu'un—qqn (*someone*)

une chose—quelque chose—qqch (*something*)

assister à qqch	convenir à qqch / qqn	demander à qqch / qqn	déplaire à qqn
désobéir à qqch / qqn	être à qqn	faire attention à qqch / qqn	se fier à qqch / qqn
goûter à qqch	s'habituer à qqch / qqn	s'intéresser à qqch / qqn	jouer à qqch
manquer à qqn	nuire à qqch / qqn	obéir à qqch / qqn	s'opposer à qqch / qqn
penser à qqch / qqn	plaire à qqn	réfléchir à qqch / qqn	répondre à qqch / qqn
résister à qqch / qqn	ressembler à qqch / qqn	réussir à qqch	téléphoner à qqch / qqn

Maurice **assiste à** tous les concerts de Mozart. (*Maurice goes to all Mozart concerts.*)

Marie **manque à** Marc terriblement. (*Marc misses Marie a lot. Note that the order is reversed in French: Marie is lacking to Marc; therefore, he misses her!*)

Raphaël **ressemble à** son père qui ressemble à un éléphant! (*Raphaël resembles his father who resembles an elephant!*)

Théodore **téléphone à** son partenaire. (*Théodore calls his partner.*)

Principal Verbs Followed by *DE* + Noun of Person/Thing

une personne—quelqu'un—qqn (*someone*)

une chose—quelque chose—qqch (*something*)

s'agir de	s'approcher de	changer de	dépendre de
qqch	qqch / qqn	qqch / qqn	qqch / qqn
douter de	féliciter de	jouer de	jouir de
qqch / qqn	qqch	qqch	qqch / qqn
manquer de	se méfier de	se moquer de	s'occuper de
qqch / qqn	qqch / qqn	qqch / qqn	qqch / qqn
partir de	se passer de	se plaindre de	remercier de
qqch / qqn	qqch / qqn	qqch / qqn	qqch
se rendre compte de	se servir de	se soucier de	se souvenir de
qqch	qqch / qqn	qqch / qqn	qqch / qqn

Dans les romans de Balzac, il **s'agit de** la société bourgeoise au dix-neuvième siècle. (*Balzac's novels are about nineteenth-century bourgeois society.*)

Peggy ne **dépend** pas **de** ses parents; elle travaille à mi-temps. (*Peggy does not depend on her parents; she works part time.*)

Je peux me **passer de** certaines personnes mais pas de mes chats. (*I can live without some people but not without my cats.*)

Sophie se **soucie de** tout le monde; c'est une sainte. (*Sophie cares about everyone; she is a saint.*)

> ### IMPORTANT!
> **To listen <u>to</u> the radio**—Écouter <u>la</u> radio
> **To <u>call one's</u> parents**—Téléphoner <u>à</u> ses parents
>
> Never assume that prepositions are used in French as they are in English even though they all have an equivalent translation.
>
> **Always verify in your dictionary which preposition to use (if any).**

Overview: Tables for Review
French-English Differential Table of Verbs + Prepositions

Never assume a preposition. Memorize the verbs most useful to you and verify all others, if you have any doubt. Prepositions are crucial in order to use the correct pronouns.

> Refer to the chapter on
> **Personal Pronouns.**
> See, also, Chapter 9

DIFFERENCES OF USE OF PREPOSITIONS BETWEEN FRENCH AND ENGLISH VERBS	
No Preposition in French	
attendre	to wait for
chercher	to look for
demander	to ask for
écouter	to listen to
essayer	to try—to try on
habiter	to live at (in)
mettre	to put on
payer	to pay for
regarder	to look at
reprocher	to blame for

DE in French	
jouer de + instrument	to play
s'apercevoir de	to notice
s'approcher de	to approach
avoir besoin de	to need
changer de	to change
discuter de	to discuss
douter de	to suspect
s'emparer de	to grab
jouir de	to enjoy
manquer de	to lack
se servir de	to use
se souvenir de	to remember
se tromper de	to make a mistake
À in French	
assister à	to attend
convenir à	to suit
se fier à	to trust
jouer à	to play a game
nuire à	to harm
(dés)obéir à	to (dis)obey
pardonner à	to forgive
(dé)plaire à	to (dis)please
renoncer à	to renounce
répondre à	to answer
résister à	to resist
ressembler à	to resemble
téléphoner à	to call

Principal Verbs + Prepositions Answer Key

PRINCIPAL VERBS DIRECTLY FOLLOWED BY AN INFINITIVE							
adorer (*adore*)	aimer (*love*)	aller (*go*)	compter (*expect*)	croire (*believe*)	descendre (*come down*)	désirer (*desire*)	détester (*hate*)
devoir (*have to*)	écouter (*listen to*)	entendre (*hear*)	entrer (*come in*)	envoyer (*send*)	espérer (*hope*)	faillir (*almost do*)	faire (*do*)
falloir (*must*)	laisser (*let*)	monter (*go up*)	oser (*dare*)	paraître (*seem*)	partir (*go off*)	penser (*think*)	pouvoir (*can*)
préférer (*prefer*)	prétendre (*pretend*)	se rappeler (*remember*)	regarder (*look at*)	rentrer (*come back in*)	savoir (*know*)	sembler (*seem*)	sentir (*feel*)
sortir (*go out*)	souhaiter (*wish*)	valoir mieux (*be better*)	venir (*come*)	voir (*see*)	vouloir (*want*)		

PRINCIPAL VERBS FOLLOWED BY <u>À</u> AND THE INFINITIVE				
aider à (*help*)	s'amuser à (*enjoy*)	apprendre à (*learn to*)	s'apprêter à (*get ready to*)	arriver à (*manage to*)
s'attendre à (*expect*)	avoir à (*have to*)	chercher à (*try to*)	commencer à (*begin to*)	consentir à (*consent*)
consister à (*consist of*)	continuer à (*continue to*)	se décider à (*decide to*)	demander à (*ask*)	encourager à (*encourage*)
enseigner à (*teach*)	forcer à (*force*)	s'habituer à (*get used to*)	hésiter à (*hesitate to*)	s'intéresser à (*be interested in*)
inviter à (*invite to*)	se mettre à (*start to*)	obliger à (*force*)	parvenir à (*manage*)	passer du temps à (*spend time . . . ing*)
penser à (*think about*)	persister à (*persist*)	pousser à (*urge to*)	préparer à (*prepare to*)	renoncer à (*give up*)
rester à (*remain . . . ing*)	réussir à (*succeed in*)	servir à (*be used for*)	songer à (*think about*)	tenir à (*care for*)

PRINCIPAL VERBS FOLLOWED BY <u>DE</u> AND THE INFINITIVE				
<u>s'agir de</u> (*to be about*)	<u>avoir peur de</u> (*be afraid of*)	<u>cesser de</u> (*stop . . . ing*)	<u>continuer de</u> (*continue to*)	<u>craindre de</u> (*dread . . . ing*)
<u>décider de</u> (*decide to*)	<u>demander de</u> (*ask*)	<u>se dépêcher de</u> (*hurry to*)	<u>essayer de</u> (*try to*)	<u>finir de</u> (*finish . . . ing*)
<u>garantir de</u> (*guarantee*)	<u>jouir de</u> (*enjoy*)	<u>manquer de</u> (*lack*)	<u>se méfier de</u> (*mistrust*)	<u>offrir de</u> (*offer to*)
<u>persuader de</u> (*persuade to*)	<u>prier de</u> (*ask to*)	<u>promettre de</u> (*promise to*)	<u>refuser de</u> (*refuse to*)	<u>regretter de</u> (*regret . . . ing*)
<u>remercier de</u> (*thank for . . . ing*)	<u>se servir de</u> (*use*)	<u>se souvenir de</u> (*remember . . . ing*)	<u>tâcher de</u> (*attempt to*)	<u>venir de</u> (*just did*)

PRINCIPAL VERBS FOLLOWED BY <u>À</u> AND A NOUN OF PERSON OR THING			
quelqu'un—qqn (*someone = s.o.*) quelque chose—qqch (*something = sthg*)			
assister à 　　　　qqch (*to attend sthg*)	convenir à 　　　qqch / qqn (*to suit sthg / s.o.*)	demander à 　　　qqch / qqn (*to ask sthg / s.o.*)	déplaire à 　　　　qqn (*to diplease s.o.*)
désobéir à 　　qqch / qqn (*to disobey sthg / s.o.*)	être à 　　　　qqn (*to belong to s.o.*)	faire attention à 　　　qqch / qqn (*to pay attention to sthg / s.o.*)	se fier à 　　　qqch / qqn (*to trust sthg / s.o.*)
goûter à 　　　qqch (*to taste sthg*)	s'habituer à 　　　qqch / qqn (*to get used to sthg / s.o.*)	s'intéresser à 　　　qqch / qqn (*to be interested in sthg / s.o.*)	jouer à 　　　　qqch (*to play sthg*)
manquer à 　　　　qqn (*to miss s.o.*)	nuire à 　　　qqch / qqn (*to hurt sthg / s.o.*)	obéir à 　　　qqch / qqn (*to obey sthg / s.o.*)	s'opposer à 　　　qqch / qqn (*to oppose sthg / s.o.*)
penser à 　　qqch / qqn (*to think about sthg / s.o.*)	plaire à 　　　　qqn (*to please s.o.*)	réfléchir à 　　　qqch / qqn (*to think over sthg / s.o.*)	répondre à 　　　qqch / qqn (*to answer sthg / s.o.*)
résister à 　　qqch / qqn (*to resist sthg / s.o.*)	ressembler à 　　qqch / qqn (*to resemble sthg / s.o.*)	réussir à 　　　　qqch (*to succeed in sthg*)	téléphoner à 　　　qqch / qqn (*to call sthg / s.o.*)

PRINCIPAL VERBS FOLLOWED BY <u>DE</u> AND A NOUN OF PERSON OR THING			
<u>s'agir</u> <u>de</u> qqch *(to be a matter of sthg)*	<u>s'approcher</u> <u>de</u> qqch / qqn *(to approach sthg / s.o.)*	<u>changer</u> <u>de</u> qqch / qqn *(to change sthg / s.o.)*	<u>dépendre</u> <u>de</u> qqch / qqn *(to depend upon sthg / s.o.)*
<u>douter</u> <u>de</u> qqch / qqn *(to doubt sthg / s.o.)*	<u>féliciter</u> <u>de</u> qqch *(to congratulate for sthg)*	<u>jouer</u> <u>de</u> qqch *(to play sthg)*	<u>jouir</u> <u>de</u> qqch / qqn *(to enjoy sthg / s.o.)*
<u>manquer</u> <u>de</u> qqch / qqn *(to miss sthg / s.o.)*	<u>se méfier</u> <u>de</u> qqch / qqn *(to mistrust sthg / s.o.)*	<u>se moquer</u> <u>de</u> qqch / qqn *(to make fun of sthg / s.o.)*	<u>s'occuper</u> <u>de</u> qqch / qqn *(to take care of sthg / s.o.)*
<u>partir</u> <u>de</u> qqch / qqn *(to leave sthg / s.o.)*	<u>se passer</u> <u>de</u> qqch / qqn *(to do without sthg / s.o.)*	<u>se plaindre</u> <u>de</u> qqch / qqn *(to complain about sthg / s.o.)*	<u>remercier</u> <u>de</u> qqch / qqn *(to thank for sthg / s.o.)*
<u>se rendre compte</u> <u>de</u> qqch *(to realize sthg)*	<u>se servir</u> <u>de</u> qqch / qqn *(to use sthg / s.o.)*	<u>se soucier</u> <u>de</u> qqch / qqn *(to care about sthg / s.o.)*	<u>se souvenir</u> <u>de</u> qqch / qqn *(to remember sthg / s.o.)*

Practice What You Learned

Exercises are rated according to four levels of difficulty:

- Beginner easy [*]
- Beginner challenging [**]
- Intermediate [***]
- Advanced [****]

1. Complete with the logical preposition: **dans, sur, sous, à,** etc. [*]

    A. Le chat est _____ la cuisine ou _____ le balcon?

    B. Charles est assis _____ un fauteuil _____ la télé, son journal est _____ la chaise _____ lui.

    C. J'ai vu "Urgence" _____ le Dr. Carter _____ la télévision mais I.A. _____ Spielberg _____ cinéma.

    D. Veux-tu faire un pique-nique _____, _____ l'herbe mais _____ les arbres _____ l'ombre?

2. Spell the date information out using a preposition each time, if necessary, according to the model or by completing the sentence. [*]

Example:

Simone de Beauvoir (9/01/1908)—**le** 9, **en** janvier, **en** 1908.

    A. Marilyn Monroe (1/6–siècle)—_____, _____, _____.

    B. Albert Einstein (14/03/1879/siècle)—_____, _____, _____, _____.

    C. Le prochain jour de l'an sera _____, _____, _____.

    D. Quel jour êtes-vous né-e? *Je suis né-e le* _____, _____, _____.

3. Insert the appropriate definite article according to the gender of the country or the state [*]

_____ France	_____ Japon	_____ Chine
_____ Texas	_____ Chili	_____ Russie
_____ Pakistan	_____ Hongrie	_____ Pérou
_____ États-Unis	_____ Suède	_____ Mexique
_____ Portugal	_____ Canada	_____ Virginie
_____ Mississippi	_____ Tibet	_____ Brésil

4. Indicate in which country the city is located using the correct preposition.[*]

Example:

Pise—Pise est **en** Italie.

A. Caracas est _____ Vénézuela.

B. Athènes est _____ Grèce.

C. Copenhague est _____ Danemark.

D. Munich est _____ Allemagne.

E. Tel Aviv est _____ Israël.

F. Osaka est _____ Japon.

G. Bagdad est _____ Irak.

H. Amsterdam est _____ Pays-Bas—_____ Hollande.

5. Complete the sentences in the following paragraph with **à**, **de**, **environ**, **vers**, or other appropriate prepositions. [**]

A. Je suis hotesse d'accueil _____ Roissy, _____ l'aéroport, _____ premier étage.

B. Je commence _____ 15 heures précises.

C. Je suis en meeting _____ une heure, une heure et quart.

D. Parfois je travaille sans interruption _____ 19 heures le lundi _____ 3 heures le mardi. Je n'ai pas de voiture et vais _____ travail _____ car, ça prend _____ une heure s'il n'y a pas d'encombrement.

6. Complete the sentences in the following paragraph with **parmi** or **entre**. [**]

A. Choisissez au hasard _____ ces cartes.

B. Des bateaux circulent _____ Marseille et les pays d'Afrique du Nord.

C. _____ la ville et la campagne, je préfère la campagne.

D. À Paris il n'y a plus de métro _____ 1h et 5h 30 du matin.

E. _____ tous les moyens de transport, je préfère la marche à pied!

7. Complete the sentences with **dans**, **depuis**, **pour**, **il y a**, **en**, **pendant**. [***]

A. Nous reviendrons _____ dix jours.

B. Vous avez loué une villa en Provence _____ deux mois.

C. Elle a improvisé un excellent repas _____ moins d'une heure.

D. Philippe doit présenter sa thèse de Doctorat _____ quinze jours; j'ai soutenu la mienne _____ sept ans.

E. Les enfants dorment _____ plus de deux heures: quel calme!

F. Olivier va travailler _____ tout l'été.

Chapter 5

FUNCTIONS OF NOUNS

Introduction

Think of a word in sentences as you think of yourself in your life. You only have one **nature**, that is who you are regardless of the environment: a human being. However, you may do many things. You take on different roles depending upon the context in which you evolve. During the day, you may **function** as a member of your family, a professional, a student, a friend, a political figure, an athlete on a team, an actor, etc.

Words, too, have a **nature**: they can be a noun, a pronoun, an article, an adjective, a verb, an adverb, a preposition, or a conjunction. And when they are put in their contexts, the various sentences, some of them can take on different **functions**.

Nouns can have only two functions—subject and complement—but within these categories there are many nuances to translate a great number of situations.

The Noun as a Subject

Nature and Characteristics

Mandatory Subject

The subject is one of the two mandatory elements—subject and verb—that make up most simple sentences. It is mandatory because it cannot be removed without the sentence becoming impossible to understand.

If nouns used as complements are taken out of a sentence, the meaning of the sentence changes but the sentence itself remains grammatical, and it still makes sense.

On the contrary, removal of the noun used as a subject leads to loss of meaning. In the following examples, only the first sentence is destroyed by the removal of the noun because it is the subject. The other sentences lose only in precision but they retain their meaning.

Sujet + **Verbe** + **Complément** (**Subject** + **Verb** + **Complement(s)**)	**Suppression of Various Nouns**
Ma chatte Vanille boit de l'eau dans sa fontaine le matin.	boit de l'eau dans sa fontaine le matin (Sentence does not make sense.)
Ma chatte Vanille boit de l'eau dans sa fontaine le matin.	Ma chatte Vanille boit de l'eau dans sa fontaine. (Sentence is still correct, after removing the circumstantial complement of time.)

Sujet + **Verbe** + **Complément** (Subject + Verb + Complement(s))	**Suppression of Various Nouns**
Ma chatte Vanille boit de l'eau ~~dans sa fontaine le matin~~.	Ma chatte Vanille boit de l'eau. (Sentence is still correct, after removing the circumstantial complement of place and time.)
Ma chatte Vanille boit ~~de l'eau dans sa fontaine le matin~~.	Ma chatte Vanille boit. (Sentence is still correct, after removing all complementary information.)
(My cat Vanille drinks water from her fountain in the morning.)	

NOTE Suppressing the subject is only possible when giving a command. In these cases, what is important is that the action be done (or not done); therefore the subject is suppressed to focus directly on the verb or its negation:

> Regarde! Fais tes exercices! Ne dépensons pas trop d'argent! (*Look! Do your exercises! Let's not spend too much money!*)

These sentences are special though: their verb or negative adverb start with a capital letter and they are in the imperative mood.

> *Refer to the chapter on* **Infinitive, Indicative, and Imperative Moods**

Superiority of the Noun

The subject rules over the verb; it imposes its person and number on the verb.

Nombre (Number)	Personne (Person)	Sujet + Verbe – Phrase (Subject + Verb – Sentence)
Singular	1st	je travaille—je finis—je vends I work—I finish—I sell
	2nd	tu manges—tu vieillis—tu prends You eat—You age—You take
	3rd	Paola danse—il obéit—elle comprend Paola dances—He obeys—She understands

Nombre (Number)	Personne (Person)	Sujet + Verbe – Phrase (Subject + Verb – Sentence)
Plural	1st	nous hésitons—nous agissons—nous répondons We hesitate—We act—We reply
	2nd	vous déjeunez—vous choisissez—vous perdez You have lunch—You choose—You lose
	3rd	Paul et Pélagie patinent—elles réfléchissent—ils attendent Paul and Pélagie skate—They think—They wait

TIP BOX

When the subject is a noun with a complement of a noun that represents a group of people or things, the verb can be used

- **in the singular** to insist on the fact that they form one united group:

  Un **groupe** d'enfants jou**e** dans le parc. (*A group of children plays in the park.*)

Or

- **in the plural** to insist on the number of individuals forming the group:

  Une foule de **fans** se précipit**ent** vers la limousine d'Isabelle Adjani. (*A group of fans **rush** toward Isabelle Adjani's limousine.*)

Placement in the Sentence

- The noun or nominal group as subject is always placed before the verb. Changing the order of the subject and the complement can result in sentences that remain grammatical but change meaning or even become meaningless:

  Jean voit Julie. Julie voit Jean. (*Jean sees Julie. Julie sees Jean.*)

  Le garçon mange un oignon. (*The boy eats an onion.*)

  L'oignon mange le garçon. (*The onion eats the boy.*) (meaningless)

- The noun or nominal group can nevertheless be separated from the verb by a noun or nominal group set between commas:

    > **Edgar a écrit** un poème à Émilie. *(Edgar wrote a poem to Émilie.)*

    > **Edgar**, amoureux fou de sa fiancée, **a écrit** un poème à Émilie.
    > *(Edgar, madly in love with his fiancée, has written a poem for Émilie.)*

> **NOTE** Special Cases: Verb + Noun
> **There are special cases in which the subject follows the verb, mostly:**
>
> - **In** dialogues: **"Tu es gentil", dit Paul à son papa.** *("You are nice," Paul says to his dad.)*
> - **In** exclamations in the subjunctive: **Puissiez-vous gagner au loto!** *(May you win the lottery!)*
> - **In administrative or** legal statements: **Sont admis au baccalauréat les candidats suivants...** *(Having passed the baccalauréat exam, the following candidates...)*
> - **After** certain adverbs: **Il travaille,** aussi **viendra-t-il plus tard.** *(He works, thus he will come later.)*

The Subject Performs the Action

There are various types of subjects that rule over the verb and perform the action. These are nuances but the same rule remains: the grammatical subject of the verb is also the person, thing, or concept responsible for the concrete or abstract action.

Real Subject—Real Action

The subject is animated and performs the action actually expressed by the verb.

> **Chantal** joue aux échecs. *(Chantal plays chess.)*

> **Elle** lance une balle à son chien Loulou. *(She throws a ball to her dog Loulou.)*

> **On** dit que les Français sont cyniques et les Américains optimistes. *(It is said that the French are cynical and the Americans optimists.)*

Inanimate Subjects—Resulting Action

Certain grammatical subjects are things and cannot therefore perform anything; a result is nevertheless generated.

> **La pomme** tombe de l'arbre. *(The apple falls from the tree.)*

Les Volvos ont une réputation de grande sécurité. *(Volvos have a reputation for being very safe.)*

La santé de Saturnin s'améliore. *(Saturnin's health is improving.)*

Impersonal Subject—Concrete or Abstract Result

These subjects may not actually refer to an agent; they are generally neuter, that is, third person masculine and singular. They may also, in fact, replace a noun in the sentence.

Il fait très beau sur la Côte d'Azur toute l'année.—No real subject, impersonal pronoun. *(The weather is beautiful all year long on the French Riviera.)*

Il manque de **l'argent** dans la caisse de la banque.—Impersonal pronoun to designate the money. *(Money is missing from the cash register.)*

Il y a **des moments** difficiles dans la vie de tout le monde.—Impersonal pronoun to designate the moments. *(There are difficult moments in everyone's life.)*

> *Refer to Chapter 17 for*
> **Subjunctive Mood**

The Subject Receives the Action

Grammatical subjects of the verb may not always be the performers of the action. The same idea can be expressed through two different constructions:

1. The Active Voice

The subject of the verb **performs** the action expressed by this verb:

Le chat attrappe le pompon. *(The cat catches the pompom.)*

L'architecte a construit cette cathédrale en 1680. *(The architect built this cathedral in 1680.)*

2. The Passive Voice

The subject of the verb **receives** the action. The actual performer of the action can be implied or stated in the sentence. It is then introduced by the preposition **par** (by) and is called the **agent**:

Le pompon est attrappé par **le chat**. *(The pompom is caught by the cat.)*

The pompom is the *subject* of the verb but the cat does the catching: **Le pompon** is the subject; **le chat** is the agent.

> *Cette cathédrale* a été construite en 1680. *(This cathedral was built in 1680.)*

The cathedral is the subject of the verb but the builder is implied.

In order to transform the subject of the verb into the receiver of the action, the verb must be conjugated in the passive voice.

The passive voice is composed of the auxiliary verb **être** (*to be*) conjugated in the desired tense and the **participe passé** (*past participle*).

PASSIVE VOICE The past participle always agrees **in gender and number with the subject of the verb in the** passive voice.

TIP BOX

When in doubt, rely on the terminology used to describe the grammar rules. **Passive** implies not doing anything: in the passive voice, the subject does nothing (namely, not the action).

Also, the word passive is used with *to be* in English: one *IS* passive (it is a state since it is not an action), so the passive voice will need the auxiliary verb *to be* (**être**) to be formed.

Finally, since being passive reflects a state of the subject, the second component of the passive voice, namely the past participle, will agree in gender and number with this noun as subject.

The Noun as Complement

Types of Complements

Complements are divided into two main categories that correspond to the information they provide about the action:

1. **Les compléments d'objet (object complements or objects)** represent the person or thing that the action affects.
2. **Les compléments circonstanciels (circumstantial complements)** inform about the various circumstances surrounding the action. These are called prepositional phrases in English grammar since they start with a preposition.

Each type of complement answers to a specific question posed after the verb in the sentence. As in English there are seven main questions to ask after pronouncing the verb:

TYPES OF COMPLEMENTS		
VERB +	1. What—whom? (Quoi?—Qui?) and its variations • To what—whom? (À quoi—À qui?) • Of what—whom? (De quoi—De qui?)	Complément d'objet direct Complément d'objet indirect
	2. When? (Quand?)	Complément circonstanciel de TEMPS (*time*)
	3. Where? (Où?)	Complément circonstanciel de LIEU (*place*)
	4. How? (Comment?)	Complément circonstanciel de MANIÈRE (*manner*)
	5. With what? (Avec quoi?)	Complément circonstanciel de MOYEN (*means*)
	6. Why? (Pourquoi?)	Complément circonstanciel de CAUSE (*cause*)
	7. With which purpose? (Dans quel but?)	Complément circonstanciel de BUT (*purpose*)

Noun as Object Complement

Verb Types

Object complements are nouns, nominal groups, or pronouns that answer the questions **Quoi—Qui?** (What—whom) or **À / De quoi?** (To / of what—whom).

Transitive Verbs

Verbs that can have an object complement are called **verbes transitifs** (transitive verbs); it is possible to ask the questions *what—whom?* or *to/of what—whom?* after the verb and insert a complement.

> L'écureuil mange.
>
> L'écureuil **mange quoi**? Une noisette. *(The squirrel eats a hazelnut.)* The verb has an object complement; it is transitive.
>
> Je parle à ma mère.
>
> Je **parle à qui**? À ma mère. *(I speak to whom? To my mother.)* The verb has an object complement; it is transitive.

Intransitive Verbs

Verbs that CANNOT have an object complement are called INtransitive.

> L'écureuil tombe.

> L'écureuil **tombe quoi**? No possible answer; one does not fall something. This verb is INtransitive.

In the order of the sentence, the object complement always follows the conjugated verb. In the sentence structure, this complement can be placed **directly after the verb** or **indirectly after the verb**.

You are going to the movies with friends.

How would you go there directly?

_____

How would go there indirectly?

_____

House to Theater
Verb to Noun as Object Complement: DIRECT
(House ☞ Theater) = (Verb ☞ Complement)

House to automated teller machine to theater (House ☞ **Bank** ☞ Theater)
House to pick up a friend to theater (House ☞ **Friend's house** ☞ Theater)
Verb to **Preposition** to Noun as Object Complement: INDIRECT
(House ☞ **Bank** ☞ Theater) = (Verb ☞ **Preposition** ☞ Theater)

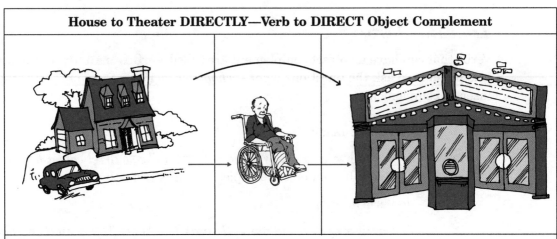

House to Theater DIRECTLY—Verb to DIRECT Object Complement

House to Friend to Theater INDIRECTLY—
Verb to Preposition to INDIRECT Object Complement

Types of Object Complement

Direct Object Complement: Complément d'Objet Direct = COD

When it is placed directly after the verb, it is a direct object complement.

- Noun Subject + Conjugated **Verb** + **Object** as Direct Complement

> Les Français **aiment l'informatique**—Verbe + **COD**. *(The French like computer science.)*
>
> Norbert **utilise son ordinateur** tous les jours—Verbe + **COD**. *(Norbert uses his computer every day.)*
>
> Lionel **préfère les MacIntosh**; Florence **adore son PC**—Verbe + **COD**. *(Lionel prefers Macs; Florence loves her PC.)*

Indirect Object Complement: Complément d'Objet Indirect = COI

After the preposition **À** or **DE** as demanded by the verb or the context of the sentence, it is an indirect object complement.

- Noun Subject + Conjugated **Verb** + **Preposition** + *Indirect Object Complement*

> Les Français **parlent DE** *l'informatique*—Verbe + Préposition **DE** + *COI* *(The French talk about computer sciences.)*
>
> Norbert **parle À** *son ordinateur* via un micro—Verbe + Préposition **À** + COI *(Norbert talks to his computer through a microphone.)*
>
> Lionel **a besoin D**'un PC, mais il **se fie** plus **aux** MacIntosh—Verbe + Préposition **DE** + *COI*—Verbe + Préposition **À** + *COI*. *(Lionel needs a PC, but he trusts Macs more.)*

NOTE The presence of the word **DE** in front of a noun object complement does not systematically make this complement an indirect one.

The same word can have different functions and natures. De can be a preposition but also a component of the partitive article du, de la, de l'.

| Lola boit | de l'eau | —boire + COD |

De l'eau means some water and it is a direct object complement because it answers the question: quoi?

Lola boit quoi? In de l'eau, de **is part of the partitive article, so water** (l'eau) **follows the verb directly.**

| Lola a besoin | de | ta voiture | —avoir besoin de + COI |

De ta voiture means that Lola is in need of your car. It is an indirect object complement because it answers the question DE quoi?

Lola a besoin de quoi? In **de ta voiture, de** is the preposition necessary with the verb **avoir besoin de.** The complement (ta voiture) is therefore indirectly following the verb (**a besoin**) through the preposition **de.**

- A French dictionary specifies how the verb is to be used. It lists verbs as *v. tr.*—transitive verb or *v. intr.*—intransitive verb. That will help you make sure that the object complement is direct or indirect.
- Remember also to learn the basic list of verbs constructed with the preposition À or DE that were provided in the preposition chapters. These will tell you which main verbs need an indirect object complement.

Refer to Chapter 4 for **Prepositions**

IMPORTANT!

Knowing the difference between **direct and indirect object** complements is key to being able to choose the **appropriate personal pronouns** that can replace them.

There are two different lists of personal pronouns that replace nouns as direct object or indirect object complements.

Since, as we have seen in the **preposition** chapter, **transitive or intransitive verbs** in English are not necessarily the same in French, always verify the construction of the French verbs in the dictionary.

Noun as Circumstantial Complement

Characteristics

Circumstantial complements are easy to use and identify because

- They are not necessary: They can be deleted from the sentence without it being grammatically destroyed. Suppressing a circumstantial complement removes information about the action that may be crucial to you, but it does not affect the structure of the sentence itself.
- They are not fixed: Circumstantial complements can be displaced in the sentence; their position puts more or less emphasis on the information they provide but it does not change their function:

Mes chattes mangent des croquettes **sur la terrasse**. *(My cats eat crunchies on the terrace.)*

> **Sur la terrasse**, mes chattes mangent des croquettes. *(On the terrace, my cats eat crunchies.)*

- On the contrary, object complements have a fixed place in the sentence:

  > Mes chattes mangent **des croquettes**.

  > **Des croquettes** mangent mes chattes. *(When positioned before the verb the noun becomes its subject—Dry food crunchies eat my cats!)*

- The normal position of the circumstantial complement is **after** the verb toward the **end** of the sentence. Consequently, the closer it is to the beginning of the sentence, the more attention is drawn to it:

  > Benjamin mange une brioche **avec plaisir**. *(Benjamin eats a brioche with pleasure.)*

Benjamin	**mange**	**une brioche**	**avec plaisir**.
Subject	Verb	Complément d'Objet Direct—COD (Complement of Direct Object)	CC Manière (Circumstantial Complement of Manner)
Benjamin,	**avec plaisir,**	**mange**	**une brioche.**
Subject	CC Manière (Circumstantial Complement of Manner)	Verb	Complément d'Objet Direct—COD (Complement of Direct Object)
Avec plaisir,	**Benjamin**	**mange**	**une brioche.**
CC Manière (Circumstantial Complement of Manner)	Subject	Verb	Complément d'Objet Direct—COD (Complement of Direct Object)

- There can be many circumstantial complements in the sentence, although more than three complements can make a sentence sound quite awkward.

Marine	se lève	**le matin**	**pour une promenade**	**à pied**	mais **avec rapidité**	**au bord de mer**	**pour sa santé.**
Subject	verb	CC **Temps**	CC **But**	CC **Moyen**	CC **Manière**	CC **Lieu**	CC **Cause**

- In most cases, the circumstantial complement is introduced **after** the verb by a preposition—but the preposition is not always mandatory:

> Lionel travaille **durant** la nuit et dort **pendant** le jour. (*Lionel works during the night and sleeps during the day.*)

> Lionel travaille **de** nuit et dort [φ] le jour. (*Lionel works at night and sleeps in the day.*)

Use

Specified Circumstances

Circumstantial complements inform principally about the time, location, way, means, cause, and purpose of the action.

These notions correspond to specific questions *when, where, how, with, what, why,* and *with which* purpose. Responses to the questions are introduced by prepositions that also express time, location, way, means, cause, and purpose of the action.

OVERVIEW TABLE: CIRCUMSTANCES SPECIFYING PREPOSITION	
CC **Temps**	**à, vers, pendant, durant, en, lors de** . . . Il arrivera **vers** 8 heures. (*He will arrive around 8 o'clock.*)
CC **Lieu**	**à, dans, sur, près de, derrière** . . . Mes clés sont **dans** la voiture fermée! (*My keys are in the locked car!*)
CC **Manière**	**avec, en, dans** . . . Elle déguste sa crêpe **avec** délicatesse. (*She eats her crêpe delicately.*)
CC **Moyen**	**avec, au moyen de, grâce à** . . . Elle coupe sa crêpe **avec** un couteau **en** argent massif. (*She cuts her crêpe with a knife made of pure silver.*)
CC **Cause**	**pour, à cause de, en dépit de, de** Ces enfants tremblent **de** froid. (*These children are shivering of cold.*)
CC **But**	**dans le but de, pour, afin de** Fab ne mange plus de chocolat **pour** son régime. (*Fab no longer eats chocolate for her diet.*)

Contextual Circumstances

Prepositions are also relatively independent from the notion expressed by the circumstantial complement.

The circumstantial information results from a combination of the preposition and the entire context of the sentence—or the conversation.

Contexte (*Context*)	Préposition (*Preposition*)
CC **Temps**	**dans, en** Aurore fera ses devoirs **dans** une heure. (*Aurore will do her homework in an hour.*) Aurore fera ses devoirs **en** une heure. (*It will take Aurore an hour to do her homework.*)
CC **Lieu**	**dans, en** Aurore fera ses devoirs **dans** la bibliothèque. (*Aurore will do her homework in the library.*) Aurore partira **en** Afrique. (*Aurore will leave for Africa.*)
CC **Manière**	**dans, en** Aurore fera ses devoirs **dans** la joie. (*Aurore will do her homework joyfully.*) Aurore décide **en** son âme et conscience. (*Aurore decides according to her soul and conscience.*)
CC **Moyen**	**avec** Aurore fera ses devoirs **avec** ses dictionnaires. (*Aurore will do her homework with her dictionaries.*)
CC **Cause**	**avec** Aurore fera ses études **avec** le désir de réussir. (*Aurore will study with the desire to succeed.*)
CC **Manière**	**avec** Aurore fera ses devoirs **avec** plaisir. (*Aurore will do her homework with pleasure.*)

Nuanced Circumstances

Inversely, the same circumstance can be expressed by a variety of prepositions that add only a particular nuance.

Je verrai Philippe	**à** 1 heure	(*at 1 P.M.*)
	vers 1 heure	(*around 1 P.M.*)
	dans une heure	(*in an hour*)
	pendant une heure	(*for an hour*)
	environ une heure	(*about an hour*)
	de 1 heure **à** 3 heures	(*from 1 to 3*)

> **MAGIC METHOD** The following Magic Method shows you how to identify a complement in six easy steps. It will also be very helpful when you need to replace nouns by the pronouns corresponding to their various functions.

> *Refer to Chapter 8 for*
> **Personal Pronouns**

Identification of Complements

IDENTIFICATION OF COMPLEMENTS ABC MAGIC METHOD				
1	**A**	**rrange**	the sentence so it follows the French normal structure.	Subject + Verb + Complement
2	**B**	**reak off**	the sentence after the verb and stop.	Subject + Verb ✄
3	**C**	**ontinue**	the sentence with a question.	☞ + ?
4	**D**	**ecide**	which question will be answered by the rest of the sentence.	Quoi—Qui? (*What—Who?*)
				À quoi—À qui? (*To what—whom?*)
				De quoi—De qui? (*Of what—whom?*)
				Quand? (*When?*)
				Où? (*Where?*)
				Comment? (*How?*)
				Avec quoi? (*With what?*)
				Pourquoi? (*Why?*)
				Dans quel but? (*With what purpose?*)

5	E	quate	the question with its corresponding complement.	Quoi—Qui?	COD *Direct Object*
				À quoi—À qui?	COI *Indirect Object*
				De quoi— De qui?	COI *Indirect Object*
				Quand?	CC Temps *Time*
				Où?	CC Lieu *Location*
				Comment?	CC Manière *Manner*
				Avec quoi?	CC Moyen *Means*
				Pourquoi?	CC Cause *Cause*
				Dans quel but?	CC But *Purpose*
6	F	ind	the nature of the complement.	Remember it when you have to replace the complements by a pronoun.	

Find examples of application of the ABC Magic Method in Practice Exercise 4 following this chapter. Complete the exercise by following the 6 steps above.

Practice What You Learned

Exercises are rated according to four levels of difficulty:

- Beginner easy [*]
- Beginner challenging [**]
- Intermediate [***]
- Advanced [****]

SUBJECTS; OBJECTS; CIRCUMSTANTIAL COMPLEMENTS			
Sujet Le meurtrier	**Objet = COD** La victime	**Moyen = CC** L'arme du crime	**Lieu = CC** Le lieu du crime
Professeur Violet	Madame Leblanc	la corde	le grand salon
Colonel Moutarde	Mlle Rose	le poignard	la véranda
Mlle Rose	Docteur Olive	le révolver	la cuisine
Docteur Olive	Colonel Moutarde	le chandelier	le petit salon
Mlle Pervenche	Professeur Violet	la matraque	la salle à manger
Madame Leblanc	Mlle Pervenche	la clé anglaise	le studio
			la bibliothèque
			le bureau
			le hall

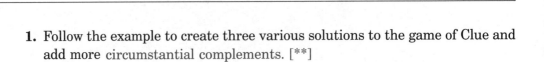

1. Follow the example to create three various solutions to the game of Clue and add more circumstantial complements. [**]

Example:

Madame Leblanc a dit à Mlle Rose qu'elle a tué le Colonel Moutarde, dans la cuisine, avec la matraque, en silence, à minuit, à cause de sa haine pour l'armée mais aussi pour la gloire du ketchup!

Madame Leblanc	a dit	à Mlle Rose	qu'elle a tuè	le Colonel **Moutarde**
Sujet	Verbe	Complément **d'Objet Indirect COI**	Sujet Verbe	Complément **d'Object Direct COD**
dans la **cuisine**,	avec la **matraque**,	en **silence**,	à **minuit**,	
Complément Circonstanciel CC de **Lieu**	Complément Circonstanciel CC de **Moyen**	Complément Circonstanciel CC de **Manière**	Complément Circonstanciel CC de **Temps**	
à cause de sa **haine** pour l'armée,		mais aussi pour la **gloire** du ketchup!		
Complément Circonstanciel CC de **Cause**		Complément Circonstanciel CC de **But**		

A. _____

B. _____

C. _____

2. Insert the correct subject in the following sentences. Be careful, there are more words than necessary. Use all the information (gender, number, verb ending, etc.) in the sentence to make the correct choice. [***]

Emmanuelle—Je—le garçon—il—un parasol—nous—les choix—ma crème brulée—Je—elle—ils—une glace au chocolat—Une glace

A. _____ sommes arrivés au café.

B. _____ y avait beaucoup de monde sur la terrasse.

C. _____ me suis assise sous un parasol et mon amie

D. _____ a regardé les choix de desserts.

E. _____ étaient nombreux.

F. _____ a choisi une glace.

G. _____ été apportée par le garçon.

H. _____ était délicieuse.

3. Identify the following object complements as direct or indirect. [**]

A. Votre petit ami achète des fleurs. _____

B. Je me sers de mon ordinateur tous les jours. _____

C. Veux-tu mes clés? _____

   D. Cette robe va bien à Marie. _____

   E. Il ne prend pas de sucre dans son café. _____

4. Ask the question that is answered by the complement in the sentence and identify its type in French. [**]

Example:

Je n'**achète** ✂ pas de fromage: **acheter quoi**? pas de **fromage**: de = partitive article; fromage = complément d'objet **direct**

   A. Elle **se déplace** ✂ en limousine: _____

   B. Valérie **adore** ✂ la vanille: _____

   C. Blanche **parle** ✂ de ses vacances: _____

   D. Barbara **part** ✂ à Bali: _____

   E. Florentin **ressemble** ✂ à Séverin: _____

   F. Les yaourts de Yolande **sont** ✂ pour son régime: _____

   G. **Donne**-moi ✂ du chocolat: _____

   H. Elisabeth peut **lire** ✂ à toute vitesse: _____

   I. Thierry **t'envoie** ✂ des tartes tatin: _____

   J. Étienne **étudie** ✂ en vue de ses examens: _____

5. Find all the complements in the following text and identify them. [****]

Restauration rapide
McDonald's recrute

Les postes proposés sont de vrais emplois permettant d'intégrer le monde du travail.

McDonald's France embauche près de 3 000 personnes chaque année. Il s'agit en majorité de jeunes de 18 à 30 ans. Il n'y a pas de profil type, car les fonctions, variées, font appel à différentes compétences. Aux équipiers, qui préparent les commandes derrière le comptoir, et aux hôtesses, qui s'occupent de l'accueil et organisent les anniversaires, on demande d'avoir l'esprit d'équipe, du tonus et de la courtoisie. Les assistants administratifs, chargés de la comptabilité et de la gestion, ont en général un BTS commercial ou comptable. Quant aux directeurs de restaurant (50 % de femmes), ils ont soit intégré l'enseigne avec un niveau bac+2 ou+3, soit gravi tous les échelons après avoir débuté comme équipier. Les possibilités de progression sont rapides, à condition d'avoir le sens du service aux clients et des aptitudes au management. Les employés bénéficient tous d'une formation sur le terrain (au restaurant) afin d'acquérir les connaissances nécessaires en hygiène et sécurité alimentaire, ou au siège de McDonald's France pour les fonctions d'encadrement. Au niveau des salaires, les postes de base sont payés au Smic horaire augmenté de 10 %. Les assistants administratifs gagnent entre 1 200 et 1 500 € brut par mois, et les directeurs de restaurant entre 2 500 et 3 000 €. ∎

M.-J. Coutanceau

Les candidatures sont à déposer auprès des restaurants ou des ANPE locales, en cas d'ouverture d'un McDonald's dans le secteur. Ou sur le site www.mcdonalds.fr, rubrique « emploi ».

Complement	List each noun you think corresponds to the category
Direct Object 18 complements	_____ – _____ – _____ – _____ – _____ _____ – _____ – _____ – _____ – _____ _____ – _____ – _____ – _____ – _____ _____ – _____ – _____ – _____ – _____
Indirect Object 13 complements	_____ – _____ – _____ – _____ – _____ _____ – _____ – _____ – _____ – _____ _____ – _____ – _____
CC Location 10 complements	_____ – _____ – _____ – _____ – _____ _____ – _____ – _____ – _____
CC Time 2 complements	_____ – _____
CC Manner 5 complements	_____ – _____ – _____ – _____ – _____
CC Means 1 complement	_____
CC Purpose 1 complement	_____

Chapter 6

QUALIFYING ADJECTIVES

Introduction

Adjectives are part of the nominal group. Think of them as accessories that enhance a plain outfit or options added to a basic car. Some may be indispensable, such as air conditioning in Nevada; a possessive adjective may make a huge difference—for instance, I have a date with my husband tonight vs. I have a date with your husband tonight! Others may be used for more aesthetic or descriptive reasons:

> "Rien ne bougeait encore dans les rues engourdies d'Orsenna, les grands éventails des palmes s'épanouissaient plus larges au-dessus des murs aveugles: l'heure sonnant à la cathédrale éveillait une vibration sourde et attentive dans les vieilles façades."
>
> <u>Le Rivage des Syrtes</u>, Julien Gracq
>
> *(Nothing was moving yet in the sleepy streets of Orsenna, the large fans of palm trees spread out further over the blind walls: the hour ringing at the cathedral was creating a dull and attentive vibration in the old facades.*

Definition: A qualifying adjective expresses any quality or characteristic of the person, thing, or concept that the noun it accompanies represents.

Rules of Use

Regardless of the category to which they belong, adjectives always accompany nouns and are closely linked to them. Their form is therefore dependent upon the characteristics of those nouns.

Agreement

Because they belong to the nominal group, adjectives must be in harmony with all their elements. Consequently, adjectives must match—agree with—the gender and number of the nouns they accompany.

Gender Agreement

Adjectives are learned in the masculine singular form since it is also the neuter one. The feminine form is modified on the basis of the masculine one.

> **NOTE** Most adjectives are changed into their feminine form by adding an **e** at the end of the masculine one.
>
> Adjectives whose masculine form already ends in **e** do not change:
>
> un stylo **noir**—un**e** voiture **noire**; un oiseau **libre**—un**e** décision **libre**

Other changes are made to adjectives with a certain ending. It is always recommended that you check the feminine form in a dictionary, but these are the main variations:

PARTICULAR PATTERNS OF FEMINIZATION	
Masculine in	Feminine Form in
. . . . . **c**	. . . . . que or . . . . che: public—publique / laïc—laïque *(public, secular)* blanc—blanche / sec—sèche *(white, dry)*
. . . . . **[t]eur**	. . . . . euse or . . . . trice: menteur—menteuse / trompeur—trompeuse séducteur—séductrice *(lying, cheating, seducing)* **Some exceptions**: majeur—majeure / supérieur—supérieure *(major, upper)*
. . . . . **x**	. . . . . se: heureux—heureuse / onéreux—onéreuse *(happy, expensive)* **Some exceptions**: faux—fausse / vieux—vieille / doux—douce *(false, old, soft)*
all vowels . . . . . **i**, ... **ai**, ... **u**	. . . . . e: vrai—vraie / poli—polie / dru—drue *(true, polite, straight)*
. . . . . **on**, ... **ien** . . . . . **el**, ... **ul**, ... **eil** . . . . . **et** . . . . . **s**, ... **t**	final consonant is doubled + e: bon—bonne / ancien—ancienne *(good, ancient)* cruel—cruelle / nul—nulle / pareil—pareille *(cruel, null, similar)* muet—muette / bas—basse / sot—sotte *(dumb, low, silly)* **Some exceptions**: inquiet—inquiète / discret—discrète *(worried, discreet)*
. . . . . **er**	. . . . . ère: léger—légère / premier—première *(light, first)*
. . . . . **f**	. . . . . ve: vif—vive / neuf—neuve *(vivacious, new)*

A few adjectives have irregular feminine forms:

malin—**maligne** / frais—**fraîche** / jumeau—**jumelle** / long—**longue** *(evil, fresh, twin, long)*

Number Agreement

Adjectives are learned in the masculine singular form since it is also the neuter one. The plural form is modified from it.

> **NOTE** Most masculine adjectives are changed into their plural form by adding an **s** at the end of the singular one. Regular feminine adjectives also have an **s**.
>   Adjectives whose masculine form already ends in **s** or **x** do not change.
>
> > **le chien est <u>gros</u> mais <u>peureux</u>. Les chiens sont <u>gros</u> mais <u>peureux</u>.** (*The dog is big but fearful. The dogs are big but fearful.*)

Other changes are made to adjectives with certain endings. It is always recommended that you check the plural form in a dictionary, but these are the main variations:

REVIEW TABLE: PARTICULAR PATTERNS OF PLURALIZATION	
Singular in	**Plural Form in**
. . . . . **al**	. . . . . aux: royal—**royaux**/ légal—**légaux** **Some exceptions**: final—**finals** / naval—**navals** / fatal—**fatals**
(*royal, legal*) (**Some exceptions**: *final, naval, fatal*)	
. . . . . **eau**	. . . . . eaux: beau—**beaux**
(*beautiful*)	

Nonagreeing Adjectives

A few adjectives are usually invariable. This means they do not change with feminine or plural nouns.

> snob, marron, impromptu *(snob, brown, impromptu)*

Adjectives describing a color with compounded words are also invariable:

> une voiture **bleu foncé**, un pantalon **bleu foncé**, des pantalons **bleu foncé** *(a dark blue car, dark blue pants)*

In case of doubt about a feminine or plural form, it is best to verify it in a dictionary.

Position

> **TIP BOX**
>
> French qualifying or descriptive adjectives, as opposed to English ones, are usually placed **after** the noun.
>
> Adjectif Français: generally **AF**ter the noun
>
> Only **BAGS** (*Beauty, age, goodness, size*) come *Before* the noun.

The placement and organization of adjectives depends upon their function. All qualifying adjectives accompany the noun, but they can do so in three ways:

1. **Épithète**: directly after—or before—the noun
2. **Mis en apposition**: separated from the noun by a comma
3. **Attribut**: separated from the noun by an auxiliary or a verb expressing a state of the subject

Choosing to use the adjective in one way or the other changes the emphasis put on the quality it describes or affects the stylistic level of language.

Epithetical Adjectives

- Epithetical adjectives express a quality without any particular insistence on it, so they can be suppressed from the sentence without grammatically affecting it.

> Mes **quatre** chattes ont des yeux **bleus**. (*My four cats have **blue** eyes.*)

> La maman chat Tofa a des poils **gris**, Vanille un nez **rose**, Fripouille une queue très **trouffue** et Cléa une fourrure couleur de chocolat **foncé**. (*The mama cat Tofa has **gray** hair, Vanille a **pink** nose, Fripouille a very **puffy** tail, and Clea's coat is of a **dark** chocolate color.*)

- Most epithet qualifying adjectives follow the noun, with the exception of the adjectives known as **BAGS** *that precede the noun*.

	BAGS	
B	EAUTY	*beau, joli . . .* C'est un **beau** chien. Tu as une **jolie** coupe de cheveux. *(This is a beautiful dog. Your haircut is pretty.)*
A	GE	*jeune, nouveau, vieux . . .* Mon **jeune** ami et moi . . . Ce **vieux** philosophe s'appelle Socrate. *(My young friend and I . . . This old philosopher's name is Socrates.)*
G	OODNESS	*bon, gentil, méchant* Marc est de **méchante** humeur. Quelle **bonne** mousse au chocolat! *(Marc is in a bad mood. What a good chocolate mousse!)*
S	IZE	*grand, court, gros, long . . .* Le **long** nez de Cléopâtre est aussi célèbre que le **gros** ventre d'Obelix. Ce **grand** géant va manger le **petit** homme comme un glace au cornet! *(Cleopatra's long nose is as famous as Obelix' big belly. This big giant is going to eat the little man as if he were an ice cream cone!)*

> **NOTE** The meaning of a few adjectives changes if they are placed before or after the noun.

DOUBLE MEANING	
BAGS: **Before the noun**	**Adjectif Français: AFter the noun**
un *grand* homme **a remarkable man**	un homme **grand** **a tall man**
un *petit* homme **a short man**	un homme **petit** **a miserable little man**
un *brave* garçon **a nice guy**	un garçon **brave** **a courageous boy**
un *ancien* professeur **a former teacher**	des meubles **anciens** **old furniture**
un *curieux* enfant **a strange kid**	un enfant **curieux** **a curious child**
mon *cher* fils **my dear son**	un livre **cher** **an expensive book**
un *certain* jour **some day**	un jour **certain** **a definite day**
la *même* chose **the same thing**	la liberté **même** **the very freedom**
ma *propre* volonté **my own will**	les mains **propres** **clean hands**
un *vrai* héros **a real hero**	une histoire **vraie** **a true story**
la *seule* façon **the only way**	un homme **seul** **a lonely man**

- When a noun is accompanied by two qualifying adjectives, two cases are possible.
  - Both are coordinated with a <u>conjunction of coordination</u> (mais, ou, et, donc, or, ni, car) and placed after the noun. They normally express qualities of a comparable category.

    C'est une femme **juste** <u>et</u> **sensible**. *(She is a fair and sensitive woman.)*

    C'est un juge **strict** <u>mais</u> **impartial**. *(He is a strict but impartial judge.)*

  - One is placed before and one after the noun; their quality is of a different order.

    J'aime cette ***grande*** maison **victorienne**. *(I like this large Victorian house.)*

Regarde ces *belles* voitures **noires**. *(Look at the beautiful black cars.)*

Le SIDA est un *véritable* fléau **moderne**. *(AIDS is a true modern plague.)*

Apposed Adjectives

- Qualifying adjectives are placed in apposition when the speaker or writer wishes to emphasize them. Because they are isolated in the sentence by a comma, or by a pause in speech, the attention is drawn to the quality they express.
- Apposed adjectives can be placed anywhere in the sentence provided their location does not create any ambiguity about the noun they qualify.

Examples:

L'enfant joyeux croquait sa sucette dans la cour de l'école.

Joyeux, l'enfant croquait sa sucette dans la cour de l'école.

L'enfant croquait sa sucette, **joyeux**, dans la cour de l'école.

L'enfant croquait sa sucette dans la cour de l'école, **joyeux**.

(The joyful child was chewing his lollipop in the schoolyard.)

In these examples there cannot be any ambiguity about who is happy here, since the adjective is masculine singular and no other word but **l'enfant** is.

On the contrary, in the following example,

L'homme triste contemplait le paysage de Cézanne. *(The sad man was contemplating Cezanne's countryside.)*

Cezanne was a famous impressionist artist who painted numerous southern hills and countrysides around the town of Aix-en-Provence.

The only way of putting the adjective in apposition is:

Triste, l'homme contemplait le paysage de Cézanne.

because:

- *L'homme contemplait le paysage, triste, de Cézanne* is grammatically correct but may mean the countryside was sad.
- *L'homme contemplait le paysage de Cézanne, triste* is grammatically correct but may mean Cézanne was sad.

Attributive Adjectives

- An attributive adjective expresses a quality of a noun by means of a verbal element. This verbal element can be the auxiliary verb **être** or a verb expressing a state of the noun that the adjective accompanies.

MAIN VERBS FOLLOWED BY AN ATTRIBUTIVE ADJECTIVE	
Attribute with Auxiliary Verb **Être**	
Marie **est mariée**. Fabrice **est fatigué**.	*(Mary is married.)* *(Fabrice is tired.)*
Attribute with Verbs of State	
paraître, sembler, demeurer, devenir, rester Cette pomme **paraît parfaite**. Le saumon **semble salé**. Damien **demeure muet**. Delphine **devient difficile** à vivre. Rémi **reste sourd** à tes demandes.	*(This apple appears to be perfect.)* *(The salmon seems salty.)* *(Damien remains speechless.)* *(Delphine is becoming difficult to live with.)* *(Remi stays deaf to your requests.)*
Être considéré comme, **passer** pour Les français **passent** pour **arrogants**. C'**est considéré** comme **vrai**.	*(The French are said to be arrogant.)* *(This is considered a true fact.)*
Avoir l'air Elle **a l'air libérée** de ses problèmes.	*(She seems to have solved her problems.)*
Être traité de Ils **sont traités de tricheurs**.	*(They are accused of cheating.)*

- Because it also belongs to the verbal group, contrary to epithet or apposed adjectives, the attribute is mandatory for the sentence to remain grammatical and make sense.

> ~~Le saumon semble~~ *(The salmon seems) is an incomplete sentence.*
>
> ~~Nous sommes considérées comme~~ *(We are considered as) is an incomplete sentence.*

- Like epithets and apposed adjectives, attributes agree in gender and number with the noun they qualify.

THINK!

Using the **attributive adjectives** and relying on the information they provide, locate the various cheeses described below. All <u>other adjectives</u> are underlined.

Le Murol est **troué** comme un bagel.

Les Roves paraissent **ronds** comme des balles de ping pong.

Le Valençay semble **brulé** comme du charbon.

En <u>demi</u>–cercle, les Mimolettes sont considérées **bonnes** pour les enfants.

Les <u>deux</u> Banons passent pour **meilleurs** que <u>tous</u> les fromages de chèvre. Ils sont **enveloppés** comme des <u>petits</u> cadeaux dans des feuilles de vigne <u>vert foncé</u>.

Le Munster devient **mou** et **puant**. Il est **gros**, **rond** et **orange**.

France has more than 300 kinds of cheese. Most of them are specific to different regions, but they are available countrywide. Cheeses generally occupy an entire aisle at the supermarket.

The solution is at the end of the practice section, page 80.

Degrees of Qualifying Adjectives

Adjectives express qualities of a person, a thing, or a concept. This characteristic, however, can be more or less marked or strong. There are two possibilities of comparisons:

1. between one element and another one
2. between one element and all the other ones in the same group

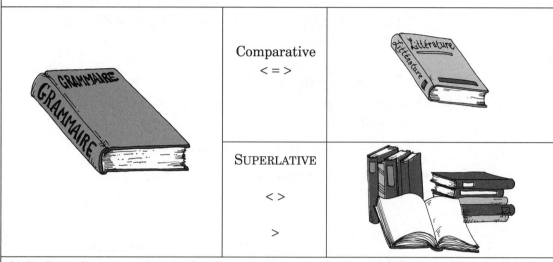

1. Le livre de grammaire est **plus gros que** celui de littérature. *(The grammar book is bigger than the literature one.)*

	Comparative < = >	
	SUPERLATIVE < > >	

2. Le livre de grammaire est **le plus gros de** tous les livres. *(The grammar book is the biggest of all the books.)*

The Comparative Degree

It expresses a comparison between two elements that share a characteristic within a group. There are three possible results to the comparison:

1. Comparatif de supériorité (Comparative Structure of Superiority)
   One object's quality is superior to the other's:

   > Le livre de grammaire est **plus *intéressant* que** celui de littérature *(more interesting than).*

2. Comparatif d'infériorité (Comparative Structure of Inferiority)
   One object's quality is inferior to the other's:

   > Le livre de littérature est **moins *intéressant* que** celui de grammaire *(less interesting than).*

3. Comparatif d'égalité (Comparative Structure of Equality)
   One object's quality is equal to that of the others:

   > Le livre de grammaire est **aussi *intéressant* que** celui de littérature *(as interesting as).*

The Superlative Degree

This expresses a comparison between one element and all the other elements of a category. The results of the comparison can be that one element is:

• The most (Superlative Structure of Superiority)

One object's quality is superior to that of ALL the others:

> Le livre de grammaire est le **plus *intéressant* de** tous les livres *(the most interesting of all).*

- **The least (Superlative Structure of Inferiority)**

One object's quality is inferior to that of ALL the others:

> Le livre de physique est **le moins** *intéressant* **de** tous les livres *(the least interesting of all).*

- **The absolute superlative (Absolute)**

One object's quality is superior in the absolute sense, without specification of the other elements of the comparison:

> Ce livre de grammaire est **le meilleur** *(the best).*

All the possibilities can be summarized in the following table:

SUMMARY TABLE: TYPES OF COMPARISON		
Element of Comparison **One element against:**	**Degree of Comparison**	**Result of Comparison**
Another element in the same group	Degré comparatif comparative	Supériorité Infériorité Égalité
All the elements in the category	Degré superlatif superlative	Supériorité Infériorité Absolu

Results of comparison in French are similar to English ones. But French uses an adverb of quantity (*plus, moins, aussi*) and a conjunction (*que*) surrounding the word instead of a suffix (. . . *er;* . . . *est*) added to the end of the adjective as in English.

TIP BOX

To construct a correct comparative structure of superiority in French, always think of the form used with long adjectives in English:

> Le Saint Nectaire est **plus** gros **que** le Picodon. *(The Saint Nectaire is [**more** large **than**] the Picodon.)*
>
> larger than

COMPARATIVE STRUCTURES OVERVIEW TABLE		
Degree of Comparison	**Result of Comparison**	**Structure of Comparison**
Degré comparatif One against One	Comparatif de Supériorité	plus [*adjectif*] que: > Le lion est plus ***gros*** que le chat. *(The lion is bigger than the cat.)*
	Comparatif d' Infériorité	moins [*adjectif*] que: Le chat est moins ***gros*** que le lion. *(The cat is less big than the lion.)*
	Comparatif d' Égalité	aussi [*adjectif*] que: = Les chats sont aussi ***beaux*** que les lions. *(Cats are as beautiful as lions.)*
Degré superlatif One against everyone	Superlatif de Supériorité	le—la—les plus [*adjectif*] de: Le lion est le plus ***beau*** de tous les animaux. *(The lion is the most beautiful of all animals.)* La lionne est la plus ***tendre*** des mamans. *(The lioness is the most tender mother.)* Les pandas sont les plus ***jolis*** des ours. *(Pandas are the cutest bears.)*
All the other elements can be stated in the sentence or they can be implied	SUPERLATIF d' Infériorité	le, la, les, moins [*adjectif*] de: Le chat est le moins ***sauvage*** des félins. *(The cat is the least wild of felines.)* La fourmi semble la moins ***sale*** des insectes. *(The ant is the less dirty insect.)* Les insectes sont les moins ***aimés*** des animaux. *(Insects are the least loved of all animals.)*
	SUPERLATIF |ABSOLU| Some examples of absolute adverbs:	**très** [ADJECTIF] Tofa est **TRÈS SENSIBLE**. *(Tofa is very sensitive.)* **super** [ADJECTIF] Vanille est SUPER MIGNONNE. *(Vanille is super cute.)* **merveilleusement** [ADJECTIF] Fripouille est **MERVEILLEUSEMENT** DRÔLE. *(Fripouille is marvelously funny.)* **extrêmement** [ADJECTIF] Mes chattes sont **EXTRÊMEMENT** DOUCES. *(My cats are extremely gentle.)* **exceptionnellement** [ADJECTIF] Cléa est **EXCEPTIONNELLEMENT** BELLE. *(Cléa is exceptionally beautiful.)*

TIP BOX

Comparative and superlative structures resemble sandwiches.

Les poils des chats Siamois sont **plus** courts **que** ceux des Ragdolls. *(shorter)*

La race Ragdoll est **moins** célèbre **que** la race Siamois. *(less famous)*

Les chats Siamois sont **aussi** affectueux **que** les Ragdolls. *(as loving)*

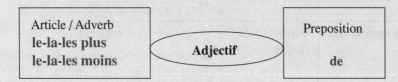

Le Ragdoll est **le plus** docile **des** chats. *(most docile)*

Les Siamois sont **les plus** intelligents. *(most intelligent)*

Les Persans sont **les moins** faciles à entretenir **des** chats à poils longs. *(least easy to take care of)*

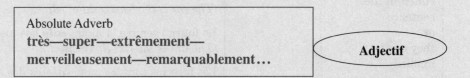

Cléa, ma chatte Ragdoll, est **extrêmement** jolie. *(extremely pretty)*

IMPORTANT!

BON and **MAUVAIS** have specific comparative and superlative forms.

- Bon: **MEILLEUR** que—**le meilleur de**
- Mauvais: **plus mauvais que** or **PIRE** que—**le plus mauvais de** or **le pire de**

Le chaource est bon, il est meilleur que le brie. *(better)*

À mon avis, le meilleur des fromages c'est le Boursault. *(the best)*

Le Pont-l'Évèque sent mauvais; le Munster sent pire! *(worse)*

C'est la pire des odeurs. *(the worst)*

Practice What You Learned

Exercises are rated according to four levels of difficulty:

- Beginner easy [*]
- Beginner challenging [**]
- Intermediate [***]
- Advanced [****]

1. Rewrite the adjectives with a feminine subject. [*]

Example:

Franz est allemand et gentil. Hilda est allemande et gentille.

A. Alex est jeune et timide. **Alexandra** est _____.

B. L'infirmier est aimable et compétent. **L'infirmière** est _____.

C. Le boulanger est mignon et drôle. **La boulangère** est _____.

D. Cet exercice est simple mais idiot. **Cette leçon** est _____.

E. Ton frère est fort et bronzé. **Ta soeur** est _____.

F. Ce tissu est blanc et doux. **Cette étoffe** est _____.

G. Ken est canadien et sportif. **Barbie** est _____.

H. Éric est menteur et manipulateur. **Érica** est _____.

2. Rewrite the adjectives with a plural subject. [*]

Example:

Franz est allemand. **Hilda et Franz** sont allemands.

A. Arthur est petit. **Arthur et Jean** sont _____.

B. Jimmy est roux. **Ses parents** sont _____.

C. Charles est original. **Charles et Paul** sont _____.

D. Charles est original. **Charles et Marie** sont _____.

E. Françoise est originale. **Françoise et Marie** sont _____.

F. Ce pull est marron. **Ces costumes** sont _____.

G. Ken est beau mais banal. **Ken et Frank** sont _____.

H. La voiture est bleue. **La voiture et le camion** sont _____.

3. Compare the qualities using the adverbs that are logically applicable to the context of the comparison. [**]

A. La durée de vie moyenne est _____ longue _____ pendant le Moyen-Âge.

B. La nourriture est _____ naturelle aujourd'hui _____ avant.

C. Les femmes sont _____ indépendantes dans les grandes villes _____ dans les campagnes.

D. Les garçons sont _____ intelligents _____ les filles.

4. Create a comparison between the following two items, then complete the sentence with a superlative of your choice. Pay attention to the gender and number agreements. [***]

Example:

argent / or—précieux—le métal précieux

> **L'argent est moins précieux que l'or; le platine est le plus précieux des métaux précieux.**

A. la soie / le lin / le tulle—léger—le tissu _____

B. Le charbon / le pétrole / l'uranium—rare—la ressource _____

C. les pommes / les poires / les cerises—cher—les fruits _____

D. le train / l'avion / la fusée—rapide—les moyens de transport _____

Fromages (Cheese)

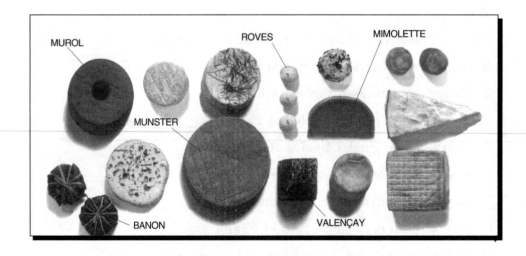

MUROL
ROVES
MIMOLETTE
MUNSTER
BANON
VALENÇAY

Chapter 7

DETERMINATIVE ADJECTIVES

Introduction

Definition: An adjective is a word that adds complementary information to a noun or a pronoun.

Determinative adjectives do not add a quality to the noun they accompany; they increase its specificity. They are classified in six categories that correspond to the specification they provide.

Determinative adjectives can

1. count the number of objects or persons designated by the noun; they are numeral adjectives. (These are referred to as ordinal and cardinal numbers in English, but they are adjectives nonetheless.)
2. point to designate an object or person; these are demonstrative.
3. clarify the owner of the object or person; these are possessive.
4. pose questions about the object or person; these are interrogative.
5. emphasize the importance of the object or person; these are exclamatory.
6. convey the indeterminacy of the object or person; these are indefinite.

Numeral Adjectives

Cardinal and ordinal numbers are expressed by corresponding numeral adjectives.

Cardinal Numeral Adjectives

Function

- Cardinal adjectives simply count the number of objects or persons:

    un, deux, vingt, cinquante, mille *(one, two, twenty, fifty, one thousand)*

- They can be used by themselves:

    Carine a quatre cadeaux. *(Carine has four presents.)*

    Didier achète cent CD pour son ordinateur. *(Didier buys a hundred CDs for his computer.)*

- They can be juxtaposed simply, with a hyphen, or coordinated:

> Francis a **six cent** centimes, c'est à dire six euros. *(Francis has six hundred cents, that is six euros.)*

> Yolande veut **quarante-cinq** crayons de couleur. *(Yolande wants forty-five colored pencils.)*

> Monique compte des moutons pour s'endormir: vingt et un, vingt-deux ... trente et un ... cinquante-trois ... quatre-vingt-un ... cent douze ... mille un ... sept mille ... un million trois cent mille ... deux milliards ... *(Monique counts sheep to go to sleep: twenty-one, twenty-two, thirty-one, fifty-three, eighty-one, one hundred and twelve, one thousand and one, seven thousand, one million three hundred thousand, two billion.)*

- In dates, French uses cardinal numbers when English uses ordinal numbers, with the *exception* of the first day:

> le vingt octobre *(the twentieth of October)*

Exception: Le premier janvier, Le Premier de l'An *(the first of . . .)*

Use

USE OF NUMERAL ADJECTIVES	
Agreement	• Cardinal numeral adjectives do not agree in number. J'ai **quatre** chattes. *(I have four cats.)* L'ère chrétienne a plus de deux **mille** ans. *(The Christian era is more than two thousand years old.)* • Cardinal numeral adjectives do not agree in gender except when they include un/une. Il y a **vingt** garçons dans ce gymnase et **quarante et une** filles. *(There are twenty boys in this gym and forty-one girls.)*
Mille Million Milliard	They are written with spaces, not with commas as in English: 8 000—huit mille 3 000 000—trois millions 6 700 000—six milliards sept cent millions
Vingt Cent	They take no **s** at the end with a plural noun when they are followed by another number: Thérèse a **vingt trois** ans. *(Thérèse is twenty-three years old.)* Sa grand-mère Simone aurait **cent cinq** ans. *(Her grandmother would be one hundred and five.)*

	They take no **s** at the end in dates: Mille neuf cent—Deux mille deux They take an **s** at the end with a plural noun when they are multiplied in a round number: Thérèse a **six cents** saucisses. (elle est bouchère) *(Thérèse has six hundred sausages. (she is a butcher))* Thérèse a **quatre-vingts** vaches. *(Thérèse has eighty cows.)* Jérôme a six cent soixante journaux. (il est libraire) *(Jérôme has six hundred and sixty newspapers. (he owns a bookstore))* Il vend vingt huit livres par jour en moyenne. *(He sells twenty-eight books a day as an average.)*
Mille Cent	Mille is invariable. Mille francs = 150 euros Mille and cent do not take **et** with **un**: **Cent un** soleils éclairent ce ciel. *(A hundred and one suns were lighting up the sky.)* Ce poème a **mille un** vers. *(This poem has one thousand and one verses.)* ***Exception: "Les mille et une nuits"***
Million Milliard	They are nouns; therefore they are followed by a noun and the preposition **de**: **Mille** femmes et hommes, **un million de** soldats, **des milliards de** morts ne suffisent pas à arrêter les guerres. *(One thousand women and men, a million soldiers, billions of dead are not sufficient to stop wars.)*

NOTE French numbers do not necessarily use the same type of numeral adjective as English ones:

Le deux janvier (cardinal)—the second of January (ordinal)

Moreover, numbers are not necessarily read in the same way.

Ordinal Numeral Adjectives

As their name indicates, they specify the order of the object or person in a list.

Function and Use

- They are formed by removing the final **e** of the cardinal number (if it ends in **e**) and adding the suffix **-ième**. The suffix is simply added to the adjectives with a final consonant:

     deux—deuxième; douze—douzième; trente—trentième; vingt et un—vingt et unième

     Exceptions
     un: premier—première
     deux: deuxième or second-seconde
     cinq: cinquième
     neuf: neuvième

- Ordinal numeral adjectives agree in gender and number with the noun they specify:

     le premier enfant, la première fille *(first child, first daughter)*

     Les dixièmes auditeurs qui appellent la station de radio gagnent.
     (Every tenth listener who calls the radio station wins.)

- Ordinal adjectives are abbreviated as 1er, 2ème, and so on.
- When both a cardinal and an ordinal adjective are used, their order is the opposite of English.

les	**cinq (5)**	premiers (1ers)	jours
the	first (1st)	**five (5)**	days

Particular Cases

These numeral words have a double nature; they are **adjectives** when they accompany a noun, but they are also <u>nouns</u> that can be used by themselves:

J'ai **quatre** chattes: <u>trois</u> ont des poils longs; <u>la quatrième</u> a des poils courts.
(I have four cats: three have long hair; the fourth one has short hair.)

Demonstrative Adjectives
Function and Use

As in English, demonstrative adjectives direct attention to a specific object to distinguish it from a group or another similar object.

Gender and Number

Demonstrative adjectives agree in gender and number with the noun they specify.

DEMONSTRATIVE ADJECTIVES		
Genre Nombre	**Masculin**	**Féminin**
Singulier	**CE** + consonnant . . . **CET** + vowel / mute h	**CETTE**
Pluriel	**CES**	

> Irène regarde **ce** renard roux. *(Irène looks at this red fox.)*
>
> Sylvestre sait que **cet** hôpital est excellent. *(Sylvester knows that this hospital is excellent.)*
>
> Tatiana travaille chez Dior, **cette** maison de haute couture célèbre. *(Tatiana works at Dior, the famous high-fastion store.)*
>
> Denis déguste **ces** éclairs et **ces** tartelettes avec délice. *(Denis eats those eclairs and little pies with delight.)*

Suffixes *-ci* and *-là*

When comparing or opposing two elements or series of elements, the demonstrative adjectives can be reinforced by the hyphenated suffixes **-ci** and **-là**. As in the English "this" and "that":

- **-ci** is closer to you in space or time or type of connection.

- **-là** is further or more removed / foreign to you.

> Ce livre-**ci** est de Sartre, ce livre-**là** est de Heidegger, mais ces philosophes sont tous deux des existentialistes. *(This book here is by Sartre, this one over there is by Heidegger, but both philosophers are existentialists.)*
>
> Nathalie est toujours copine avec cet ex fiancé-**ci**, mais elle déteste cet ex fiancé-**là**! *(Nathalie is still friends with this ex-fiancé [here], but she detests that ex-fiancé [there]!)*

Ce texte est écrit en Grec ancien. Jayme est un imbécile: il ne veut apprendre aucune langue et ne comprend rien à cette langue-là! *(This text is written in classical Greek. Jayme is a moron: he does not want to learn any language and knows nothing about that language (Greek)!)*

TIP

If you forget what the demonstrative adjectives are in French, remember in English: thiSSSSS "sssss" sound.

    In French: demonSSSSStratif: "sssss" = **CE** sound
démonstratif = démonCEtratif = demon**CET**ratif—**ce**—**cet**—**cette**—**ces**

      -cI indicates proxImIty (as in **iCI**: *Here* or th**I**s)

      -lÀ is used for the most distAnt element of the comparison (as in **LÀ-bas**: *Over there* or th**A**t)

Possessive Adjectives
Function and Use

Contrary to English, possession cannot be indicated by simply adding a suffix at the end of a word. In French one always uses

- the long expression with "of"

      Barry<u>'s</u> teddy bear—the teddy bear <u>of Barry</u>: le nounours <u>de Barry</u>

- or a possessive adjective or pronoun.

Consequently, possessive adjectives are very precise in determining who possesses the object or what is owned. The forms of the adjectives vary to indicate each possible combination of owners and properties.

Possession Components

Possession implies one or more owner-s and one or more object-s owned.

Owner = Person	Property = Object

Gwladys vient de réussir **son** concours d'ingénieur comme le montre **son** diplôme, **sa** toque universitaire et **son** programme de la cérémonie. *(Gwladys just passed her engineering exams as her diploma, cap, and graduation program show.)*

There are four different possible cases in a relationship of possession:

1. One person owning one object
2. One person owning two (or more) objects
3. Two (or more) persons owning one object
4. Two (or more) persons owning two (or more) objects

	Object	1 Object	2 or more Objects
Person			
1 Person			
2 or more Persons			

	Object	1 Object	2 or more Objects
Person			
Jessica		un bonsaï	deux voitures
Patrick et Philippe		une maison	deux raquettes

Jessica adore les plantes et les voitures; elle a un bonsaï et deux voitures, une coccinelle Volkswagen et une Ford de collection. *(Jessica loves plants and cars; she has a bonzai and two cars, a Bug and a vintage Ford.)*

Patrick et Philippe sont architectes; ils viennent de construire leur maison avec vue sur la mer sur la Côte d'Azur. Le week-end, ils jouent au tennis pour compenser toutes leurs heures de travail! *(Patrick and Philippe are architects; they just built their house with a view of the sea on the Riviera. On weekends, they play tennis to compensate for their long hours of work!)*

The four different possibilities of possession (1 person owning 1 object—1 person owning 2 objects—2 persons owning 1 object—2 persons owning 2 objects) are conveyed by each possessive adjective. Each element (person, object) is displayed in the adjectives.

- The first letter refers to the owner.
- The rest of the word refers to the property.

Adjective Formation

Here are various ways of summarizing the formation of possessive adjectives:

List by Owner

1 person: mon, ma, mes; ton, ta, tes; son, sa, ses
2 persons: notre, nos; votre, vos; leur, leurs

TABLE OF POSSESSIVE ADJECTIVES						
Object	**1 Object**				**2+ ObjectS**	
Person	**Masculine**		**Feminine**		**Masc.-Fem.**	
1 Person	**Mon**	My	**Ma**	My	**Mes**	My
	Ton	Your	**Ta**	Your	**Tes**	Your
	Son	His/Her	**Sa**	His/Her	**Ses**	His/Her
2 PersonS	**Notre**	Our			**Nos**	Our
	Votre	Your			**Vos**	Your
	Leur	Their			**Leurs**	Their

Person Indicator List

PERSON INDICATORS IN POSSESSIVE ADJECTIVES					
			OBJECT-S		
PERSON			**1 Object**		**2+ ObjectS**
1 Person—Singulier			**masc.**	**fem.**	**masc.-fem.**
1ère	Je (me)	**M**	ON	A	ES
2ème	Tu (te)	**T**	ON	A	ES
3ème	Il, Elle (se)	**S**	ON	A	ES
2 Persons—Pluriel					
1ère	Nous	**N**	OTRE		OS
2ème	Vous	**V**	OTRE		OS
3ème	Ils, Elles	**L**	EUR		EURS

Object Indicator List

OBJECT INDICATORS IN POSSESSIVE ADJECTIVES			
Object	1 Object		2+ ObjectS
1 Person	Masculine mON, tON, sON	Feminine mA, tA, sA	Masc.—Fem. mES, tES, sES
M T S	ON	A	ES
2 Persons	nOTRE, vOTRE		nOS, vOS
N V	OTRE		OS
	lEUR-S		
L	EUR		EURS

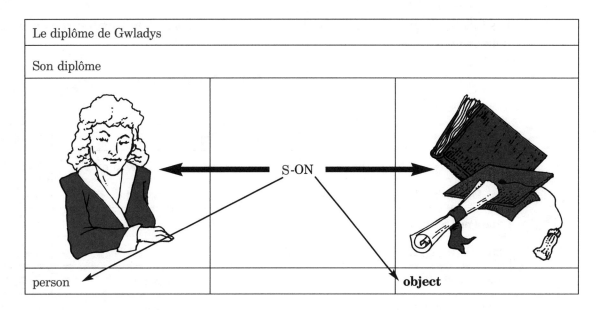

| Le diplôme de Gwladys |
| Son diplôme |
| person | object |

The first letter tells you if there are one or more owners and the adjective endings tell you if there are one or more objects and their gender. Feminine and masculine forms are the same in the plural, since the masculine always takes over. By default, the language assumes there is at least one masculine element in a group and that is enough to make the entire group masculine.

> **MAGIC METHOD** To find the correct adjective once you have memorized the table, write it down as a 2 × 2 matrix (1 person—2 persons / 1 object—2 objects), identify the owner, and simply go to the relevant intersection Person + Gender and Number of Objects.

Le parapluie de Patrice: 1 object, masculine singular—1 owner, 3rd person singular (Patrice—il) ⇒ son parapluie

$$\text{Patrice} \Leftarrow \text{S ON} \Rightarrow \text{parapluie}$$

	Object	1 Object		2⁺ Objects
Letter corresponding to the Person		Masculine	Feminine	Masc.-Fem.
1st Pers. Sing. JE	M	Mon	Ma	Mes
2nd Pers. Sing. TU	T	Ton	Ta	Tes
3rd Pers. Sing. IL, ELLE	S	Son	Sa	Ses
1st Pers. Pl. NOUS	N	Notre		Nos
2nd Pers. Pl. VOUS	V	Votre		Vos
3rd Pers. Pl. ILS, ELLES	L	Leur		Leurs

Les filles de François et moi: 2+ objects—2 owners, 1st person singular (François et moi—nous) ⇒ nos filles

François et moi ⇐ N OS ⇒ filles

	Object	1 Object		2⁺ Objects
Letter corresponding to the Person		Masculine	Feminine	Masc.-Fem.
1st Pers. Sing. JE	M	Mon	Ma	Mes
2nd Pers. Sing. TU	T	Ton	Ta	Tes
3rd Pers. Sing. IL, ELLE	S	Son	Sa	Ses
1st Pers. Pl. NOUS	N	Notre		Nos
2nd Pers. Pl. VOUS	V	Votre		Vos
3rd Pers. Pl. ILS, ELLES	L	Leur		Leurs

La voiture de Olivier et toi: 1 object, feminine singular—2 owners, second person plural (Olivier et toi = vous) ⇒ votre

Olivier et toi ⇐ V OTRE ⇒ voiture

	Object	1 Object		2⁺ Objects
Letter corresponding to the Person		Masculine	Feminine	Masc.-Fem.
1st Pers. Sing. JE	M	Mon	Ma	Mes
2nd Pers. Sing. TU	T	Ton	Ta	Tes
3rd Pers. Sing. IL, ELLE	S	Son	Sa	Ses
1st Pers. Pl. NOUS	N	Notre		Nos
2nd Pers. Pl. VOUS	V	Votre		Vos
3rd Pers. Pl. ILS, ELLES	L	Leur		Leurs

Les livres que tu as achetés: 2+ objects—1 owner (Tu—2nd person singular)—tes livres

$$\text{Toi} \Leftarrow \text{T ES} \Rightarrow \text{livres}$$

	Object	1 Object		2$^+$ Objects
Letter corresponding to the Person		Masculine	Feminine	Masc.-Fem.
1st Pers. Sing. JE	M	Mon	Ma	Mes
2nd Pers. Sing. TU	T	Ton	Ta	Tes
3rd Pers. Sing. IL, ELLE	S	Son	Sa	Ses
1st Pers. Pl. NOUS	N	Notre		Nos
2nd Pers. Pl. VOUS	V	Votre		Vos
3rd Pers. Pl. ILS, ELLES	L	Leur		Leurs

 Once you know that the first part of the possessive adjectives refers to the owner and the rest refers to the property, there are two conclusions you can draw from the fact that the adjectives' endings change.

1. You can conclude that, as opposed to English possessive adjectives, French possessive adjectives **agree in gender and number with the object** that is possessed and not with the person owning them.

   > The shirt of Paul—*His* shirt because Paul is a man.

   > La chemise de Paul—**SA** chemise because <u>la chemise</u> is a feminine noun.

2. You can conclude that if there are many propertie**s**, your possessive adjective needs to be in the plural as well; therefore it ends with an **s**. They all do: me**s**, te**s**, se**s**, no**s**, vo**s**, leur**s**, with multiple object**s** owned.

Interrogative Adjectives

Function and Use

Interrogative adjectives help determine which object is designated among a group.

- Interrogative adjectives agree in gender and number with the noun they specify:

INTERROGATIVE ADJECTIVES: OVERVIEW		
Genre **Nombre**	**Masculin**	**Féminin**
Singulier	**QUEL**...?	**QUELLE**...?
Pluriel	**QUELS**...?	**QUELLES**...?

- Interrogative adjectives are used regardless of the function of the noun in the sentence (subject or complement).

Direct / Indirect Question

The same adjectives allow a direct or indirect interrogation about a noun: A direct question ends with a question mark; an indirect question may be inserted within an affirmative sentence.

The interrogative adjectives remain the same, regardless of the function of the noun they accompany.

Quel film passe en ce moment? *(Which movie is in the theater right now?)*	Direct interrogation	*film* is subject
Je me demande **quel** film tu as vu récemment. *(I wonder which movie you have seen recently.)*	Indirect interrogation	*film* is complement of direct object
Quelle robe vas-tu porter pour le Réveillon de Noël? *(Which dress are you going to wear for Christmas?)*	Direct interrogation	*robe* is complement of direct object
Rosa ne sait pas <u>de</u> **quelle** robe elle a besoin pour ce bal. *(Rosa does not know what dress she needs for this ball.)*	Indirect interrogation	*robe* is complement of <u>indirect</u> object
Peggy est allée <u>dans</u> **quels** pays pendant son voyage? *(Peggy went to which countries during her trip?)*	Direct interrogation	*pays* is circumstantial complement of <u>location</u>
Claire explique <u>avec</u> **quelles** armes on joue au Cluedo. *(Claire explains with which weapons one plays Clue.)*	Indirect interrogation	*armes* is circumstantial complement of <u>means</u>

Exclamatory Adjectives

Function and Use

Exclamatory adjectives put an emphasis on the noun they specify.

Since they function in a similar way to the interrogative adjectives (they accentuate the noun instead of questioning it), the same list of adjectives is used.

- Exclamatory adjectives agree in gender and number with the noun they specify:

EXCLAMATORY ADJECTIVES		
Genre **Nombre**	**Masculin**	**Féminin**
Singulier	**QUEL...!**	**QUELLE...!**
Pluriel	**QUELS...!**	**QUELLES...!**

Functions of the Noun

Exclamatory adjectives are used regardless of the function of the noun in the sentence (subject or complement).

Quel film magnifique est ce dernier Resnais! *(What a magnificent movie, this last Resnais!)*	*film* is subject
Quelles journées aventureuses j'ai passées à Cannes! *(What adventurous days I have spent in Cannes!)*	*journées* is complement of direct object
À **quelle** voisine bizarre vous parlez! *(What a strange neighbor you are talking to!)*	*voisine* is complement of indirect object
Tu as vu la largeur de leurs épaules? **Quels** athlètes ces nageurs olympiques! *(Did you see the size of their shoulders? What athletes these Olympic swimmers are!)*	*athlètes* is subject

Indefinite Adjectives

Function and Use

Indefinite adjectives are different from the rest of the determinative adjectives because they are more heterogeneous.

- Their category is composed of various words that do not seem to have a common element like the **ce** for the demonstrative or the person marker for the possessive.

  certain, quelque, aucun, nul, chaque, différents, plusieurs, tout, tel, autre, même
  (certain, some, none, no, each, different, a few, all, such, other, same)

- They agree in gender with the noun they specify, although some of them have a similar form in the masculine and the feminine. They also agree in number when it is logical. Some have the same form in the singular and the plural.

MAIN INDEFINITE ADJECTIVES		
Masculin S. P.	**Féminin S. P.**	**Traduction-s**
certain—certains	certaine—certaines	some / certain
quelque—quelques		some / a few
aucun—only singular	aucune—only singular	no
nul—only singular	nulle—only singular	none / no
chaque—only singular		each / every
différents—only plural	différentes—only plural	various / different
plusieurs—only plural		many
tout—tous	toute—toutes	all / every / any
tel—tels	telle—telles	such
autre—autres		other
même—mêmes		same

Particular Cases

Some indefinite adjectives have particular characteristics.

Chaque, plusieurs, quelque, aucun, nul, certains (Each, a few, some, no, none, certain)

They are used without an article.

Chaque culture est intéressante. *(**Each** culture is interesting.)*

Plusieurs cultures sont basées sur une religion. *(A few cultures are based on a religion.)*

Certaines cultures sont plus le résultat d'une histoire politique. *(Certain cultures are more the result of political history.)*

Tout (All)

It is followed by an article.

Tous les jours je travaille. *(I work every day.)*

Je me lève **tout le** temps à 6 heures 30 du matin. *(I always get up at 6:30 A.M.)*

Elle peut travailler **toute une** journée sans s'arrêter. *(She can work all day long without a break.)*

Autre et tel (Other and Such)

They come after an article.

Les **autres** cadeaux sont arrivés. *(The other presents have arrived.)*

Avoir une **telle** énergie est rare! *(To have such energy is rare!)*

Même (Same, even, very, self)

It has four different meanings depending on its position in the sentence:
Before the article: même = even

Même le président est un homme comme tout le monde. *(Even the president is a man like anyone else.)*

Before the noun or after a verb: même = same

Plus ça recommence, plus c'est la **même** chose. *(The more it starts again, the more it is the same.)*

Mes amies sont les **mêmes** depuis des années. *(I have had the same friends for years.)*

After the noun: même = very

Ce que je te dis est la vérité **même**. *(What I am telling you is the honest truth.)*

Hyphenated after a pronoun: même = self

Tu as fait ce gâteau **toi-même**, c'est incroyable! *(You made this cake yourself; that's incredible!)*

NOTE The best way to learn these indefinite adjectives is to force yourself to use them systematically in numerous sentences. Also pay special attention when you encounter them in a sentence; refer to the section of this chapter (page 96) and see to which rule or behavior the indefinite adjective conforms and why.

REVIEW TABLE: DETERMINATIVE ADJECTIVES	
Adjectifs Cardinaux (Numeral Cardinal Adjective)	Un, deux, vingt et un, cent un, deux mille . . . *(One, two, twenty-one, a hundred, two thousand . . .)*
Adjectifs Ordinaux (Numeral Ordinal Adjective)	Le premier, la deuxième . . . *(the first, the second . . .)*

Adjectifs Démonstratifs (Demonstrative Adjective)

Dem.	Masculin	Féminin
Singulier	Ce, Cet	Cette
Pluriel	Ces	

(this—that, these)

Adjectifs Possessifs (Possessive Adjective)

Poss.	1 Object	
	Masculin	Féminin
1 Owner	Mon, Ton, Son	Ma, Ta, Sa
2 Owners	Notre, Votre, Leur	
	2 objects	
1 Owner	Mes, Tes, Ses	
2 Owners	Nos, Vos, Leurs	

(my, your, his—her—its, our, your, their)

Adjectifs Interrogatifs? (Interrogative Adjective?)

Adjectifs Exclamatifs! (Exclamatory Adjective!)

Int./Excl. ? / !	Masculin	Féminin
Singulier	Quel	Quelle
Pluriel	Quels	Quelles

(what/which . . . ? what . . .!)

Adjectifs Indéfinis (Indefinite Adjective)	certain, quelque, aucun, nul, chaque, différents, plusieurs, tout, tel, autre, même *(certain, some, no, none, each, different, a few, all, such, other, same)*

Practice What You Learned

Exercises are rated according to four levels of difficulty:

- Beginner easy [*]
- Beginner challenging [**]
- Intermediate [***]
- Advanced [****]

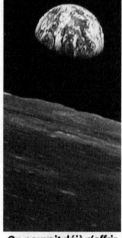

Pour joindre l'inutile à l'agréable

Envie de faire un cadeau très original ? Achetez un bout de lune ! Une société française permet en effet d'acquérir une surface de 4 000 m² de Lune pour un prix de base de 35 € (achat par tél. au 08 00 90 11 94 ou www.luneimmo.com). Autre idée : vous rédigez un message (par e-mail ou courrier*), qui sera placé à bord d'un satellite mis en orbite fin 2003. Le but ? Laisser un souvenir à nos descendants (s'il y en a) lorsque l'engin redescendra sur Terre dans… 50 000 ans !

* Sur le site www.keo.org ou par courrier KEO, BP 100, 75262 Paris Cedex 06. Tél. : 01 44 32 19 00.

On pouvait déjà s'offrir une étoile, désormais, on pourra aussi décrocher un bout de lune !

1. Write down and spell out all the numbers in the article.[*]

_____

_____

_____

_____

_____

_____

_____

_____

2. Spell out the following numbers. [**]

Example:

101 = cent un

A. 400 = _____

B. 200 000 = _____

C. 92 = _____

D. 17 461 = _____

E. 5 948 203,29 = _____

3. Complete with the appropriate possessive adjective. Remember to pay attention to the owner and the property. [***]

A. Bernard et Bernadette partent pour _____ voyage de noces.

B. _____ valises sont prêtes.

C. Bernadette appelle _____ frère qui lui a prété _____ voiture Jeep pour _____ voyage.

D. Ils partent en Afrique, Bernard va voir _____ parents qui y habitent et présenter _____ femme.

4. Combine the following elements of the possession relationship. [**]

Example:

Paul et Marie—les enfants: leurs enfants

A. Marc et toi—la maison: _____

B. Fabienne et Sophie—le prénom: _____

C. Karine—les livres: _____

D. Amélie—le film: _____

E. Éliane et Caroline—le script: _____

5. Complete with the corresponding demonstrative adjective. [*]

A. _____ poires sont jaunes.

B. _____ roman est passionnant.

C. _____ hôpital a une bonne réputation.

D. _____ histoire est si triste.

E. _____ bâtiments sont très laids.

6. Oppose the two elements with the corresponding demonstrative adjective. [*]

Example:

Ce danseur-**ci** est excellent; cette danseuse-**là** est superbe.

A. homme gentil—méchant

_____

B. tableau beau—cher

_____

C. Éclair au café—au chocolat

_____

7. Complete the following text with the logical indefinite article. Pay attention to the gender and the number of the nouns they accompany. [***]

Certains—chaque—différentes—nul—toutes—autre

A. _____ être humain est unique mais _____ individu n'est parfait.
B. _____ hommes sont banals mais tous ont _____ qualités.
C. _____ les femmes ne sont pas originales non plus, mais c'est une _____ histoire!

8. Underline all the adjectives in the following text. Write them in a table and give all the details you can about them. There are 40 adjectives. [****]

Example:

jeune = adjectif qualificatif masculin singulier, épithète

Hervé, jeune écrivain, était un garçon très sensible, particulièrement doué pour la littérature et cette forme de romans que différents critiques appellent intimistes. Ses premiers mois à Paris ont été difficiles, mais il a vite rencontré d'importantes personnalités de la société parisienne des années quatre-vingt. Il prenait de superbes photos de chaque personne célèbre qui devenait son ami: Michel, Isabelle et autres intellectuels ou artistes. Il mentionne sept ou huit de ces connaissances dans son roman le plus célèbre À *l'ami qui* . . . Quels hommes ou femmes se cachent sous chaque pseudonyme? Quelques noms sont transformés, plusieurs personnages restent plus mystérieux. Mais tous les acteurs de ce livre autobiographique, vivants ou disparus, restent gravés dans la mémoire de ses lecteurs. Hervé est mort trop tôt, de cette maladie atroce appelée le SIDA. Quelle perte pour la scène culturelle d'une telle époque.

Chapter 8

PERSONAL AND IMPERSONAL PRONOUNS

Introduction

Definition: A pronoun is used to
- replace a noun
- replace a nominal group
- replace an entire clause

Pronouns are part of the nominal group. **Pro** in Latin means "for" or "in favor of" as in *Pros* and *Cons* (what is in favor of something and what is against, counter to it). They are pro-noun, that is, used for a noun that may be alone, accompanied by an adjective, or at the core of a clause:

> Audrey adore dessiner. [**Audrey**] **Elle** peint très bien aussi. *(Audrey loves to draw. She paints very well too.)*

> Ses tableaux sont magnifiques. [**Ses tableaux**] **Les siens** sont magnifiques. *(Her paintings are splendid. Hers are splendid.)*

> Joachim a acheté ce tableau-ci. Joachim voulait [**ce tableau-là**] **celui-là** aussi. *(Joachim bought this painting. He wanted that one too.)*

> L'exposition d'Audrey a beaucoup de succès. Tout le monde **en** parle [du fait que **l'exposition d'Audrey a beaucoup de succès**]. *(Audrey's exhibit has a lot of success. Everyone talks about it.)*

Nouns in French have a gender and a number. They can have various functions, and can be specified in numerous ways. There are consequently multiple lists of pronouns from which to choose, so that none of the characteristic of the noun is lost during its replacement by a pronoun.

Nature

Personal pronouns refer to either persons or objects.

- Their particular role is double:
  1. They replace a noun or a nominal group to avoid repetition.
  2. They indicate who acts, and about whom, or to whom the action is performed.

- There are five lists of personal pronouns, each corresponding to the function the pronoun has in its sentence.

  1. Subject: Sujet du verbe
  2. Direct Object Complement: Complément d'Objet Direct
  3. Indirect Object Complement: Complément d'Objet Indirect
  4. Reflexive or Reciprocal Complement: Complément d'une action réflexive ou réciproque
  5. Emphatic or Disjunctive: Après une préposition qui accentue leur importance

- There are two additional personal pronouns used after the prepositions **À** and **DE**: Nonattribution or inanimate objects and location: **Y** and **EN**

Personal Pronouns as Subject

Use

Personal pronouns have a gender and a number and correspond to the person doing the action. The third person singular **on** is used for impersonal subjects, unidentified groups, or neutral entities. It is masculine and singular.

PERSONAL PRONOUNS BY FUNCTION					
Fonction **Personne**	**Sujet**	**COD** **(Direct** **Object)**	**COI** **(Indirect** **Object)**	**Reflexif** **Réciproque** **(Reflexive/** **Reciprocal)**	**Emphatique** **Disjoint** **(Emphatic/** **Disjunctive)**
1ère Sing.	Je	Me	Me	Me	Moi
2ème Sing.	Tu	Te	Te	Te	Toi
3ème Sing.	Il—Elle- On	Le—La—L'	Lui	Se	Lui—Elle
1ère Pl.	Nous	Nous	Nous	Nous	Nous
2ème Pl.	Vous	Vous	Vous	Vous	Vous
3ème Pl.	Ils—Elles	Les	Leur	Se	Eux—Elles

Subject: *I, You, He—She—It, We, You, They*

Direct / Indirect Object Complement: *Me, You, Him—Her—It, Us, You, Them*

Reflexive: *Myself, Yourself, Himself—Herself—Itself, Ourselves, Yourselves, Themselves*

Reciprocal: *Each other*

Emphatic: *Me, You, Him—Her—It, Us, You, Them*

Function

Personal pronoun subjects are placed before the conjugated verb of which they are the subjects.

PERSONAL PRONOUNS AS <u>SUBJECT</u>		
Fonction **Personne**	**Sujet**	
1ère Sing.	**Je**	I
2ème Sing.	**Tu**	You
3ème Sing.	**Il—Elle** **On**	He—She One/We
1ère Pl.	**Nous**	We
2ème Pl.	**Vous**	You
3ème Pl.	**Ils—Elles**	They

Je ne peux écrire ce livre que pendant le week-end. *(I can write this book only on the weekend.)*

Tu liras ce livre pour apprendre le français. *(You will read this book to learn French.)*

(Claudine) **Elle** a acheté ce livre dans une librairie. *(She bought this book in a bookstore.)*

(Julien) **Il** avait acheté ce livre sur l'internet. *(He had bought this book on the Internet.)*

On considère tous les livres de Barron's très pratiques. *(Barron's books are considered very practical.)*

(Ed et moi) **Nous** avons développé un logiciel: PDAbs. *(We have developed a software: PDAbs.)*

(Ton ami et toi) **Vous** serez contents de ce livre. *(You will be pleased with this book.)*

(Claudine et Julien) **Ils** vont améliorer leur grammaire. *(They will improve their grammar.)*

(Claudine et Nathalie) **Elles** aiment étudier ce livre ensemble. *(They like to study this book together.)*

NOTE The second person plural **Vous** can be used to designate:

- A **group of people** including all women, all men, or both
- A **person** to whom one owes respect

Vous is a formal pronoun that does not exist in English. The French use it systematically:

- **When they meet someone for the first time, until the older person suggests using** tu:

> "Comment allez-**vous** Fabienne?" *("How are you doing, Fabienne?")*

> "Très bien, merci Kenneth, mais nous sommes amis maintenant. On se tutoie?" *("Very well, thank you, Kenneth, but we are friends now. Shall we say 'Tu' to each other?")*

> "Bonne idée, Fabienne. **Tu** vas bien aujourd'hui?" *("Good idea, Fabienne. You're well today?")*

> "Très bien, Ken, et **toi**, ça va?" *("Very well, Ken, what about you, everything's OK?")*

- **When a person is older**
- **In business relationships unless the person with the highest rank suggests that one use** tu.
- **With official personalities**

As a foreigner always use **Vous** unless invited to do otherwise. Similarly, do not address people by their first name, unless the French person suggests it:

> "**Vous** pouvez m'appeler Fabienne si **vous** voulez, Monsieur Washington. Dr. Chauderlot est un peu trop formel." *("Please call me Fabienne, if you want, Mr. Washington. Dr. Chauderlot is a little too formal for me."*

> "D'accord, avec plaisir Fabienne, moi c'est Denzel." *("All right, Fabienne, with pleasure. Call me Denzel.")*

Personal Pronouns as Direct Object Complement

Function and Use

Direct object complement pronouns also take on the gender and number of the person or object they replace. **Le** is used both as masculine and as neuter. The vowels **e** and **a** are replaced by an apostrophe when **le** and **la** come before a verb starting with a vowel.

PERSONAL PRONOUNS AS DIRECT OBJECT COMPLEMENT		
Personne **Fonction**	**COD**	
1ère Sing.	**Me**	me
2ème Sing.	**Te**	you
3ème Sing.	**Le—La—L'**	him—her
1ère Pl.	**Nous**	us
2ème Pl.	**Vous**	you
3ème Pl.	**Eux—Elles**	them

TIP BOX—Reminder

Complements of direct objects answer the question **Quoi**? (*What*) or **Qui**? (*Whom*) with a noun placed *directly* after the verb they complement.

> Martial voit Paul: voit **QUI**? Paul. (*Martial sees Paul: sees WHOM? Paul.*)

> **Paul = Complement of direct object** of the verb **voit**.

> Martial vient voir un film: vient voir **QUOI**? (*Martial comes to see a film: comes to see WHAT?*)

> **Un film = Complement of direct object** of the infinitive **voir**.

Placement

Direct object personal pronouns are placed **before** <u>the verb</u> **they complement**: <u>this verb</u> can be a conjugated verb or a verb in the infinitive.

Sentence with Noun as Complement	Sentence with Pronoun as Complement
Martial <u>voit</u> **Paul**. *(Martial sees Paul.)*	Martial le <u>voit</u>. *(Martial sees him.)*
Martial <u>a vu</u> **la comédie**. *(Martial saw the comedy.)*	Martial l'<u>a vue</u>. *(Martial saw it.)*
Martial <u>verra</u> **Marie et Ève**. *(Martial will see Marie and Eve.)*	Martial les <u>verra</u>. *(Martial will see them.)*
Martial <u>aurait vu</u> **Paul**. *(Martial would have seen Paul.)*	Martial serait venu le <u>voir</u>. *(Martial would have seen him.)*
Martial <u>veut voir</u> **la comédie**. *(Martial wants to see the comedy.)*	Martial veut la <u>voir</u> *(Martial wants to see it.)*
Martial <u>avait vu</u> **Marie et Ève** *(Martial had seen Marie and Eve.)*	Martial avait aimé les <u>voir</u> *(Martial had liked seeing them.)*

PLACEMENT OF THE PERSONAL PRONOUN AS OBJECT COMPLEMENT			
Fonction **Personne**	Sujet	**COD** of conjugated verb	**COD** of infinitive verb
1ère Sing.		**me** voit	Martial vient **me** voir.
2ème Sing.		**te** voit	Martial vient **te** voir.
3ème Sing. Masculin (Paul) Féminin (Éva)		**le** voit (le = Paul) **la** voit (la = Èva)	Martial vient **le** voir. Martial vient **la** voir.
1ère Pl.	Martial	**nous** voit	Martial vient **nous** voir.
2ème Pl.		**vous** voit	Martial vient **vous** voir.
3ème Pl. Paul et Éva Paul et Philippe Marie et Éva		**les** voit	Martial vient **les** voir.

TIP BOX

To make sure that your complement personal pronoun is correctly placed, ask the question WHAT? or WHOM? after reading the verb that follows your pronoun.

Paul loue la voiture—Paul **la** loue: **rents What?** **la** = la voiture. Correct

Paul va louer une voiture—~~Paul **la** va louer~~: **is going to What?** **la** = WRONG

Paul va louer une voiture—Paul va **la** louer: **rent What?** **la** = la voiture. Correct
(Paul rents it—Paul is going to rent it.)

Personal Pronouns as Indirect Object Complement

Function and Use

They also take on the gender and number of the person or object they replace. **Lui** and **Leur** are used to replace masculine, feminine, and neutral nouns of persons or things.

PERSONAL PRONOUNS AS INDIRECT OBJECT COMPLEMENT		
Fonction **Personne**	**COI** **Preposition +**	
1ère Sing.	**Me**	me
2ème Sing.	**Te**	you
3ème Sing.	**Lui**	her—him
1ère Pl.	**Nous**	us
2ème Pl.	**Vous**	you
3ème Pl.	Leur	them

TIP BOX—Reminder

Indirect object complements answer the question **À/DE quoi?** *(To What)* or À/DE Qui? *(To Whom)* with a noun placed after the preposition **À** or **DE**. This preposition separates them from their verb, which is why they complement indirectly (that is, through the preposition first and then the noun).

IMPORTANT!

The indirect object complement personal pronouns

me—te—lui—nous—vous—leur

are used only to replace **animate beings**.

Placement

Indirect Object Pronouns with À

When verbs are used with the preposition À, indirect object personal pronouns replacing animate beings can be placed:

Before the Verb They Complement

This verb can be a conjugated verb or a verb in the infinitive. The preposition is *absorbed* by the pronoun and disappears. In this case, the complement corresponds to an attribution, and the translation of À is generally *to*.

> Paul a parlé **à Éva**. Paul **lui** a parlé. *(Paul speaks to Eva. Paul has spoken **to her**.)*

> Paul voudrait parler **à Éva**. Paul voudrait **lui** parler. *(Paul would like to speak to Eva. Paul would like to speak **to her**.)*

After the Verb They Complement

The preposition remains in the sentence. In this case, À can be translated by various prepositions such as **about**.

> Paul s'était intéressé **à Éva**.—Paul s'était intéressé **à elle**. *(Paul had been interested in Eva. Paul had been interested in her.)*

> Paul ne veut plus penser **à Éva**. Paul ne veut plus penser **à elle**. *(Paul does not want to think about Eva anymore. Paul does not want to think about her anymore.)*

Indirect Object Pronouns with *DE*

When verbs are used with the preposition **DE**, indirect object personal pronouns replacing animate beings are placed after the preposition. In this case, the personal pronouns used are the emphatic/disjunctive ones:

> Éva parle **DE Paul**. Éva parle **DE lui**. *(Eva speaks about him.)*

> Éva et Paul se souviennent **DE Marc**. Éva et Paul se souviennent **DE lui**. *(Eva and Paul remember him.)*

Mes étudiants se souviennent. *(My students remember me.)*	**de** moi
Tes parents parlent souvent. *(Your parents often speak of you.)*	**de** toi
Cette cause charitable a besoin. *(This charitable cause needs him/her.)*	**de** lui **d'**elle
Notre réussite dépend. *(Our success depends upon us.)*	**de** nous
Voilà ce que j'attends. *(Here is what I expect from you.)*	**de** vous
Tu sais ce que je pense. *(You know what I think of them.)*	**d'**eux **d'**elles

Reflexive or Reciprocal Personal Pronouns

Function

As their name indicates, they are used when a subject performs the action upon itself or when two subjects perform the same action toward each other.

Reflexivity

The action reflects upon the subject (that is, comes back to the subject as in a mirror reflection).

> Je **me** lève means *I get myself out of bed.*
>
> Tu **te** coiffes means *You brush your own hair.*
>
> Il **s**'habille means *He dresses himself.*

Reciprocity

The same action is done reciprocally by one subject to the other, and vice versa.

> **Paul** regarde Éva. **Éva** regarde Paul. Ils **se** regardent. *(Paul looks at Eva. Eva looks at Paul. They look at each other.)*

Use

- Reflexive/reciprocal pronouns change only according to the person they replace, not gender. Because the two people sort of merge in the reciprocity, **SE** is used to replace both singular and plural third person.
- **Me, te, se** become **m', t', s'** in front of verbs starting with a vowel or a mute **h.**

REVIEW TABLE: REFLEXIVE AND/OR RECIPROCAL PERSONAL PRONOUNS			
Fonction Personne	**Réflexif Réciproque**	**Reflexive**	**Reciprocal**
1ère Sing.	**Me—m'**	Myself	
2ème Sing.	**Te—t'**	Yourself	
3ème Sing. Elle—Il On	**Se—s'**	Herself—Himself Oneself	
1ère Pl.	**Nous**	Ourselves	One another Each other
2ème Pl.	**Vous**	Yourselves	One another Each other
3ème Pl.	**Se**	Themselves	One another Each other

- Reflexive/reciprocal personal pronouns are placed before the verb they complement; this verb can be a conjugated verb or a verb in the infinitive:

  > Je **me** lève tôt le matin. J'aime **me** lever tôt le matin. (*I get up early in the morning. I like to get up early in the morning.*)

  > Paul parle à Éva. Éva parle à Paul. Paul et Éva **se** parlent. (*Paul speaks to Eva. Eva speaks to Paul. Paul and Eva speak to each other.*)

  > Paul veut parler à Éva. Éva veut parler à Paul. Paul et Éva veulent **se** parler. (*Paul wants to speak to Eva. Eva wants to speak to Paul. They want to speak to each other.*)

Intermediate—Advanced Topic

Agreement of Past Participle with Personal Pronoun

Verbs are used in the reflexive voice, with a reflexive/reciprocal pronoun, when the action comes back to the person or thing that performs it like a boomerang.

Direct Object Pronoun

The subject of the verb is also its direct object complement if the verb is transitive:

> Elle **s'est** maquillée: **se** = **COD** (maquiller + direct object complement)

Indirect Object Pronoun

The subject of the verb is its indirect object if the verb is used with a preposition:

> Elles **se** sont parlé: **se** = **COI** (parler + **À** + complement)

Se maquiller : Maquiller soi-même
Se = *Direct Object Reflexive Pronoun*

Se parler : X parle à Y—Y parle à X
Se = *Indirect Object Reciprocal Pronoun*

> ### IMPORTANT!
> Due to the merging of subject and object into one person, when a verb is used in the reflexive/reciprocal form, it is always conjugated with the auxiliary verb **Être** (to be) in compound tenses.
>
> Because it is conjugated with **Être**, the question of the past participle agreement arises. The same rule as for all compound tenses applies with reflexive/reciprocal verbs. The question to ask is: Where is the direct object?

> **NOTE** Refer to the section "Agreement of the Past Participle" in Chapter 12, Past Indicative Tenses, page 218.
>
> If the verb is transitive (used with a direct object complement) and this direct object complement is placed in the sentence <u>before</u> the <u>past participle</u>, then the past participle agrees with that direct object.
>
> > **Charlotte s'est <u>maquilléE</u>** (COD = se: before the past participle—Charlotte: feminine singular maquilléE)
>
> If the direct object appears in the sentence after the past participle, it is too late to make the agreement.
>
> > **Charlotte s'est <u>lavÉ</u> *les cheveux*** (COD = les cheveux: *after* the past participle: TOO LATE! no *agreement*—lavÉ)
>
> If there is no direct object, there is no agreement of the past participle since the past participle agrees only with a DIRECT object.
>
> > **Charlotte [s']est demandé si Paul venait: [se = C O INDIRECT]** (demander À): *no agreement*—demandÉ

Personal Pronouns as Emphatic or Disjunctive

> *"Who ate all the cookies I just made? Chuck, did you do that?"*
>
> *"What? MOI, I would never eat your delicious fresh hot melting soft chewy chocolate cookies ..."*

Function

These are the pronouns that made the expression Moi?! famous in the United States. They also take on the gender and number of the person or object they replace.

EMPHATIC AND/OR DISJUNCTIVE PERSONAL PRONOUNS		
Fonction Personne	Accentué Disjoint	
1ère Sing.	Moi	Me?!
2ème Sing.	Toi	You!
3ème Sing.	Lui—Elle	Him—Her?
1ère Pl.	Nous	Us?
2ème Pl.	Vous	You . . .
3ème Pl.	Eux—Elles	Them!

They are called *emphatic* because they are used to insist on the person they designate. When you want to accentuate either the subject or the complement of the action, you can use an emphatic pronoun:

> Ursule adore les géraniums. **Toi**, tu détestes ces fleurs! *(Ursula loves geraniums. You, you hate these flowers!)*

> "Gautier, as-tu cassé mon vase en cristal?" "**Moi**? certainement pas!" *("Gautier, did you break my crystal vase?" "Who, me? Certainly not!")*

Use

They are also called *disjunctive* because they are often sent to the end of the sentence, sometimes after a preposition. Their being the final word puts even more emphasis on the person:

> "Pour ton gâteau, Léon l'a mangé: le coupable, c'est **lui**!" *("About your cake: Léon ate it: he is the culprit!")*

> "Ah non, alors, je ne partirai pas en vacances avec Pierrette; je préfère rester ici, avec **toi**." *("Not a chance, I will not go on vacation with Pierrette; I'd rather stay here, with you.")*

EN and *Y* for Inanimate Beings

When the indirect complement is an inanimate being, it is not possible to use the regular pronouns: ~~Me, Te, Lui, Nous, Vous, Leur~~.

They are substituted by neuter pronouns that do not show a difference between genders or numbers.

Y with Preposition À

If the verb uses the preposition À, the pronoun used is **Y**:

Je pense **à mon examen**. J'**y** pense. *(I think about my exam / it.)*

Mon examen = (indirect object complement) COI inanimate:

Je vais **à Èze**. J'**y** vais. *(I go there.)*

Èze = (Circumstantial complement of location) CC lieu inanimate

EN with Preposition DE

If the verb uses the preposition **DE**, the pronoun used is **EN**.

Je parle **DE mon examen**. J'**en** parle. (*I talk about my exam. I talk about it.*)

Mon examen = (indirect object complement) COI inanimate:

Je viens **D'Èze**. J'**en** viens. (I come from Èze. I come from there.)

Èze = (Circumstantial complement of location) CC lieu inanimate

EN as Quantity

~~EN is also used to replace undetermined quantities, namely a noun that was originally~~ used with a partitive article. When there is a need to specify the quantity, it is added at the end of the sentence:

Vous buvez du café? Non je n'**en** bois pas. *(Do you drink coffee? No, I don't.)*

Avez-vous **un** dictionnaire de français? Oui, j'**en** ai **deux**. *(Do you have a French dictionary? Yes, I have two of them.)*

TIP BOX

Associate **EN** with the idea of a sourcE-origiN from which you are deriving the information and you will see the common point between its various uses:

- J' **EN** parle (*I speak about it*): There is a topic out there and I am drawing information from it in order to speak.
- J' **EN** viens (*I come from there*): There is a place out there and I am coming from it.
- J' **EN** bois (*I drink some of it*): There is an indefinite quantity of liquid out there and I am taking some out of it to drink.
- J' **EN** ai deux (*I have two of them*): There is a large quantity of objects available in this category and I obtained two of them from that source.

All of these are origins from which to extract yourself or something.

From what you have seen so far in terms of adjectives and pronouns, can you recognize a common pattern that would help you remember the correct form of pronouns for each person?

TIP BOX

To each person are assigned one or two specific letters that start most determinative adjectives and personal pronouns.

Remember these common beginnings when you forget a list. If you start by writing the correct letter, chances are the rest of the word will automatically follow.

Je	M	mon, me, moi
Tu	T	ta, te, toi
Elle Il	S—L	ses, se, soi, lui, elle
Nous	N	notre, nous
Vous	V	vos, vous
Ils Elles	L—S	leur, les, se, elles

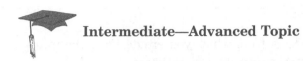

Intermediate—Advanced Topic

Order of Multiple Personal Pronouns

Since there may be more than one complement in a sentence, there may be multiple pronouns replacing them.

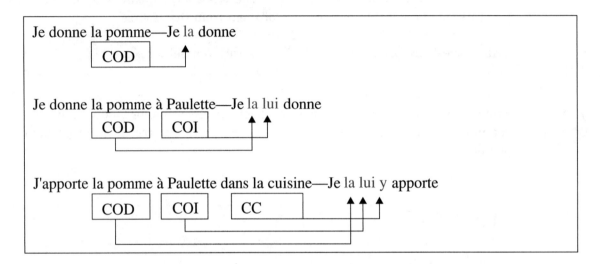

General Order of Precedence

The general rule is that personal pronouns always come **before** the conjugated or the infinitive verb that they complement, but some take precedence over others:

REVIEW TABLE: ORDER OF PERSONAL PRONOUNS BY FUNCTION						
Indirect Object Or Reflexive/Reciprocal		Direct Object	Indirect Object **3rd Persons**	**Prep. À**	**Prep. DE**	**VERB**
me—m'	me—m'					
te—t'	te—t'	le—l' la—l' les	lui leur	y	en	Conjugated or Infinitive verb
lui	se					
nous	nous					
vous	vous					
leur	se					

Typical Examples

Consider the examples below. To form the various sentences, let us assume that Boris is the subject of all the actions.

COD	COI	Prep. DE	Prep. À Location	Verb
les bonbons	(à) moi		dans ma chambre	apporter
les	**me**		**y**	
Boris apporte les bonbons à moi dans ma chambre. (*Boris brings candy to me in my bedroom.*) Boris **me les y** apporte. (*Boris brings them to me.*) Indirect—Direct—Y				
	(à) toi	des bonbons	à ton école	apporter
	te	**en**	**y**	
Boris t'apporte des bonbons à ton école. (*Boris brings you candy to your school.*) Boris **t'y en** apporte. (*Boris brings you some there.*) Indirect—y—en				
la clé	(à) Sarah			donner
la	**lui**			
Boris donne la clé à Sarah. (*Boris gives the key to Sarah.*) Boris **la lui** donne. (*Boris gives it to her.*) Direct—Indirect because indirect object is 3rd person				
la clé	(à) vous			confier
la	**vous**			
Boris confie la clé à vous. (*Boris turns the key over to you.*) Boris **vous la** confie. (*Boris turns it over to you.*) Indirect—Direct				
les clés	(à) Nadia et moi		sur le parking	rendre
les	**nous**		**y**	
Boris rend les clés à Nadia et moi sur le parking. (*Boris gives the keys back to us on the parking lot.*) Boris **nous les** y rend. (*Boris gives them back to us.*) Indirect—Direct—y				

la corde	(à lui)		au cou	mettre
la	**se**		**y**	

Boris met la corde au cou à lui. *(French colloquialism that means to get married!)*
Boris **se l'y** met. *(Boris puts it on himself.)* Reflexive—Direct—y

les cartes	(à) Nadia et Julie		à Marseille	envoyer
les	**leur**		**y**	

Boris envoie les cartes à Nadia et Julie à Marseille. *(Boris sends the cards to Nadia and Julie in Marseille.)*
Boris **les leur y** envoie. *(Boris sends it to them there).* Direct—Indirect—y (Indirect object is 3rd person)

	(à) Natacha	des promesses	sous son balcon	faire
	lui	**en**	**y**	

Boris fait des promesses à Natacha sous son balcon. *(Boris makes promises to Natacha under her balcony.)*
Boris **lui y en** fait. *(Boris makes them to her there.)* Indirect—y—en

You can memorize the above ordering table, or try to remember the following story: *Il était une fois Enceladus . . .*

MAGIC METHOD D. I. Y. EN

Il était une fois, en boîte *(Once upon a time, in a bar)*

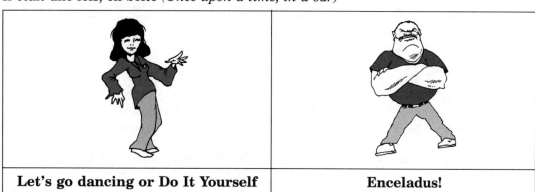

Let's go dancing or Do It Yourself	Enceladus!

A friend and you have just taken a tough Greek Mythology exam. So you decide to go dancing to relax. At the door of a popular bar stands a giant bouncer, with huge muscles. It is late and the line is long. When you finally get to the door, you are a bit tired. So is the big guy who has been standing here for hours, to make sure no one under 21 sneaks in on him.

Without even saying "Hi," the big guy indirectly shouts at you:

"I. D."

As it is taking you a while to get your license out of your small purse/wallet, the guy indirectly yells again:

"I. D.!"

You find that very rude, so you just hand him out your purse/wallet and say, looking directly at him:

"**D**o **I**t **Y**ourself, **E**nceladus!"

Enceladus is a giant with a hundred arms who fought against Zeus. He was thought by the Ancient Greeks to be responsible for seismic terror and volcanoes.

Moral of the story:
Get a bigger purse or wallet or go to a bar with a smaller bouncer!
Conclusion of the story:
I.D.-I.D.-D. I. Y. EN is the order of the pronouns.

ORDER OF OBJECT COMPLEMENT PERSONAL PRONOUNS BY PERSON					
I.D.	1st pers. Indirect	Indirect	Direct		
I.D.!	2nd pers. Indirect	Indirect	Direct		
D. I. Y. Enceladus	3rd pers. Indirect	Direct	Indirect	Y	EN
I.D.	1st pers. Indirect	me—nous	le—la—les		
I.D.!	2nd pers. Indirect	te—vous	le—la—les	Y	EN
D. I. Y.! Enceladus	3rd pers. Indirect	le—la—les	lui—leur		

I.D. Le videur rend le permis de conduire **à** moi.	1st pers. Indirect me		Le videur **me le** rend. Indirect—Direct *(The bouncer gives it back to me.)*
I.D.! Le videur rend le permis de conduire **à** toi.	2nd pers. Indirect te		Le videur **te le** rend. Indirect—Direct *(The bouncer gives it back to you.)*
D. I. Y.! Enceladus Le videur rend le permis de conduire **à** Marc.		3rd pers. Indirect lui	Le videur **le lui** rend. Direct—Indirect *(The bouncer gives it back to him.)*
D. I. Y.! Enceladus Le videur rend le permis **à** Marc devant la boîte.		3rd pers. Indirect lui	Le videur **le lui y** rend. Direct—Indirect—Y *(The bouncer gives it back to him there.)*
D. I. Y.! Enceladus Le videur rend **de** la monnaie **à** Marc et Paul devant la boîte.		3rd pers. Indirect leur	Le videur **leur y en** rend. Indirect—Y—EN *(The bouncer gives some back to them there.)*

NOTE Indirect complements of object follow the story:
I.D.—I.D.—D.I. **Y** comes before **EN**.
EN is always closest to the verb.

Order in Negative Sentences

In negative sentences, the direct object and indirect complements or reflexive/reciprocal personal pronouns remain closer to the verb. They therefore come after the first part of the negation **ne**:

- before the verb conjugated in a simple tense
- before the auxiliary verb if the verb is conjugated in a compound tense
- **before the infinitive verb to which they actually relate.**

Affirmative	Negative		
	Simple Tense	Compound Tense	**Infinitive**
COD Paul **le** voit.	Paul <u>ne</u> **le** voit <u>pas</u>. (*Paul does not see him.*)		
	Paul <u>ne</u> l'a <u>pas</u> vu. (*Paul did not see him*)		
Paul **l'**a vu.	Paul <u>ne</u> veut <u>pas</u> **le** voir. (*Paul does not want to see him.*)		
	Paul n'a pas voulu **le voir**.		
COI Paul **me** parle. Paul **m'**avait parlé.	Paul <u>ne</u> **me** parle <u>pas</u>. (*Paul does not speak to me.*)		
	Paul <u>ne</u> **m'**avait <u>pas</u> parlé. (*Paul had not spoken to me.*)		
	Paul <u>ne</u> veut <u>pas</u> **me** parler. (*Paul does not want to speak to me.*)		
	Paul <u>n'</u>avait <u>pas</u> voulu **me parler**. (*Paul had not wanted to speak to me.*)		
Ref./Rec. Paul **se** brosse.	Paul <u>ne</u> **se** brosse <u>pas</u>. (*Paul does not brush himself.*)		
	Paul <u>ne</u> **s'**était <u>pas</u> brossé. (*Paul did not brush himself.*)		
Paul **s'**était brossé	Paul <u>n'</u>essaie <u>pas</u> de **se** brosser.		
	Paul <u>n'</u>a <u>pas</u> essayé de **se brosser**. (*Paul did not try to brush himself.*)		

Particular Cases: *Nous and Vous*

IMPORTANT!

Picturing in your mind the entire group of personal pronouns as subjects, direct object complements, indirect object complements, reflexive or emphatic, isn't there something that strikes you?

Je, Tu, Il—Elle—On, Nous, Vous, Ils—Elles
Me, Te, Le—La, Nous, Vous, Les
Me, Te, Lui, Nous, Vous, Leur
Me, Te, Se, Nous, Vous, Se
Moi, Toi, Lui—Elle, Nous, Vous, Eux—Elles

What is striking: Nous and **Vous** are common to ALL lists.

Since most of these personal pronouns are placed before the conjugated or infinitive verb to which they relate, with the exception of the emphatic pronouns, you should always be careful when conjugating your verb.

Only one time out of five is the pronoun **Nous** or **Vous** that you see before the verb actually the subject of that verb; 80 percent of the time **Nous** or **Vous** is the complement of the verb.

They can be direct or indirect object complement, reflexive, or reciprocal. Always make sure to ask the question: "Who/What does the action?" before choosing your verb ending.

Tu nous téléphon**es**   —   **Nous** te téléphon**ons**

Subject

<u>Nous</u> lis**ons** le chapitre sur les pronoms; <u>**vous**</u> lis**ez** le chapitre sur les pronoms. *(We read the chapter on pronouns; you read the chapter on pronouns.)*

Direct Object Complement

(Ce chapitre) Il **nous** intéress**e** · <u>Il</u> **vous** intéress**e**. *(This chapter: it interests us · It interests you.)*

Indirect Object Complement

<u>Vous</u> **nous** parl**ez** du chapitre · <u>Je</u> **vous** par**le** du chapitre. *(You talk to us about the chapter · I talk to you about the chapter.)*

Reflexive Complement

<u>Nous</u> **nous** souven**ons** **de** ce chapitre · <u>Vous</u> **vous** souven**ez** **de** ce chapitre. *(We remember this chapter · You remember this chapter.)*

Because the **-ons** and **-ez** endings are easy to remember, a common tendency is to add them routinely when one sees **nous** or **vous** in front of the verb. As the examples above demonstrate, this often leads to a mistake.

Impersonal Pronouns

When certain personal pronouns are used in conjunction with specific verbs or in particular idiomatic expressions, they no longer refer to a precise person or thing. They designate a vague and unidentified entity and function as subjects of the verb, although they do not actually replace a noun.

In this case, they are called *impersonal*. The main impersonal pronouns are **Il, Y,** and **Ce—C'** or **Ça.**

Il y a (There Is / There Are)
Use

The impersonal expression **Il y a + Noun** is always singular. Contrary to English, even when the noun is in the plural, the expression itself remains in the singular because its actual grammatical subject is **IL**, impersonal, third person masculine singular.

Il y a un arbre. **Il y a** des arbre**s**. *(There is a tree. There are trees.)*

Il serves only as the subject of the auxiliary verb **avoir**. It does not refer to any specific person or object. It is therefore neuter.

Use

Contrary to English, French does not use the auxiliary verb **être** (to be) to designate the presence of a person or a thing in a location, but the impersonal construction with **avoir**— **Il y a** (There *has*).

> **Il y a** des arbres en fleurs dans ma rue. *(There are blossoming trees in my street.)*

> **Il y a** un livre, trois stylos et une tasse de thé vert sur mon bureau. *(There are a book, three pens, and a cup of green tea on my desk.)*

Although **y** signifies the presence (being there) of the person or object designated by the noun, it is not necessarily visible or actually present in the context.

> En Afrique, **il y a** des lions magnifiques. *(In Africa, there are magnificent lions.)*

Ce + *être* (This Is / These Are)

Use

Ce + Être (Ce in Front of Être)

Ce is used as an impersonal pronoun in front of the auxiliary verb **être**. The final **e** is dropped in front of a form of **être** starting with a vowel.

> **C(e)'est** la vie. **Ce** sont des choses qui arrivent. *(That's life. These things happen.)*

Ça + autres verbes (Ça in Front of All Other Verbs)

With any other verb used impersonally, the pronoun changes to **ça**. The final **a** is never dropped.

> **Ça a**rrive. **Ça v**enait de Belgique. **Ça t**e dirait d'aller au ciné? **Ça** encourage. *(It happens. This came from Belgium. Feel like going to the movies? That's encouraging.)*

Function

The impersonal expressions **C'est** and **Ce sont** serve to identify visible persons or things. **C'est** is used with a singular noun. **Ce**, as a demonstrative pronoun, takes on the gender and number of the noun it replaces. Therefore, **Ce sont** (third person plural) is used with a plural noun.

> Regarde cet arbre; **c'est** un palmier. *(Look at this tree; it's a palm tree.)*

> Mes voisins, **ce sont** les Duplessy. *(My neighbors are the Duplessys.)*

After Il y a

C'est and **Ce sont** can help specify a person or a thing introduced by **il y a**.

> Devant le musée du Louvre, **il y a** une construction étrange; **c'est** une pyramide toute en verre. *(In front of the Louvre museum, there is a strange construction; it is a pyramid made entirely of glass.)*

> **Il y a** deux posters que j'adore chez Fabrice; **ce sont** des reproductions de Magritte. *(There are two posters that I really like at Fabrice's place; they are reproductions of Magritte's paintings.)*

Introduction

C'est and **Ce sont** are used to introduce people or oneself.

> Je vous présente ma Directrice de Production, **c'est** Magali Lemercier. *(Let me introduce to you my Production Director, Magali Lemercier.)*

> "Allô, Monsieur Legrand? Bonjour, **c'est** Fabienne. Comment allez-vous?" *(Hello, Mr. Legrand? Good morning, this is Fabienne. How are you?)*

Profession

C'est and **Ce sont** establish the profession of a person.

> Voilà le Dr. Arnaud; **c'est** mon médecin. **C'est** un généraliste mais il a fait aussi de l'acuponcture. *(Here is Dr. Arnaud; he is my doctor. He is a general practitioner, but he also does acupuncture.)*

> Les Schweitzer? **Ce sont** tous des avocats: de père en fils et de mère en fille! *(The Schweitzers? They are all lawyers: fathers to sons and mothers to daughters.)*

> **NOTE** When stating the profession of a specific person and using **Il** or **Elle** to replace that person, **Il** or **Elle** is a personal pronoun and the profession is never preceded by an article.

> Magali Lemercier est Directrice de Production. **Elle** est **ingénieur** de Polytechnique. *(She is an engineer from the Polytechnic School.)*

Professions are used in the same way as an attributive adjective:

Il est professeur. / **Il est** blond.

On the contrary, **c'est** is followed by an article.

Albert Einstein était un génie. **C'est le** mathématicien le plus célèbre. Il était professeur à MIT. *(Albert Einstein was a genius. He is the most famous mathematician. He was a professor at MIT.)*

Practice What You Learned

Exercises are rated according to four levels of difficulty:

- Beginner easy [*]
- Beginner challenging [**]
- Intermediate [***]
- Advanced [****]

1. Complete the text with the appropriate personal or impersonal pronoun subject. Pay attention to the verb ending or the agreements to make sure they match your choice. [**]

   A. Allô, Marc? Bonjour, _____ est Marie.

   B. _____ suis à Nice avec mon mari François.

   C. _____ est ingénieur et veut travailler à Sophia-Antipolis. Nos enfants Charles et Julien sont ici aussi.

   D. _____ veulent te voir.

   E. _____ pouvons aller à Grasse chez toi cet après-midi.

   F. Est-ce que _____ es libre?

   G. Si _____ voulez, ta femme et toi, _____ pourrions tous aller visiter les grandes parfumeries.

   H. _____ sont si célèbres!

2. Replace the *subject* and the **direct object complement** by a pronoun. [**]

   Example

   Karine connait **Valérie**. Elle la connait.

   A. *Ed et moi* arrosons **les fleurs** le samedi. _____

   B. *Philippe* garde **sa petite nièce**. _____

   C. *Guy et toi* n'aimez pas **les sandwiches** au beurre de cacahuète. _____

3. Replace the *subject* and the **indirect object complement** by a pronoun. [**]

    A. *Sylvie et Sophie* téléphonent <u>à leur mère</u>. _____

    B. *Ton frère et ta soeur* répondent <u>au professeur</u>. _____

    C. *Leur ami* n'écrit pas <u>à ton frère et ta soeur</u>. _____

    D. *Ken et toi* envoyez des fleurs <u>à Barbie et moi</u>. _____

4. Answer the questions according to the model and the *yes or no* opening. [***]

Example

Tu me prêtes ton livre, Jean? Non, je ne te le prête pas.

    A. Vous m'envoyez la lettre par télécopie? Oui, _____

    B. Tu laisses les clés à ta camarade de chambre? Oui, _____

    C. Charles vous vend sa moto? Non, _____

    D. Françoise te prête ses robes? Oui, _____

5. Rewrite the sentences replacing all the nouns by pronouns and EN. [***]

    A. Mon ami m'offre des fleurs. _____

    B. Maman m'apporte du chocolat français à Noël. _____

    C. Pierre et toi empruntez de l'argent. _____

    D. Les professeurs donnent des exercises. _____

6. Answer in the negative form while replacing all the nouns by direct object, indirect object, or en pronouns. [****]

Examples

Tu prêtes votre voiture à votre voisine? Non, je ne la lui prête pas.
Vous parlez de votre voiture à votre voisine? Non, nous ne lui en parlons pas.

    A. Tu laisses tes clés à ces idiots? _____

    B. Tu donnes tes bijoux à Marie et moi? _____

    C. Vous achetez des bonbons à vos enfants? _____

    D. Tu donnes du chocolat à ton chien? _____

7. Replace the *À* + noun group by the pronoun *Y*. [**]

    A. Vous allez à l'aéroport maintenant? _____

    B. Nous sommes à Paris pour une semaine. _____

    C. Elle s'intéresse à la peinture surréaliste. _____

    D. Je pense souvent au sens de la vie. _____

8. Answer with the appropriate pronoun: **le, la, les, lui, leur, en, y**. [****]

A. Utilisez-vous ces ordinateurs? Oui, _____

B. Tu vas à ce cocktail? Non, _____

C. Robert parle à son frère? Non, _____

D. Les enfants veulent des glaces? Oui, _____

E. Cette couleur va bien à ta soeur? Non, _____

F. Faites-vous de l'exercice? Oui, _____

G. As-tu téléphoné à tes cousines? Non, _____

9. Translate with the appropriate reflexive or reciprocal pronoun. Be careful to use a pronominal verb in French. [**]

A. Bernard and Bernadette love each other. _____

B. You get up early. _____

C. They dress themselves. _____

D. I ask myself many questions. _____

E. We often write each other. _____

F. They dress each other. _____

10. Use **ce** or **ça** or **il** when appropriate. [**]

A. Roger est mon ami. _____ est un homme bon et admirable.

B. _____ est médecin cancérologue.

C. _____ 'est une profession difficile.

D. _____ demande beaucoup de gentillesse pour les patients.

E. Être cancérologue, _____ n'est pas comme les autres spécialités.

F. _____ confronte à tant de souffrances.

G. Et _____ exige du courage et de l'abnégation.

Chapter 9

DEMONSTRATIVE, POSSESSIVE, INTERROGATIVE, INDEFINITE PRONOUNS

Introduction

Pronouns are part of the nominal group. They are pro-noun, that is used for a noun that may be alone, accompanied by an adjective, or at the core of a clause:

> **Audrey adore dessiner. (Audrey) Elle peint très bien aussi.**

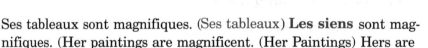

> Ses tableaux sont magnifiques. (Ses tableaux) **Les siens** sont magnifiques. (Her paintings are magnificent. (Her Paintings) Hers are magnificent.)

> Joachim a acheté ce tableau-ci. Joachim voulait (ce tableau-là) **celui-là** aussi. (Joachim bought this painting. Joachim wanted (that painting) that one as well.)

> L'exposition d'Audrey a beaucoup de succès. Tout le monde **en** parle (du fait que l'exposition d'Audrey a beaucoup de succès). (Audrey's exhibit is very successful. Everyone speaks about it.)

Nouns in French have a gender and a number; they can have various functions, and can be specified in numerous ways. There are consequently multiple lists of pronouns from which to choose so that none of the characteristic of the noun is lost during its replacement by a pronoun. Nonpersonal pronouns, like all pronouns, are used to replace a noun. They are necessary when the noun they replace originally was specified by a determinative adjective. Because the pronoun must retain as much of the original information as possible, there is a category of pronoun that corresponds to each determinative adjective:

CORRESPONDANCE BETWEEN DETERMINATIVE ADJECTIVES—NONPERSONAL PRONOUNS		
Adjective **Demonstrative** Adjective **Possessive** Adjective **Interrogative** Adjective **Indefinite** Adjective	+ *Noun*	Pronoun **Demonstrative** Pronoun **Possessive** Pronoun **Interrogative** Pronoun **Indefinite** Pronoun

Demonstrative Pronouns

Function

As in English, demonstrative pronouns direct the attention of the reader, or speaker, to a specific object to distinguish it from a group or another similar element. In order to avoid repeating it, they replace a noun that was originally accompanied by a demonstrative adjective.

Gender and Number

Demonstrative pronouns take on the gender and number of the noun they replace.

Nombre / Genre	Masculin	Féminin	
Singulier	**CELUI**	**CELLE**	This—That The one
Pluriel	**CEUX**	**CELLES**	These—Those The ones

Adjective + Noun Replacement

Demonstrative pronouns replace a noun that originally was specified by a demonstrative adjective.

DEMONSTRATIVE ADJECTIVES AND PRONOUN EQUIVALENTS EXAMPLES				
	Adjectif Démonstratif	+	Nom	**Pronom** Démonstratif
Masc. Sing.	**Ce** **Ce livre** est intéressant.	+	livre	**Celui** **Celui-ci** est intéressant.
(This book is interesting.)				*(This one is interesting.)*
Fem. Sing	**Cette** **Cette amie** est fabuleuse.	+	amie	**Celle** **Celle-ci** est fabuleuse.
(This friend is fabulous.)				*(This one is fabulous.)*
Masc. Pl.	**Ces** **Ces enfants** sont à Paul.	+	enfants	**Ceux** Ce sont **ceux de** Paul.
(These children are Paul's.)				*(These are Paul's.)*
Fem. Pl.	**Ces** J'adore **ces chattes** qui parlent.	+	chattes	**Celles** J'adore **celles qui** parlent.
(I love these cats that speak.)				*(I love those that speak.)*

REVIEW TABLE: DEMONSTRATIVE ADJECTIVES AND PRONOUNS					
Genre Nombre	**Masculin**		**Féminin**		
	Adjectif	Pronom	**Adjectif**	Pronom	
Singulier	**Ce—Cet**	CELUI ci/là—de—qui	**Cette**	CELLE ci/là—de—qui	This—That The one
Pluriel	**Ces**	CEUX ci/là—de—qui	**Ces**	CELLES ci/là—de—qui	These—Those The ones

Use with Suffix, Preposition, or Relative Pronoun

> ### IMPORTANT!
> Demonstrative pronouns never stand alone in the sentence. They must be followed by a suffix, a preposition, or a relative pronoun.

Demonstrative Pronouns with Suffixes -ci / -là

These suffixes are used when there is an opposition or a comparison between two elements:

> Ce cheval est blanc, ce cheval est noir mais ils sont tous deux superbes. **Celui-ci** est blanc, **celui-là** est noir mais ils sont tous deux superbes. *([This horse] This one is white, [that horse] that one is black but both are superb.)*

Demonstrative Pronouns with Prepositions DE, À, or EN

- **De** designates the owner of the object replaced by the pronoun:

  > Cette voiture est à mon professeur. C'est **celle de** mon professeur. *(This car belongs to my professor. It is the one of my professor. It is my professor's.)*

- **EN** indicates the matter of the object replaced by the pronoun:

  > Vous voulez quel pull? **Celui en** cachemire. *(Which sweater do you want? The cashmere one.)*

- **À** refers to the price replaced by the pronoun:

  > Je préfère ces chaussures, **celles à** 48€. *(I prefer these shoes, the ones that cost 48 €uros.)*

Simple/Compound Relative Pronouns with Demonstrative Pronouns

The pronoun replaces the noun in the subordinate clause. It can be either subject of or complement in the relative clause:

> Cet examen est difficile; c'est **celui qui** fait peur aux étudiants. *(This exam is difficult; it's the one that scares the students.)*

> Cet examen est difficile; c'est **celui que** tu as passé hier. *(This exam is difficult; it's the one that you took yesterday.)*

> Cet examen est difficile; c'est **celui dont** tout le monde parle. *(This exam is difficult; it's the one that everyone is talking about.)*

> Cet examen est difficile; c'est **celui pour lequel** il faut beaucoup réviser. *(This exam is difficult; it's the one for which we must review a lot.)*

TIP BOX

If you forget what the demonstrative pronouns are in French, remember in English: thiSSSSS "sssss" sound—

> in French: demon**SSSSS**tratif: "sssss" = **celui-ci**
> démon**s**tratif = démon**CET**ratif

celui—celle—ceux—celles all start with a ce sound, like the adjectives.

Possessive Pronouns

Function

Possessive pronouns replace nouns that were originally accompanied by a possessive adjective. They are also used to determine who possesses the object or person they replace, in an opposition, a comparison, etc.

Possession implies an owner and an object owned. Once again, returning to the example of 1 owner and 1 object:

Owner = Person	Property = Object

Gwladys vient de réussir <u>son</u> examen d'ingénieur. Ce diplôme est **le sien**, la toque **la sienne** aussi. Mais ce programme est **le mien**. *(Gwladys recently passed her engineer exams. This diploma is **hers**, the cap is **hers** too. But this program is **mine**.)*

Possession Relationships

There are four variations in a relationship of possession. They result from the various possible combinations of the two components of this relationship between an owner and an object.

- One person owning one object
- One person owning two (or more) objects
- Two (or more) persons owning one object
- Two persons owning two (or more) objects

The following diagram summarizes all the possessive situations.

POSSESSION MATRIX		
Object Person	1 Object	2 or more Objects
1 Person		
2 or more Persons		

Object Person	1 Object	2 or more Objects
Jessica	un bonsaï	deux voitures
Patrick et Philippe	une maison	deux raquettes

Use and Formation

The four different possibilities of possession (1 person owning 1 object; 1 person owning 2 objects—2 persons owning 1 object, 2 persons owning 2 objects) are conveyed by each possessive pronoun. Each element (person, object) is made visible by the pronouns. Possessive pronouns result from the combination of two elements:

- the definite article
- the possessive marker.

Definite Article in the Possessive Pronoun

Definite articles are used with the possessive markers to form the possessive pronoun.

Nombre Genre	Masculin	Féminin
Singulier	**Le**	**La**
Pluriel	**Les**	

Contrary to English, they agree in gender and in number with the object that is owned. This is similar to the possessive adjectives whose ending corresponds to the object, and not to the owner.

> Paul's chair—His chair. *His* is masculine because Paul (the owner) is a man.

> La chaise de Paul—Sa chaise. *Sa* is feminine because *la chaise* (the object) is feminine.

Possessive Pronoun

The second word is the actual possessive pronoun and, like possessive adjectives, it refers both to the owner and the object owned. The first letter refers to the owner; the rest of the word refers to the property.

Here are two ways of summarizing the possessive pronouns list:

> le mien; le tien; le sien—la mienne; la tienne; la sienne (*mine, your, his—hers—its*)

> les miens; les tiens; les siens—les miennes; les tiennes; les siennes (*mine, your, his—hers—its*)

> le nôtre; le vôtre; le leur—la nôtre; la vôtre; la leur (*ours, yours, theirs*)

> les nôtres; les vôtres; les leurs—les nôtres; les vôtres; les leurs (*ours, yours, theirs*)

REVIEW TABLE: POSSESSIVE PRONOUN FORMATION AND OWNER MARKERS

Object / Person	1 Object				2⁺ ObjectS		
	Masculine		Feminine		Masc. Fem.	Masc.	Fem.
1 Person *Mine* *Yours* *His—Hers*	Le	Mien Tien Sien	La	Mienne Tienne Sienne	Les	Miens Tiens Siens	Miennes Tiennes Siennes
	Masc.	Fem.	Masculine Feminine		Masc. Fem.	Masculine Feminine	
2 Persons *Ours* *Yours* *Theirs*	Le	La	Nôtre Vôtre Leur		Les	Nôtres Vôtres Leurs	

REVIEW TABLE: POSSESSIVE PRONOUN FORMATION AND PROPERTY MARKERS

Object / Person	1 Object		2⁺ ObjectS	
	Masculine	**Feminine**	**Masculine**	**Feminine**
1 Person	Le mien Le tien Le sien	La mienne La tienne La sienne	Les miens Les tiens Les siens	Les miennes Les tiennes Les siennes
2 Persons	Le nôtre Le vôtre Le leur	La nôtre La vôtre La leur	Les nôtres Les vôtres Les leurs	

TIP BOX

Remember that each person is associated with a letter. This letter is the same for possessive adjectives and pronouns as well as other pronouns. Please find the equivalent letters in the table on page 115 in Chapter 8, Personal and Impersonal Pronouns.

NOTE The possessive adjectives notre and votre **are spelled with a regular o. Only the possessive pronouns** le—la—les nôtres **and** le—la—les vôtres **are spelled with a circumflex accent over the ô.**

TIP BOX

If you can't remember if the adjective or the pronoun takes the "^" accent, the answer is:

If there is NO Article with **NOtre** then there is NO Accent on **Notre**: notre livre
If there *is* AN ArticLe then there is AN AcceNt: **Le n** **ô** **tre**

MAGIC METHOD   Whenever you are wondering which pronoun to use, remember that possession implies one or more people owning one or more objects. Mentally diagram the relationship for each situation as below, if you cannot instantly remember which pronoun to use. Find the intersection between the person and the object that corresponds to the particular situation (A, B, C, or D). This should help you remember which letter starts the pronoun. Then make sure you know the gender of the object, which will determine the article.

To find the correct pronoun, always start by going to the relevant intersection of the column and the row.

	1 Object	2+ Objects
1 Person	? A m t s	? B m t s
2+ Persons	? C n v l	? D n v l

Then try to remember the possessive words themselves.

TIP BOX

French possessive pronouns are very helpful. The words themselves represent the possession relationship. The first letter refers to the owner, while the article and the rest of the word replace the property

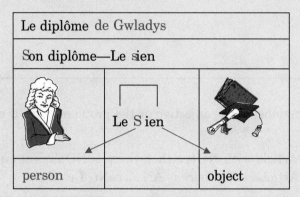

Le diplôme de Gwladys
Son diplôme—Le sien

person   Le S ien   object

The first letter tells you if there is one or more owners. The article and pronoun endings tell you if there is one object that is feminine or masculine or if there are more objects. The feminine pronoun is formed in the singular or plural by doubling the final consonant (n) and adding an "e" or "es," which is a common way to feminize certain words.

Example 1:

Le parapluie de Patrice: 1 object masculine singular—1 owner, 3rd person singular (Patrice = il)—(son parapluie) = le sien

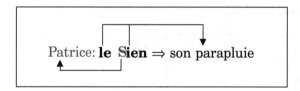

Patrice: **le Sien** ⇒ son parapluie

	Object	1 Object		2⁺ Objects	
Letter corresponding to the **Person**		Masculine	Feminine	Masculine	Feminine
1st Pers. Sing. JE	**M**	Le mien	La mienne	Les miens	Les miennes
2nd Pers. Sing. TU	**T**	Le tien	La tienne	Les tiens	Les tiennes
3rd Pers. Sing. IL—ELLE	**S**	Le sien	La sienne	Les siens	Les siennes
1st Pers. Pl. NOUS	**N**	Le nôtre	La nôtre	Les nôtres	Les nôtres
2nd Pers. Pl. VOUS	**V**	Le vôtre	La vôtre	Les vôtres	Les vôtres
3rd Pers. Pl. ILS—ELLES	**L**	Le leur	La leur	Les leurs	Les leurs

Example 2:

Les filles de François et moi: 2+ objects—2 owners, 1st person plural (François et moi = nous)—(nos filles) = les nôtres

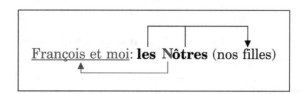

François et moi: **les Nôtres** (nos filles)

	Object	1 Object		2⁺ Objects	
Letter corresponding to the Person		Masculine	Feminine	Masculine	Feminine
1st Pers. Sing. JE	**M**	Le mien	La mienne	Les miens	Les miennes
2nd Pers. Sing. TU	**T**	Le tien	La tienne	Les tiens	Les tiennes
3rd Pers. Sing. IL—ELLE	**S**	Le sien	La sienne	Les siens	Les siennes
1st Pers. Pl. NOUS	**N**	Le nôtre	La nôtre	Les nôtres	Les nôtres
2nd Pers. Pl. VOUS	**V**	Le vôtre	La vôtre	Les vôtres	Les vôtres
3rd Pers. Pl. ILS—ELLES	**L**	Le leur	La leur	Les leurs	Les leurs

Example 3:

La voiture de Olivier et toi: 1 object feminine singular—2 owners, 2nd person plural (Olivier et toi = vous)—(votre) la vôtre

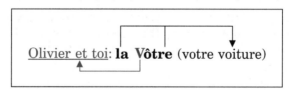

Olivier et toi: **la Vôtre** (votre voiture)

	Object	1 Object		2⁺ Objects	
Letter corresponding to the Person		Masculine	Feminine	Masculine	Feminine
1st Pers. Sing. JE	**M**	Le mien	La mienne	Les miens	Les miennes
2nd Pers. Sing. TU	**T**	Le tien	La tienne	Les tiens	Les tiennes
3rd Pers. Sing. IL—ELLE	**S**	Le sien	La sienne	Les siens	Les siennes
1st Pers. Pl. NOUS	**N**	Le nôtre	La nôtre	Les nôtres	Les nôtres
2nd Pers. Pl. VOUS	**V**	Le vôtre	La vôtre	Les vôtres	Les vôtres
3rd Pers. Pl. ILS—ELLES	**L**	Le leur	La leur	Les leurs	Les leurs

Example 4:

Les livres que tu as achetés: 2+ objects—1 owner (Tu = 2nd person singular)—(tes livres) = les tiens

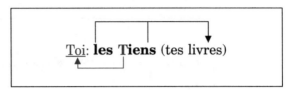

Toi: **les Tiens** (tes livres)

	Object	1 Object		2⁺ Objects	
Letter corresponding to the Person		Masculine	Feminine	Masculine	Feminine
1st Pers. Sing. JE	**M**	Le mien	La mienne	Les miens	Les miennes
2nd Pers. Sing. TU	**T**	Le tien	La tienne	Les tiens	Les tiennes
3rd Pers. Sing. IL—ELLE	**S**	Le sien	La sienne	Les siens	Les siennes
1st Pers. Pl. NOUS	**N**	Le nôtre	La nôtre	Les nôtres	Les nôtres
2nd Pers. Pl. VOUS	**V**	Le vôtre	La vôtre	Les vôtres	Les vôtres
3rd Pers. Pl. ILS—ELLES	**L**	Le leur	La leur	Les leurs	Les leurs

---

IMPORTANT!

The article accompanies the noun of the property; therefore it takes on its gender and number. The structure of the possessive pronoun is:

Property	Owner	Property
Article agreeing with the property in gender and number **Le—La—Les**	**Letter corresponding to the person of the owner** **M—T—S—N—V—L**	**Ending matching the property's gender and number:** **ien/iens—ienne/iennes** **ôtre/ôtres—eur/eurs**

Think of it as the owner being "sandwiched" between her—his objects.

Interrogative Pronouns

Function

Interrogative pronouns replace a noun that was originally accompanied by an interrogative adjective. They can also ask questions about the subject or the complements of an action to identify them or in cases of options, choices, etc.

There are two types of interrogative pronouns: simple and compound. Simple means that the pronoun is made of one word; compound means that it is formed by combining two words.

Simple Interrogative Pronouns

Simple interrogative pronouns ask questions about the subjects or complements of an action.

Their form varies depending upon:

- what is in question: a person, an animal, or a thing
- the function of the interrogative pronoun in the sentence

OVERVIEW TABLE: ANIMATE AND INANIMATE INTERROGATIVE PRONOUNS		
	Personne (person)	Chose (*thing*)
Sujet (*Subject*)	QUI (*Who*)	
COD (*Direct Object Complement*)	QUI (*Whom—That*)	QUE (*That*)
COI (*Indirect Object Complement*)	à / de QUI (*Whom*)	à / de QUOI (*What*)
CC (*Circumstantial Complement*)	préposition + QUI (*Whom*)	préposition + QUOI (*What*)

ANIMATE AND INANIMATE INTERROGATIVE PRONOUNS: EXAMPLES		
Paul a cassé ce vase. (*Paul broke this vase.*)	Paul = Personne / Sujet	QUI a cassé ce vase? (*Who broke this vase?*)
J'ai vu **Ida**. (*I saw Ida.*)	Ida = Personne / COD	QUI as-tu vu? (*Whom did you see?*)
Bob veut **un chien**. (*Bob wants a dog.*)	un chien = Chose / COD	QUE veut Bob? (*What does Bob want?*)
Vous avez parlé **à Anne**. (*You talked to Anne.*)	à Anne = Personne / COI	À QUI avez-vous parlé? (*To whom did you talk?*)
Nous avons parlé **de tout**. (*We talked about everything.*)	de tout = Chose / COI	De QUOI avez-vous parlé? (*About what did you talk?*)
Daniel a dansé **avec Sue**. (*Daniel danced with Sue.*)	avec Sue = Personne / CC	Avec QUI Daniel a-t-il dansé? (*With whom did Daniel dance?*)
Guy se lave **dans du lait**! (*Guy washes himself in milk!*)	dans du lait = Chose / CC	Guy se lave dans QUOI??? (*Guy washes himself in what???*)

Qui . . . ? (Interrogative Pronoun)

- **Qui** is used with a question about a human being or an animal that is personified, regardless of the functions it has in the sentence:

> **Qui** appelles-tu ce soir? *(Who are you calling tonight?)*

> **Qui** est le plus joli chat du monde? C'est Tofa! *(Who is the cutest cat in the world? Tofa!)*

- It can be combined with any preposition (à, de, pour, avec, chez, sans):

> **À qui** penses-tu? *(Whom are you thinking about?)*

> **Pour qui** est ce gros cadeau? *(For whom is this big present?)*

Que . . . ? and Quoi . . . ? (Interrogative Pronouns)

- **Que** and **quoi** are used with questions about things (or animals that are more generic).

- **Que** and **quoi** function as complements in the interrogative sentence.

Que

- **Que** is used without a preposition:

> **Que** veux-tu manger ce soir? *(What do you want to eat tonight?)*

> **Que** devient-elle ces jours-ci? *(What is going on with her these days?)*

Quoi

- When there is a preposition, **quoi** must be used:

> **Avec quoi** prépares-tu cette vinaigrette? *(With what do you make this salad dressing?)*

> **Dans quoi** ranges-tu ces timbres de collection? *(In what do you keep these collectible stamps?)*

Intermediate—Advanced Topic

Compound Interrogative Pronouns

Oral Interrogative Structure

Use

- A longer form of the same pronouns is commonly used in oral French.
- Its main advantage is that it does not require inverting the order of the subject and the verb.
- This inversion is already done among the components of the pronoun itself.
- These pronouns can always be used instead of the simple forms. Their use reflects, however, a more familiar level of language because they do not sound very elegant.

Formation

As a compound form, these pronouns combine three elements:

1. a first simple interrogative pronoun following the rule explained above:

Qui	Person
Que	Thing
Quoi	Preposition + Thing

2. the inversion of the neutral pronoun **ce** and the 3rd person of the auxiliary verb **être**, which indicates the interrogation (**c'est**): **est-ce?**
3. the repetition of **qui** if it is the subject of the question or **que** if there is another subject in the sentence.

> **NOTE** In fact, in
>
> > "Qui est-ce qui vient ce soir?", "Qui est-ce que tu as invité?",
> > "Qu'est-ce qui te ferait plaisir?", "Qu'est-ce que tu as préparé?"
>
> **qui and que are relative pronouns that help combine the two clauses into a compound sentence.**
>
> The structure, therefore, is similar to that of relative subordinate clauses:
>
> > **Principal clause** + qui + **conjugated verb**
> >
> > **Principal clause** + que + **subject** + **conjugated verb**

> **Although a similar structure does not exist in English (unless one really wants to emphasize the question), an equivalent would be**
>
> *Who is it that you have invited?* Whom did you invite?
>
> *Who is it that you saw?* Whom did you see?
>
> *What is it that would make you happy?* What would make you happy?
>
> *What is it that you prepared?* What did you prepare?

> *Refer to Chapter 16 for*
> **Relative Clauses**

Context

The compound interrogative pronoun therefore indicates

- first, if a person/animal or a thing is in question, and
- second, if this person/animal or thing is the subject or the object of the action expressed in the question.

COMPOUND INTERROGATIVE PRONOUNS STRUCTURE		
Remplacement (Replacement of)	une **Personne** (Person)	une **Chose** (Thing)
Sujet (Subject)	**QUI** est-ce QUI	**QU(E)**'est-ce QUI
COD (Direct Object Complement)	**QUI** est-ce QUE	**QU(E)**'est ce QUE
COI (Indirect Object Complement)	à / de **QUI** est-ce QUE	à / de **QUOI** est-ce QUE
CC (Circumstantial Complement)	preposition + **QUI** est-ce QUE	preposition + **QUOI** est-ce QUE

COMPOUND INTERROGATIVE PRONOUNS EXAMPLES)		
Ta soeur a téléphoné. *(Your sister called.)*	Ta soeur—Personne / Sujet	**QUI** est-ce **QUI** a téléphoné? *(Who [is it that] called?)*
J'ai vu **Ida**. *(I saw Ida.)*	Ida—Personne / COD	**QUI** est-ce **QUE** tu as vu? *(Whom did you see?)*
Un accident est arrivé. *(An accident happened.)*	Un accident—Chose / Sujet	**QU**(E)'est ce **QUI** est arrivé? *(What [is it that] happened?)*
Bob veut **un chien**. *(Bob wants a dog.)*	Un chien—Chose / COD	**QU**(E)'est ce **QUE** Bob veut? *(What does Bob want?)*
Vous avez parlé **à Pam**. *(You talked to Pam.)*	à Pam—Personne / COI	**À QUI** est-ce **QUE** vous avez parlé? *(To whom did you talk?)*
Nous avons parlé **de tout**. *(We talked about everything.)*	de tout—Chose / COI	**De QUOI** est-ce **QUE** vous avez parlé? *(About what did you talk?)*
Daniel a dansé **avec Diane**. *(Daniel danced with Diane.)*	avec Diane—Personne / CC	**Avec QUI** est-ce **QUE** Daniel a dansé? *(With whom did Daniel dance?)*
Guy mange ses frites **avec du lait!** *(Guy eats his fries with milk!)*	avec du lait—Chose / CC	**Avec QUOI** est-ce **QUE** Guy mange ses frites? *(With what does Guy eat his fries?)*

Direct or Indirect Interrogation

Interrogative Pronoun *Lequel* ...

These pronouns result from the combination of the definite articles and the interrogative adjective **quel**. Consequently, both parts of the pronoun vary to reflect the gender and number of the noun they replace.

Nombre \ Genre	Masculin	Féminin
Singulier	LEQUEL...?	LAQUELLE...?
Pluriel	LESQUELS...?	LESQUELLES...?

FORMATION OF INTERROGATIVE PRONOUNS LEQUEL / LAQUELLE					
Component	Definite Articles		Interrogative Adjectives		Interrogative Pronouns
Gender Number	Masculine	Feminine	Masculine	Feminine	Masculine	Feminine
Singular	Le	La	quel	quelle	Lequel	Laquelle
Plural	Les	Les	quels	quelles	Lesquels	Lesquelles
	The		*which*		*Which one / ones?*	

- **Lequel** replaces a noun that originally was accompanied by the interrogative adjective **quel**.
- The **lequel** series allows a direct or indirect interrogation about a noun when it is part of a group and a choice is possible.
- **Lequel—laquelle—lesquels—lesquelles** can be used by themselves or after any preposition **except À** and ~~DE~~.

INTERROGATIVE ADJECTIVES VS. PRONOUNS STRUCTURES WITH LEQUEL: EXAMPLES		
Interrogative Adjective + Noun	**Interrogative Pronoun**	
Quel film d'Isabelle Adjani passe en ce moment? *(Which Adjani movie is in the theater these days?)*	**Lequel** passe en ce moment? *(Which one [movie] is in the theater these days?)*	Direct interrogation
Je me demande quelle actrice tu préfères. *(I wonder which actress you like best.)*	Je me demande **laquelle** tu préfères. *(I wonder which one you like best.)*	Indirect interrogation
Claire explique <u>avec</u> quelles armes on joue au Cluedo. *(Claire explains with which weapons one plays Clue.)*	Il y a beaucoup d'armes. **Avec lesquelles** joue-t-on au Cluedo? *(There are a lot of weapons. **With which ones does one play Clue?**)*	Direct interrogation
Tu as travaillé beaucoup pour quels examens? *(You worked a lot for your exams?)*	Tu as eu tes examens. **Pour lesquels** as-tu travaillé beaucoup? *(You took your exams. **For which ones did you work a lot?**)*	Direct interrogation

Interrogative Pronoun *Auquel / Duquel* . . .

À + [le]quel = auquel (Formation of <u>Auquel</u>)

When the interrogative pronoun replaces a noun that originally followed the preposition **À**, or when it is used as the complement of a verb that requires **À**, the **Lequel** series must be modified. Since **lequel** is composed of **le—la / les**, it falls under the rule of the contraction between **à** and the definite articles.

> *Refer to Chapter 3 for*
> **Articles**

FORMATION OF INTERROGATIVE PRONOUNS WITH À: AUQUEL / À LAQUELLE							
Component	Preposition	Contracted Definite Articles		Interrogative Adjectives		Interrogative Pronouns	
Gender Number		Masculine	Feminine	Masculine	Feminine	Masculine	Feminine
Singular	À	Le	La	quel	quelle		
		AU	À la			Auquel	À Laquelle
Plural		Les		quels	quelles		
		AUX				Auxquels	Auxquelles

DE + [le]quel = duquel (Formation of <u>Duquel</u>)

When the interrogative pronoun replaces a noun that originally followed the prepositions **DE**, or when it is used as the complement of a verb that requires **DE**, the **Lequel** series must be modified. Since **lequel** is composed of **le—la / les**, it falls under the rule of the contraction between **DE** and the definite articles.

FORMATION OF INTERROGATIVE PRONOUNS WITH DE: DUQUEL							
Component	Preposition	Contracted Definite Articles		Interrogative Adjectives		Interrogative Pronouns	
Gender Number		Masculine	Feminine	Masculine	Feminine	Masculine	Feminine
Singular	DE	Le	La	quel	quelle		
		DU	DE la			Duquel	DE Laquelle
Plural		Les		quels	quelles		
		DES				Desquels	Desquelles

INTERROGATIVE ADJECTIVES VS. PRONOUNS STRUCTURES WITH AUQUEL—DUQUEL: **EXAMPLES**	
Interrogative Adjective + Noun	**Interrogative Pronoun**
De quel film d'Isabelle Adjani parles-tu? *(About which Adjani movie are you talking?)*	**Duquel** parles-tu? *(About **which one** are you talking?)*
Je me demande à quelle amie je vais téléphoner d'abord. *(I wonder which friend I am going to phone first.)*	Je me demande à **laquelle** je vais téléphoner d'abord. *(I wonder **which one** I am going to phone first.)*
Claire explique de quelles armes elle a besoin au Cluedo. *(Claire explains which weapons she needs to play Clue.)*	Il y a beaucoup d'armes. **Desquelles** Claire a-t-elle besoin au Cluedo? *There are many weapons.* *(**Which ones** does Claire need to play Clue?)*
Tu as pensé beaucoup à quels examens? *(About which exams did you think a lot?)*	**Auxquels** as-tu pensé beaucoup? *(About **which ones** did you think a lot?)*

Interrogative Pronouns in Choices, Options, or Preferences

The **lequel** series can also be used when a choice is implied, that is, even if the noun that is recalled was not accompanied by an interrogative adjective in the original sentence.

- In this case, it is not a simple substitution of **quel** + noun but a replacement of the reference by the interrogative pronoun.
- The pronoun then takes on the gender of the noun it replaces but its number is decided by the context of its own sentence or clause.

  ○ Single option among numerous objects: J'ai beaucoup de disques compacts de Julien Clerc. **Lequel** préfères-tu? *(I have many records by Julien Clerc. Which one do you prefer?)*

  ○ Preference: Il y a plusieurs plages entre Cannes et Nice. **À laquelle** veux-tu aller? *(There are several beaches between Cannes and Nice. To which one do you want to go?)*

  ○ Multiple option among numerous objects: Tous mes dictionnaires sont accessibles; **desquels** as-tu besoin? *(All my dictionaries are available to you; which ones do you need?)*

  ○ Choice: Vous organisez deux soirées de Réveillon du Jour de l'An; cette robe, c'est **pour laquelle** des deux? *(You are organizing two New Year's Eve parties; this dress is for which of them?)*

Indefinite Pronouns

Function and Use

As their name indicates, indefinite pronouns are used to replace vague entities—a person, a thing, or a group of either and both.

Because they refer to a vague being or object, they may be considered as a whole. They are perceived as indiscriminate, and therefore are masculine—singular since this combination is also used as neuter.

Some indefinite pronouns have the same form as their corresponding adjectives; others are unique.

PRINCIPAL INDEFINITE PRONOUNS			
Indefinite Adjective	INDEFINITE PRONOUNS		
	Masculin Singulier Masculin Pluriel	Féminin Singulier Féminin Pluriel	Translation
chaque	chacun	chacune	each one
certain—certains certaine—certaines	certain certains	certaine certaines	some/ certain
aucun—aucune	aucun	aucune	no
	plusieurs		many
	tout tous	— toutes	everything all
quelque—quelques	quelqu'un quelques uns	— quelques-unes	someone some
	on		one, you, they, we
	quiconque		whoever—anybody
	n'importe qui		anyone
	personne		nobody
	l'un . . . l'/d' autre les uns les/d'autres	l'une . . . l'/d' autre les unes les/d'autres	one . . . the other
	quelque chose		something
	rien		nothing

Particular Cases

Aucun, personne, et rien (None, Nobody, Nothing)

Aucun, personne, and **rien** are negative. Since the negative form in French requires two negative elements, **aucun, rien,** and **personne** have a specific construction.

> *Refer to Chapter 15 for*
> **Sentences and Clauses**

1. As Subject

When they are the subject of the verb, they are the first element of the negation and must be followed by the second one: **ne**

> Il y a trois films à la télé; **aucun ne** m'intéresse. *(There are three movies on TV; none interests me.)*

> Cette vidéo en russe est gratuite mais **personne ne** la veut. *(This Russian video is free but no one wants it.)*

> **Rien ne** sert de courir; il faut partir à point! *(No need to run; just leave on time!) (This is a famous proverb.)*

2. Complement of the Verb

As complements, they come after a verb that is previously negated by **ne**. They form the second element of the negative "sandwich":

> Je **n'**ai **aucune** envie de discuter politique avec toi. *(I have no desire to talk politics with you.)*

> Il **ne** veut voir **personne.** *(He does not want to see anybody.)*

> Antoine **ne** dit **rien** d'intéressant. *(Antoine says nothing interesting.)*

Certains, tous—toutes, quelques-uns—quelques-unes, les uns . . . les autres—les unes . . . les autres (Plural Indefinite Pronouns)

When the pronouns are plural (**certains, tous—toutes, quelques-uns—quelques-unes, les uns . . . les autres—les unes . . . les autres**), they are naturally followed by a verb in the **plural** if they are its subject:

> J'ai différents types d'étudiants. **Certains** arriv**ent** toujours à l'heure. **Quelques-uns sont** systématiquement en retard. **Les uns** prenn**ent** beaucoup de notes; **d'autres** n'écriv**ent** pas une ligne. Mais **tous** pos**ent** la même question: "Qu'est-ce qu'il faut faire pour avoir un A?" *(I have different types of students. Some always arrive on time. Others are systematically late. Some take a lot of notes; others do not write a single line. But all ask the same question: "What do I need to do to get an A?")*

NOTE The best way of learning these indefinite pronouns is to force yourself to use them regularly in numerous sentences. Also pay special attention when you encounter them while reading: refer to the section of this chapter and review them all every time.

REVIEW TABLE	
Règle (Rule)	Most of these pronouns replace the structure: corresponding adjective + noun
Pronoms Démonstratifs (Demonstrative Pronouns)	**Celui, Ceux—Celle, Celles** Always followed by one of the following: • the suffix **-ci** or **-là** • the preposition **de** or **à** or **en** • a relative pronoun (**qui, que, dont, où, lequel, auquel, duquel**) *(this—that one; the one of, to, in; the one which . . .)*
Pronoms Possessifs (Possessive Pronouns)	le mien, le tien, le sien—la mienne, la tienne, la sienne les miens, les tiens, les siens—les miennes, les tiennes, les siennes le nôtre, le vôtre, le leur—la nôtre, la vôtre, la leur les nôtres, les vôtres, les leurs *(mine, yours, his—hers—its; ours, yours, theirs)*

Possessive Relationship (Structure of the Possessive Pronoun)

Article agrees with the property (gender and number)	1st letter designates the owner	Ending designates the property (gender and number)
le—la les	M—T—S N—V L	ien(s)—ienne(s) ôtre(s) eur(s)

Pronoms Interrogatifs (Interrogative Pronouns)

• Simple: qui—que—quoi
• Compound with inversion **est-ce**

Qui est-ce qui—Qui est-ce que
Qu(e)'est-ce qui—Qu(e)'est-ce que

• **Lequel** for a choice among a group

No preposition		À		DE	
lequel	laquel	auquel	à laquelle	duquel	de laquelle
lesquels	lesquelles	auxquels	auxquelles	desquels	desquelles

(which one, to which one, of which one)

Pronoms Indéfinis (Indefinite Pronouns)

certain, quelqu'un, aucun, nul, chacun, plusieurs, tout, tous, tel, on, quiconque, quelque chose, personne, n'importe qui, n'importe quoi, rien . . .
(certain, someone, none, no one, each one, several, all, such, one, anyone, something, nobody, anybody, anything, nothing . . .)

Practice What You Learned

Exercises are rated according to four levels of difficulty:

- Beginner easy [*]
- Beginner challenging [**]
- Intermediate [***]
- Advanced [****]

1. Complete the sentences with the demonstrative pronoun appropriate to the context. Add the necessary suffix, relative pronoun, or preposition. [***]

    A. Ta maison est très belle, mais je préfère _____ _____ Mathieu.

    B. Ce garçon-ci est roux, _____ _____ est blond.

    C. Je voudrais ces boucles d'oreilles argentées et aussi _____ _____ or.

    D. Tous _____ _____ Kévin portent sont des costumes Armani, _____ _____ Monsieur Alex Trebek viennent de Perry Ellis, je crois.

2. Find the possessive adjectives and pronouns corresponding to the owner(s) and object(s). Make sure to verify the gender of the object if necessary. [**]

    Example:

    Toi—les stylos: tes stylos—les tiens

    A. Tatiana—la tante: _____-_____

    B. Nicolas et Ninon—l'anniversaire: _____-_____

    C. Toi et moi—les livres: _____-_____

    D. Vous et moi—les libertés: _____-_____

    E. Toi et ton ami—l'appartement: _____-_____

3. Respond in an affirmative or negative way to the question, using a possessive pronoun. [***]

    Example:

    Ces clés sont à toi? Oui, ce sont les miennes.

    A. Cette ceinture est à Saturnin?—Non, _____

    B. Ces livres sont aux étudiants?—Oui, _____

    C. Cet ordinateur est à vous, Odette?—Non, _____

    D. Cet ordinateur est à vous, Odile et Didier?—Oui, _____

4. Create an opposite case with the possessive pronoun corresponding to the (person of the) owner. [**]

Example:

Ma mère est brune, la tienne est blonde (toi).

A. Les enfants d'Annie sont adorables; _____ sont des démons (Valérie)

B. Vos chattes sont mignonnes mais _____ sont splendides (moi)

C. La valise de Viviane est légère; _____ pèse une tonne (Aline et Aude)

D. Ton bureau est loin; _____ est tout à côté (Luc et moi)

5. Complete the questions with the appropriate interrogative pronoun and preposition if needed from the list below: [***]

> **qui—lequel—à laquelle—que—desquelles—à quoi**

A. J'ai un Mac et un PC. _____ veux-tu utiliser?

B. _____ penses-tu en ce moment?

C. Qui est-ce _____ va venir ce soir?

D. Je vais acheter des piles, tu as besoin _____ ?

E. _____ est-ce que Léa veut pour son anniversaire?

F. Elle ressemble à une actrice, mais _____ ?

6. Complete the paragraph with the indefinite pronoun that makes the most sense within the context of the story. [****]

> **on—plusieurs—personne—certains—tous—quelqu'un—
> n'importe quoi—rien—tout—quelque chose**

A. Gaëtan est un enfant très gaté. Il veut toujours _____ .

B. Ses parents lui ont offert beaucoup de jouets, et il en a cassé _____ .

C. Dès qu'il voit _____ à la télé, un jeu, un ours, un ballon, _____ , il pleure pour qu' _____ lui achète.

D. Il a tous les jeux électroniques, _____ même en double bien que _____ valent très cher!

E. _____ dans sa famille devrait refuser ses caprices, mais dans les magasins, il crie très fort et _____ ne l'arrête.

F. Alors _____ ne lui résiste.

Chapter 10

SIMPLE TENSES—*ÊTRE* AND *AVOIR* AUXILIARY VERBS

Verbs

Introduction

If the sentence were a person, the noun would be the head and the verb the body. Verbs make the subject act, move, change, etc., or they express a state of its body.

Nature of Verbs

Verbs can be classified in three different categories according to how they behave with other verbs.

- Verbes d'Action et d'État (General Verbs: Action and State)
  They express either an action or a state of the subject.
  Most verbs are action verbs.
  There are six main state verbs:
  Être, paraître, sembler, devenir, demeurer, rester *(To be, to appear, to seem, to become, to remain, to stay)*

General verbs are conjugated by themselves and cannot be followed directly by another verb in the infinitive.

- Les Modaux (Modal Verbs)
  Modal verbs are general verbs that can be used by themselves and also be combined with other verbs. They function like auxiliaries do, not to situate the action in time but to express a wider range of meanings.
  They are followed by a dependent verb in the infinitive, never by a verb in the past participle.
  There are only five French modal verbs: Devoir *(must)*, Pouvoir *(can)*, Savoir *(to know)*, Vouloir *(to want)*, Falloir: Il faut (only used in the third person singular *(it is necessary)*.
  Can, could, may, might, should, had better, must, will, would, have to, ought to are the English ones.

A few other verbs can be used as modal verbs and may be followed by an infinitive:
faire, dire, penser, voir *(to do, to say, to think, to see)*
Je fais réparer ma voiture. *(I have to have my car repaired.)*

- Les Auxiliaires (Auxiliary Verbs)

Characteristics of Auxiliary Verbs

Use

Être and Avoir

There are two auxiliary verbs in French:

- Être—To be
- Avoir—To have

Both **to be** and **to have** are also auxiliary verbs in English, but they are grouped with other auxiliaries called modals (can, must, will, etc.). In French, auxiliary verbs and modal verbs are clearly separated but they function in the same way as their English counterparts.

Verb vs. Auxiliary

As their name indicates, auxiliary verbs are words that are used both as:

1. Verbe (Verb)

They function like general verbs **by themselves**:

> Francis **est** français. Il **a** trois frères. *(Francis is French. He has three brothers.)*

The meaning of the sentences is given by the conjugated verbs **être** and **avoir**.

2. Auxiliaire (Auxiliary)

These are used not for their own meaning but to **help conjugate <u>other verbs</u>**. That is why they are known in English as *helping verbs*:

> Francis **est** <u>né</u> en France. *(Francis was born in France.)*

The meaning of the sentences is given by the verb **naître**. The use of **être** is auxiliary.

> Il **a** <u>élevé</u> ses frères. *(He raised his brothers.)*

The meaning of the sentence is given by the verb **élever**. The use of **avoir** is auxiliary.

IMPORTANT!

Although **Être** and **Avoir** appear at first to be associated more frequently with certain verbs, there are various factors to consider before choosing between them when they are used as auxiliaries. This choice does not depend solely on the verb with which they are used.

Refer to Chapter 12, **Agreement of the Past Participle** *for* **"Auxiliary Choice and Agreement Decision Flowchart"**

Function of the Auxiliary Verbs *Être* and *Avoir*

The basic use and purpose of all languages is to communicate the experiences a person (the subject) has in the surrounding world (made of a series of other persons including oneself and an infinite number of objects).

The variety of experiences one can have within the world is communicated through numerous verbs:

Paul **a mangé** une pomme.

Sophie **fait** du surf.

Robert **est** en retard.

Guy **a** la grippe.

Choosing and conjugating a verb is the way to best translate each specific situation or action in the world that each person can have.

Difference between Être and Avoir

Être and Avoir can be used as auxiliary verbs to help form the compound tenses of general verbs. When they are used by themselves as verbs, Être and Avoir express two crucial relationships:

ÊTRE The subject is a part of his or her world. Personal States of the Subject	AVOIR The subject relates to part of the world. Relation of Subject to External Object

Consequently, **être** is associated with events that happen to or affect the subject:

> Pélagie **est** pâle. Pélagie **est** partie à l'hôpital. (*Pelagie is pale. Pelagie has left for the hospital.*)

Both being pale and being gone affect Pélagie.

On the contrary, **avoir** is used when events have an impact on the outside world.

> Pélagie **a** une Peugeot. Pélagie **a** acheté une moto aussi. (*Pélagie has a car. She has bought a motorcycle too.*)

Both events (having and buying) concern the car and the motorcycle.

TIP BOX

When you are not sure which auxiliary verb to use, try drawing a little picture representing the situation of the subject in his or her world and how this person interacts with it. **After having learned in this chapter what type of** connection **with the world** **être** and **avoir** convey, the illustration of the subject/world relationship will show you which auxiliary verb is most appropriate.

> **NOTE** Think about how the subject is relating to her or his world to decide which auxiliary verb to use. It is safer than simply translating. Here is a list of the most common expressions that use the opposite auxiliary verb in each language:

TO BE **EXPRESSIONS TRANSLATED BY** AVOIR **EXPRESSIONS**	
To be _____ years old	Avoir _____ ans
To be hot	Avoir chaud
To be lucky	Avoir de la chance
To be hungry	Avoir faim
To be cold	Avoir froid
To be ashamed	Avoir honte
To be sick to one's stomach	Avoir mal au coeur
To be afraid	Avoir peur
To be right	Avoir raison
To be wrong	Avoir tort
To be thirsty	Avoir soif
To be sleepy	Avoir sommeil

Our conception of our place in and relation to the world is also dictated by the way our language allows us to express them. English and French viewpoints are not always equivalent, and that is the source of various cultural differences.

Choosing between Auxiliary Verbs

Être as Verb

Être describes how the subject is in its world:

> Fabrice **est** fatigué. (*Fabrice is tired.*)

> Les enfants **sont** en train de jouer dans le jardin. (*The children are playing in the garden.*)

Être as Auxiliary Verb

In compound tenses, **être** is used with verbs that express

Displacement

Être is used with an action whose result is to displace the subject that performs it. This change of place can be

- physical:

> Sarah **est** sortie des Urgences. *(Sarah walked out of the ER.)*

- social or symbolic:

> Sarah **est** devenue Médecin-Chef. *(Sarah became Chief of Medicine.)*

Reflection

Être is used with an action that reflects upon the subject that performs it (the verb is then called a *reflexive verb*):

> Sarah **s'est** réjouie de cette promotion. *(Sarah ["rejoiced herself"] was pleased about this promotion.)*

Être and Past Participle

Compound Tenses

- **Être** is combined with the past participle to form all compound tenses.
- With **être**, the agreement of the past participle follows the Golden rule explained in detail in the passé composé chapter and stated on page 223.

Passive Voice

- **Être** is combined with the past participle to form the passive voice.
- The passive voice is the opposite of the active voice. In the active voice, the grammatical subject of the verb is also the person or thing that performs the action:

> Les enfants mangent la tarte aux pommes. *(The children eat the apple pie.)*

In the sentence in the active voice, the noun **Les enfants** is the subject of the verb **mangent**.

In reality, the children are the ones eating.

- The passive voice is used when the subject of a verb is not doing the action expressed by the verb; it is submitted to it:

> La tarte **est** mangée **par les enfants**. *(The apple pie is eaten by the children.)*

In the sentence in the passive voice, the action is actually performed by a noun or pronoun that is not the subject of the verb. It is called the **agent**. In the sentence in the passive voice, the noun **La tarte** is the subject of the auxiliary verb **Être**.

But, in reality, it is not the apple pie that eats, but the children. The apple pie receives the action performed by the agent: **les enfants**.

○ Because **être** generally expresses an action that reflects back on the subject, it is used to form the passive voice since, in that case, the action also affects the subject.

○ The action is put in the past participle form and it describes what happens to the subject. The past participle form therefore agrees in gender and number with this subject.

○ In the passive voice, the past participle functions in the structure of the sentence like an adjective does, which is also why it agrees with its subject:

La tarte **est** mangée. La tarte **est** bonne. *(The apple pie is eaten. It is good.)*

COMPARATIVE OVERVIEW OF ACTIVE AND PASSIVE VOICES	
Passive voice = Être (conjugated) + Participe Passé of ALL verbs Être can be conjugated in all simple or compound tenses.	
The word that is the Subject of the verb in the	
Active Voice: Performs the action	**Passive Voice: Is submitted to the action**
Action Performer = Subject of Verb	**Action Performer ≠ Subject of Verb** **Action Performer = Agent ≠ Subject**
The agreement of the past participle follows the golden rule.	**Past Participle always agrees with the Subject of the sentence.**

Avoir as Verb

Avoir shows what the subject has in its world:

Vincent **a** deux voitures et six vélos. *(Vincent has two cars and six bikes.)*

Avoir describes the subject's interaction with its world and the effect they have on each other:

Vincent **a** vendu ses deux motos parce qu'il **a eu** un accident. *(Vincent sold his motorcycles because he had an accident.)*

Maintenant, Vincent **a** une peur irrationelle de la vitesse. *(Now, Vincent has an irrational fear of speed.)*

Avoir as Auxiliary Verb

In compound tenses, most verbs are conjugated with **avoir**.

Action of the Subject on an Object

Because **avoir** expresses an event that is performed by a subject and affects the world outside or around it, **avoir** is used with most verbs. When a verb is conjugated with **avoir**, its subject and the object of the action it expresses are different.

Avoir and Past Participle

With **avoir**, the agreement of the past participle depends on the presence of a direct object complement in the sentence and the position of the direct object complement in the sentence.

The agreement of the past participle follows the general rule explained in detail in Chapter 12, Past Indicative Tenses—Perfect and Agreement of the Past Participle.

COMPARATIVE OVERVIEW OF ÊTRE AND AVOIR	
ÊTRE	**AVOIR**
Indicative of a state	Indicative of possession
If followed by a verb, it is in the past participle; **être** and **avoir** are never followed directly by an infinitive.	
Helps conjugate verbs in the passive voice	Helps conjugate **être** and **avoir** in compound tenses
Être and **avoir** help conjugate verbs in compound tenses.	
Action or state reflects back to the subject: **The subject is also the object of the action: S = O**	Action or possession reach out and away from the subject: **They concern a subject different from its object: S ≠ O**
When conjugated with **être**, verbs express personal or intimate actions. **Être** implies an internal process.	When conjugated with **avoir**, verbs express a gesture that the subject directs toward the outside world. It implies an external object.

Conjugations
Formation of Conjugations

To conjugate a verb is to put it in the specific form corresponding to all the factors that are necessary to produce and express an action. There are three elements to combine to select the correct conjugation form:

1. Who performs the action = the **Person**
2. When the action was, is, or will be performed = the **Tense**
3. If the completion of the action is potential, real, imperative, conditioned, or subjective = the **Mood**

Person

The person marker varies according to the subject of the verb.

Number

- The person may represent only one performer of the action: 1st, 2nd, or 3rd person singular:

> Je suis professeur. *(I am a professor.)*
>
> Tu as ce livre. *(You have this book.)*
>
> On est meilleur en français grâce à ce livre. *(One gets better in French thanks to this book.)*

- Or it designates a group of people: 1st, 2nd, or 3rd person plural!

> Nous sommes américains. *(We are Americans.)*
>
> Vous avez des enfants. *(You have children.)*
>
> Ils sont gentils—Elles sont intelligentes. *(They are nice. They are intelligent.)*

Gender

The person also represents female, male, or neuter subjects: 1st person singular feminine or masculine, 2nd person singular masculine or feminine, 2nd person singular feminine or masculine:

> (Fabienne) Je suis professeur. *(I am a professor.)*
>
> (Un étudiant) Tu as ce livre. *(You have this book.)*
>
> Loy est meilleur en français grâce à ce livre. *(Loy is better in French thanks to this book.)*
>
> On a des exercices à faire. *(We have homework to do.)*

Vous as Form of Respect

Finally, the 2nd person plural is used to address a single, respected person. There is no equivalent to this formal pronoun in English.

> Monsieur, vous êtes un mauvais président. *(Sir, you are a bad president.)*

REVIEW TABLE: CONJUGATIONS AND PERSONS			**Masculine**	**Feminine**	**Super-Person**
Persons			**Masculine**	**Feminine**	**Super-Person**
I	Singular	1st Person	JE		
You		2nd Person	TU		VOUS
He— It/One —She		3rd Person	IL—ON	ELLE	
We		1st Person	NOUS		
You	Plural	2nd Person	VOUS		
They		3rd Person	ILS	ELLES	

Tense

Chronology

The tense places actions along a chronological line. It organizes them in terms of past, present, and future time.

LE TEMPS (TIME LINE)		
Past	**Present**	Futur
Audrey travaille aujourd'hui. *(Audrey works today.)*		
Irène a travaillé hier. *(Irène worked yesterday.)*		
Denis travaillera demain. *(Denis will work tomorrow.)*		

Relativity

The markers vary according to each specific tense. The various tenses are relative to the moment in which the action is enunciated. Tenses place the action relatively when one is speaking.

LES TEMPS (TENSES)				
Prior	**Before**	**Now**	Before	Later
Plus-que-Parfait	**Imparfait** **Passé Composé** **Conditionnel Passé** **Subjonctif Passé**	**Indicatif Présent** **Conditionnel Présent** **Subjonctif Présent**	Future Antérieur	Futur
	Hier	Aujourd'hui		Demain
Audrey travaille aujourd'hui. *(Audrey works today.)*				
Irène a travaillé hier. *(Irène worked yesterday.)*				
Sabine avait travaillé la semaine d'avant. *(Sabine had worked the week before.)*				
Denis travaillera demain. *(Denis will work tomorrow.)*				
Audrey aura travaillé avant lui. *(Audrey will have worked before him.)*				

Mood

The mood expresses the level of reality of an action. Actions can be more or less real and objective, or potential and subjective.

The Infinitive

The **infinitive** is the mood of *potential* actions.

Infinitive actions are concepts—to eat, to laugh, to work—but they have not actually been performed by anyone. So they are not yet anchored in time.

The Indicative

The **indicative** is the mood of *real* actions.

Indicative actions are happening now, or they have or will happen. There is no doubt about their being performed at some point in time.

The Imperative

The **imperative** is the mood of commands.

Imperative actions are demanded by a subject from another subject.

The Conditional

The **conditional** is the mood of a cause-consequence relationship.

Conditional actions depend on another action to be performed before they can themselves become real.

The Subjunctive

The **subjunctive** is the mood of subjectivity.

Subjunctive actions are very far above the level of reality because they depend on the decision of another person over which one has no control.

TENSES AND MOODS COORDINATE AXIS			PAST	PRESENT	FUTURE
MOODS = Y Ordinate					
↑ *y*	**SUBJUNCTIVE**		Past	Present	
	CONDITIONAL		Past	Present	
	IMPERATIVE		Present		
	INDICATIVE		Past	Present	Future
REALITY					→ *x*
TENSES = X Axis					
	INFINITIVE		*Past*	*Present*	

Verb Types

Categories

General verbs can be of two categories:

Regular Verbs

Regular verbs follow an entirely predictable pattern. This conjugation is determined by the way their infinitive form ends. There are three regular infinitive endings.

Irregular Verbs

Irregular means that these verbs follow no systematic pattern:

- There is no way to predict their stems (the part of the word to which the ending is added).
- There may be no way either to predict the ending that is added to them in the past participle form.

Verb Groups

Regular verbs are organized in three groups. Each group is characterized by the form of its infinitive and its sets of endings.

1. 1st Group and Conjugation

1ST GROUP ENDINGS	
Infinitive ending in —**ER**	Past Participle ending in —É

- Most French verbs belong to this first group:

    apprécier, danser, changer, monter, admirer, arriver, etc. *(to appreciate, to dance, to change, to go up, to admire, to arrive)*

    J'ai apprécié, tu as dancé, Charles a changé, Véra est arrivée

- When a new verb is needed to describe a new action, it is always created according to this model. All invented or imported verbs enter the French conjugations as 1st group:

    zapper, surfer, magnétoscoper, beamer *(to zap or to change channels with the remote control, to surf, to record on the VCR, to beam files off a personal digital assistant)*

    Sophie a surfé sur internet toute la soirée. *(Sophie surfed on the Internet all evening long.)*

2. 2nd Group and Conjugation

2ND GROUP ENDINGS	
Infinitive ending in —**IR**	Past Participle ending in —I

- This is the second-largest group of verbs:

    finir, haïr, agir, applaudir *(to finish, to hate, to act, to applaud)*

    Nous finissons, nous avons fini

    Nous agissons, nous avons agi

- In rare cases, new verbs can be created in the second group

alunir = to land on the moon was made similarly to **atterrir** (to land on the earth)

3. 3rd Group and Conjugation

3RD GROUP ENDINGS	
Infinitive ending in —**RE**	Past Participle ending in —U

- The verbs ending in -re and having a past participle form in -u form this small group:

  vendre—vendu; tendre—tendu; pendre—pendu; descendre—descendu
  (to sell, to tighten, to hang, to go down)

- There are no new verbs created in this group. This conjugation is said to be dead like languages that are no longer spoken:

  Le latin et le grec ancien sont des langues mortes; la conjugaison du troisième groupe est morte aussi.

NOTE To belong to one of the regular groups, both the infinitive and the past participle forms must be predictable.

Many verbs end in **-re**, but they do not belong to the third group if their past participle does not end in **-u**, or if their stem changes to form the past participle. Verbs like the following are irregular verbs; they do not belong to the third group.

COMMON IRREGULAR PAST PARTICIPLES	
Infinitive	**Irregular Past Participle**
prendre	**pris**
dire	**dit**
vivre	**vécu**
coudre	**cousu**
craindre	**craint**
boire	**bu**
naître	**né**
Always verify the past participle form in a dictionary or a conjugation book such as Barron's *501 French Verbs*.	

Stems

The stem is the part of the verb that does not change. The various sets of endings that correspond to each tense are added to this stem.

All verbs have four stems:

1. the infinitive stem
2. the past participle stem
3. the future stem
4. the subjunctive stem

Regular verbs have predictable stems that correspond to their group. The stems of irregular verbs are not predictable, although there are still some patterns one can distinguish among them.

PRINCIPAL VERB STEMS				
	Infinitive	**Past Participle**	FutuRe	Subjunctive
To go	Aller	**allé**	iR-	**aill- / all-**
To be	Être	**été**	seR-	**soi- / soy-**
To do	Faire	**fait**	feR-	**fass-**
To eat	Manger	**mangé**	mangeR-	**mang-**
To end	Finir	**fini**	finiR-	**finiss-**
To leave	Partir	**parti**	partiR-	**part-**
To say	Dire	**dit**	diR-	**dis-**
To write	Écrire	**écrit**	écriR-	**écriv-**
To put	Mettre	**mis**	mettR-	**mett-**
To take	Prendre	**pris**	prendR-	**prenn- / pren-**
To have	Avoir	**eu**	auR-	**a-**
Must	Devoir	**du**	devR-	**doiv-**
Can	Pouvoir	**pu**	pourR-	**puiss-**
To know	Savoir	**su**	sauR-	**sach-**
To want	Vouloir	**voulu**	voudR-	**veuill- / voul-**
To read	Lire	**lu**	liR-	**lis-**
To hold	Tenir	**tenu**	tiendR-	**tienn- / ten-**
To come	Venir	**venu**	viendR-	**vienn- / ven-**
To know	Connaître	**connu**	connaitR-	**connaiss-**
To believe	Croire	**cru**	croiR-	**croi- / croy-**
To sell	Vendre	**vendu**	vendR-	**vend-**

Formation of Tenses

Elements of Simple Tenses

Stems

Simple tenses are called simple not because they are easy to learn but because they are formed with one single word.

General and Modal Verbs

For general as well as auxiliary verbs, the simple tenses are formed by adding a fixed set of suffixes—or endings—to the stem of the verb.

Regular verbs have two stems:

1. The stem used for all tenses and moods except the future and the conditional: the infinitive minus the -er, -ir, or -re ending.
2. The stem used for the future and the conditional is the entire infinitive for -er and -ir verbs, or the infinitive minus -e for -re verbs.

In short, the stem for the futu**R**e and the conditional must end in an **-R**.

SIMPLE TENSE FORMATION ON EACH GROUP'S STEM	
Stem + Ending	
Indicative except Future	Future—Conditional
INFINITIVer + Ending	InfinitivER + Ending
INFINITIVir + Ending	InfinitivIR + Ending
INFINITIVre + Ending	InfinitivRe + Ending

Auxiliary Verbs

The conjugations of **Être** and **Avoir** in the simple tenses must simply be learned.

Être (To Be)

The actual stem of Être is

- **ét-** for its regular forms and the past participle
- **ser-** in the future and the conditional.

But the conjugations of Être are also characterized by their beginning simply with the letter **s**.

Avoir (To Have)

The actual stem of Avoir is

- **av-** for its regular forms
- **aur-** in the future and the conditional.

But the conjugations of Avoir are also characterized by their beginning simply with the letter **a**.

Endings

The ending of all types of verbs is determined by their subject, namely the 1st, 2nd, or 3rd person singular or plural.

> *Refer to Chapter 8 for*
> **Personal and**
> **Impersonal Pronouns**

TIP BOX

Once you have learned the conjugation of the present indicative, use the 1st person plural form (**nous**) as the stem of irregular verbs. It is more accurate than the infinitive in their case because certain verbs have a dual stem. Generally, the 1st person plural stem is used in more conjugations:

DEVoir: Je dois, **Nous DEV**ons—**POUV**oir: Je peux, **Nous POUV**ons—**ALL**er: Je vais, **Nous ALL**ons, **SAV**oir: Je sais, **Nous SAV**ons—**VEN**ir: je viens, **Nous VEN**ons

---

Each set of endings is specific to the combination of the three factors needed to express an action: the person, the tense, and the mood.

The ending you need is found at the intersection of:

- The **person**—shows who performs the action,

- The **tense**—indicates when the action was, is, or will be performed,

- The **mood**—reveals if the completion of the action is potential, real, imperative, conditional, or subjective.

Components of Compound Tenses

Auxiliary Verbs Être and Avoir

Compound tenses are called *compound* because they require the combination of two separate verbal elements.

The auxiliary verbs Être and Avoir are conjugated in a simple tense.

The compound tense that is obtained from the combination auxiliary verbs in Simple Tense + Past Participle depends on the simple tense in which the auxiliary verb is conjugated.

ELEMENTS OF SIMPLE AND COMPOUND TENSES		
Temps Simple Être or Avoir	Participe Passé Verbe à conjuguer	Temps Composé Verbe Conjugué
Indicatif Présent	Participe Passé	**Indicatif Passé Composé**
Je suis J'ai	parti travaillé	Je suis parti J'ai travaillé *(I left, I worked)*
Indicatif Imparfait	Participe Passé	**Indicatif Plus-que-Parfait**
Tu étais Tu avais	sorti fini	Tu étais sorti Tu avais fini *(You had left, worked)*
Indicatif Futur	Participe Passé	**Indicatif Futur Antérieur**
Il sera Il aura	venu appris	Il sera venu Il aura appris *(He will have come, learned)*
Conditionnel Présent	Participe Passé	**Conditionnel Passé**
Nous serions Nous aurions	arrivés voulu	Nous serions arrivés Nous aurions voulu *(We would have arrived, wanted)*
Subjonctif Présent	Participe Passé	**Subjonctif Passé**
que vous soyez que vous ayez	revenus réussi	que vous soyez revenus que vous ayez réussi *(that you had come back, succeeded)*

The Past Participle

The compound tense is composed with the past participle form of the verb to be conjugated in that tense.

For regular verbs, the past participle depends on the verb group.

INFINITIVE AND PAST PARTICIPLE BY VERB GROUP		
1st: Infinitive in —ER	**2nd: Infinitive in** —IR	**3rd: Infinitive in** —RE
stem + É **manger** — mang + é **travailler** — travaill + é	stem + I **finir** — fin + i **applaudir** — applaud + i	stem + U **descendre** — descend + u **attendre** — attend + u

For irregular verbs, the past participle must be learned systematically.

> **NOTE** Because tenses are linked to the past, present, or future, one does not always find all of them in each mood. It is not necessary, for instance, to have a past imperative—what would be the point of ordering someone to do something . . . yesterday!

Conjugations

Principal Simple Tenses

There are seven simple tenses but only **five** are used in everyday communication; one is literary, and one has practically disappeared. We will focus only on these five mandatory tenses.

Mood	PRINCIPAL SIMPLE TENSES		
Indicative	Present *I work, I am working*	1. Présent	
	Imperfect *I worked, I was working,* *I used to work*	2. Imparfait	
	Past historic *I worked*	Passé Simple	Literary
	Future *I will work, I shall be working*	3. Futur	
Conditional	Present *I would/should work*	4. Conditionnel Présent	
Subjunctive	Present *May I work*	5. Subjonctif Présent	
	Imperfect *I might work*	Subjonctif Imparfait	Archaic

All simple tenses are formed by adding an ending to the appropriate stem.

Auxiliary Verbs in Simple Tenses

Auxiliary verbs can be conjugated in all the simple tenses by themselves to express a state of the subject or an action performed by the subject.

Some of their endings follow the general patterns presented in the chapters corresponding to each mood; they are underlined in the tables. Other endings do not.

Être (**Simple Tenses of** *To Be*)

CONJUGATION OF ÊTRE IN SIMPLE TENSES			
Indicative	Présent **s- / e- + ending**	Je suis	Nous sommes
		Tu es	Vous êtes
		Il—Elle—On est	Ils—Elles sont
		Indicatif Présent	
Indicative	Imparfait **ét- + imparfait ending**	J'étais	Nous étions
		Tu étais	Vous étiez
		Il—Elle—On était	Ils—Elles étaient
		Indicatif Imparfait	
Indicative	Futur **ser- + futur ending**	Je serai	Nous serons
		Tu seras	Vous serez
		Il—Elle—On sera	Ils—Elles seront
		Indicatif Futur	
Conditional	Conditionnel Présent **ser- + imparfait** **ending**	Je serais	Nous serions
		Tu serais	Vous seriez
		Il—Elle—On serait	Ils—Elles seraient
		Conditionnel Présent	
Subjunctive	Subjonctif Présent **s- + endings**	Je sois	Nous soyons
		Tu sois	Vous soyez
		Il—Elle—On soit	Ils—Elles soient
		Subjonctif Présent	

Avoir (Simple Tenses of *To Have*)

CONJUGATION OF AVOIR IN SIMPLE TENSES			
Indicative	Présent **a- / av- + ending**	J'ai	Nous av<u>ons</u>
		Tu as	Vous av<u>ez</u>
		Il—Elle—On a	Ils—Elles <u>ont</u>
		Indicatif Présent	
Indicative	Imparfait **av- + imparfait ending**	J'av<u>ais</u>	Nous av<u>ions</u>
		Tu av<u>ais</u>	Vous av<u>iez</u>
		Il—Elle—On av<u>ait</u>	Ils—Elles av<u>aient</u>
		Indicatif Imparfait	
Indicative	Futur **aur- + futur ending**	J'aur<u>ai</u>	Nous aur<u>ons</u>
		Tu aur<u>as</u>	Vous aur<u>ez</u>
		Il—Elle—On aur<u>a</u>	Ils—Elles aur<u>ont</u>
		Indicatif Futur	
Conditional	Conditionnel Présent **aur- + imparfait ending**	J'aur<u>ais</u>	Nous aur<u>ions</u>
		Tu aur<u>ais</u>	Vous aur<u>iez</u>
		Il—Elle—On aur<u>ait</u>	Ils—Elles aur<u>aient</u>
		Conditionnel Présent	
Subjunctive	Subjonctif Présent **a- + ending**	J'ai<u>e</u>	Nous ay<u>ons</u>
		Tu ai<u>es</u>	Vous ay<u>ez</u>
		Il—Elle—On ai<u>t</u>	Ils—Elles ai<u>ent</u>
		Subjonctif Présent	

Principal Compound Tenses

Use

- A compound tense corresponds to each simple tense.

- All compound tenses are formed by conjugating the appropriate auxiliary verb in a simple tense. It is then followed by the past participle form of the verb to conjugate in the compound tense.

> ### IMPORTANT!
> It is the auxiliary verb that is conjugated but the real action is expressed by the verb in the past participle form.

Formation

FORMATION OF PRINCIPAL COMPOUND TENSES				
Simple Tense of Auxiliary Verb	+	**Past Participle of Verb to Put in Compound Tense**	=	**Compound Tense of Verb**

Simple Tenses		Compound Tenses	
Auxiliary		**Verb to be conjugated**	**in**

						Passé Composé
Indicatif Présent	J'ai	Nous avons	PARTICIPE PASSÉ	J'ai travaillé		
	Tu as	Vous avez		Tu as fini		
	Il—Elle—On a	Ils—Elles ont		Il est arrivé		
	Je suis	Nous sommes		Nous sommes sortis		
	Tu es	Vous êtes		Vous êtes restés		
	Il—Elle—On est	Ils—Elles sont		Elles ont déménagé		

(I have worked—You finished—He has arrived—We left—You have stayed—They moved)

				Plus-Que Parfait
Indicatif Imparfait	J'avais	Nous avions	PARTICIPE PASSÉ	J'étais partie
	Tu avais	Vous aviez		Tu avais bu
	Il—Elle—On avait	Ils—Elles avaient		Elle avait chanté
	J'étais	Nous étions		Nous étions tombés
	Tu étais	Vous étiez		Vous aviez joué
	Il—Elle—On était	Ils—Elles étaient		Ils étaient entrés

(I had left—You had drunk—She had sung—We had fallen—You had played—They had entered)

				Futur Antérieur
Indicatif Futur	J'aurai	Nous aurons	PARTICIPE PASSÉ	J'aurai parlé
	Tu auras	Vous aurez		Tu seras venue
	Il—Elle—On aura	Ils—Elles auront		Il aura perdu
	Je serai	Nous serons		Nous serons parvenus
	Tu seras	Vous serez		Vous aurez compris
	Il—Elle—On sera	Ils—Elles seront		Elles auront lu

(I will have talked—You will have come—He will have lost—We will have reached—You will have understood—They will have read)

				· Conditionnel Passé
Conditionnel Présent	J'aurais	Nous aurions	**PARTICIPE PASSÉ**	Je serais née
	Tu aurais	Vous auriez		Tu aurais entendu
	Il—Elle—On aurait	Ils—Elles auraient		Elle aurait gagné
	Je serais	Nous serions		Nous aurions bu
	Tu serais	Vous seriez		Vous seriez monté
	Il—Elle—On serait	Ils—Elles seraient		Ils auraient filmé

(I would have been born—You would have heard—She would have won—We would have drunk—You would have come up—They would have filmed)

				Subjonctif Passé
Subjonctif Présent	J'aie	Nous ayons	**PARTICIPE PASSÉ**	QUE
	Tu aies	Vous ayez		j'aie fini
	Il—Elle—On ait	Ils—Elles aient		tu sois venu
	Je sois	Nous soyons		elle soit sortie
	Tu sois	Vous soyez		nous ayons dit
	Il—Elle—On soit	Ils—Elles soient		vous ayez écrit
				ils soient retournés

(That I had finished—you had come—she had left—we had said—you had written—they had gone back)

IMPORTANT!
The criterion of choice of the auxiliary verb is the same for all compound tenses.

The agreement of the past participle is the same for all compound tenses.

Refer to Chapter 12 for
**Passé Composé—
Compound Tenses**

FORMATION OF ALL COMPOUND TENSES AND THEIR COMPONENTS

Auxiliary		Verb to be conjugated in the compound tense		
Présent Present	+		⟶	**Passé Composé** Perfect
Imparfait Imperfect	+		⟶	**Plus-Que-Parfait** Pluperfect
Futur Future	+	**Participe Passé**	⟶	**Futur Antérieur** Future perfect (anterior)
Conditionnel Présent Conditional Present	+	Past Participle	⟶	**Conditionnel Passé** Conditional perfect (past)
Subjonctif Présent Conditionnal Perfect	+		⟶	**Subjonctif Passé** Subjunctive perfect (past)

Moods	MAIN SIMPLE AND **COMPOUND** TENSES		
	Passé	Présent	Futur
Subjonctif	**Subjonctif Passé**	Subonctif Présent	
Conditionnel	**Conditionnel Passé**	Conditionnel Présent	
Impératif		Impératif Présent	
Indicatif	**Indicatif Plus-Que Parfait** **Indicatif Passé Composé** Indicatif Imparfait	Indicatif Présent	**Indicatif Futur Antérieur** Indicatif Futur
			Tenses
Infinitif	**Infinitif Passé**	Infinitif Présent	

Practice What You Learned

Exercises are rated according to four levels of difficulty:

- Beginner easy [*]
- Beginner challenging [**]
- Intermediate [***]
- Advanced [****]

1. Using the context of the sentence, identify the words that serve as time markers and indicate in which French tense you would conjugate the verb. [*]

A. Je [aller] _____ à la banque demain. _____

B. Marc fait la vaisselle tous les jours pendant que Marie [préparer] _____ le diner. _____

C. Quand elle [être] _____ jeune, Mère Thérésa [aider] _____ déjà les gens malheureux. _____

2. Insert the form of être or avoir in the present indicative that corresponds to the person of the subject. [*]

A. Charlotte et Serge _____ en voyage.

B. C' _____ le mois d'août et il y _____ beaucoup de gens en vacances.

C. Ils _____ trois filles: Christiane, Célestine et Sissy.

D. Christiane _____ 9 ans.

E. Célestine _____ plus jeune.

F. Nous _____ leurs voisins à Antibes et nous _____ trois garçons.

G. Christiane, Célestine et Sissy disent toujours: "Vous _____ nos maris."

H. Et nos fils répondent "Nous _____ célibataires!"

3. Translate the story below using the appropriate French **avoir + quelque chose** to translate *To be* + Adjective. Pay attention to the meaning as well as the tense. [***]

A. When he was 10 years old, Hector was always hungry.

_____

B. At 10 A.M., he was first hot then cold; he needed food.

_____

C. His parents were afraid for him.

_____

D. He told them: "I am ashamed; when I do not eat, I am very sleepy.

_____

E. Today, Oscar knows he is wrong to be afraid.

_____

F. He will eat when he is hungry and will drink when he is thirsty.

_____

4. Complete the sentences with **être** or **avoir** in the **imparfait** and insert the following time markers. [***]

La semaine dernière—hier—il y a trente-cinq ans—au siècle précédent—avant

A. Aujourd'hui je suis au bureau.— _____ j' _____ au bureau.

B. Dans cinq ans nous irons sur Mars. _____ nous _____ sur la lune.

C. La grippe était encore une maladie dangereuse en 1900. _____, les médecins n' _____ pas d'antibiotiques.

D. Vous êtes blonde cette semaine; _____, vous _____ rousse!

E. _____ tu _____ souvent du chocolat mais tu es toujours au régime ces jours-ci.

5. Put the following text in the **future tense**: 15 changes to make. [****]

Aujourd'hui, je suis au Cap d'Antibes avec mes amis Vincent et Vladimir. Nous sommes

_____

à l'Hôtel du Cap. Vincent n'a pas de rendez-vous et Vladimir est en vacances. Ils ont

_____

une partie de tennis prévue. Puis Vincent et moi avons un grand diner à préparer.

_____

Vincent et Vladimir sont des chefs excellents. Il y a un concours de cuisine à vingt

_____

heures. Les juges sont célèbres dans la région. Les invités ont déjà leur place à table et

_____

nous sommes à leur service. Tout le monde est en tenue de soirée. La soirée et les

_____

invitations sont intitulées: "Vous avez faim? Bon Appétit!"

_____

Chapter 11

INFINITIVE, INDICATIVE, AND IMPERATIVE MOODS—PRESENT INDICATIVE

Introduction

As described in the previous chapter, the mood is one of the three pieces of information necessary to choose the right conjugation form of the verb.

- The *person* indicates who performs the action.
- The *tense* anchors the action in time: past, present, or future.
- The mood is a more subtle concept. Actions are perceived to be more or less feasible, more or less real. Each mood functions as a marker of the level of reality of the action.

VARIOUS LEVELS OF REALITY REPRESENTED BY EACH MOOD		
Least real	*Subjunctive*	Action is completely up to someone else's decision—*out of one's control*.
	Conditional	Action is dependent upon the realization of another action first—various degrees of dependency.
	Imperative	Action is not yet realized but **strongly recommended**.
Most real	Indicative	Action is real.
	Infinitive	Action is only potential but completely feasible.

 (THINK!) Le mode—mood was compared to **la mode**—fashion. Just like moods, clothes are subtle markers of various levels of reality as well: the person's social status, association with a certain group (yuppies, surfers, punk, Gap crowd, etc.), even a person's moods (sad, happy, exuberant, etc). If you were to explain what a mood is, how else could you illustrate it? You will find sample suggestions at the end of the chapter.

The Infinitive Mood

Meaning of Infinitive

Potential Action

When a verb is put in the infinitive, the message conveyed by this mood is that the action expressed by the verb is potential, but no one has yet realized it.

Think of the infinitive as a warehouse for actions; it is full of potential events but no one has yet taken them out of storage.

Timeless Action

The infinitive action has not been claimed by a specific subject; it has not been inscribed on the time line of history. It is *infinite*.

In our fashion analogy, the infinitive verb would be dressed like a Greek god for instance, or a ghost, to signify its immortality or eternal wandering, as well as the fact that both gods and ghosts can [theoretically] be embodied on earth.

Infinitive Markers	
1st Group:	-ER
2nd Group:	-IR
3rd Group:	-RE

Use

A verb is put in the infinitive either by itself or because of its context in the sentence.

Endings of New Verbs

A verb is in the infinitive when you first learn it. "To" precedes English infinitives. French verbs signal to you they are in the infinitive when they end in

- **-er, -ir,** or **-re** for regular verbs of the first, second, and third groups
- various other endings (**-oir, -oire, -re, -dre**) for irregular ones.

> **TIP BOX**
> The infinitive form of both regulaR and iRRegulaR veRbs include an R somewhere at the ReaR of the veRb: mangeR, finiR, attendRe, devoiR, êtRe, croiRe, . . .

Verb Sequence

When two general verbs follow each other, or a verb follows a modal verb, the second verb is always in the infinitive. The reason for this is that, if they are one right after the other, they share the same subject. So there is no need to "waste" an extra conjugation ending on the second verb since it would be the same as for the first verb. The first verb is conjugated with all person, tense, and mood markers and the second is in the infinitive—the mood by default.

The markers are added to the first verb but automatically distributed over the second one:

> Patrick **souhaite piloteR** un petit planeur. *(Patrick wishes to pilot a little hanglider.)*
>
> Il **veut atterrIR** à Menton. *(He wants to land in Menton.)*
>
> Il **sait sautER** en parachute. *(He knows how to jump with a parachute.)*
>
> Il **va prendRE** une leçon demain! *(He is going to take a lesson tomorrow.)*

After the Prepositions À, DE, POUR, SANS

When a verb follows the prepositions À, DE, POUR, and SANS, it is always written in the infinitive:

> Marianne est parvenue À avoiR une audition à Nice. Elle rêve DE deveniR danseuse à l'opéra. Elle s'exerce tous les jours POUR êtRE en excellente forme. Aucun succès n'est possible SANS faiRE beaucoup d'efforts. *(Marianne has managed to get an audition in Nice. She dreams of becoming a ballet dancer at the opera. She practices every day to be in excellent shape. No success is possible without making a lot of efforts.)*

> **NOTE** An auxiliary verb can never be followed by a verb in the infinitive.
>
> ~~Auxiliary + Infinitive:~~
>
> Think instead: Auxiliary + Past Participle

Past Infinitive and Present Participle

Sequence of Actions by the Same Subject

When a series of actions is performed by the same subject in a chronological order, it is not necessary to conjugate each verb and duplicate the person or tense markers, since they are the same for all actions:

Trois fois par semaine, Dorothée fait la même série de choses:
aller au gymnase; marcher sur le tapis roulant; écouter de la musique;
prendre une douche. 1. (*goes to the gym*) 2. (*listens to music while she walks on the treadmill*) 3. (*takes a shower*)

These actions are made in a certain order but by the same subject, so there is no need to conjugate them all. Only the action on which to focus is normally conjugated:

1. The action happening **before** the focus action on the time line follows the preposition **Après** and is put in the **infinitive passé, since it is in its past**.
2. The action happening at the same time as another action follows the preposition **En** and is put in the **participe présent**, since it is happening in its present.
3. The action happening **after** the focus action follows the preposition **Avant de** and is put in the **infinitive** like all verbs following **De**.

1. aller au gymnase	2. marcher sur le tapis 2. écouter de la musique	3. prendre une douche
"to go to the gym" happens	"to walk on the treadmill" and "to listen to music" happen	to take a shower happens
in the past of [before] taking a shower	simultaneously	in the future of [after] going to the gym

Formation

As it name indicates the **Infinitif Passé** is formed with:

PAST INFINITIVE FORM	
Infinitive **of the Auxiliary Être or Avoir**	**Participe Passé** **of the anterior action**
Dorothée prend une douche **APRÈS être allée** au gymnase Dorothée prend une douche **APRÈS avoir marché** sur le tapis	
(*Dorothée takes a shower after having gone to the gym—having walked on the treadmill.*)	

The Participe Présent is formed with EN + . . . ANT!

To form the Participe Présent—En—Ant, the suffix -ant is added to the PrésENt stem of the verb:

PRESENT PARTICIPLE/GERUND FORM	
Racine du Présent	-ANT
Dorothée marche sur le tapis EN écoutANT la musique (écout—ant) Dorothée écoute de la musique EN marchANT sur le tapis roulant (march—ant)	
(Dorothée walks on the treadmill while listening to the music.) *(Dorothée listens to music while walking on the treadmill.)*	

Any action happening in the future follows **AVANT DE** and is put in the **infinitive**

ACTION IN THE FUTURE OF THE PAST INFINITIVE AND THE PRESENT PARTICIPLE	
AVANT DE	Infinitif
Dorothée va au gymnase **AVANT DE marcher** sur le tapis roulant Dorothée marche sur le tapis **AVANT DE prendre** une douche	
(Dorothée goes to the gym before walking on the treadmill.) *(Dorothée walks on the treadmill before taking a shower.)*	

NOTE The Participe Présent is impersonal so it does not vary in gender or number.

If there is an opposition, or a contrast, between the two actions that are performed simultaneously, the adverb TOUT is added to reinforce EN

Elle fait des études de médecine TOUT en élevANT ses trois enfants seule.

She is pursuing her medical studies while raising her three children by herself.

IMPORTANT!

To form the Infinitif Passé, the choices between the Infinitif of Être and Avoir and the agreement of the participe passé follow the standard rules for all compound tenses.

Refer to Chapter 12 for
Past Indicative Tenses—Perfect, and
Agreement of the Past Participle

The Indicative Mood

Meaning of Indicative

Fact and Index

Consider the **indicatif** as your basic, generic mood: **i n d i c a t i f**

- It serves to indic **a t** e that an action is not a matter of opinion, judgment, or appreciation but is to be considered a **f a c t**.
- If you were to write an **i n d** ex of all the events contained in the big book of human history, you would use the **i n d i c a t i v e**.
- When you want to give **i n d i c a t i** ons to help someone find, do, or understand something without any ambiguity, use the **i n d i c a t i v e**.

Moment of Utterance

Within this general ground level mood, the actions are placed along the line that generally represents time. They are organized according to:

Narrator as Absolute Point of Reference

That reference is given by the narrator of the story, or the subject of the sentence.

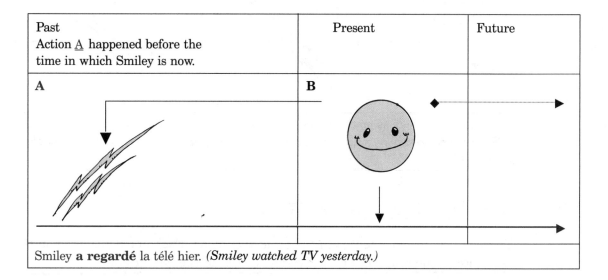

Past Action <u>A</u> happened before the time in which Smiley is now.	Present	Future
A B		
Smiley **a regardé** la télé hier. *(Smiley watched TV yesterday.)*		

Another Action as Reference

The indicative is also used when there is a relative point of reference: an action is organized on the time line according to another action.

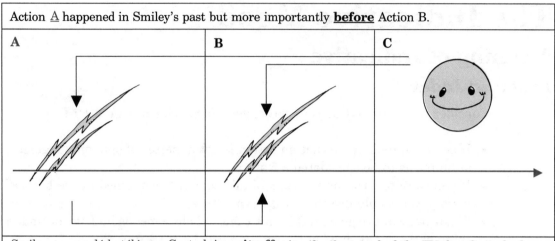

Action A̲ happened in Smiley's past but more importantly **before** Action B.

Smiley a regardé la télé que Greta lui **avait offerte**. *(Smiley watched the TV that Greta had given him.)*

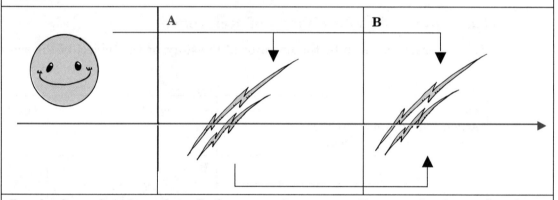

Both Actions A̲ and B will happen in Smiley's future, but Action A must have happened before Action B.

Pour les Oscars le mois prochain, Smiley portera le costume qu'il **aura acheté** ce week-end. *(For the Oscar ceremony next month, Smiley will wear the suit that he will have bought this weekend.)*

Tenses of the Indicative Mood

There are six primary tenses in the indicative mood. Each one depends upon the point of reference in the sentence or the overall context of the paragraph.

TIP BOX

In case of doubt about which tense to use, draw a time line and locate your actions on it "around" the person, thing, or object that is the central reference.

TIME LINE: CHOICE OF INDICATIVE TENSE					
Indicative Mood			😊		
Simple Tenses		Imparfait	PRÉSENT		Futur
Compound Tenses	Plus-Que-Parfait	Passé Composé		Futur Antérieur	
Action Order	#1	#2		#1	#2
	Happened before Passé Composé or Imparfait	Happened before Moment of Utterance		Happens before **Futur**	Will Happen after Moment of Utterance

Although there are many tenses in the indicative, the mood itself grounds the action in reality and gives it a sense of solidity, evidence, neutrality. For this reason, I would "dress" my indicative verb in a pair of jeans and sneakers, the most average outfit that anyone can wear without making any fashion statement.

À LA—LE MODE INDICATIF: VERB FASHION

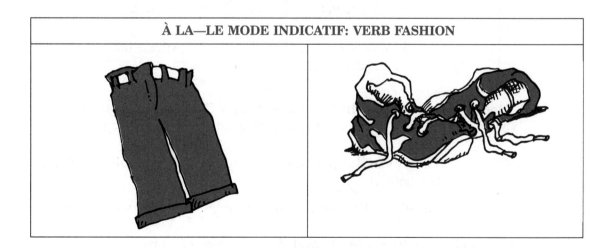

The Present Indicative

Use

- The French present of the indicative mood translates both the regular and the progressive present in English (to be + -ing—gerund form of the verb):

  Je travaille = *I work—I am working*

- A verb is put in the present to indicate that the action is being performed as the sentence is uttered:

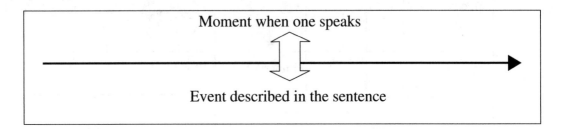

Special Use of the Present: *Aller* and *Venir De* + Infinitive)

The verbs **aller** and **venir** can be combined with the infinitive of any other verbs to represent an action that is very close to the present on either the past or future side. When **aller** and **venir** are conjugated in the présent, they form the **passé immédiat** and the **futur proche**.

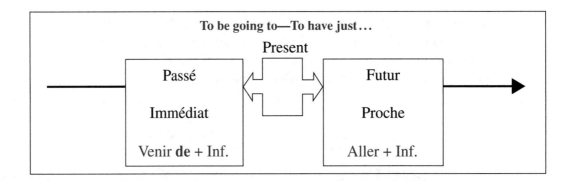

Aller in the présent + **infinitive** translates the English: *I am going to . . .*
Venir in the présent + **DE** + **infinitive** translates the English: *I just . . .*

> Tu **vas étudier** pendant deux heures. (You **are going to** study for two hours.)

> Elle **vient d'étudier** toute la journée. (She **just studied** all day.)

Aller and **venir de** can be conjugated in all tenses of all moods.

Formation of Indicative Present

Regular Verbs

As with all simple tenses, the indicative present is formed by adding an ending to the stem of the verb.

SET OF INDICATIVE PRESENT ENDINGS					
	Persons in the Singular Je—Tu—Elle/Il			**Persons in the Plural** Nous—Vous—Ils/Elles		
	1st	**2nd**	**3rd**	**1st**	**2nd**	**3rd**
-ER aimer	-E	-ES	-E	-ONS	-EZ	-ENT
-IR finir	-IS	-IS	-IT	-ISSONS	-ISSEZ	-ISSENT
Variation Mentir	-S	-S	-T	-ONS	-EZ	-ENT
-RE Vendre	-S	-S	d	-ONS	-EZ	-ENT
Je mangE—tu travaillES—elle dirigE—nous chantONS—vous dansEZ—ils passENT Je finIS—tu punIS—elle bannIT—nous haISSONS—vous salISSEZ—ils blanchISSENT Je parS—tu menS—elle courT—nous partONS—vous sortEZ—ils courENT Je vendS—tu pendS—elle attenD—nous entendONS—vous descendEZ—ils dépendENT						

Irregular Verbs

The ending depends on the group to which the verb belongs if it is regular. For irregular verbs, both endings and stems may vary.

INDICATIVE PRESENT FORMATION					
Infinitive	**1st Group** -ER	**2nd Group** -IR	**3rd Group** -RE	**Sample Irregular Verbs**	
JE	port-E	fini-S	descend-S	Je vais	Nous allONS
				Tu vas	Vous allEZ
				Il va	Elles vont
TU	aime-ES	puni-S	vend-S	Je peux	Nous pouvONS
				Tu peux	Vous pouvEZ
				Il peut	Elles peuvENT
ELLE— IL—ON	travaill-E	atterri-T	atten-d	Je dois	Nous devONS
				Tu dois	Vous devEZ
				Il doit	Elles doivENT

NOUS	déjeun-ONS	fini-SSONS	entend-ONS	Je sais	Nous savONS
				Tu sais	Vous savEZ
				Il sait	Elles savENT
VOUS	écout-EZ	puni-SSEZ	pend-EZ	Je tiens	Nous tenONS
				Tu tiens	Vous tenEZ
				Il tient	Elles tiennENT
ILS— ELLES	dans-ENT	atterri-SSENT	tend-ENT	Je prends	Nous prenONS
				Tu prends	Vous prenEZ
				Il prend	Elles prennENT

NOTE Many irregular verbs are, in fact, semiregular. Semiregular verbs have their 1st and 2nd person of the plural (**nous** and **vous**) formed on the normal stem (the infinitive minus the infinitive ending) and they take the regular **-ons** and **-ez** ending. Always verify the conjugations of **-IR** and **-RE** verbs even if they seem regular:

Finir: je finis—nous finissons / Mentir: je mens—nous mentons
Entendre: j'entends—nous entendons / Prendre: je prends—nous prenons

> Dev-**oir**: **Je dois**—nous Dev-**ONS**, vous Dev-**EZ**
> Ten-**ir**: **je tiens**—nous Ten-**ONS**, vous Ten-**EZ**
> Sav-**oir**: **je sais**—nous Sav-**ONS**, vous Sav-**EZ**

MODELS OF 22 REGULAR AND IRREGULAR MAIN VERBS IN THE PRESENT INDICATIVE					
Infinitive	**JE**	**TU**	**IL**	**NOUS**	**VOUS**	**ELLES**
Aimer	aime	aimes	aime	aimons	aimez	aiment
Aller	vais	vas	va	allons	allez	vont
Avoir	ai	as	a	avons	avez	ont
Connaître	connais	connais	connaît	connaissons	connaissez	connaissent
Croire	crois	crois	croit	croyons	croyez	croient
Devoir	dois	dois	doit	devons	devez	doivent
Dire	dis	dis	dit	disons	disez	disent
Écrire	écris	écris	écrit	écrivons	écrivez	écrivent
Être	suis	es	est	sommes	êtes	sont
Faire	fais	fais	fait	faisons	faites	font
Finir	finis	finis	finit	finissons	finissez	finissent
Lire	lis	lis	lit	lisons	lisez	lisent
Mettre	mets	mets	met	mettons	mettez	mettent
Partir	pars	pars	part	partons	partez	partent
Pouvoir	peux	peux	peut	pouvons	pouvez	peuvent
Prendre	prends	prends	prend	prenons	prenez	prennent
Savoir	sais	sais	sait	savons	savez	savent
Tenir	tiens	tiens	tient	tenons	tenez	tiennent
Vendre	vends	vends	vend	vendons	vendez	vendent
Venir	viens	viens	viens	venons	venez	viennent
Vouloir	veux	veux	veut	voulons	voulez	veulent

Make separate files of these conjugations so you can refer to them easily until you know them by heart.

The Imperative Mood

When you are in the mood to order people around, become the emperor and USE the imperative mood! An imperative verb could be dressed like Napoleon, a general, or a dictator.

IMPERATIVE VERBS DRESS TO COMMAND!

Meaning of Imperative

The Nature of Commands

Commands have their own mood because, although they can be forcefully expressed, they are not real. It is not because you give an order to someone that the person will actually perform the requested action; as much as I repeat "Make a file of all conjugations of the most common verbs," I can never be sure that students will do it. So, contrary to what may be intuitive, a command has a lesser degree of reality than a simple fact.

Persons in the Imperative Mood

The imperative is an attempt to suppress a person or a group's ability to choose. The "Emperor" addresses others as his inferiors to tell them it is *imperative* they do something.

A command is given as part of a dialogue, so it can be directed only to the one or more persons to whom one is talking; consequently, there are only three persons in the imperative:

CONJUGATION BY PERSONS IN THE IMPERATIVE MOOD		
1 familiar person	A group of people (including the Emperor)	A group of people A Superior Person
2nd Person Singular TU	1st Person Plural NOUS	2nd Person Plural VOUS
Viens! Sors! Danse! *(Come! Get out! Dance!)*	Allons-y! Chantons! *(Let's go! Let's sing!)*	Entrez! Arrêtez! *(Come in! Stop!)*

THINK! Could there be other persons to give a command to? Could I give myself a command, for instance? Find the response at the end of the section.

Formation of the Imperative

No Subject

Since, in a command, what matters is that the action be realized, there is no subject in the imperative.

> **TIP BOX**
>
> Remember that grammar rules were not only created to make young French people or American students of French suffer, although they are pretty good at doing that. They follow a certain logic. If you forget the rule, try to think about what is really going on in your sentence. In the case of the imperative, for instance, imagine you see a child on a balcony. There is danger there, so you cannot waste any time. The imperative needs to convey just such immediacy and emergency; therefore, there is no time to try to remember the child's name. You need to go directly to what matters: the action without a subject: "Stop!" and, start with the negation, if necessary, "Don't run!" "Wait for me!"

Imperative Conjugations

Endings

Because a command is always given at the same time of its utterance, the **imperative** is formed on the **indicative present** conjugation, with a slight modification.

- In the imperative, the final **s** of the present 2nd person singular for **-ER** ending verbs is normally dropped.

    Indicative Present: tu travailles—tu entres—tu ranges ta chambre.

    Imperative Present: Travaille!—Entre!—Range ta chambre!

- The **s** is reintroduced if the imperative is followed by the pronoun **EN** or **Y**. In this case, keeping the final **s** and making a liaison facilitates the pronunciation and makes the group of words sound better: so the grammar rule bends!

    Va!—Vas-y! [va zi] (*Go! Go There!*)

    Mange! Manges-en! [mãʒə zã] (*Eat! Eat some!*)

- If the action should not be performed, the imperative is used in the negative form. The sentence starts with **Ne**, as negating the possibility of the action is most important. All standard negative adverbs can be used and they are placed normally, surrounding the entire imperative verb group as described in the Negative Sandwich Sections in Chapter 14: Negative Sentences.

Present Tense Only

Because it is useless to order something for yesterday (it is a bit late!) there is no imperative past.

And because there is always some time between the command and the realization of the action, there is no need for an imperative future either; the future component is built in. Therefore, the imperative mood has only one tense: the present.

Use of Pronouns in the Imperative

The imperative can be used by itself or with complements.

- Complements that are full nouns always come after the verb in an affirmative command or after the second negative component in a negative command.

> Regarde Carla! *(Look at Carla!)*

> Ne regarde pas Caroline! *(Do not look at Caroline!)*

- If the complements are personal pronouns, their selection and place is different in an affirmative or a negative command.

TIP BOX

Sometimes there is no obvious explanation for rules. The choice and place of personal pronouns will not necessarily make sense to you, so *Just Learn it*! But you can also try to say the sentence out loud. If it does not sound right to you, chances are pronouns and/or place are incorrect.

Negative Imperative

With negative commands, the type and order of the personal pronouns is similar to that in standard sentences:

TYPE AND ORDER OF PRONOUNS IN NEGATIVE IMPERATIVE SENTENCES							
NEGATIVE COMPONENT #1	Direct Object		Indirect Object 3rd Persons	Prep. À	Prep. De	COMMAND!	NEGATIVE COMPONENT #2
NE	me— m' te— t' nous vous	le—l' la—l' les	lui leur	y	en	**Verb in the Imperative**	**PAS JAMAIS PLUS** ...

You must therefore first identify which type of complement your pronoun is going to replace. There are four possibilities:

1. Direct Object Complement (D.O.): me, te, le-la, nous, vous, les
2. Indirect Object Complement (I.O.): me, te, lui, nous, vous, leur
3. Location Complement: Y
4. [Stated or implied] preposition DE complement: EN

Once you have identified which complement it is, verify if there is a third person complement and organize all pronouns around it.

NEGATIVE IMPERATIVE SENTENCES WITH PRONOUNS: EXAMPLES		
Identify the complement	**Complement** **Direct** *Indirect* **Person**	**Negative Imperative**
Donner <u>le bonbon.</u>	<u>D.O.</u> = 3rd p.	Ne <u>le</u> donne pas! (*Don't give it!*)
Donner *à Bruno.*	*I.O.* = 3rd p.	Ne *<u>lui</u>* donne pas! (*Don't give to him!*)
Donner <u>le bonbon</u> *à Bruno.*	<u>D.O.</u> - *I.O.* = 3rd p.	Ne <u>le</u> *lui* donne pas! (*Don't give it to him!*)
Parler *à moi.*	*I.O.* = 3rd p.	Ne *me* parle pas! (*Don't talk to me!*)
Donner <u>le bonbon</u> à moi.	<u>D.O.</u> - *I.O.* = 3rd p.	Ne *me* <u>le</u> donne pas! (*Don't give it to me!*)
Donner **des bonbons** *à Bruno.*	**Prep. De** = *I.O.*	Ne *lui* **en** donne pas! (*Don't give him any!*)
Donner **des bonbons** *à moi.*	**Prep. De** = *I.O.*	Ne *m'***en** donne pas! (*Don't give me any!*)
Descendre *<u>à la cave.</u>*	*<u>Location</u>*	N'*<u>y</u>* descends pas! (*Don't go down there!*)
Descendre <u>les livres</u> *<u>à la cave.</u>*	<u>D.O.</u> = *<u>Location</u>*	Ne <u>les</u> *y* descends pas! (*Don't take them down there!*)

Positive Imperative

With positive commands:

- All object pronouns follow the verb.
- The object pronouns are hyphenated (-) to the verb and to each other.
- Two pronouns are changed: ~~me~~ and ~~te~~ are replaced by **moi** and **toi**.
- Before en, moi and toi become **m' and t'**, which is not hyphenated.

TYPE AND ORDER OF PRONOUNS IN AFFIRMATIVE IMPERATIVE SENTENCES				
COMMAND!	Direct Object	Indirect Object	Prep. À	Prep. DE
Verb in the Imperative	le—l' la—l' les	moi—m'	y	en
		toi—t'		
		lui		
		nous		
		vous		
		leur		

The possibilities of complements remain the same as for negative imperative sentences.

Organize multiple pronouns according to the "D.I.Y. EN" rule and around the third person complement.

AFFIRMATIVE IMPERATIVE SENTENCES WITH PRONOUNS: EXAMPLES		
Identify the complement	**Complement** **Direct** *Indirect* **Person**	**Negative Imperative**
Donner le bonbon.	D.O. 3rd p.	Donne-le! (*Give it!*)
Donner *à Bruno.*	I.O. = 3rd p.	Donne-lui! (*Give him!*)
Donner le bonbon *à Bruno.*	D.O. - I.O. = 3rd p.	Donne-le-lui! (*Give it to him!*)
Donner *à moi.*	I.O. = 3rd p.	Donne-moi! (*Give me!*)
Donner le bonbon *à moi.*	D.O. - I.O. = 3rd p.	Donne-le-moi (*Give it to me!*)
Donner **des bonbons** *à Bruno.*	**Prep. De** = I.O.	Donne-lui-en! (*Give him some!*)
Donner **des bonbons** *à moi.*	**Prep. De** = I.O.	Donne-m' en! (*Give me some!*)
Descendre *à la cave.*	*Location*	Descends-y! (*Go down there!*)
Descendre les livres *à la cave.*	D.O. = *Location*	Descends-les-y! (*Take them down there!*)

8 Steps to Form the Imperative

1. Conjugate the verb in the present of the indicative.
2. Choose the 2nd person of the singular (tu), the 1st person of the plural (nous), or the 2nd person of the plural (vous):

   tu viens—nous marchons—vous sortez *(you come—we walk—you go out)*
3. Suppress the subject:

   viens—marchons—sortez
4. Remove the final **s** at the end for the second person singular if you are conjugating an **-er** ending verb (marcher, acheter, amener, apporter, aller . . .):

   marche**x**—achète**x**—amène**x**—apporte**x**—va**x**—regarde**x**—écoute**x**
5. Capitalize the first letter of the verb or the first negative component:

   Achète—Ne regarde
6. Add the appropriate pronouns after the verb for a positive command:

   Achète-la-lui
7. Add the appropriate pronouns before the verb and the second component for a negative command:

   Ne la regarde plus
8. Conclude your sentence by an exclamation point!

   Achète-la-lui!—Ne la regarde plus! *(Buy it for her! Do not look at her any longer!)*

Imperative Forms of *Être* and *Avoir*

The imperative forms of the auxiliary verbs are not similar to their present indicative conjugation but to their subjunctive present.

They are used in the same way as regular verbs.

IMPERATIVE FORMS OF THE AUXILIARY VERBS *ÊTRE* AND *AVOIR*		
	ÊTRE	**AVOIR**
2nd Person Singular	**SOIS!** Sois sage! (Be good!)	**AIE!** Aie un peu de courage! (Have some guts!)
1st Person Plural	**SOYONS!** Soyons gentils avec les animaux! (Let's be kind with animals!)	**AYONS!** Ayons de la patience! (Be patient!)
2nd Person Plural	**SOYEZ!** Soyez attentive aux règles de grammaire! (Pay attention to grammar rules!)	**AYEZ!** Ayez beaucoup d'amis si possible! (Have many friends if possible!)

Can there be other persons in the imperative than the three above? No, there cannot be another person in the imperative. Even if I give an order to myself, I treat myself as I would another person. I give an order to me.

I have the choice: I can say **Tu** to myself, if I am my friend. Or I can talk to myself as a superior person and use the formal **Vous**. The latter option may indicate some mild form of schizophrenia or megalomania, however.

Practice What You Learned

Exercises are rated according to four levels of difficulty:

- Beginner easy [*]
- Beginner challenging [**]
- Intermediate [***]
- Advanced [****]

1. Complete the sentence with the verb conjugated in the present indicative. [*]

A. Je [aller: _____] à la banque.

B. Félicie [arriver: _____] à huit heures tous les jours.

C. Karine et toi [finir: _____] vos exercices.

D. Tu [accepter: _____] sa proposition.

E. Nous [dîner: _____] au restaurant ce soir.

F. Elle [entendre: _____] l'océan dans le coquillage.

G. Jean-Paul et Jean-Jacques [prendre: _____] un filet de tennis.

H. Les gentils parents [ne punir: _____] jamais leurs enfants.

I. Tu [vendre: _____] des olives sur le marché d'Antibes.

J. Cette société [fournir: _____] des ordinateurs gratuits aux écoles.

K. Je [ne croire: _____] plus ce garçon.

L. Vous [devoir: _____] trois livres à la bibliothèque.

2. Complete the paragraph with the logical verb left in the infinitive or conjugated in the present according to the context. [**]

> Aller—Prendre—Être—Répondre—Faire—Se lever—Connaître—Se promener—Utiliser—Dire—Mettre—S'entraîner—Venir—Partir—Voir—Devoir

George _____ tôt pour _____ tous les jours au gymnase. Il _____ un survêtement et _____ son sac. Son ami Gérard et lui _____ entraîneurs. Je les _____ bien parce que nous nous _____ en vélo souvent. Je _____ sur le tapis roulant avant de _____ au bureau. Quand George et Gérard me _____, ils me _____: "Fab, tu _____ aussi _____ de la muscu mais sans _____ des poids très lourds." Je leur _____: "D'accord, mais vous, _____ à mon cours d'aérobic alors!"

3. Put the following verb in the affirmative or negative imperative according to the context. [**]

> Manger—Sortir—Étudier—Ranger—Arrêter—Danser

A. Ton petit frère est dans ta chambre, il joue et il crie. Tu dois étudier, tu lui dis:

_____

B. Tes parents vont rentrer de vacances et la maison est en désordre. Tu dis à ton frère et à ta soeur: _____ la maison!

C. Ton ami joue du piano et cela te plaît, tu lui demandes: _____ s'il te plaît!

D. La cigale a chanté tout l'été, la méchante fourmi, qui n'est pas son amie, lui dit: Eh bien, _____ maintenant!

E. Il y a trop de sel dans la soupe et ton patron invité à diner déteste le sel, tu lui recommandes: _____ la soupe!

F. Votre prof dit toujours aux étudiants: _____

4. Conjugate the verbs in the affirmative and negative imperative and replace the nouns with the appropriate pronoun. [***]

Example:

Amener la cousine à l'aéroport, 2nd p. sing: **Amène-la!—Ne l'amène pas!**

A. Acheter le pain, 2nd p. pl.

_____

B. Apporter de la glace, 1st p. pl.

_____

C. Donner aux voisins, 2nd. p. sing.

_____

D. Écouter mon ami et moi, 2nd p. pl.

_____

E. Monter les livres au grenier, 2nd p. sing.

_____

F. Rendre sa veste à Vladimir, 2nd p. sing.

_____

G. Avoir de la tolérance, 2nd p. plu.

_____

H. Se cacher dans le garage, 1st p. plu.

_____

I. Prêter de l'argent à moi, 2nd p. sing.

_____

J. Être à la mode, 1st p. plu.

_____

5. In the following grid, locate the six imperative forms of the auxiliary verbs. They can be horizontal, vertical, or diagonal, up or down, left or right. [**]

j	f	s	t	x	o	s	i
q	y	s	h	a	i	e	p
a	y	o	n	s	a	d	s
e	r	y	k	u	c	n	k
g	m	e	r	s	o	l	z
i	a	z	c	y	i	i	g
a	s	i	o	s	x	u	h
v	o	s	a	z	e	y	a

Chapter 12

PAST INDICATIVE TENSES—PASSÉ COMPOSÉ (PERFECT) AND AGREEMENT OF THE PARTICIPE PASSÉ (PAST PARTICIPLE)

Introduction

The **passé composé**, the **imparfait**, and the **plus-que-parfait** are the three past tenses of the indicative mood. They have equivalent forms in English: the *perfect*, the *imperfect*, and the *pluperfect* tenses, but their use sometimes differs in French. It is therefore safer to learn when to use each past tense and why, rather than simply memorizing their formation.

This chapter will focus specifically on the **passé composé**:

- as interrelated to the other past tenses of the indicative
- in comparison and contrast to its "rival," the **imparfait**
- as the exemplary tense for the rule of agreement of the **participe passé** (*past participle*), since this rule remains the same throughout all compound tenses.

Past Indicative Tenses: Characteristics of the Perfect

Chronological Order

The **passé composé** is a tense of the past used for actions that happened directly before the moment they are mentioned.

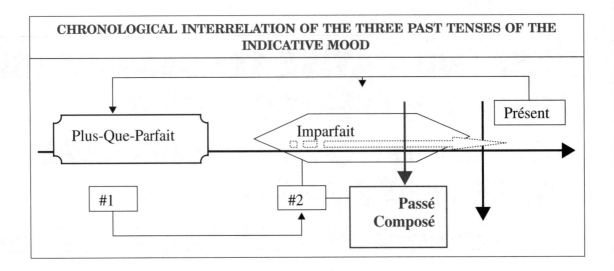

CHRONOLOGICAL INTERRELATION OF THE THREE PAST TENSES OF THE INDICATIVE MOOD

- Both **passé composé** and **Imparfait** actions may happen at the same time in the past, but if they happen together, the action in the **passé composé** is understood as interrupting the one in the **imparfait**.
- The **plus-que-parfait** represents an action that has happened in the past of an already past action. The action in the **plus-que-parfait** did not happen directly before the moment it was mentioned, but prior to another action itself happening before that mention. The **plus-que-parfait** takes the subject of the action back twice. It precedes actions that are conjugated in the **imparfait** or in the **passé composé**.

TIP BOX

Rely on the grammatical terms themselves to remember the rule that comes with them:

Parfait comes from the Latin *perficio–perfectum*. Perfect was not used to mean ideal or without flaw. Originally it meant made (*factum*) through (*per*), that is, made all the way, completely finished.

So the imperfect is the tense for actions that are not perfect, that is, the action was done in the past but may not be completely finished. It may extend into the present.

The **perfect** (**passé composé**) is the tense for actions that are completely finished, started and concluded in the past: perfect = over, done all the way through. Perfect actions cannot be still happening now.

The word **plus-que-parfait** means literally "**more than perfect, that is more than finished.**" The **pluperfect** is the tense for actions that are doubly past, over before an already past action started. As its name indicates, the **plus-que parfait** is "more than past."

Definition of Compound Tense

The **passé composé** is the most commonly used past tense in everyday French.

One finds it more and more often in novels and formal discourses as well, since it is gradually replacing its literary equivalent, the *passé simple*.

- **Simple** means that the conjugation is formed with a single element: the appropriate ending.
- **Composé** signifies that two elements are necessary: an auxiliary verb and a past participle.

COMPARATIVE OVERVIEW OF SIMPLE AND COMPOUND TENSES				
Simple Tense	Compound Tenses			
Stem + Ending	Auxiliary verb conjugated in one of the simple tenses			Past participle of the verb to conjugate in the compound tense
Présent **Stem + Present Endings**	Passé Composé Auxiliary Verb in Present + **Participe Passé**			
Stem +	-e	Je suis	J'ai	—É
	-es	Tu es	Tu as	
	-e	Elle est	On a	—I
	-ons	Nous sommes	Nous avons	
	-ez	Vous êtes	Vous avez	—U
	-ent	Ils sont	Ils ont	

Use

The **passé composé** is used to indicate that an action was performed in the past.

The amount of time that has elapsed since the event is not important in choosing the **passé composé**.

IMPORTANT!

Your choice to conjugate a verb in the **passé composé** should not be dictated by the action itself. All verbs can be conjugated both in the **passé composé** and the imparfait depending on the aspect of the action you want to emphasize.

- Il **a couru** pendant trois heures puis il est allé à la fac. *(He ran for three hours, then went to the university.)*
  Emphasis is on the FACT that he ran, as one of his activities—**passé composé**.
- Il courait un marathon quand il a eu cette idée. *(He was running when he had this idea.)*
  Emphasis on his running as the EXTENDED period of time during which he had an idea—**imparfait**.
- Il **est tombé** de l'échelle. *(He fell from the ladder.)*
  Emphasis on BRIEF, occasional, OVER action—**passé composé**.
- Il tombait de son lit tous les jours. *(He used to fall from his bed every day.)*
  Emphasis on REPETITION—**imparfait**.

What matters is that actions had one or more of the four characteristics explained below.

1. *Completed Action*

When the action started in the past and ended in the past, you must use the **passé composé**. The action in the **passé composé** is **over**.

Le téléphone a sonné. *(The telephone rang.)*

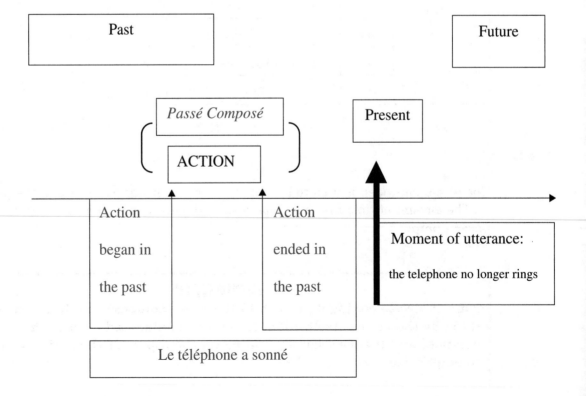

2. *Action Perceived as Brief*

Because the action belongs entirely to a time gone by, the action is perceived as being relatively brief.

- The action in the **passé composé** is not considered extended. The **passé composé** makes the action feel like a point in time:

   > Le téléphone a sonné pendant 10 minutes. *(The phone rang for ten minutes.)*

- The event is described as a block. It is perceived as a vertical line crossing the horizontal stretch of time, even if it lasted for a while.

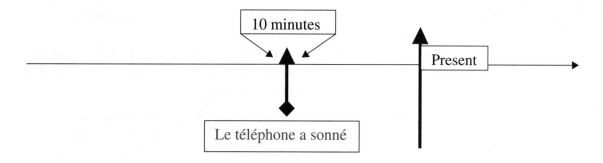

3. *Interrupting Action*

Logically then, when two actions happened in the past at the same time, the "short" one interrupts the "longer" one. This interrupting action must be conjugated in the **passé composé**.

- The **passé composé** is perceived as the brief interrupting event:

   > Je faisais une sieste quand le téléphone a sonné. *(I was taking a nap when the phone rang.)*

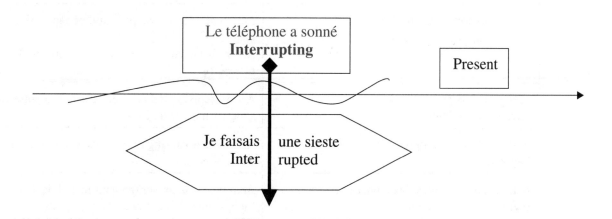

4. Occasional Action

Finally, the **passé composé** is used to indicate that the action was occasional.

- An action in the **passé composé** did not happen on a regular basis.

- The **passé composé** indicates that the action was not in a series. In the following example, what is conveyed is that Sophie normally does not take naps, and this was a singular event:

> Sophie a fait une sieste la semaine dernière. *(Sophie took a nap last week.)*

> **NOTE** Perceived recurrence vs. individual action **is one of the major differences between the imparfait and the passé composé:**
>
> Je suis allée à la piscine l'année dernière: **I may have gone swimming more than once but it was not something I want to describe as a regular event.**
>
> J'allais à la piscine l'année dernière: **It may have been daily, weekly, or even monthly, but it happened regularly and it is something I want to present as systematic when I tell my story in the past.**

TIP BOX

Anytime you can think of your action in the English past as something you *used to* do, it *cannot* be translated by the **passé composé** since it was some sort of a habit.

COMPARATIVE DESCRIPTION OF ACTIONS IN THE IMPARFAIT AND THE PASSÉ COMPOSÉ	
IMPARFAIT	**PASSÉ COMPOSÉ**
Action started in the past but may be continuing in the present	Action started in the past and ended in the past Action is boxed in before the moment of utterance
Action that is perceived to be lasting, ongoing for a while	Action represented as a short event, a point in time without extension
Action being interrupted while it was happening	Action interrupting an extensive action as it was happening
Action that may have been part of a series; regular, recurrent action	Action that is presented as unusual, isolated, independent from any pattern

> **IMPORTANT!**
> The English *preterit* can translate either the French **imparfait** or the **passé composé**. The English *perfect* (I have done—You have been) is actually rarely used these days, but the **passé composé** is very common. Do not translate the tenses directly; look at each action and identify its characteristics according to the previous summarizing table.

Components of the *Passé Composé*

Formation

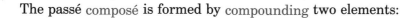

The passé composé is formed by compounding two elements:

- The auxiliary verbs **être** and **avoir** conjugated in the present of the indicative.
- The **participe passé** of the verb to be put in the **passé composé**.

FORMATION OVERVIEW			
Auxiliary	Auxiliary **in the Indicatif Présent**	**Past Participle Participe Passé**	**Passé Composé**
Être	Je suis Tu es Elle, il, on est Nous sommes Vous êtes Ils, elles sont	**Participe passé*** = p.p. . . . +é . . . +i . . . +u . . . +p.p. of irregular verb ^	Je suis **née** Tu es **allé** Elle est **arrivée** Nous nous sommes **lavés** Vous vous êtes **téléphoné** Ils sont **parties**
Avoir	J'ai Tu as Elle, il, on a Nous avons Vous avez Ils, elles ont	*May or may not agree ^Must be learned for each verb	J'ai **travaillé** Tu as **peint** Il a **appris** Nous avons **fini** Vous avez **rêvé** Elles ont **couru**

Auxiliary Verbs *Être* and *Avoir*

Choosing between **être** and **avoir** does not depend on the tense but on the type of action to be put in the **passé composé**.

> **IMPORTANT!**
> The choice between the two auxiliary verbs is ruled by the same criteria in all the moods. Learning these criteria for the passé composé will help you form all other compound tenses.

Characteristics of the Auxiliary Verb Avoir

- **Avoir** applies to actions that are directed from the subject toward an external object.
- **Avoir** is used with most verbs, as most actions are performed by the subject onto something or someone else in the world.

J'ai parlé à ma mère.	me—my mother	*(I talked to my mother.)*
Tu as fini tes exercices.	you—your homework	*(You finished all your homework.)*
Sophie a voulu un biscuit.	Sophie—a cookie	*(Sophie wanted a cookie.)*
Philippe a pris le train pour Cannes.	Philippe—the train	*(Philippe took the train for Cannes.)*
Nous avons connu son frère en vacances.	us—his brother	*(We met his brother on vacation.)*
Vous avez fait un excellent diner.	you—the dinner	*(You made an excellent dinner.)*
Ils ont pu partir à l'heure.	them—ability	*(They were able to leave on time.)*
Tes soeurs ont mis une robe bleue.	my sisters—dress	*(Your sisters put on a blue dress.)*

Characteristics of the Auxiliary Verb Être

Reflection of Action on its Subject

- **Être** expresses a state of the subject.
- **Être** is therefore used with actions that are performed by the subject but also affect it. **Être** verbs "boomerang" back to the subject. They are used with a reflexive or reciprocal pronoun.

Je me suis levé(e).	me—myself	*(I got out of bed.)*
Tu t'es vu(e) dans le miroir.	you—yourself	*(You saw yourself in the mirror.)*
Karine s'est habillée tout en blanc.	Karine—herself	*(Karine dressed all in white.)*
Rodolphe s'est dépêché.	Rodolphe—himself	*(Rodolphe hurried up.)*
On s'est cru perdu.	we—us	*(We thought we were lost.)*
Nous nous sommes rencontré(e)s régulièrement.	we—each other	*(We saw each other regularly.)*
Vous vous êtes connu(e)s en Provence.	you—you	*(You met in Provence.)*
Les enfants se sont tenus tranquilles.	the kids—themselves	*(The children behaved.)*
Elles se sont photographiées sur le grand escalier du Palais des Festivals.	the girls—each other	*(They took pictures of each other on the steps of the Palais des Festivals.)*

Displacement of the Subject

Change of Place Concept

- **Être** is also used when the action displaces the subject that performs it.
- **Être** actions are intransitive verbs that result in some form of change for the subject.

Intransitive means the verb does not take a direct object.
Displacement means that the main purpose of the action is to place the subject in another place, whether physical or psychological.

Here are some examples of the displacement concept:

1. Descendre: Subject from up to down *(To go down)*
2. Revenir: Subject from somewhere back to here *(To come back)*
3. Sortir: Subject from in to out *(To go out)*
4. Tomber: Subject from on something to off and down from it *(To fall)*
5. Naître: Subject from inside the womb to out in the world *(To be born)*

In all these cases, the subject doing the action ends up somewhere else.

IMPORTANT!

Beware: Some verbs imply motion yet their primary purpose is not really to displace the subject. Displacement is secondary to a more important characteristic of the action: speed, height, etc. Such verbs are not conjugated with être.

Emphasis on Fact THAT Subject Is Moved ÊTRE	Emphasis on **HOW** the Motion Happens **AVOIR**

For instance, **entrer, sortir, monter, passer, partir**, etc. are displacement verbs, because their purpose is to displace the subject from point A, that is out, in, down, away, to point B, in, out, up, closer, etc.
 	
   The only purpose of these actions is a change of location of the subject that performs it.
	For instance, **courir**, **sauter**, **ramper**, **marcher**, etc. are *not displacement* verbs, because their purposes are to go fast, to go high or over, to lower oneself, to stroll casually when running or jumping is possible.
	
	   They do not simply put the subject elsewhere; they add a special effect to the change of place.

These displacement verbs are sometimes called "motion" verbs, which is misleading, or "house verbs," because they describe how a person can change place toward, within, around, and out of a house. The most correct category for them is Change of Place of the Subject.

Change of Place Verbs

The most common and useful displacement verbs can easily be remembered as belonging to the Dr. Patricia and Mr. Patrick Vandertramp's family.

DR. PATRICIA & MR. PATRICK VANDERTRAMP'S VERB FAMILY						
				Venir		*(To come)*
				Aller		*(To go)*
				Naître		*(To be born)*
				Devenir		*(To become)*
				Entrer		*(To come in)*
Descendre Revenir	Passer	Monter Rester	Partir	Retourner	Sortir	*(To go back)*
				Tomber		*(To fall)*
				Rentrer		*(To come back in)*
				Arriver		*(To arrive)*
				Mourir		*(To die)*
				Parvenir		*(To reach)*
(To go down) *(To come back)*	*(To pass by)*	*(To go up)* *(To stay)*	*(To leave)*		*(To go out)*	

Dr. Patricia and her husband, Mr. Patrick, Vandertramp's beautiful foundation is located on the famous Cap d'Antibes. Here is her story:

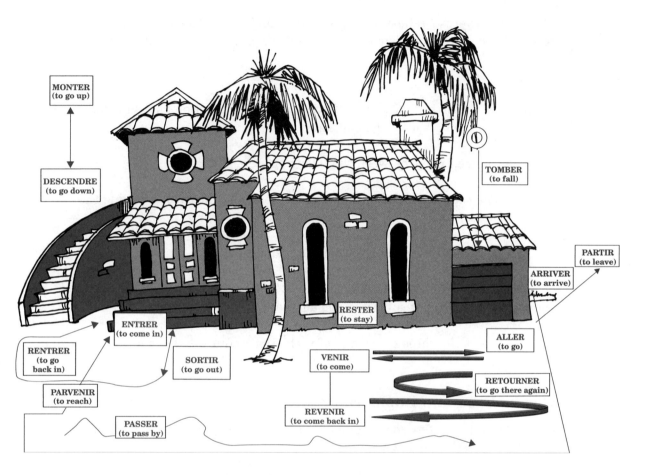

The house of Dr. Patricia and Mr. Patrick Vandertramp

Patricia **est née** en Allemagne en 1925. Ses parents **sont arrivés** à Munich en 1920. Son père **est entré** à l'université pour enseigner la philosophie classique, et sa mère **est retournée** à l'université pour finir ses études. Lorsque le parti de Hitler **est monté** au pouvoir, et que les nazis **sont passés** dans les classes pour imposer leur propagande, beaucoup d'intellectuels **sont tombés** sous leur contrôle. Les parents de Patricia **sont restés** fidèles à leurs principes éthiques, et ils **sont partis** pour ne pas collaborer au régime. D'allemagne, le père de Patricia **est descendu** dans le sud de la France pour devenir espion et aider la résistance au régime hitlérien, pendant que Patricia et sa mère **sont allées** aux États-Unis par sécurité. Patricia et sa mère **sont devenues** professeurs de philosophie et de droit, et le père **est sorti** des services secrets à la libération. Il **est venu** aux États-Unis et, tous les trois, ils **sont parvenus** à créer une fondation grâce à de généreuses donations. Maintenant, les parents de Patricia **sont morts**, mais elle **est rentrée** en Europe. Patricia, son mari Patrick et leurs enfants **sont revenus** à Antibes pour agrandir la fondation: ils luttent pour faire respecter les droits de l'homme dans le monde entier.

Reasons to Use Être

Since most verbs use **Avoir**, it is easier to understand why some need **Être**.

- Why do these verbs—reflexive/reciprocal and subject displacement—require **Être**?
- Do they have a common element that groups them in the **Être** category?

Rationale

Être expresses either a state/status of the subject or an action that affects its subject. **Être** implies an event that is personal, intimate.

What is the common point between the following?

> The cat is happy, the cat is on the table, and the cat is entering the house?

Happy, on the table, and entering, all reflect a condition.

- All states and events apply to the cat.
- The word cat is also the subject of the auxiliary *To be*.

Looking closely at the three categories of verbs that require **Être**, one can see a similar common factor.

Reflexive Pronoun: Boomerang Effect

A verb is used with a reflexive pronoun because the action performed by the subject comes back to this subject—like a boomerang:

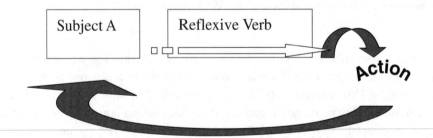

Je me lève: I get up = I pull myself out of my bed.

Tu te rases: You shave = Your own face ends up being shaved by you.

Elle se fiance à Marc: She gets engaged = she promises herself to Marc in marriage.

Elle se voit dans l'écran de son ordinateur: She sees herself in her monitor screen.

Reciprocal Pronoun: Mutual Effect

A verb is used with a reciprocal pronoun because the action performed by subject A toward subject B is also performed in return by subject B toward subject A. The reciprocity of the action made each person both the subject and the object of the same action.

(**Ma mère et moi**) Nous nous sommes rencontrées toutes les semaines.

My mother met me—she was the subject of the action *to meet*. I was its object.

But, at the same time, I met her—I was the subject of the action *to meet*. She was its object.

Angelina et Brigitte se sont saluées.

Angelina greeted Brigitte—she held out her hand. Brigitte was the object of the handshake.

At the same time, Brigitte shook Angelina's hand and she was also a subject.

Reciprocal ÊTRE

Action

Subject A
Object A

Subject B
Object B

Angelina A a serré la main de Brigitte B.
A Subject—B Object

Brigitte B a serré la main de Angelina A.
B Subject—A Object

Elles se sont saluées.
They greeted each other.

Angelina is both the subject and the object of the handshake.

> Brigitte is both the object and the subject of the handshake. *(They shake each other's hand.)*

As in the reflexive case, the action comes back, although indirectly via the other person, to the subject who performed it. The subject of the verb is also the object of the action.

Because **Être** expresses a status or a state of the subject, when the action is directed back to the person or thing that performs it, as in a U-turn, the auxiliary **Être** is necessary. The person or thing doing the action also receives it.

Change of Place: Displacing Effect

So why is **Être** also used to conjugate the **passé composé** of intransitive verbs of ~~motion~~, as they are wrongly known, **displacement** as they should be called?

- For the same reason: by this ~~motion~~ displacement, the subject does something to herself or himself and it ends up somewhere else, displaced.
- The subject is both performing and receiving the action.

> **Je suis entré.** I came in = I was out, I entered myself, and now I am inside.
>
> **Tu es allé à Nice.** You went to Nice = You were in Cannes, you went to Nice, and now find yourself in a different city.
>
> **Paul est monté dans sa chambre.** Paul went up to his bedroom = Paul was in the living room, he went up, his body is now upstairs at a different place.

Mélanie est devenue médecin. Mélanie became a doctor = Mélanie was a student, she graduated, and became an M.D. She is at a different place in her life.

In all these cases, the subject of the verb did something and ended up elsewhere.

Instead of motion, let's call these verbs *change of place of the subject* or *displacement* verbs. They all have one thing in common: after acting, the subject is relocated to another place—physical or social.

TIP BOX

Even if you forget the **Dr. P. & Mr. P. Vandertramp's** verbs memorizing tool, try to visualize the various changes in physical place, spatial situation, or social position generated by these verbs. When you need to conjugate a verb in a compound tense, put yourself in the shoes of the subject. If you end up at another place as a result of the action, you must use the auxiliary verb **Être**.

	REVIEW: DISPLACEMENT VERBS		
D	**D**escendre To go down		**Elle est descendue à ski de la montagne.** *(She was on the summit; she is in the valley.)*
R	**R**evenir To come back	Cannes . . . . Nice . . . .▶ ◀—————————— Cannes . . . . Nice	**Paul est revenu de Nice.** *(Paul was in Nice; he is back in Cannes.)*
P	**P**asser To pass by		**Patricia et sa mère sont passées par la Californie.** *(Patricia and her mother crossed California on their fund-raising trip around the USA.)*
M	**M**onter To go up		**Sylviane est montée sur une échelle.** *(Sylviane was on the ground; she is perched on the ladder.)*
R	**R**ester To remain		**Annie est restée pour lire.** *(Annie stayed home in order to read.)* 0 is a zero quantity. No change of place is a change = 0

P	Partir To leave	La Sorbonne	**François est parti à la fac à pied.** *(Francois was at his office; he left for the university.)*
V	Venir To come		**L'étoile est venue du ciel.** *(The star was in the sky; it is now on earth.)*
A	Aller To go		**Sylvia est allée à Paris en avion.** *(Sylvia lives in Nice; she flew to Paris.)*
N	Naître To be born		**Bébé Mélodie est née.** *(The baby was in the womb; she is now out in the world.)* Major change of place!
D	Devenir To become		**Dominique est devenue ingénieur le jour de la remise des diplômes.** *(Dominique was a student; she became an engineer.)* Change of place in society.
E	Entrer To come in		**Céline est entrée en chantant.** *(Celine was out; she is now inside the box.)*
R	Retourner To go back	Cannes . . . . Nice Cannes . . . . Nice Cannes . . . . Nice	**Nous sommes retournés à Nice.** **TIP** (Aller à—revenir de—retourner à) 　Retourner = Second trip to Nice Aller and Retourner go in the same direction! 　Retourner is a "faux-ami": it does not mean "to return" but "to go there again."

T	*T*omber To fall		**L'eau est tombée sur les fleurs de Megumi** *(Water was high in the watering can; it is falling down on the flowers.)*
R	*R*entrer To come back in		**Vous êtes rentrés tard du cinéma.** Entrer—sortir—rentrer *(You were home, went to the movies, and are coming back home.)*
A	*A*rriver To arrive		**Jean-Marc est arrivé à toute allure.** *(Jean-Marc was gone; he ran and arrived at home quickly.)*
M	*M*ourir To die		**La pilote est morte pour son pays.** *(She was in this world; she is now in another one.)*
P	*P*arvenir To reach		**Georgia et Michel sont parvenus ensemble au sommet de l'Everest.** *(They were in the valley and it was a hard climb, but they reached the summit.)*
S	*S*ortir To go out		**Marine est sortie du Lycée heureuse après la cérémonie.** *(Marine was in the high school; she is now outside.)*

TO BE OR NOT TO BE?	
After the action was performed, who was affected by it?	
The person/thing who performed the action	Someone/something different from who/what performed the action
Être	**Avoir**

When you need to conjugate the verb in the **passé composé** and do not remember which auxiliary verb to use—être or **avoir**—ask yourself this question:

"After the action is performed, who or what is affected by it?"

If the answer is: "The person or the thing who actually performed the action," then use **être**.

> **Elle est entrée dans mon bureau**—Displacement of the subject
>
> She came into my office: Who ended up in my room? She = the subject.
>
> **Ils se sont regardés tendrement**—Reciprocal action toward each subject
>
> They looked at each other tenderly: Who was affected by the look? They were = the subjects.
>
> **Je me suis maquillée**—Reflexive action toward the subject
>
> I put my makeup on: Who ended up with eye shadow and lipstick? I did = the subject.

When you ask yourself the question:

> **"After the action is performed, who or what is affected by it?"**

If the answer is "someone or something different from the subject," then use **avoir.**

Reasons to Use Avoir

Rationale

Avoir is used with all verbs, including both auxiliary verbs **Être** and **Avoir**, except the reflexive/reciprocal and displacement verbs, because in all other cases, the action affects an external object.

    Avoir implies a relationship of possession. A person or a thing possesses another person or thing. This relationship implies a separation between the subject of **avoir** and its object:

> J'**ai** quatre chattes, Tofa, Vanille, Fripouille and Cléa.
> The subject is separate.
> As much as I love them, "**I**" the subject is different from the cats.

Consequently, all verbs expressing an action performed by a subject that goes out to a separate object require **Avoir**.

> **TIP BOX**
> The Auxiliary Equation
> Who is affected by the action performed by the Subject? The Object
>
> If Object = Subject use Être
>
>   **If Object ≠ Subject use Avoir**

> ### IMPORTANT!
> The action of some verbs can be directed either back to the subject or toward an external object. Therefore, these verbs can be conjugated either with
>
> **Être**, if Subject = Object
>
> OR
>
> **Avoir**, if Subject ≠ Object

VERBS CONJUGATED WITH EITHER ÊTRE OR AVOIR: MONTER—LAVER— SORTIR (TO GO/TAKE UP—TO SHOWER/WASH—TO LEAVE/TAKE OUT)	
I can take **myself** and go up. Je **suis** montée.	I can bring **books** upstairs. **J'ai** monté les livres.
Paul can wash **himself**. Paul **s'**est lavé.	Paul can wash the **dishes**. Paul **a** lavé la vaiselle.
Marianne and Marina **can get** themselves out of the house. Marianne et Marina **sont** sorties.	Marianne and Marina can take their dress out of the closet. Marianne et Marina **ont** sorti leur robe du placard.

J'ai lavé ma voiture. What was affected by the washing? My car—the object of the action.

Tu as fini tes exercices. What was completed? My exercises—the object of the action.

Il a installé son logiciel. What was installed? The application—the object of the action.

Elle a aperçu l'oiseau-mouche. What was seen? The humming-bird—the object of the action.

Nous avons choisi le français. What was chosen? French—the object of the action.

Vous avez fait une tarte. What was baked? A pie—the object of the action.

Ils ont pu acheter la maison de leurs rêves. What was bought? The dream house.

All these objects that received the action are separate from the subjects that performed it.

Intermediate—Advanced Topic

Agreement of the Past Participle

Certain words like *articles* and *adjectives* are dependent on the noun they accompany. They therefore take on the same gender (feminine or masculine) and the same number (singular or plural) as the noun they qualify:

>   Les vagues sont bleues—feminine/plural *(The waves are blue.)*
>
>   Le ciel devient gris—masculine/singular *(The sky is turning gray.)*
>
>   Les grands oiseaux volent—masculine/plural *(The big birds fly.)*
>
>   Isolée, la barque disparaît à l'horizon—feminine/singular *(The isolated boat disappears in the horizon.)*

The reason for the agreement is that nouns, articles, and adjectives are logically very closely connected. Blue describes the waves, gray is the color to which the sky is changing, these birds are big, and there is only one lonely boat out there. All these elements belong to the same nominal group: article, adjective, and noun, and they need to match. They must get along, match, and agree with the dominant element: the noun.

TIP BOX

Think about fashion again. When you dress, one of the clothing pieces dictates what you are going to wear with it. If you are going to a prom, the color of your gown has to be matched by your jacket, or purse, or jewelry, and chances are you will not wear sneakers or slippers with it. It is the same thing for the nominal group; whatever gender and number the name "wears," the other elements around it must agree with it so they do not clash.

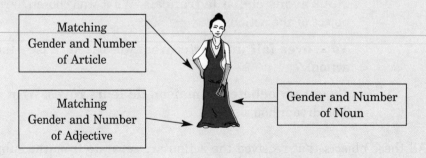

Rationale

Using the **participe passé** follows the same rule. Since the past participle describes an action applying to a noun, it will match this noun. The past participle and the object of the action expressed in the **passé composé** must agree because they are part of the same process. But we can only make the past participle match this noun if we know it and, consequently, can choose the harmonizing color for the **participe passé**.

Participes passés come in four colors: masculine-singular, **masculine-plural**, feminine-singular, or **feminine-plural**.

Unfortunately, we do not always know what was affected by the action, because we cannot necessarily see that noun in the sentences. The **participe passé** then remains as transparent as possible, that is, in the combination that is also neutral: masculine-singular.

Irrelevance of the Auxiliary Verb

Because the agreement of the past participle is the sign of the connection between the action and its object, the decision to make it agree does not depend upon which auxiliary verb is used. There can be agreement or nonagreement of the past participle whether the compound tense is formed with **être** or with **avoir**.

In the following two sentences, the adjective **bleues** and the past participle **tombées** function in the same way and both apply to the subject: waves.

> Les vagues sont bleu**es**. *(The waves are blue.)*
>
> Les vagues sont tomb**ées** sur le surfer. *(The waves have fallen on the surfer.)*

So it is seems logical that both adjective and participle have to agree.
But in the following sentences, the past participle used with **Être** does not agree with the subject:

> Elles se sont serr**é** la main. *(They shook hands.)*

while the one used with **Avoir** agrees with the complement of the direct object:

> Les fleurs que tu as achet**ées** sont magnifiques. *(The flowers you bought are splendid.)*

And that is not intuitive at all. So when does the **participe passé** need to agree?

Past Participle Agreement Rule
The "Official" Rule and Exceptions

The traditional official rule is something like this:

> The **past participle** *agrees with the* **subject** *when the* **passé composé** *is conjugated with* **Être.** *When the* **passé composé** *is conjugated with* **Avoir,** *the* **past participle** *agrees with the* **direct object complement** ***if*** *and only if the complement is situated* **before** *the past participle in the sentence.*

This rule has been given to generations of French and foreign students to memorize. It is quite difficult to remember and not completely true.

We can summarize it in the following table, which will make it somewhat easier. It will still not be exact, however.

THE TRADITIONAL BUT INCORRECT RULE OF THE AGREEMENT OF THE PAST PARTICIPLE	
Participe passé = p. p. COD = complément d'objet direct (direct object complement)	
Subject + Être in present + **p. p.**	**p.p.** agrees with **subject** = takes on the gender and number of the noun/subject of the verb
Ma soeur s'est lavéE sous la pluie. (*My sister washed herself in the rain.*) **Paul et Pierre se sont saluéS.** (*Paul and Pierre greeted each other.*) **Sophie est arrivéE** à huit heures. (*Sophie arrived at 8 o'clock.*) **Les enfants sont montéS** dans leur chambre. (*The children went up to their room.*)	
Subject + **Avoir** in present + <u>COD</u> + **p. p.** <u>Direct object</u>: before the participe passé	**p.p.** agrees with **COD** = takes on the gender and number of the noun/<u>direct object of the verb</u>
Les chocolats **que tu as achetéS** sont délicieux. (*The chocolates you bought are delicious.*) J'adore ces cerises, **je <u>les</u> ai mangéES** en classe. (*I love cherries. I ate them in class.*)	
Subject + **Avoir** in present + p. p. + <u>COD</u> <u>Direct object</u>: after the participe passé	p.p. does not agree with anything and remains neutral = masculine/singular
Tu as acheté des <u>chocolats</u> délicieux. (*You bought delicious chocolates.*) **Martine a adoré** mes <u>cerises</u> aussi. (*Martine loved my cherries too.*)	

But look at the sentence below; although the auxiliary verb is **être** and the subject is feminine plural, the past participle must be neuter = masculine singular. Why?

Elles se sont serré la main. (*They shook hands.*)

A simple answer is that **there are exceptions**. Not all past participles agree with the subject when conjugated with Être. In the following cases, the past participles remain neuter, in the masculine singular, although the subject is feminine singular, or masculine plural.

But that does not help you avoid making mistakes.

Moreover it is incorrect: Elles se sont serré la main is not an exception. It is a different type of sentence: Although the auxiliary verb must be used, the subject of the action is different from its object.

Flaw with this Rule

In fact, the traditional rule is wrong.

The agreement of the **Participe Passé** does not depend on **être** or **avoir** but on having enough information about the dress to match the shoes and the gloves.

Since the **Participe Passé** expresses an action or a state, we must know whom or what is affected. To know this, the **noun** directly affected by the action or represented by the state must be present in the sentence **before** we write the past participle so we have enough information about its color. Here are some examples:

> Ma soeur s'est [laver] les mains sous la pluie.

> Paul et Pierre se sont [envoyer] une lettre.

Agreement or not?

> **Ma soeur** s'est **lavé <u>les mains</u>** sous la pluie.

> **Paul et Pierre** se sont **envoyé <u>une lettre</u>.**

These verbs must be used with Être since they are reflexive/reciprocal verbs.

However, their action, in both cases, does not come back to the subject. It affects a <u>direct</u> object complement that is different from the subject:

> **Ma soeur** s'est **lavé** <u>les mains</u>: Subject ≠ <u>Object</u>

> Subject of the action = ma soeur

> <u>Direct object</u> of the action = <u>les mains</u>

Although the verb needs a reflexive pronoun (it concerns a body part), what is washed are the hands and not my sister as in:

> **Ma soeur** <u>s</u>'est **lavée**: Subject = Direct Object (**s'** = ma soeur)

Yet, if the direct object complement were a pronoun, it would be before the past participle:

> Ma soeur se <u>les</u> est **lavé<u>es</u>**: Subject ≠ Object

> Subject of the action = ma soeur

> <u>Direct Object</u> of the action = <u>les mains</u>

So the past participle would agree with the direct object.

In short, the agreement of the past participle depends on the position of the object that is directly affected by the action, not on the auxiliary verb.

IMPORTANT!

Remember that the <u>direct object complement</u> can appear under three forms:

1. The noun itself
2. A personal pronoun replacing it: le—la—les
3. A relative pronoun: que

   J'ai acheté <u>trois pommes</u>—Je <u>les</u> ai acheté<u>es</u>—Les pommes <u>que</u> j'ai acheté<u>es</u> sont vertes. Since pronouns are located before the verb in the sentence they generally trigger **the** agreement of the past participle. **Make sure to look for them in your sentences every time you have a compound tense.**

Refer to Chapter 8 for
Personal and Impersonal Pronouns
and Chapter 16 for
Relative Clauses

Claire et Sarah se sont [envoyer] une robe du soir.
Agreement or not?

> Claire et Sarah se sont **envoyé** <u>une robe du soir.</u>
>
> Subject of the action = Claire and Object = Sarah.
>
> Subject of the action = Sarah and Object = Claire.

The verb **Envoyer** is constructed with the preposition à, thus Claire and Sarah are replaced by the pronoun **se**, which is an object complement but INDIRECT.

   The DIRECT object complement is <u>une robe</u>. It is different from the subjects Claire and Sarah. And it comes <u>after</u> the past participle in the order of the sentence; when I had to write the past participle **envoyé**, I had no idea of the object sent. It could have been **des livres** masculine plural, or **des fleurs** feminine plural. I did not know the "color" so I could not match it with my outfit. I left the **participe passé** in a neutral color: the neuter form of the masculine singular so that it does not clash with anything: Claire et Sarah se sont envoyé /<u>une robe du soir.</u>

New and Improved: The Fault-Proof Rule with No Exceptions

Summary of Agreement Assumptions

In order to decide the agreement, regardless of the auxiliary verb, you need to consider the following logical elements:

- The past participle expresses the action performed by a subject on an <u>object.</u>
- This action expressed by the past participle affects the <u>object.</u>
- It makes sense to think that the past participle should then match this <u>object</u> it directly affects.

- To agree with a noun/<u>direct object</u> we need to know its gender and number (so the past participle can match them).
- The noun/<u>object</u> can be either the subject performing the action (if it comes back to it) or something different (if it is external to the subject).

Conclusion

What is the element common in all these statements? The <u>direct object</u>.

> *For a definition of direct vs. indirect object complement refer to Chapter 5,* **Functions of Nouns**

So let's modify the old rule:

> ***Old Rule:*** *The past participle agrees with the subject when the passé composé is conjugated with Être. When the passé composé is conjugated with **avoir**, the past participle agrees with the direct object complement if and only if the complement is situated before the past participle in the sentence.*

The Golden Rule of the Agreement of the Past Participle

> Regardless of the **auxiliary** verb, the past participle agrees with the **object** that is **directly affected** by the action. But to make it match, this noun/direct object must appear in the sentence **before** the past participle so you know its **gender and number**. **Then the past participle can and must be harmonized with the direct object.**
>
> If the **noun/direct object** has **not** appeared **before** the past participle, there is **no way** of knowing which gender and number to give the past participle. So the **participe passé** must stay in its most neutral form: the masculine singular. It remains as transparent as possible so as not to clash with any color that the upcoming object may have.

TIP BOX

An easier way of remembering the rule: One cannot affect the past participle retroactively. If the direct object shows up in the sentence once the past participle has already been written, too bad! The direct object should have come earlier if it was to have an influence on the past participle. At this point it's too late—the past participle is already written in the neutral form and it stays that way.

Example:

J'ai mang**é**.......... ???

Mangé affects something but . . . What??? It could be

    . . . des cerises—feminine plural
    . . . un éclair au chocolat—masculine singular
    . . . des bonbons—masculine plural
    . . . une glace à la vanille—feminine singular

You may know what you ate, but the words in the sentence cannot read your mind. If you cannot see what has been eaten when you write **mangé**, too bad—leave the past participle as is, neuter in the original masculine singular form you learned.

The Tip

Before actually writing the past participle in your sentence and adding the feminine/masculine and singular/plural markers or not, ask yourself this simple question: "Where is the direct object?"

    Picture yourself walking along the words of your sentence and getting to the **participe passé**. Stop, turn around, and look back to the beginning of the sentence/path. Do you see a direct object complement?

- If you can find a direct object in your partial sentence, apply its gender and number to the past participle when you get to it.

Les fleurs que j'ai (STOP) acheté? achetés? achetées? sont belles.

bought what? que = the flowers = direct object complement feminine plural: achet**éES**

- If you cannot see anything that is directly affected by the action you want to put in the **participe passé**, do not touch it; keep running and pass by it. The past participle will stay in the neuter gender: masculine singular.

J'ai (STOP) acheté? achetés? achetées? des fleurs magnifiques ce matin

bought what? I cannot see what I bought before writing the past participle so I bypass it: acheté.

> **Note** Never modify the past participle if you do not have sufficient elements to do so; you need a written proof of the gender and number of the directly affected object.

REVIEW TABLE: PAST PARTICIPLE WITH A DIRECT OBJECT COMPLEMENT: ALL POSSIBLE CONTEXTS		
Être + Reflexive verb	Sophie s'est / maquillée. Object directly affected = s(e) = Sophie = feminine/singular	Where is the direct object? Before the past participle in the order of the sentence: maquillé + **e**
	Sophie s'est maquillé / les yeux. Object directly affected = les yeux— masculine/plural but Too Late!	Where is the direct object? After the past participle in the order of the sentence. past participle unchanged: maquill**é**
	Sophie s'est écrit / une lettre. S(e) is an indirect object: écrire à Object directly affected = une lettre— feminine singular but Too Late!	Where is the direct object? After the past participle in the order of the sentence. Past participle unchanged: écri**t**
Être + Reciprocal verb	Sophie et Éliane se sont / maquillées. Object directly affected = se = Sophie et Éliane—feminine plural	Where is the direct object? Before the past participle in the order of the sentence: maquillé + **e** + **s**
	Sophie et Éliane se sont maquillé / les paupières. Object directly affected = les paupières— feminine plural but Too Late!	Where is the direct object? After the past participle in the order of the sentence. Past participle unchanged: maquill**é**
Être + Change of place of the Subject	Sophie et Éliane sont montées au studio. Object directly affected = Subject = Sophie et Éliane—feminine plural (who ends up upstairs?)	Where is the direct object? It is implied but equal to the subject. Before the past participle in the order of the sentence: monté + **e** + **s**
Avoir + COD After PP	Ton frère **a monté** / les boites au grenier. Object directly affected = les boites— feminine plural but Too Late!	Where is the direct object? After the past participle in the order of the sentence. Past participle unchanged: mont**é**
Avoir + COD Before PP	Ton frère les **a montées.** Object directly affected = les = les boites—feminine plural	Where is the direct object? Before the past participle in the order of the sentence: monté + **e** + **s**
	Les boites que ton frère **a montées** sont au grenier. Object directly affected = que = les boites—feminine plural	Where is the direct object? Before the past participle in the order of the sentence: monté + **e** + **s**

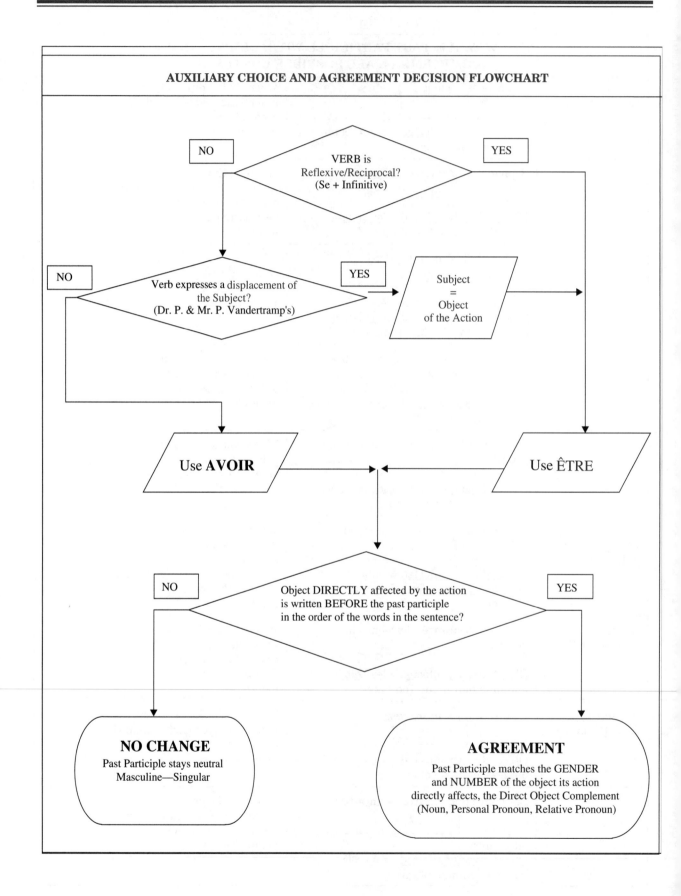

AUXILIARY CHOICE AND AGREEMENT DECISION FLOWCHART

NO

YES

VERB is
Reflexive/Reciprocal?
(Se + Infinitive)

NO

YES

Verb expresses a displacement of
the Subject?
(Dr. P. & Mr. P. Vandertramp's)

Subject
=
Object
of the Action

Use **AVOIR**

Use ÊTRE

NO

YES

Object DIRECTLY affected by the action
is written BEFORE the past participle
in the order of the words in the sentence?

NO CHANGE

Past Participle stays neutral
Masculine—Singular

AGREEMENT

Past Participle matches the GENDER
and NUMBER of the object its action
directly affects, the Direct Object Complement
(Noun, Personal Pronoun, Relative Pronoun)

Practice What You Learned

Exercises are rated according to four levels of difficulty:

- Beginner easy [*]
- Beginner challenging [**]
- Intermediate [***]
- Advanced [****]

1. Write sentences in the **passé composé** with **avoir** according to the following model. Change the subject every time and add some relevant information. [**]

> acheter du pain—hier: Hier, j'ai acheté du pain à la boulangerie.

A. retirer de l'argent—ce matin: _____.

B. téléphoner à une copine—hier soir: _____.

C. manger une tarte—cet après-midi: _____.

D. avoir une panne de voiture—la semaine dernière: _____.

E. finir vos exercices—déjà!: _____.

F. tourner un film—l'été passé: _____.

2. Write sentences in the **passé composé** with **être** according to the following model. Change the subject every time and add some relevant information. Make the necessary agreements. [**]

Example:

> Partir—à 6h: ils sont partis à 6h.

A. arriver en retard—hier: _____.

B. se lever tôt—ce matin: _____.

C. aller en boîte—hier soir: _____.

D. sortir à 16 heures—cet après-midi: _____.

E. devenir parents—la semaine dernière: _____.

F. passer devant cet immeuble trois fois—déjà!: _____.

G. se marier—l'été passé: _____.

3. Write sentences in the **passé composé** with **avoir** or **être** according to the verb. Explain why you chose **être** and make the necessary agreements. [***]

Example:

> Le président meurt dans son lit. Le Président **est mort** dans son lit.
> (Displacement)

A. Je cours sous la pluie. _____.

B. Nous inventons un programme de fitness. _____.

C. Elles montent dans un taxi. _____.

D. Tu te dépêches de rentrer. _____.

E. Vous entrez sur la scène. _____.

F. Sissi casse le vase de Soisson. _____.

G. Cet homme tombe amoureux fou. _____.

H. Tu attends l'autobus. _____.

I. Isabelle et Nicolas se saluent. _____.

J. Ils prennent un café au lait. _____.

K. Les touristes partent enfin. _____.

4. Complete the sentences with the **passé composé** of the pronominal verbs. Indicate all possible agreements. [***]

Example:

> Votre femme et vous (se lever) très tard.
>
> **Votre femme et vous <u>vous</u> êtes levés très tard.**

A. Vous (s'habiller) en tenue de soirée. — _____.

B. Mes collegues (se mettre) au travail. — _____.

C. Ta fille (s'amuser) pour son anniversaire. — _____.

D. Nous (se promener) sur le sable — _____.

E. Elles (se perdre) dans cette grande ville. — _____.

5. Complete the sentences with **être** or **avoir**. [**]

A. Les techniciens _____ démonté la machine.

B. Ils _____ allés vérifier l'alimentation.

C. Ils _____ passé deux heures à la cave.

D. Je _____ posé beaucoup de questions.

E. Un ingénieur _____ expliqué la panne.

F. Nous _____ écouté et nous _____ allés acheter la pièce de rechange.

G. Ces gens _____ enfin partis et le calme _____ revenu.

6. Underline the direct object of the action and decide to make the agreement or not in the following **passés composés** with **être**. [**]

A. Karine (se lever) _____ à huit heures.

B. Elle (se faire) _____ un café.

C. Elle (se dépêcher) _____ de s'habiller.

D. Elle (se maquiller) _____ les yeux en bleus et elle (se brosser) _____ .

E. Quand elle (se regarder) _____ dans la glace, elle (se rendre) _____ compte qu'elle ne (se plaire) pas _____ dans cette couleur de Tee-shirt.

F. Elle (se changer) _____ et (s'ajouter) _____ du rouge à lèvres.

7. Conjugate all the missing verbs in the **passé composé**. Underline the direct object of the action if it triggers the agreement of the past participle. [****]

La semaine dernière, mes amies et moi, nous (aller) _____ faire un pique-nique et nous (apporter) _____ des sandwichs. Nous les (manger) _____ rapidement parce que les fourmis nous (trouver) _____ et elles (partir) _____ à l'attaque de nos paniers. Felicia (jouer) _____ de la guitare et (chanter) _____ les chansons qu'elle (apprendre) _____ en Espagne. Nous (rencontrer) _____ un groupe de garçons qui (passer) _____ près de nous. Ils (se promener) _____ dans la forêt et (ramasser) _____ des champignons. Mais ceux qu'ils (trouver) _____ étaient vénéneux alors nous les (jeter) _____ . Deux mecs sympas (rester) _____ pour nous aider à tout ranger. Ils nous (proposer) _____ de les revoir. Nous (prendre) _____ rendez-vous pour la semaine prochaine. On (se séparer) _____ sur le parking et je (penser) _____ qu'on (passer) _____ une excellente journée. Nous (s'amuser) _____ tous et toutes comme des fous!

8. In the following article about a tragic "Fait Divers" identify the **passé composé** and the **imparfait** verbs and explain why they are conjugated in this tense. [***]

Example:	**a tué**: passé composé, single event, rapid action that is over now and not ongoing in the present, interrupts the normal life.
"Malade, ma nièce a tué son fils qu'elle adorait" Ma nièce est dans une situation épouvantable. Elle est en prison pour avoir tué son fils. Un enfant qu'elle adorait. Ma nièce était en instance de divorce, accablée par les dettes et sa maladie, une sclérose en plaques. Le jour où le drame a eu lieu, elle n'était pas elle-même. Elle avait mélangé médicaments et alcool et son cerveau a disjoncté. Elle s'était enfermée dans sa maison avec ses enfants, sa fille a pu s'échapper pour demander de l'aide, car elle voyait que sa mère n'était pas comme d'habitude. Quand elle s'est retrouvée en garde à vue, elle se demandait ce qu'elle faisait là. Les gendarmes lui ont expliqué les faits, et elle s'est effondrée. Si je vous écris, c'est parce que ma nièce se laisse mourir. La seule raison de se battre serait qu'elle puisse voir sa fille plus souvent, mais je ne sais pas comment faire. On ne peut pas s'imaginer ce que c'est la prison. On est coupé du monde. Alors, si des personnes ont vécu une telle atrocité ou ont souffert d'avoir perdu un enfant, qu'ils lui écrivent pour la réconforter. Bien amicalement. **André, réf. 951.02**	

Chapter 13

INDICATIVE MOOD PAST AND FUTURE TENSES: IMPERFECT—PLUPERFECT / FUTURE—FUTURE PERFECT

Introduction

The **imparfait** and **plus-que-parfait** are on one (past) side of the present moment. The **futur** and **futur antérieur** are on the other (future) side. They are however, similar in two ways: how they are organized in regard to the present and how they are formed.

Key Aspects of Past and Future Indicative Tenses

Simple vs. Compound: Common Points

A **tense (the simple one)** is used to form the other one (the compound tense).

Auxiliary in the Im**parfait**	+	Participe Passé	=	Plus-que-**Parfait**
Auxiliary in the **Futur**				**Futur** Antérieur

A tense (the compound one) is used for actions that took place before the other **one (the simple tense)**.

ORDER OF EVENTS	
#1	**#2**
Plus-que-Parfait	**Imparfait**
Futur Antérieur	**Futur**

Chronological Order

- **Imparfait** and **Futur** are simple tenses. Chronologically, they happen **after** the compound tenses they form with the **Participe Passé**: the Plus-que-Parfait and the Futur Antérieur.
- The Plus-que-Parfait represents, therefore, an action that has taken place in the past of an already past action. It takes the subject of the action back *twice*.
- The futur antérieur also represents an action that has happened in the past but of a future action.

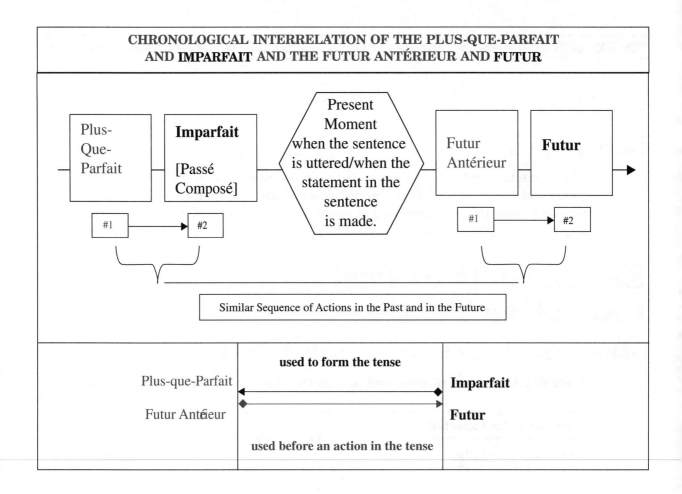

CHRONOLOGICAL INTERRELATION OF THE PLUS-QUE-PARFAIT AND IMPARFAIT AND THE FUTUR ANTÉRIEUR AND FUTUR

Plus-Que-Parfait — Imparfait [Passé Composé] — Present Moment when the sentence is uttered/when the statement in the sentence is made. — Futur Antérieur — Futur

#1 → #2

#1 → #2

Similar Sequence of Actions in the Past and in the Future

	used to form the tense	
Plus-que-Parfait	←	Imparfait
Futur Antérieur	→	Futur
	used before an action in the tense	

The Imperfect of the Indicative

- The **imparfait** is very common, in both everyday and literary or elevated language. It can describe a past action that is either close to the present or very remote.

Use of the *Imparfait*

Type of Action in the Imparfait

Context

As a general rule, the **imparfait** does not specify the beginning or the end of an action; it is used to describe the circumstances surrounding an action. There is no exact equivalent in English; the **imparfait** is translated in different ways.

Time is not a criterion either in choosing to use the **imparfait** instead of the **passé composé**. As in the case of the **passé composé**, what matters are the characteristics of the action. An **imparfait** action can have one or any combination of the following aspects.

Open-Ended Action

If you use the **imparfait**, you communicate two sorts of information:

1. The action happened in the past, but
2. This action may also still be happening in the present.

What you are considering is the past of the event but, contrary to the **passé composé**, the **imparfait** does not exclude the possibility for this action to be continuing in the present. We know that it happened in the past, which is what matters.

> Quand j'**étais** jeune, je **faisais** de la danse. *I was dancing when I was young*: Perhaps I am no longer dancing; perhaps I am. The point is, what matters is that I was dancing then.

Extension in Time

- The **imparfait** describes an action in its extension. Contrary to the **passé composé**, it is not a point in time. The action is not necessarily long by itself but conjugating the verb in the **imparfait** forces one to focus on the unfolding of the event. The impression conveyed by the **imparfait** is that the event stretched in time:

> Pour mes versions latines, je **travaillais** pendant des heures. *(I was working for hours to do my Latin translations.)*

> Tess **regardait** toujours la télé, l'air hébété et les yeux grand ouverts. *(Tess would always look at the TV, looking puzzled and with her eyes wide open.)*

- Because it conveys a sense of duration, the **imparfait** is often used in descriptions of circumstances surrounding events, places, moments, emotions:

> Le ciel **était** d'un bleu intense et les rares nuages qui se **promenaient** lentement **ressemblaient** à des barbes-à-papa, ces grosses boules de coton sucré. Le vert tendre de la colline **ajoutait** à la

douceur de sa vision. Il **était** encore tôt mais les cigales **s'affairaient** et leur crissement lancinant **hypnotisait** Solange. Le soleil écrasait déjà les rangs violets des lavandes en fleurs. Elle se **sentait** bien. Il n'y **avait** rien de mieux que passer son été en Provence. *(The sky was intensely blue and the rare clouds that were walking along it looked like big round puffs of sweet cotton candy. The tender green of the hillside made this even softer to the sight. It was very early still but the cicadas were busy and their insistent songs were slowly hypnotizing Solange. The sun was already smashing down the purple rows of blooming lavender. She felt at ease. There was nothing better than spending one's summer in Provence.)*

Segment in Time

Since the **imparfait** extends in time and presents the event as lasting, even for a little while, it is always long enough to be interrupted by another action. The interrupting action is conjugated in the **passé composé**:

> Jennifer **faisait** du jogging quand l'orage <u>a commencé</u>. *(Jennifer was jogging when the rain started.)*

> Son ami <u>est arrivé</u> en retard comme Pierre le **pensait**. *(His friend arrived late, as Pierre thought he would.)*

 Which English verb form is used to convey such a sense of extension in time?

_____ See the answer at the end of this section (page 239)

Habitual or Repetitive Action

If the action was regular, planned, or habitual, it must be conjugated in the **imparfait**. Anytime you can think of the action in terms of "used to," use the **imparfait**:

> *Refer to the table*
> **Comparative Description of Actions in the Imparfait and the Passé Composé**
> *in Chapter 12.*

Tous les matins, mon père m'**apportait** une tasse de café pour me réveiller. *(Every morning, my father would bring me a cup of coffee to wake me up.)*

Il y **avait** toujours des roses rouges dans ce jardin. *(There always were red roses in this garden.)*

James n'**était** heureux que sur une planche de surf. *(James was happy only when he was on a surfboard.)*

Special Uses of the Imparfait

Depuis, depuis que, il y a (Adverbs of Time)

The very common adverbs of time, *for* and *since*, are translated in French by **depuis**, **depuis que**, or **il y a**. In English, they are followed by a pluperfect that can also be continuous—pluperfect of the auxiliary + gerund of the verb (verb + -ing). In French, the equivalent adverbs are used with the **imparfait**.

For—Since—**Pluperfect**	Depuis—Il y a—**Imparfait**
I **had been waiting for** two hours when you finally arrived.	**J'attendais depuis** deux heures quand tu es finalement arrivé.
I **had known** him **for** three years.	**Il y avait** trois ans que je le **connaissais.**
Henri **had been** a lot happier **since** his promotion.	Henri **était** beaucoup plus heureux **depuis** sa promotion.
Marie **had not seen** her friend **since** Sylvie had started working nights.	Marie ne **voyait** plus son amie **depuis que** Sylvie travaillait la nuit.

Aller + infinitive – *venir DE* + infinitive (near Future and Recent Past in the Past)

The **Futur Proche** and **Passé Immédiat** concepts that were presented as a particular use of the **Present Indicative** also apply to past actions. **Aller** and **venir** are simply conjugated in the **imparfait** to indicate something one was about to do or had just done.

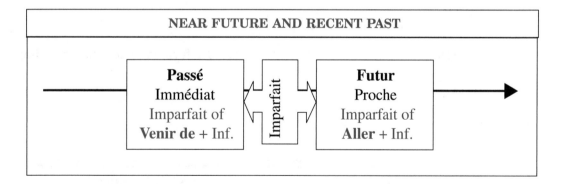

Je **venais** de rentrer. *(I had just come home.)*

Tu **allais** partir. *(You were going to leave.)*

Near Future in the Past

The near future (formed by combining the verb **aller** and the infinitive of the action just about to be performed) is conjugated in the **Imparfait** in French, while it is in the continuous past or marked by "about" in English.

> Françoise **allait** rentrer. *(Françoise was going / about to come home.)*

Immediate Past of a Past Action

The recent past (formed by combining the verb **venir de** and the infinitive of the action just performed) is conjugated in the **imparfait** in French, while it is in the **perfect** in English.

> Françoise **venait de** déménager. *(Françoise had just moved.)*

Cause or Condition

The **imparfait** is the tense used to express the condition of another action. When action B depends on an action A being performed, and that action is possible, action A follows the <u>condition marker</u> SI and is conjugated in the **imparfait**.

<table>
<tr>
<td>

Refer to Chapter 17 for
the **Conditional Mood**

</td>
<td>

<u>Si</u> tu **venais** ce soir, on pourrait réviser l'examen ensemble. *(If you came tonight, we could review for the exam together.)*

</td>
</tr>
</table>

<u>Si</u> j'**avais** une maison avec un grand jardin, j'aurais beaucoup d'animaux: un mouton, deux chiens, trois lapins, quatre alpacas, cinq canards et six chats de plus! *(If I had a house with a big garden, I would have a lot of animals: a sheep, two dogs, three rabbits, four alpacas, five ducks, and six more cats!)*

Formation of the *Imparfait*

The **Imparfait** is a simple tense. It is therefore formed by adding an ending to the basic stem of the verb.

Endings

> **NOTE** When conjugating a verb in a simple tense:
>
> - the stem **of the verb conveys the** meaning **of the** action;
> - the **ending of the verb indicates the person, the tense, and the mood of the conjugation.**

The **Imparfait** endings sound and look like the tense itself.

TIP BOX—Imparfait Endings

IMPARFAIT	
	AIS
	AIS
IMPARF-	AIT
	IONS
	IEZ
	AIENT

FORMATION OF THE IMPARFAIT OF REGULAR VERBS

1st Group -ER	2nd Group -IR	3rd Group -RE
Stem = 1st person plural of the Indicative Present minus the "nous" ending: -ons **Endings = ais, ais, ait, ions, iez, aient**		
Stem Présent: Nous portons -ons **port** + -ending	Stem Présent: Nous finissons -ons **finiss** + -ending	Stem Présent: Nous vendons -ons **vend** + -ending
Je port -ais Tu commenç -ais* Il—Elle—On mange -ait* Nous dans -ions Vous chant -iez Elles—Ils arriv -aient	Je finiss -ais Tu finiss -ais Il—Elle—On finiss -ait Nous finiss -ions Vous finiss -iez Elles—Ils finiss -aient	Je vend -ais Tu vend -ais Il—Elle—On vend -ait Nous vend -ions Vous vend -iez Elles—Ils vend -aient

*NOTE Verbs ending in **-ger** (manger) and **-cer** (commencer) are modified when the first letter of the ending is an **a** or an **o**.

- -ger verbs keep the e in front of **ons, ais, ait, aient**, etc.
- -cer verbs have a cedilla: ç, added to the c.

The point is to keep the soft c [s] or g [ʒ] sound so this change is valid in all tenses.

Je mange: Nous mangeons, Il mangeait—Je commence: Tu commençais

Irregular Verb Stems

A verb is irregular because:

- it is not possible to guess its stem (the part to which the ending is added) by simply removing the infinitive marker: stem of devoir: ~~dev-oir~~

    devoir: je dois (~~je dev xxx~~)

    connaître: je connaissais (~~je connaît ais~~)

- it is not possible to predict its endings:

    devoir: il dOIT

    vouloir: il vEUT

    falloir: il fAUT

- it may have both irregular and **regular** stems, irregular and **regular** endings

    devoir: je dOIS—nous **devONS**

IMPORTANT IRREGULAR VERBS IN THE IMPARFAIT OF THE INDICATIVE						
Infinitive Stem	JE	TU	IL	NOUS	VOUS	ILS/ELLES
	Endings					
Aller	allais	allais	allait	allions	alliez	allaient
Avoir	avais	avais	avait	avions	aviez	avaient
Connaître	connaissais	connaissais	connaissait	connaissions	connaissiez	connaissaient
Croire	croyais	croyais	croyait	croyions	croyiez	croyaient
Devoir	devais	devais	devait	devions	deviez	devaient
Dire	disais	disais	disait	disions	disiez	disaient
Écrire	écrivais	écrivais	écrivaient	écrivions	écriviez	écrivaient
Être	étais	étais	était	étions	étiez	étaient
Faire	faisais	faisais	faisait	faisions	faisiez	faisaient
Lire	lisais	lisais	lisait	lisions	lisiez	lisaient
Mettre	mettais	mettais	mettait	mettions	mettiez	mettaient
Partir	partais	partais	partait	partions	partiez	partaient
Pouvoir	pouvais	pouvais	pouvait	pouvions	pouviez	pouvaient
Prendre	prenais	prenais	prenait	prenions	preniez	prenaient
Savoir	savais	savais	savait	savions	saviez	savaient
Tenir	tenais	tenais	tenait	tenions	teniez	tenaient
Venir	venais	venais	venait	venions	veniez	venaient
Vouloir	voulais	voulais	voulait	voulions	vouliez	voulaient

Which English verb form is used to convey a sense of extension in time?
The gerund: auxiliary verb **to be** conjugated + verb stem -ing.

> Jennifer **was jogging** when the storm started.

> His friend was late as **he was thinking** [he would be.]

 Intermediate–Advanced Topic

The *Plus-que-Parfait* of the Indicative

Use of the *Plus-que-Parfait*

The **plus-que-parfait**, as its name indicates is more than perfect, more than finished, further in the *past than past*. The pluperfect action is in the **past** of a **past** action. On the time line, the **plus-que-parfait** makes you jump **backward twice.**

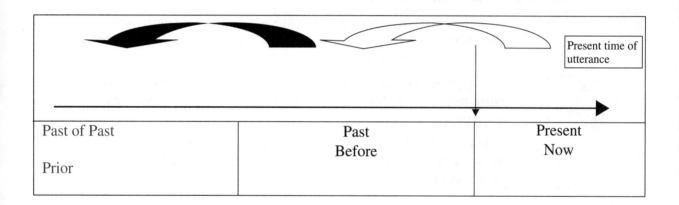

Past of Past Prior	Past Before	Present Now

Present time of utterance

Type of Action in the Plus-que-Parfait

Double Removal from the Present

The **Plus-que-Parfait** is the exact equivalent of the English *Pluperfect*. It is used to describe actions that are doubly removed from the present because they precede an already past action. **Plus-que-Parfait** means more than perfect, not ideal or godly, but more than complete, "super" finished. The pluperfect action was finished before an action that is finished did even start.

CHRONOLOGICAL ORDER OF THE PLUS-QUE-PARFAIT

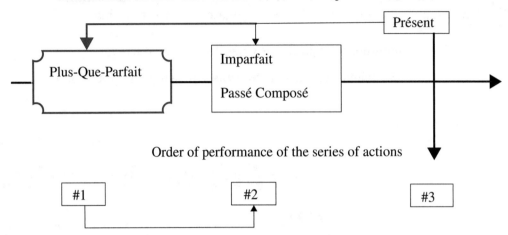

Precedence in the Past

The **Plus-que-Parfait** is therefore used when two past actions are described and one is *anterior* to the other. It indicates the first of a sequential series of events in the past. These events can be in the **imparfait**, in the **passé composé** as well as in the **plus-que-parfait** itself.

> [plus-que-parfait] J'**avais détesté** le film que **tu regardais** [imparfait] avec tant de plaisir. *(I had hated the movie you were watching with so much pleasure.)*

> [plus-que-parfait] J'**avais détesté** le film qui **a gagné** [passé composé] l'Oscar hier soir. *(I had hated the movie that won the Oscar last night.)*

> [plus-que-parfait] J'**avais détesté** le film qui **avait lancé** [plus-que-parfait] cette actrice. *(I had hated the movie that had launched that actress.)*

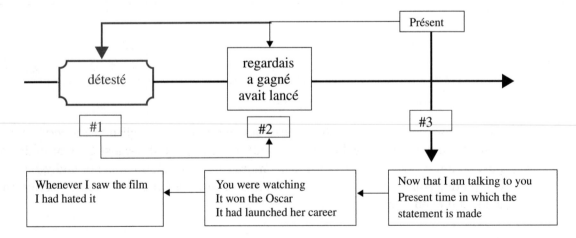

> À ton mariage samedi dernier, j'**ai** enfin **porté** cette robe que j'**avais achetée** à Paris il y a deux ans mais que je n'**avais** jamais **mise** avant! *(For your wedding last Friday, I finally wore this dress that I had bought in Paris two years ago but had never worn before!)*

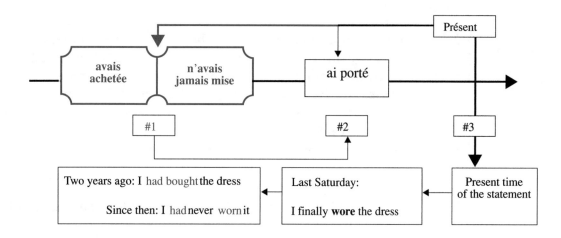

Displacement of Sequence of Action

The Plus-que-parfait is also used when a combination of present and past actions is displaced further into the past. If you slide a sequence of actions toward the past, along the time line, the present action is put in the past (**passé composé** or **imparfait**) and what was the previous action is put in the plus-que-parfait. The same time gap between the two actions is therefore maintained; it is simply displaced in the past.

> Maintenant il sait que tu as téléphoné. (*Now he knows you (have) called.*)
>
> Hier il savait que tu **avais téléphoné**. (*Yesterday, he knew you had called.*)

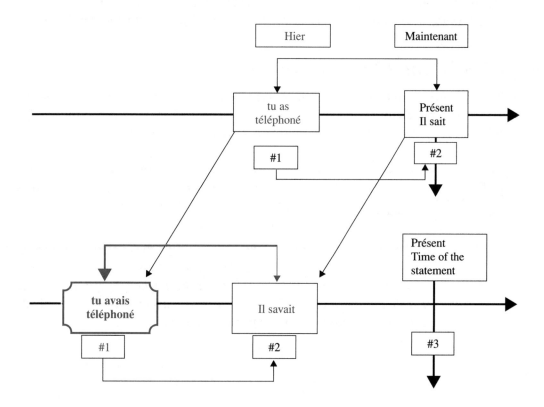

> **NOTE** Conjugation changes due to the displacement of the point of reference along the time line are part of a series of rules called **Concordance des Temps** (correspondence between tenses.)
>
> These rules are beyond the scope of this book but you can intuitively apply many of them by representing the various actions in your sentence on a time line.

[Aujourd'hui] **Je dis que tu as écouté CD que tu** as acheté hier.

HIER tu as écouté tu as acheté	AUJOURD'HUI je dis

AVANT-HIER tu avais écouté	**HIER** je disais

[Hier] **Je disais que tu** avais écouté **le CD que tu** avais acheté avant-hier.

(Today) I say you listened to the CD you bought yesterday.
Je dis que tu as écouté le CD que tu as acheté hier.
(Yesterday) **Je disais que tu avais écouté le CD que tu avais acheté avant-hier**.
I was saying that you had listened to the CD you had bought the day before.

Special Use of the Plus-que-Parfait

The **plus-que parfait** is also a tense used to express the condition of another action. When action B depends on action A being performed, but action A has not taken place, action A follows the condition marker SI and is conjugated in the **plus-que-parfait**.

> *Refer to Chapter 17 for* the **Conditional Mood**

Si tu **étais venu** ce soir, on aurait pu réviser l'examen ensemble. (*If you had come by tonight, we could have reviewed for the exam together. But you did not come, so we did not do it.*)

Si j'**avais eu** une maison avec un grand jardin, j'aurais eu beaucoup d'animaux: un mouton, deux chiens, trois lapins, quatre alpacas, cinq canards et six chats de plus! (*If I had had a house with a big backyard, I would have had a lot of animals. But I never was able to afford such a house, so I never had my personal zoo.*)

Formation of the *Plus-que-Parfait*

As all compound tenses, the **plus-que-parfait** is formed by conjugating the auxiliary verbs **être** or **avoir** and combining them with the **Participe Passé** of the verb to put it in the **plus-que-parfait**. It is composed of

- The auxiliary verb, conjugated in a **past** tense: the **imparfait**,
- The **past** participle.

This makes the result a **double past** and therefore corresponds to the **plus-que-parfait** being twice removed from the present.

Indicatif Imparfait (Past)		Past participle (Past)	Plus-que-Parfait (More Past than Past)
Être	J'étais Tu étais Elle, il, on était Nous étions Vous étiez Ils, elles étaient	**Participe Passé*** = p.p. . . . + é . . . + i . . . + u . . . + p.p. of irregular verb**	J'étais **née** Tu étais **allé** Elle était **arrivée** Nous nous étions **lavés** Vous vous étiez **téléphoné** Ils étaient **partis**
Avoir	J'avais Tu avais Elle, il, on avait Nous avions Vous aviez Ils, elles avaient	*May or may not agree **Must be learned for each verb	J'avais **travaillé** Tu avais **peint** Il avait **appris** Nous avions **fini** Vous aviez **rêvé** Elles avaient **couru**

> *Refer to Chapter 12 for the* **passé composé and agreement of past participle.**

J'**étais** déjà **arrivée** quand le tremblement de terre a commencé. *(I had already arrived when the earthquake started.)*

Tu **avais compris** que la situation <u>allait</u> être delicate. *(You had understood that the situation was going to be delicate.)*

Elle s'**était habillée** avant de se maquiller. *(She had dressed before putting on her makeup.)*

Nous **avions entendu** dire que les Ragdolls <u>étaient</u> des chats adorables. *(We had heard that Ragdolls were adorable cats.)*

Vous **aviez couru** pour ne pas manquer le début du film. *(You had run so as not to miss the beginning if the movie.)*

Ils **avaient déclaré** que la guerre ne <u>devait</u> pas avoir lieu. *(They had declared that the war should not happen.)*

> **NOTE** It is not necessary to have both past actions represented in the sentence. The **plus-que-parfait** can be used by itself when the context implies the second point of reference in the past.
>
> **J'y avais déjà pensé.** (I had already thought about that (implied: when you mentioned it).)

The *Futur* of the Indicative

The **Futur** is also called the **Futur Simple** because it is one of the simple tenses of the **Indicative** mood, along with the **Présent** and the **Imparfait**.

Use of the *Futur*

Types of Action in the Future

Posteriority of the Action

As in English, the **Futur** represents an event happening after or beyond the time when the statement in the sentence is made.

Patricia partira demain. *(Patricia will leave tomorrow: after I am saying this.)*

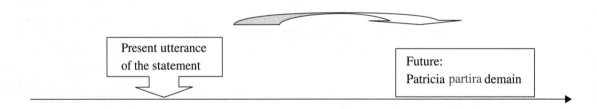

The **Futur** indicates an action that will happen after it is mentioned, but it can be used regardless of the amount of time that *separates* it from the time the sentence is uttered.

Le monde finira demain. Le monde finira dans cent mille ans. Le monde ne finira jamais. *(The world will end tomorrow. The world will end in one hundred thousand years. The world will never end.)*

Perceived Future

But the **Futur** can be replaced by the **near future** (**aller** conjugated in the present and the infinitive of the future action) if one wants to psychologically reduce or even try to deny the distance in time:

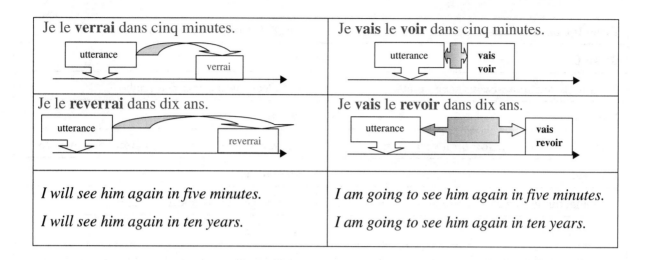

Je le **verrai** dans cinq minutes.	Je **vais** le **voir** dans cinq minutes.
Je le **reverrai** dans dix ans.	Je **vais** le **revoir** dans dix ans.
I will see him again in five minutes. *I will see him again in ten years.*	*I am going to see him again in five minutes.* *I am going to see him again in ten years.*

Special Uses of the Future

Quand, lorsque, dès que, aussitôt que, tant que, pendant que (Conjunctions of Time)

Since French conjugations are as strict a representation of reality as possible, the **Futur** is used for events that will happen *beyond* the time they are being stated in the sentence. For a very mysterious reason that puzzles French students of English, some English conjunctions are followed by the present even though the action they introduce is in the future. Sentences like: "He will retire when he **is** seventy, in 2053" make no sense for the French at all: retiring is fifty years ahead in the future yet the verb is in the present! There is no such time warp possible in French; the conjugations convey the exact time logic of the situation.

French Conjunctions + Future	English Conjunctions + Present
Quand	**When**
Nous partirons **quand** vous **serez** prêts.	We'll leave **when** you **are** ready.
Lorsque	**When**
Il veut être professeur **lorsqu'**il **sera** grand.	He wants to be a professor **when** he **grows up.**
Dès que	**As soon as**
Je changerai de travail **dès que** je le **pourrai.**	I'll change jobs **as soon as** I **can.**
Aussitôt que	**As soon as**
Aussitôt qu'elle **entrera**, nous crierons "Surprise!"	**As soon as** she **comes** in, we'll yell "Surprise!"
Tant que	**As long as**
Je serai triste **tant que** tu ne **reviendras** pas.	I'll be sad **as long as** you **don't** come back.
Pendant que	**While**
Vous chanterez **pendant que** nous **danserons.**	You'll sing **while** we **dance.**

```
                                              partirons—serez
                                              sera
                                              changerai—pourra
                                              entrera—crierons
                                              serai—reviendra
              Present time of                 chanterez—danserons
              the statement
                                  Futur
```

The Future in Past Narrations

When telling a past story, it is possible to use the **Futur** to increase the sense of suspense or destiny. Even though the general context is the past, the reader is placed in a position of not knowing yet what will happen. This particular use of the **Futur** is increasingly more common in journalism.

> Onassis **arrivera** aux États–Unis comme simple immigrant. Il **croiera** les principes du rêve américain et **se lancera** dans le monde des affaires. Il **finira** à la tête d'une des plus grosses fortunes du monder et **épousera** Jackie Kennedy, la jolie veuve du Président assassiné. Elle **deviendra** le couronnement et l'ultime symbole de sa réussite. *(Onassis was to arrive in the United States as a simple immigrant. He was to believe in the principles of the American dream and*

*throw himself into the business world. He was to end up at the control
of one of the largest fortunes in the world and to marry Jackie
Kennedy, the pretty widow of the assassinated president. She would
become the regal and ultimate symbol of his success.)*

The English equivalent is the past expression "was to" plus the infinitive used with each verb:

Onassis **was to** arrive . . . **was to** believe . . . **was to** throw himself . . . **was to** end . . . and **was to** marry . . . She **was to become** the epitome and the ultimate symbol of his success.

Formation of the *Futur*

The **Futur** is a simple tense. It is therefore formed by adding

- a specific set of endings
- to the stem of the verb.

This stem is different from the one used for the **present** and the **imparfait**.

Future Stem of Regular Verbs

The futu**R**e stem of regular verbs is the infinitive including the **R** but excluding anything after the **R**:

FUTURE STEMS AND ENDINGS OF REGULAR VERBS		
1st Group: . . . . . . -ER	2nd Group: . . . . . . -IR	3rd Group: . . . . . . -RE
. . . . . .e**R** + ending	. . . . . .i**R** + ending	. . . . . .**R**e + ending
mang**ER** + ending	fin**IR** + ending	boi**R** + ending

Future Endings

TIP BOX—futu**R**e endings

	R	A
	R	AS
FUTU	R	A
	R	ONS
	R	EZ
	R	ONT

FORMATION OF THE FUTUR OF REGULAR VERBS		
1st Group -ER	2nd Group -IR	3rd Group -RE
Stem Futur: porteR **porter** + -ending	Stem Futur: finiR **finir** + -ending	Stem Futur: vendR **vendr** + -ending
Je porte**Rai** Tu commence**Ras** Il-Elle-On mange**Ra** Nous danse**Rons** Vous chante**Rez** Elles-Ils arrive**Ront**	Je fini**Rai** Tu fini**Ras** Il-Elle-On fini**Ra** Nous fini**Rons** Vous fini**Rez** Elles-Ils fini**Ront**	Je vend**Rai** Tu vend**Ras** Il-Elle-On vend**Ra** Nous vend**Rons** Vous vend**Rez** Elles-Ils vend**Ront**

IMPORTANT!

The rule is: If you do not have an R sound in your veRb, it is not in the futuRe. This is doubly important to remember because the same stem is also used to form the conditional.

```
                         F
                         U
         C O N D I T I O N N E L
                         U
                         R
```

The conditional will have the same stem and R sound, only the endings will change.

Future Stems of Irregular Verbs

The general rule still applies: there must be an **R** sound for it to be a futuRe stem.

- Yet, it is impossible to guess at these stems for irregular verbs. They must be learned systematically with each new infinitive form.
- The set of future endings remains the same for irregular verbs.

FUTURE STEMS AND CONJUGATIONS OF SAMPLE IRREGULAR VERBS						
Infinitive	*JE*	*TU*	*IL*	*NOUS*	*VOUS*	*ILS/ELLES*
Aller **iR-**	irai	iras	ira	irons	irez	iront
Avoir **auR-**	aurai	auras	aura	aurons	aurez	auront
Connaître **connaitR-**	connaitrai	connaitras	connaitra	connaitrons	connaitrez	connaitront
Croire **croiR-**	croirai	croiras	croira	croirons	croirez	croiront
Devoir **devR-**	devrai	devras	devra	devrons	devrez	devront
Dire **diR-**	dirai	diras	dira	dirons	direz	diront
Écrire **écriR-**	écrirai	écriras	écrira	écrirons	écrirez	écriront
Être **seR-**	serai	seras	sera	serons	serez	seront
Faire **feR-**	ferai	feras	fera	ferons	ferez	feront
Lire **liR-**	lirai	liras	lira	lirons	lirez	liront
Mettre **mettR-**	mettrai	mettras	mettra	mettrons	mettrez	mettront
Partir **partiR-**	partirai	partiras	partira	partirons	partirez	partiront
Pouvoir **pouRR-**	pourrai	pourras	pourra	pourrons	pourrez	pourront
Prendre **prendR**	prendrai	prendras	prendra	prendrons	prendrez	prendront
Savoir **sauR-**	saurai	sauras	saura	saurons	saurez	sauront
Tenir **tiendR-**	tiendrai	tiendras	tiendra	tiendrons	tiendrez	tiendront
Venir **viendR-**	viendrai	viendras	viendra	viendrons	viendrez	viendront
Vouloir **voudR-**	voudrai	voudras	voudra	voudrons	voudrez	voudront

 Intermediate—Advanced Topic

The Future Perfect Indicative

The **Futur Antérieur** is called both the anterior future and *future perfect* in English. This double name indicates that this future action is both

- *anterior*: before another action, and
- *perfect*: finished before this other action.

Use of the *Futur Antérieur*

Type of Action in the Futur Antérieur

The name of the **Futur Antérieur** has two words. It is a compound tense, therefore it also needs two verbal forms. Similarly, the future anterior reaches in two directions.

Subsequence

The **future** perfect is in the **future** of the statement: The action will happen after the point of reference in time given by the sentence. The action in the future perfect (anterior) is ahead of *now*.

> J'**aurai** eu quarante trois ans le 11 août. *(By the time we get to August 11 in a few days from now, I will have turned 43.)*

Precedence

The future **perfect** is also in the **past** of a future action. It is perfect, completed, by the time this other action starts.

> J'aurai **eu** quarante trois ans quand nous serons le 12 août. *(When it is August 12, in a few days, I will have turned 43, because my birthday is on the 11th.)*

On the time line, the **Futur Antérieur** makes you contemplate two jumps ahead of you, but it is located where you land first, before (ante) the second jump.

Sequence

The **futur antérieur** is used to describe an action that will happen first when many actions are contemplated in the future. It is the first in the sequence of future actions.

> Je **vérifierai** la semaine prochaine le chapitre que j'**aurai écrit** cette semaine et que les étudiants **liront** l'an prochain. *(Next week, I will verify the chapter that I will have written this week and that students will read next year: Sequence = 1. write—2. verify—3. read.)*

> Gregory **réparera** ta voiture dès que tu lui **auras donné** les clés du garage et qu'il **recevra** les pièces détachées. *(Gregory will repair your car as soon as you will have given him the keys and he has received the parts: Sequence = 1. give—2. receive—3. repair.)*

	ANTERIOR ◄———————	┌— future
PRESENT S T A T E M E N T		
	Action #1 Anterior Future j'aurai écrit	Action #2 Future je vérifierai / les étudiants liront
	tu auras donné #1 Anterior Future	Grégory recevra / il réparera #2 Future
Now	Later but before Action #2	Even Later

Special Use with Conjunctions: quand, lorsque, dès que, aussitôt que, tant que, pendant que

In order to respect the chronological order of actions, the **Futur antérieur** may also be used after these French conjunctions although it is translated by a present or a perfect in English.

However, the **Futur antérieur** does not have to be used systematically with these conjunctions. As seen in the **Futur** section above, they can also be followed by a simple future. The choice depends on the order of the future actions:

- if they are in a **sequence**: use the **Futur Antérieur**
- if they are performed at the **same time**: use the **Futur**.

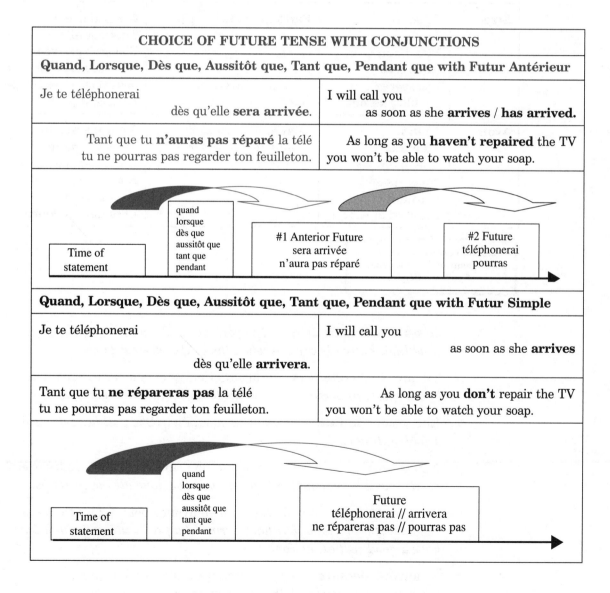

CHOICE OF FUTURE TENSE WITH CONJUNCTIONS	
Quand, Lorsque, Dès que, Aussitôt que, Tant que, Pendant que with Futur Antérieur	
Je te téléphonerai dès qu'elle **sera arrivée**.	I will call you as soon as she **arrives / has arrived.**
Tant que tu **n'auras pas réparé** la télé tu ne pourras pas regarder ton feuilleton.	As long as you **haven't repaired** the TV you won't be able to watch your soap.

quand
lorsque
dès que
aussitôt que
tant que
pendant

Time of statement

#1 Anterior Future
sera arrivée
n'aura pas réparé

#2 Future
téléphonerai
pourras

Quand, Lorsque, Dès que, Aussitôt que, Tant que, Pendant que with Futur Simple	
Je te téléphonerai dès qu'elle **arrivera**.	I will call you as soon as she **arrives**
Tant que tu **ne répareras pas** la télé tu ne pourras pas regarder ton feuilleton.	As long as you **don't** repair the TV you won't be able to watch your soap.

quand
lorsque
dès que
aussitôt que
tant que
pendant

Time of statement

Future
téléphonerai // arrivera
ne répareras pas // pourras pas

Formation of the *Futur Antérieur*

As a compound tense, the **Futur Antérieur** is formed by conjugating the auxiliary Être or Avoir and combining it with the **Participe Passé** of the verb **to be** put in the **Futur Antérieur**.

- The auxiliary verb is conjugated in a **future** tense, the **futur simple**.
- It is combined with the **past** participle.

This results in a tense that is the **past** *(participle)* of the **future** *(anterior)*.

FORMATION OF THE FUTUR ANTÉRIEUR		
Auxiliary Verb Indicatif Futur	**Past participle**	**Futur Antérieur**
Être Je serai Tu seras Elle, il, on sera Nous serons Vous serez Ils, elles seront	**Participe Passé*** = p.p. ... +é ... +i ... +u ... + p.p. of irregular verb ^	Je serai **née** Tu **seras allé** Elle **sera arrivée** Nous nous **serons lavés** Vous vous **serez téléphoné** Ils **seront partis**
Avoir J'aurai Tu auras Elle, il, on aura Nous aurons Vous aurez Ils, elles auront	*May or may not agree ^Must be learned for each verb	J'aurai **travaillé** Tu **auras peint** Il **aura appris** Nous **aurons fini** Vous **aurez rêvé** Elles **auront couru**

> *Refer to Chapter 12 for the* **passé composé and agreement of past participle.**

Je **serai** déjà **arrivée** quand la conférence de presse <u>commencera</u>.
(I will have already arrived when the conference starts.)

Tu **auras** vite **compris** que la situation <u>va</u> être delicate. *(You will have rapidly understood how delicate the situation is going to be.)*

Elle se **sera habillée** avant de se maquiller. *(She will have dressed before putting on her makeup.)*

Nous ne serons satisfaits que quand nous **aurons fait** tous les exercices. *(We will be satisfied only when we have done all the exercises.)*

Vous **serez arrivé** une demi-heure en avance pour avoir une bonne place au concert. *(You will have arrived half an hour early in order to have a good seat at the concert.)*

Ils **auront déclaré** que la guerre <u>sera</u> inutile et dangereuse.
(They will have declared that the war is useless and dangerous.)

> **NOTE** It is not necessary to have both past actions represented in the sentence. The **Futur Antérieur** can be used by itself when the context implies the second point of reference in the future.
>
> **Tu m' auras appelée ce soir.** *(You will have called me (when I get home and find your message).)*

IMPORTANT!

Both the **plus-que-parfait** and the **futur antérieur** may be used with tenses and moods other than the preterit, the perfect, or the future; for instance, with the present of the indicative, of the imperative, or tenses of the conditional. These combinations are more advanced to learn but they are common. The rule remains the same though: the choice in tense and mood depends on the chronology and the logic organizing the series of actions:

Tu **avais** vite **compris** que la situation <u>serait</u> très délicate—<u>conditional present</u>. *(You had rapidly understood that the situation would be very delicate.)*

On ne t'**avait** pas **dit** qu'elle <u>est</u> Présidente Directrice Générale de notre société?—<u>indicative present</u>. *(They hadn't told you that she is president of our company?)*

<u>Appelle-moi</u> aussitôt que tu **auras atterri** à Washington!—<u>imperative</u>. *(Call me as soon as you have landed in Washington!)*

Vous **aurez préparé** beaucoup à manger parce que vous <u>savez</u> qu'Olivier mange comme un ogre—<u>indicative present</u>. *(You will have made a lot of food because you know Oliver eats like an ogre.)*

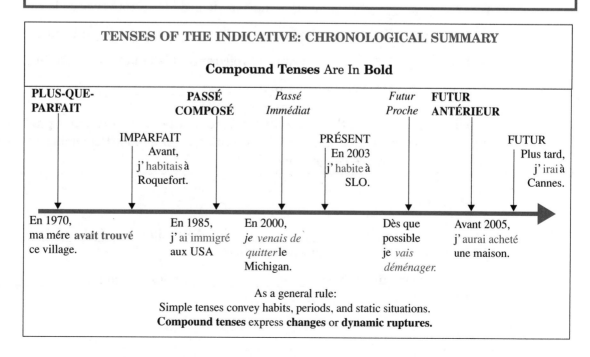

TENSES OF THE INDICATIVE: CHRONOLOGICAL SUMMARY

Compound Tenses Are In Bold

PLUS-QUE-PARFAIT	IMPARFAIT	PASSÉ COMPOSÉ	Passé Immédiat	PRÉSENT	Futur Proche	FUTUR ANTÉRIEUR	FUTUR
	Avant, j'habitais à Roquefort.			En 2003 j'habite à SLO.			Plus tard, j'irai à Cannes.
En 1970, ma mére avait trouvé ce village.		En 1985, j'ai immigré aux USA	En 2000, *je venais de quitter* le Michigan.		Dès que possible je *vais déménager.*	Avant 2005, j'aurai acheté une maison.	

As a general rule:
Simple tenses convey habits, periods, and static situations.
Compound tenses express **changes** or **dynamic ruptures**.

Practice What You Learned

Exercises are rated according to four levels of difficulty:

- Beginner easy [*]
- Beginner challenging [**]
- Intermediate [***]
- Advanced [****]

1. Identify the characteristic of the action and conjugate the verb in the **imparfait**.[*]

Il (être) une fois une princesse. _____

Les enfants (attendre) Noël impatiemment. _____

Je (arriver) à mon bureau au moment de l'attentat. _____

Pascal (travailler) comme moniteur de ski de décembre à février. _____

Il (diriger) les gentils organisateurs au Club Med tous les étés. _____

Nous (s'amuser) dans la cabane construite par mon père. _____

Vous (sembler) triste et découragé. _____

2. Complete the sentences with the logical verb in the **plus-que-parfait**. Remember to make the past participle agree if necessary. [**]

rencontrer—se fiancer—perdre—mettre—écrire

A. Mes chattes ont sorti les souris en peluche que je _____ dans leur panier de jouets.

B. Tu _____ ce stylo mais je viens de le retrouver sous le canapé.

C. J'ai revu ce célèbre philosophe que nous _____ à Irvine.

D. Fiona _____ avant d'avoir rencontré la famille de Florent.

E. Vous ne vous rappelez plus ce que vous me _____

3. Conjugate the verbs in the **imparfait**, **passé composé**, or **plus-que-parfait** according to the logical sequence of actions and the type of action. Remember to modify the past participle if there is agreement. [**]

Example:

oublier—apporter: Je _____ les fleurs que tu _____
J'ai apporté les fleurs que tu avais oubliées.

A. commencer—finir: Sylvia _____ la lessive qu'elle _____ hier.

B. ranger—nettoyer: Marc _____ le garage que tu _____ aujourd'hui.

C. partir—arriver: La voleuse _____ depuis longtemps quand les policiers _____

D. terminer—trouver: Je ne pas encore _____ mes études quand je _____ un travail.

4. Rewrite the following text in the future. [**]

Aujourd'hui, je vais à la plage. Il n'y a pas de monde parce que c'est le mois de septembre. Mais il fait toujours chaud et le soleil brille. Le vent ne souffle pas le matin et les vagues viennent doucement sur le sable. Je te téléphone pour te demander un matelas. Tu veux me rejoindre avec tes enfants mais vous ne pouvez pas à cause de ton travail. Nous prenons rendez-vous pour y retourner ensemble dimanche.

5. Create sentences with a future and a future perfect. Use a different subject for each sentence. [**]

Example:

terminer le repas—faire des crêpes
Je ferai des crêpes quand j'aurai terminé le repas.

A. passer le permis—acheter une voiture

_____

B. faire l'exercice #2—faire l'exercice #3—

_____

C. être heureuse—réussir

_____

D. plonger dans la piscine—se mettre en maillot

_____

E. débrancher—enregistrer les données

_____

F. protéger tout le monde—supprimer les véhicules tout terrain

_____

6. Complete the sentences with a *passé immédiat* or a futur proche—in the past—according to the context. [***]

La semaine dernière. . . .

A. . . . le spectacle (commencer) _____ sans moi.

B. . . . je (laver la vaisselle) _____ et il fallait déjà préparer le repas.

C. . . . vous aviez déjà oublié ce que vous (me dire) _____ .

D. . . . tu étais encore en retard, mais nous (t'attendre) _____ .

E. . . . ces idiots (répéter) _____ la même propagande alors j'ai changé de table.

7. Complete the paragraph by conjugating the verbs according to the chronological order and the type of events: use any present, past, or future tense of the indicative. Organize the events along a time line to visualize the unfolding of the story and identify the main characteristic of each action (finished, state, emotion, anterior to another one, about to happen, still happening, etc.). Check for a possible agreement of the past participles. [****]

Quand Tofa (avoir) _____ deux ans, je (chercher) _____ un futur mari pour elle. Je (vouloir) _____ des bébés chats et elle (se porter) _____ bien. Auparavant, elle (être) _____ souvent malade mais tout (aller) _____ beaucoup mieux. Je (mettre) _____ une annonce dans le journal de Ann Arbor qui (décrire) _____ une jolie blonde aux yeux bleus. On (me recommander) _____ de chercher un mari parmi les chats de sa race, mais je (décider) _____ que la personnalité et la santé du futur papa (être) _____ plus importantes que le pedigree. Un couple de gens très gentils (m'appeler) _____ . Leur chat Mittens (avoir) _____ d'immenses yeux bleus aussi et des pattes toute blanches. Si je le (désirer) _____ , ils (venir) _____ immédiatement le présenter à Tofa. Quand Mittens (arriver) _____ , il (venir) _____ tout de suite vers moi gentiment. Il (être) _____ encore plus adorable que ses "parents" le (décrire) _____ . Tofa ne pas (vouloir) _____ l'approcher parce que ce (être) _____ leur premier rendez-vous. Mais elle lui (dire) _____ : "Quand vous (revenir) _____ une fois ou deux, je vous (laisser) _____ jouer avec moi." Mittens (répondre) _____ : "D'accord, quand je vous (revoir) _____ , je vous (rappeller _____ ce que vous me (promettre) _____ ."

Tout (se terminer) _____ bien, Tofa (avoir) _____ des bébés magnifiques dont une (ressembler) _____ à son gentil papa comme une copie conforme. Elle (s'appeler) _____ Vanille parce que ces pattes (être) _____ toute blanches aussi! Naturellement, je (garder) _____ toujours toute la famille avec moi!

Chapter 14

STRUCTURE— AFFIRMATIVE, NEGATIVE, INTERROGATIVE SENTENCES AND CLAUSES

Introduction

The order of words in French is progressive, which means that the function of the words is linked to their position in the sentence. Although there are some variations, the order remains mostly the same in affirmative, negative, and interrogative sentences.

Affirmative Sentences

A sentence in the affirmative form states an action that was, is, or will be performed.

Normal Word Order

Subject

The subject is placed before the verb. The typical sentence follows the pattern:

Subject + Conjugated Verb + Complements

Noun or Pronoun

Honoré <u>achète</u> une montre *(Honoré buys a watch.)*

Complements

- Object complements follow the verb: the direct object first, the indirect object second

Subject + Conjugated Verb + Complement Object + Circumstantial Complements

Direct Object + Indirect Object

Honoré <u>achète</u> *une montre <u>à sa femme</u> (Honoré buys a watch for his wife.)*

- The order of circumstantial complements (the prepositional phrases that inform about the circumstances surrounding an event) vary according to the emphasis one wishes to give to the information. The position of strength in a French sentence is at the end, so the most important circumstantial complement will be placed last:

> **Honoré** <u>achète</u> *une montre* <u>*à sa femme*</u> pour son anniversaire.
> *(Honoré buys a watch for his wife for her birthday.)*

> **Honoré** <u>achète</u> *une montre* <u>*à sa femme*</u> chez Cartier. *(Honoré buys a watch for his wife at Cartier's.)*

Honoré achète une montre à sa femme pour son anniversaire chez Cartier. (The brand of the watch is the important information.)

Honoré achète une montre à sa femme chez Cartier pour son anniversaire. (The birthday is the important circumstance.)

"J'ai vu Marie dans la rue à 2 heures du matin!" Stresses the early hour.

"J'ai vu Marie à 2 heures du matin dans la rue!" Stresses the unexpected place.

Verb-Subject Inversion
Adverbs at the Beginning

The normal order of subject + verb must be inverted in an affirmative sentence when certain words are placed at the beginning of clauses or sentences. The main ones are:

Peut-être *(perhaps)*	À peine *(barely / just)*	Sans doute *(undoubtedly)*
Encore *(that is)*	Tout au plus *(at the very most)*	À plus forte raison *(all the more so as)*
Du moins *(at least)*	Aussi *(that is why)*	Ainsi *(thus)*

Il a mangé une boîte entière de chocolats, aussi **est-il** malade.
(He ate an entire box of chocolate candies; therefore he is sick.)

À peine Nina **entra-t-elle** dans son salon que ses amis crièrent:
Surprise!
(As soon as Nina entered her living room, her friends shouted "Surprise!")

Louis est rentré de voyage, sans doute **va-t-il** venir te voir.
(Louis is back from his trip; he is undoubtedly going to come and see you.)

- Such inversion elevates the level of language; it sounds literary and is therefore more common in written texts.
- In everyday French, the inversion is avoided and replaced by alternative constructions or conjunctions:

> Il a mangé une boîte entière de chocolats, **c'est pourquoi il est** malade. (*He ate an entire box of chocolate candies; that is why he is sick.*)

> **Nina était à peine entrée** dans son salon que ses amis ont crié: Surprise! (*Nina had barely entered her living room when her friends shouted "Surprise!"*)

> Louis est rentré de voyage, **il va sûrement** venir te voir. (*Louis is back from his trip; he is surely going to come and see you.*)

Circumstantial Complement at the Beginning

The normal order of subject + verb can also be inverted in an affirmative sentence when the complements indicating the circumstances of the action are placed at the beginning of the sentence:

> Dans un village perché, surplombant les flots azur de la Méditerranée **se trouve le Château d'Èze**, un des restaurants les plus célèbres de France. (*In a village on top of a hill, looking over the azure blue waves of the Mediterranean Sea, is located the Èze Castle, one of the most famous restaurants in France.*)

This is also a literary construction that adds a poetic dimension to the description. It should not be used orally, unless one is narrating a story.

Dialogues

The normal order of subject + verb is also inverted when reporting dialogues:

> "Je suis très fatiguée", **dit Fanny** à son frère.

> "Pourquoi?", **demanda-t-il**, "tu n'as pas bien dormi?"

> "Non, et j'ai beaucoup trop travaillé!", **répondit-elle** en baillant. (*"I am very tired," said Fanny to her brother. "Why," he asked. "You did not sleep well?" ("No," she answered, "and I worked a lot.")*)

NOTE Unlike in English, periods and commas are outside the quotation marks in French, and a comma separates the identification of the speaker from the actual words that were said.

Negative Sentences
Normal Word Order
Negative Structure

- A sentence is made negative by using the combination of two negative elements: **Ne** and a negative adverb, pronoun, or adjective.
- Most sentences are made negative when the action is negated. **Ne** and the second negative element then surround the verb.
- But the subject of the sentence can also be negative: the negative pronoun then comes first and before **Ne** that stays in front of the verb.

NEGATING THE ACTION OR THE SUBJECT				
Negation of Action	Element #1 NE	Verb	Element #2 adverb, pronoun, adjective	
Paul	NE	déteste	PAS . . .	
Negation of Subject	Negative Pronoun	Ne	Verb	
	PERSONNE	NE	déteste	Paul
	Element #1 Pronoun	Element #2 NE	Verb	

Pair of Negative Elements

The basic order of words remains the same in negative sentences, since only the verb is negated. Two elements are always necessary to negate an action:

1. **Ne**
2. A negative adverb, <u>pronoun</u>, **adjective**, or conjunction:

PRINCIPAL NEGATIVE ELEMENTS			
Guère *(hardly)*	Pas *(not)*	Plus *(no longer/more)*	Jamais *(never)*
Pas encore *(not yet)*	Pas déjà *(not already)*	Pas vraiment *(not really)*	Point *(not [literary])*
Aucun—Aucune *(none)*	Personne *(nobody)*	Rien *(nothing)*	Que *(only)*
Ni *(neither/nor)*	**Nul—Nulle** *(no/none/no one)*	Nullement *(in no way)*	<u>Nulle part</u> *(nowhere)*
adverb	<u>pronoun</u>	**adjective**	conjunction

IMPORTANT!

The negative form takes two parts in French:

NE . . . Pas — NE . . . Rien — NE . . . Que — NE . . . Jamais . . .

Personne NE . . . — Rien NE . . .

Needing two elements to form one negative adverb does not mean it is a double negative and does not result in an affirmation.

Position of Negative Elements

When the negation affects the action, the negative elements surround the verb. The position of these negative elements is dependent upon two factors:

1. the tense in which the verb is conjugated
2. negative element #2

NOTE When the verb starts with a vowel, the **E** of the negative element #1 **NE** is dropped and replaced by an apostrophe: **n'** to facilitate the pronunciation.

   The negative element **NE** tends to be dropped in everyday conversations. Be aware of it, but always try to use both parts yourself as it is always required in written discourse:

   Je N(E)' arrive pas à 8 heures. *(I don't get here at 8 o'clock.)*

   Paul N(E)' est jamais en retard. *(Paul is never late.)*

   Nous N(E)' avons rien à manger. *(We did not have anything to eat.)*

Verb Tense

Simple Tenses—Without a Pronoun

As a general rule, **NE** comes before the verb conjugated in a simple tense. The negative adverbs and pronouns or adjectives: aucun, pas, guère, plus, rien, personne, jamais, nullement, ni, nulle part, que, nul, come after the verb.

TIP BOX
Since the verb is stuck between two negative elements, one on each side, think of French negative sentences as a sandwich. There are different kinds of "Negative Sandwiches" you can order from the menu by their number:
    The negative element #1 is the bottom slice of plain bread.
    The negative element #2 is the top slice of bread with sesame seeds.
    Different words/foods can be added between these two slices: cooked meat, cheese, pieces of pickle.

PLACEMENT OF NEGATIVE ELEMENTS WITH SIMPLE TENSES		
Negative Element #1	**Conjugated Verb Simple Tense**	Negative Element #2
NE	CV	aucun, pas, guère, plus, rien, personne, jamais, nullement, ni, nulle part, que, nul
Charles NE	jouera	QUE du jazz (*Charles will only play jazz.*)
Je N(e)'	aime	PAS le beurre de cacahuètes (*I do not like peanut butter.*)
Vous N(e)'	arriviez	JAMAIS à l'heure (*You never arrived on time.*)
Cette histoire NE	concerne	PERSONNE ici (*This story is no one's business here.*)
Richard N(e)'	aura	GUÈRE de temps libre (*Richard will not have much free time.*)
Mes clés NE	sont	NULLE PART ici (*My keys are nowhere around here.*)
Stéphane N(e)'	hésite	PLUS avant de plonger (*Stéphane no longer hesitates before diving.*)
Nina NE	voudrait	NI vanille NI chocolat (*Nina would like neither chocolate nor vanilla.*)
Annick et Antoine N(e)'	ont	AUCUNE responsabilité (*Annick and Antoine have no responsibility.*)
Le médecin NE	peut	RIEN faire pour lui (*The doctor cannot do anything for him.*)
Nous N(e)'	avions	NUL désir de partir (*We had no desire to leave.*)
Il NE	s'agit	NULLEMENT d'une plaisanterie (*This is not a joke whatsoever.*)

TIP BOX
Order the Negative Sandwich #1, Hamburger only
The Verbe Conjugué = Viande Cuite (cooked meat) is placed between the two slices of bread.
   The NE slice at the bottom comes first.
   A second slice with all the sesame seeds = all the possible negative adverbs/adjectives or pronouns, after the meat.

SIMPLE TENSE—NO PRONOUN: NEGATIVE SANDWICH #1 BURGER ONLY

Sesame Seeds =
Pas, plus, personne, rien, que, jamais, ni, guère, nul, aucun . . .

NE

Verbe Conjugué = Viande Cuite
(Cooked Meat)

NOTE A verb conjugated in a simple tense is made of only one part: a chunk of meat. In this hamburger, there is only cooked meat = **VC**

Simple Tenses with Personal Pronouns

As we saw in the chapter on personal pronouns (page 102), when the verb is completed by personal pronouns they are always placed before it.

   These personal pronouns remain in their normal place and in their normal order. They are integrated into the negative "sandwich."

NOTE Personal pronouns are included within the negative brackets. In this "sandwich," the personal Pronoun Complement is like a Piece of Cheese = **PC**. This makes a cheeseburger.

TIP BOX

Order the Negative Sandwich #2, Cheeseburger

The personal Pronoun(s) Complement: Piece(s) of Cheese remain in their normal place: before the verb they complement.

SIMPLE TENSE—PRONOUN COMPLEMENT:
NEGATIVE SANDWICH #2 CHEESEBURGER

NE + Pronoun(s) Complement + Verb Conjugated in Simple Tense + poSSible adverbs

=

No sesamE + Piece(s) of Cheese + Viande Cuite + SeSame bun

Bernard **NE la** connaît **PAS**. (*Bernard does not know her.*)

Paul **NE lui en** donne **PLUS**. (*Paul no longer gives him any.*)

Il **NE leur y** apporte **JAMAIS**. (*He never brings it to them there.*)

Tu **NE me le** souhaites **NULLEMENT**. (*You do not wish that to me at all.*)

Véra **NE se** rappelle **RIEN**. (*Vera does not remember anything.*)

Ninon **N**(e)' **en** a **GUÈRE**. (*Ninon does not have much of it.*)

Compound Tenses—Without a Pronoun

When the verb is conjugated in a compound tense, adverbs can be placed

- before the past participle (for most of them)
- after the past participle (for some of them)

You need to memorize them as there is no identical explanation for all the cases.

The following adverbs surround the auxiliary verb (which is the conjugated verb, that is the cooked meat) but exclude the past participle:

NEGATIVE ELEMENT #2 **BEFORE PAST PARTICIPLE IN COMPOUND TENSES**		
Negative Adverbs	**Simple Tense**	**Compound Tense**
Ne . . . Pas	Paul NE mange PAS. *(Paul does not eat.)*	Paul N(e)' a PAS **mangé**. *(Paul did not eat.)*
Ne . . . Plus	Denise NE conduit PLUS. *(Denise no longer drives.)*	Denise N(e)' a PLUS **conduit**. *(Denise has not driven anymore.)*
Ne . . . Guère	Nous NE sortons GUÈRE. *(We hardly ever go out.)*	Nous NE serons GUÈRE **sortis**. *(We will not have gone out often.)*
Ne . . . Jamais	Elles NE viennent JAMAIS. *(They never come by.)*	Elles N(e)' étaient JAMAIS **venues**. *(They had never come by.)*
Ne . . . Nullement	Tu NE mens NULLEMENT. *(You do not lie in any way.)*	Tu N(e)' as NULLEMENT **menti**. *(You did not lie at all.)*
Ne . . . Rien	Ils NE croient RIEN. *(They do not believe anything.)*	. . . qu'ils N(e)' aient RIEN **cru**. *(. . . that they did not believe anything.)*

> ## TIP BOX
> Order the Negative Sandwich #3, Hamburger only and Pickle on the side
> **The auxiliary verb: V**erb **C**onjugué = **V**iande **C**uite (**cooked meat**) **is placed between two slices of bread.**
>   **With these adverbs the** <u>past participle</u> **is outside the negative sandwich.**
>   **The** <u>past participle</u> **= a** pickle piece **is a** <u>side order</u>**; it is not included in this hamburger.**

COMPOUND TENSE—PAST PARTICIPLE EXCLUDED: NEGATIVE SANDWICH #3, HAMBURGER AND PICKLE ON SIDE	

Neg. #1 + **V**erb **C**onjugated + Neg. #2 **Viande Cuite** (auxiliary verb)	**Past Participle** Pickle Pieces
Paul **N(e)' a PAS**	<u>**mangé**</u>
Denise **N(e)' a PLUS**	<u>**conduit**</u>
Nous **NE** serons **GUÈRE**	<u>**sortis**</u>
Elles **N(e)' étaient JAMAIS**	<u>**venues**</u>
Tu **N(e)' as NULLEMENT**	<u>**menti**</u>
Étrange qu'ils **N(e)' aient RIEN**	<u>**cru**</u>
Paul has not eaten. *Denise did not drive anymore.* *We will have not gone out much.* *They had never come.* *You did not lie to me in any way.* *It is strange that they did not believe anything.*	

Compound Tenses with Personal Pronoun—Past Participle Excluded

When the verb is completed by personal pronouns they are always placed before it. These personal pronouns remain in their normal place and in their normal order. They become part of the negative "sandwich."

TIP BOX
Order the Negative Sandwich #4 Cheeseburger & Pickle on the side
   **The Pronoun Complement: Piece of Cheese remains in its normal place—
before the verb it complements.**

**COMPOUND TENSE WITH PERSONAL PRONOUN AND PAST PARTICIPLE
EXCLUDED: NEGATIVE SANDWICH #4, CHEESEBURGER AND PICKLE ON SIDE**

NE + Pronoun(s) Complement + **V**erb **C**onjugated + po**SS**ible adverbs (+ <u>Past Participle</u>)
No sesam**E** + Piece of Cheese + **V**iande **C**uite + Se**S**ame bun (+ Pickle Piece)

Bernard NE **la** connaît PAS.	Il NE **l(a)'** avait PAS <u>rencontrée</u>.
Paul NE **lui en** donne PLUS.	Paul NE **lui en** a PLUS <u>donné</u>.
Il NE **leur y** apporte JAMAIS.	Il NE **leur y** aura JAMAIS <u>apporté</u>.
Tu NE **me le** souhaites NULLEMENT.	Tu NE **me** l'avais NULLEMENT <u>souhaité</u>.
Véra NE **se** rappelle RIEN.	Véra NE **se** soit RIEN <u>rappelé</u>.
Ninon N(e)' **en** a GUÈRE.	Ninon N(e)' **en** aurait GUÈRE <u>eu</u>.

Bernard does not know her.	*He had not met her.*
Paul no longer gives her any.	*Paul has no longer given her any.*
He never brings it to them there.	*He will never have brought it to them there.*
Don't you wish it to me at all?	*You had not wished that to me at all.*
Vera remembers nothing.	*Vera had not remembered anything.*
Ninon does not have much of it.	*Ninon would not have had much of it.*

TIP BOX
Conclusion:

Ne . . . pas — Ne . . . plus — Ne . . . jamais — Ne . . . nullement —
Ne . . . rien — Ne . . . guère: These adverbs do not like pickles!

   But other adverbs, pronouns, or adjectives must be considered individually.

Compound Tenses—Past Participle Included

The following negative elements #2 come after the past participle, which means that the past participle is included between the two negative brackets.

NEGATIVE ELEMENT #2 **AFTER PAST PARTICIPLE** IN COMPOUND TENSES		
Negative Element #1	**Compound Tense**	**Negative Element #2**
NE	Conjugated Auxiliary + PAST PARTICIPLE	PERSONNE NULLE PART QUE AUCUN—AUCUNE NUL—NULLE NI . . . NI
Il NE voit PERSONNE. Elle NE va NULLE PART. Nous NE buvons QUE ça. Tu NE veux AUCUN jeu. Je NE sens NULLE brise. Vous NE dites NI son nom NI son prénom.	Il n' a **VU** personne. Elle **ne** sera **ALLÉE** nulle part. Nous n' avions **BU** que ça. . . . que tu n' aies **VOULU** aucun jeu. Je n' ai **SENTI** nulle brise. Vous n' aurez **DIT** ni son nom ni son prénom.	
He does not see anyone. *She goes nowhere.* *We drink only this.* *You do not want any game.* *I cannot feel any air.* *You tell neither his last nor his first name.*	*He did not see anyone.* *She will have gone nowhere.* *We had drunk only that.* *. . . that you did not want any game.* *I have felt no air.* *You will have told neither his last nor his first name.*	

Compound Tenses with Personal Pronoun—Past Participle Included

When a verb is completed by one or more personal pronouns, they are always placed before it. With the above adverbs, pronouns, or adjectives, the personal pronouns also remain in their normal place and in their normal order. They become part of the negative sandwich, but so does the past participle.

TIP BOX

Order the Negative Sandwich #5, Cheeseburger with Pickles inside

Verbe **C**onjugué = **V**iande **C**uite (cooked meat) Conjugated Verb/**A**uxiliary Verb
NE = **N**o sesam**E** bread
Po**SS**ible adverbs/adjectives/pronouns = Se**S**ame bread
Personal **P**ronoun(s) **C**omplement = **P**iece(s) of **C**heese
Past **P**articiple = **P**ickle **P**ieces

COMPOUND TENSE WITH PERSONAL PRONOUN AND PAST PARTICIPLE INCLUDED: NEGATIVE SANDWICH #5, CHEESEBURGER WITH PICKLES

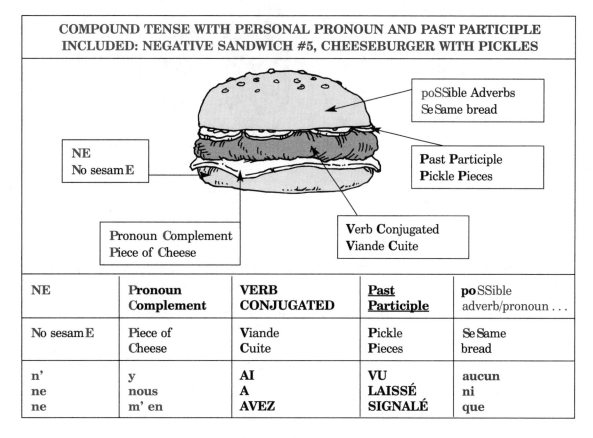

NE	Pronoun Complement	VERB CONJUGATED	Past Participle	poSSible adverb/pronoun . . .
No sesamE	Piece of Cheese	Viande Cuite	Pickle Pieces	SeSame bread
n' ne ne	y nous m' en	AI A AVEZ	VU LAISSÉ SIGNALÉ	aucun ni que

Je [n(e)' y AI <u>VU</u> **aucun**] défaut. *(I did not see any flaw in it.)*

Marie [ne **nous** A <u>LAISSÉ</u> **ni**] son nom **ni** son numéro. *(Marie left us neither her name nor her number.)*

Vous [ne **m'en** AVEZ <u>SIGNALÉ</u> **que**] trois. *(You only signaled three to me.)*

 From the following sentence, what can you conclude about Eric when he goes to a fast food restaurant with his son?

Eric ne lui a acheté aucun hamburger.

Can you draw the corresponding negative sandwich?

Conclusion: Eric has ordered the Negative Sandwich #5 and Aucun likes pickles!

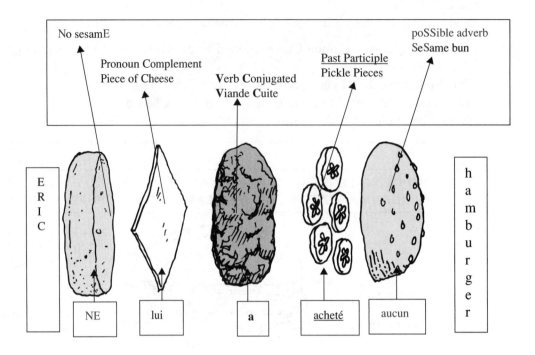

No sesamE

Pronoun Complement
Piece of Cheese

Verb Conjugated
Viande Cuite

Past Participle
Pickle Pieces

poSSible adverb
SeSame bun

E R I C | NE | lui | a | acheté | aucun | h a m b u r g e r

THINK! With all this information on negative sandwiches, what do you think can happen when the negated verb is in the infinitive as in, for example, the English equivalent?

*Paul would like **not to come** tomorrow, if possible.*

Intermediate—Advanced Topic

Negating an Infinitive

Past Participle Excluded—Infinitive Excluded

- If the verb to be negated is in the infinitive, the negative adverbs that rejected the past participle aside stay together. They stand in front of the infinitive that they also push aside.
- If the infinitive verb has a personal pronoun for a complement, the personal pronoun remains in its normal place, just before the verb it complements.

ADVERBS (PAS, GUÈRE, PLUS, RIEN, JAMAIS, NULLEMENT) EXCLUDING NEGATED INFINITIVE VERBS		
Negative elements #1 & #2	(If any) *Personal Pronoun Complement*	 *Infinitive Verb*
The slices of bread #1 and #2 stick together and they keep the meat outside because it is not cooked!		
Je peux	NE PAS	**venir** demain
Elle décide de	NE GUÈRE	**acheter** de cadeaux
Paul est désolé de	NE PLUS	*vous* **voir** au club
J'espère	NE RIEN	**regretter** dans ma vie
Il devrait	NE JAMAIS	*y* **avoir** de guerre
Le médecin conseille de	NE NULLEMENT	*te* **stresser**
The two negative elements form a block because the infinitive verb is not a Conjugated Verb (CV = cooked meat).		

Past Participle Included—Infinitive Included

- If the verb to be negated is in the infinitive, the negative adverbs that were after the past participle and included within the negative sandwich also include the infinitive verb.
- These adverbs, adjectives, or pronouns are placed around the infinitive verb and include its personal pronouns complement that remain at their normal place.

ADVERBS (PERSONNE, NULLE PART, QUE, AUCUN—AUCUNE, NUL—NULLE, NI . . . NI) INCLUDING NEGATED INFINITIVE VERBS			
	Negative Element #1	(if any) *Personal Pronoun Complement*	Negative Element #2
Tu es sûr de	NE	**détester**	PERSONNE?
Il veut	NE	***la* rencontrer**	NULLE PART
Nous voulons	N(e)'	**entendre**	QUE la vérité
Je décide de	NE	***lui* accorder**	AUCUN crédit
Elle espère	N(e)'	***en* subir**	NULLE conséquence
Marc regrette de	N(e)'	**avoir connu**	NI ton père NI ta mère

The two negative elements bracket the infinitive and its complements.

Je décide de [ne *lui* accorder aucun] crédit. *(I decide not to give him any credit.)*

Elle espère [n'*en* subir nulle] conséquence. *(She hopes not to suffer any consequence from it.)*

Conclusion: The two pieces of French bread and the raw meat make a steak tartare sandwich!

Negative Subject: Negative Pronoun or Adjective . . . NE

A sentence can be put in the negative form when its subject is negative in itself.

Personne—Rien (Nobody—Nothing)

Personne and **rien** are pronouns. They can therefore function as subject of a sentence whose meaning is negative. In this case, two negative elements are still necessary, but their order is inverted: the subject pronoun comes first and is followed by **NE**. **NE** remains just before the conjugated verb.

- The inversion of the two negative elements is the same with simple and compound tenses.
- If there are personal pronoun complements of the verb, they remain at their normal place, just before the verb.

ORDER OF THE SENTENCE WITH A NEGATIVE PRONOUN (PERSONNE—RIEN) AS SUBJECT			
Negative Elements		Normal order of the rest of the words	
#1 = Pronoun	#2 = NE	Conjugated Verb	Tense and **complements**
PERSONNE	NE	veut ce gâteau	Simple
	N(e)'	a voulu ce gâteau	Compound
	NE	*le* voit	*Pronoun Complement—* Simple
	NE	*m'*avait prévenue	*Pronoun Complement—* Compound
(No one wants this cake.) *(No one wanted this cake.)* *(No one sees him.)* *(No one had warned me.)*			
RIEN	NE	satisfait cet enfant gâté	Simple
	N(e)'	aura plu à cet enfant gâté	Compound
	NE	*lui* rappelle son passé	*Pronoun Complement—* Simple
	NE	*nous* a tenté sur ce menu	*Pronoun Complement—* Compound
(Nothing satisfies this spoiled child.) *(Nothing will have satisfied this spoiled child.)* *(Nothing reminds him of his past.)* *(Nothing sounded good to us on this menu.)*			

IMPORTANT!

When inverting these negative elements, make sure NOT to add pas **after the verb. Two and only two negative elements are necessary and Personne Ne / Rien Ne are sufficient. Pas would make a double negation therefore an affirmation.**

Personne ne veut pas ce gâteau = Nobody does not want this cake = Everyone wants it!

Aucun—aucune et nul—nulle (No—None)

Aucun—aucune as well as **nul—nulle** are indefinite adjectives accompanying a noun, or indefinite pronouns.

- They mean the same thing: **aucun—aucune** is more familiar, while **nul— nulle** is a literary form used in more formal speeches.

- They both signify a quantity equal to zero and therefore have a negative meaning. As adjectives, they may accompany a subject. As pronouns they may function as subjects themselves.
- In this case of **aucun—aucune** as well as **nul—nulle**, two negative elements are still necessary to form a negative sentence, but their order is inverted: **aucun—aucune** or **nul—nulle** come first and are followed by **NE**.
- **NE** remains just before the conjugated verb.

ORDER OF THE SENTENCE WITH A NEGATIVE PRONOUN (AUCUN-E—NUL-LE) AS SUBJECT			
Negative Elements		Normal order of the rest of the words	
#1 = Adjective	#2 = NE	*(Pronoun Complement)* Conjugated Verb	Tense and **complements**
Aucun / Nul animal **Aucune / Nulle** bête	**NE**	**fait peur à Tarzan**	Simple
Aucun / Nul film **Aucune / Nulle** vedette	**N(e)'**	**a obtenu cet Oscar**	Compound
Aucun / Nul étudiant **Aucune / Nulle** étudiante	**NE**	*le* **croit**	**Pronoun Complement—** Simple
Aucun / Nul ami **Aucune / Nulle** amie	**NE**	*t'***avait téléphoné**	**Pronoun Complement—** Compound
(No animal scares Tarzan.) *(No film received this Oscar.)* *(No student believes it.)* *(No friend had called you.)*			
#1 = Pronoun	#2 = NE	Conjugated Verb	Tense and **complements**
Aucun / Nul **Aucune / Nulle**	**NE**	**fait peur à Tarzan**	Simple
Aucun / Nul **Aucune / Nulle**	**N(e)'**	**a obtenu cet Oscar**	Compound
Aucun / Nul **Aucune / Nulle**	**NE**	*le* **croit**	*Pronoun Complement—* Simple
Aucun / Nul **Aucune / Nulle**	**NE**	*t'***avait téléphoné**	*Pronoun Complement—* Compound
(None scares Tarzan.) *(None received this Oscar.)* *(None believes it.)* *(None had called you.)*			

> **NOTE** Remember that a pronoun can be used only if the noun it replaces has been stated shortly before, or if the context clearly indicates what the pronoun replaces.
>
> Outside of its context, and used by itself, **nul** is the literary equivalent of **personne** and means *nobody*.
>
> "Nul ne fait peur à Tarzan" without its context means that no one (and not "no animal") scares Tarzan.

Ni . . . Ni (Neither . . . Nor)

- **Ni . . . Ni** are negative conjunctions that are used to link nouns, pronouns, or clauses. They can therefore also stand by the subject of a sentence.
- As always, two negative elements are still necessary to form the negative sentence, but their order is inverted: **Ni . . . Ni** come first and are followed by **NE**.
- **NE** remains just before the conjugated verb.

ORDER OF THE SENTENCE WITH A NEGATIVE PRONOUN AND NI . . . NI AS SUBJECT			
Negative Elements		Normal order of the rest of the words	
#1 = Ni . . . Ni	#2 = NE	Conjugated Verb	Tense and **complements**
Ni Dieu **ni** Diable	N(e)'	**existent**	Simple
Ni son frère **ni** sa soeur	N(e)'	**ont réussi** leur examen	Compound
Ni l'automne **ni** l'hiver	NE	*me* **plaisent**	*Pronoun Complement—* Simple
Ni l'argent **ni** la gloire	NE	*lui* **avaient suffi**	*Pronoun Complement—* Compound
(Neither God nor the Devil exist.) *(Neither his brother nor his sister have passed their exams.)* *(Neither fall nor winter are seasons I like.)* *(Neither money nor glory were enough for him.)*			

REVIEW TABLE: MOST COMMON NEGATIVE STRUCTURES WITH BOTH FUNCTIONS NE ... PERSONNE—RIEN—AUCUN-AUCUNE—NUL-NULLE—NI ... NI ... NE	
Subject **Negative Element #1** + **#2** + Verb	Complement Neg. Element #1 + **Verb** + Neg. Element #2
Personne ne déteste Stéphane. **Personne n'**avait détesté Stéphane.	Stéphane **ne** déteste **personne**. Stéphane **n'**avait détesté **personne**.
(Nobody hates Stéphane.) *(Nobody hated Stéphane.)*	*(Stéphane hates nobody.)* *(Stéphane hated nobody.)*
Rien ne plaît à Paola dans ce magasin. **Rien n'**avait plu à Paola dans ce magasin.	Paola **n'**aime **rien** dans ce magasin. Paola **n'**avait **rien** aimé dans ce magasin.
(Nothing is to Paola's taste in this store.) *(Nothing was to Paola's taste in this store.)*	*(Paola likes nothing in this store.)* *(Paola liked nothing in this store.)*
Aucun commentaire **n'**est stupide. **Aucune** question **ne** m'aura paru stupide.	Il **n'**existe **aucun** commentaire stupide. Luc **ne** m'a posé **aucune** question stupide.
(No comment is stupid.) *(No question will have sounded stupid to me.)*	*(There is no stupid comment.)* *(Luc did not ask me any stupid question.)*
Nul n'entre ici qui **n'**est géomètre (Platon). **Nul ne** serait entré à l'Académie de Platon.	Nicole **ne** voit **nulle** raison de partir. Elle **n'**avait perçu **nulle** sincérité en lui.
(Let no one unversed in geometry enter here.) (On the door to Plato's Academy) *(No one would have been accepted in Plato's Academy.)*	*(Nicole sees no reason to leave.)* *(She had seen no sincerity in him.)*
Ni le froid **ni** la pluie **ne** découragent Pierre. **Ni** le froid **ni** la pluie **n'**ont découragé Pierre.	Pierre **ne** redoute **ni** le froid **ni** la pluie. Pierre **n'**a redouté **ni** le froid **ni** la pluie.
(Neither cold nor rain discourage Pierre.) *(Neither cold nor rain have discouraged Pierre.)*	*(Pierre dreads neither cold nor rain.)* *(Pierre dreaded neither cold nor rain.)*

Reinforced Negative Adverbs *ne ... plus / ne ... jamais*

In order to insist on the negative aspect, **NE ... PLUS** and **NE ... JAMAIS** can qualify the negative elements **personne, nulle part, que, aucun-aucune, ni ... ni.**

These structures are not double negatives but *reinforced ones*.

> Tu **ne** vois **plus personne** ici. Tu **ne** vois **jamais personne** ici. *(You no longer see anyone around here. You never see anyone around here.)*

Paul **ne** va **plus nulle part**. Paul **ne** va **jamais nulle part** ces jours-ci. *(Paul no longer goes anywhere. Paul never goes anywhere these days.)*

Agnès **n'**aime **plus que** les gens snobs. Agnès **n'a jamais que** des snobs autour d'elle. *(Agnès only likes snobs these days. Agnès is always surrounded only by snobs.)*

Il **n'y a plus aucune** minute à perdre. Il **n'y a jamais aucune** minute de trop. *(There is not one minute left to waste. There is never a minute too many.)*

Je **ne** sais **plus ni** le jour **ni** l'heure. Je **ne** sais **jamais ni** la date **ni** l'heure. *(I no longer know what day or time it is. I never know the date or the time.)*

Nonnegative NE

With certain expressions, **NE** is used before the verb by itself. It does not have a negative meaning since it is not accompanied by the required second negative element. It indicates a more formal level of language. This nonnegative **NE** is often associated with the use of the subjunctive mood.

Verbs Implying Fear

A nonnegative **NE** is used with verbs expressing fear: avoir peur que, craindre que, redouter que *(to be afraid that, to fear that, to dread that)*

J'ai toujours **peur que** mes chattes **ne** tombent malades. *(I am always afraid that my cats will become sick.)*

Marie **craint que** ses parents **ne** soient déjà arrivés chez elle: elle n'a pas fait le ménage! *(Marie is worried about her parents having already arrived at her place; she has not cleaned it!)*

Conjunctions Implying Fear or Obstacles

A nonnegative **NE** is also used with the conjunctions that express fear or a possible obstacle: de peur que, de crainte que or avant que, à moins que *(for fear that, dreading that, before, unless)*

Marie a fait le ménage **de peur que** ses parents ne trouvent sa maison sale. *(Marie cleaned her house for fear that her parents find it dirty.)*

Marie va faire le ménage **avant que** ses parents ne viennent la voir. *(Marie is going to clean her house before her parents come to see her.)*

Comparative Structures

NE is also used by itself and therefore without a negative meaning in structures of comparison that mark the superiority or inferiority: plus . . . que and moins . . . que.

> **Ce comédien est** plus sérieux que vous ne le pensez, **mais cet homme politique est bien** moins intelligent que les gens ne le croient! *(This comedian is more serious than you think, but this politician is a lot less intelligent than people believe!)*

> **NOTE** The nonnegative NE tends to be dropped in everyday conversations. Be aware of it, but knowing how to use it is part of a more advanced mastering of the French language.

Interrogative Form

The interrogative form is used to ask questions. There are two main categories of questions: those asking for a yes or no answer, and those requiring specific information. These questions can be asked directly as part of a conversation or a dialogue. They can also be asked indirectly when inserted in a compound sentence.

Direct Questions

Yes or No Answers

There are four ways to ask direct questions requesting **Oui** or **Non** answers.

1. Rising Intonation

When speaking French, especially in everyday conversations in a familiar style, the most common way of asking a **Oui** *(yes)* or **Non** *(no)* question is simply to raise your voice at the end of an affirmative sentence.

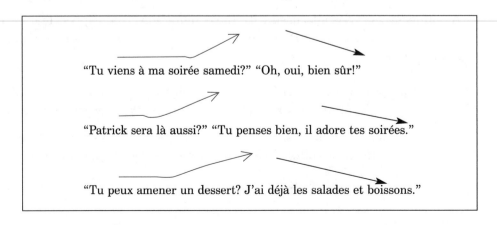

"Tu viens à ma soirée samedi?" "Oh, oui, bien sûr!"

"Patrick sera là aussi?" "Tu penses bien, il adore tes soirées."

"Tu peux amener un dessert? J'ai déjà les salades et boissons."

The answer is another affirmative sentence whose intonation falls on the two or three last syllables.

2. *Est-ce que . . . ?* Interrogative Expression

This is an idiomatic expression, that is, one peculiar to French whose exact translation *(Is it that?)* does not make sense in any other language. It allows one to transform any affirmative sentence into a question by simply adding **est-ce que** . . . at the beginning of it.

- It is very convenient and can be used almost all the time, unless you really want to appear formal.
- Est-ce que . . . can be used with sentences in any tense or mood. It can be answered by a simple "Yes" or "No," or with a more specific explanation.

TRANSFORMING A SENTENCE INTO A QUESTION WITH EST-CE QUE . . . ?	
Affirmative Sentence	Interrogative Sentence Oui or **Non** answers
Patrick est à Caracas.	Est-ce que Patrick est à Caracas?
	Oui, Patrick est à Caracas. **Non**, Patrick **n'**est **pas** à Caracas.
	Is Patrick in Caracas? *Yes, Patrick is in Caracas.* *No, Patrick is not in Caracas.*
Tu viens à ma soirée demain.	Est-ce que tu viens à ma soirée demain?
	Oui, je viens à ta soirée demain. **Non**, je **ne** viendrai **jamais** à ta soirée!
	Will you come to my party tomorrow? *Yes, I will come to your party tomorrow.* *No, I will never come to your party!*
Marie avait un petit mouton.	Est-ce que Marie avait un petit mouton?
	Oui, Marie avait un petit mouton. **Non**, Marie **n'**avait **plus** de petit mouton.
	Did Marie have a little lamb? *Marie had a little lamb.* *No, Marie did not have a little lamb any more.*
Vous irez en France cet été.	Est-ce que vous irez en France cet été?
	Oui, nous irons à Cannes cet été. **Non**, nous **n'**irons **qu'**en Italie cet été.

	Will you go to France this summer? *Yes, we will got to France this summer.* *No, we will go only to Italy this summer.*
Nous nous sommes promenées sur la Croisette et sur la Promenade des Anglais.	Est-ce que nous nous sommes promenées sur la Croisette et sur la Promenade des Anglais?
	Oui, nous nous sommes promenées sur les deux avenues. **Non**, nous **ne** sommes promenées **ni** sur la Croisette **ni** sur la Promenade des Anglais.

Did you take a walk along the Croisette in Cannes and the Promenade in Nice?
Yes, we took a walk on both avenues.
No, we took a walk neither in the Croisette nor on the Promenade.

Verb—Subject Pronoun Inversion

Subject Pronouns except Je

If the subject is any personal pronoun except the first person **Je**, you can turn an affirmative sentence into a question by simply inverting the order subject-verb.

> Vous travaillez à l'Hôtel Carlton. Travaillez-vous à l'Hôtel Carlton?
> *(Do you work at the Carlton Hotel?)*

Je as Subject

Je can only be inverted with the verbs pouvoir, devoir, être, and occasionally avoir. This inversion makes the question sound much more formal: the literary form of the first person of pouvoir—je puis instead of je peux—is used in the inversion. Most of the time, **est-ce que** is used with **Je**.

> Puis-je ouvrir la fenêtre? *(May I open the window?)*

> Dois-je aller voir mon patron? *(Must I go see my boss?)*

> Suis-je en retard? *(Am I late?)*

> Ai-je un rendez-vous demain? *(Do I have an appointment tomorrow?)*

Structure

- Since normally the position of the subject is before the verb, when inverted, the verb and its subject pronoun are linked by a hyphen. That way, one will not think that the subject is missing

> Tu travailles: Travailles-tu? *(Are you working?)*

- When the verb ends in a vowel, and the pronoun subject starts with a vowel as well, the letter -t- is inserted between verb and subject. That facilitates the pronunciation and avoids the harsh sound of two juxtaposed vowels:

  Elle arrive: Arrive - **t** - elle? *(Is she arriving?)*

- When the verb is conjugated in a compound tense, the auxiliary verb and the subject pronoun are inverted. All the other words stay in the same place:

  Nous avons chanté faux: **Avons-nous** chanté faux? *(Did we sing off-key?)*

INVERSION OF SUBJECT PRONOUN AND VERB		
Tu	Tu viens ce soir	Viens-tu ce soir?
		Oui, je viens **Non**, je **ne** viens **pas** ce soir
(Are you coming tonight?) *(Yes, I am coming.)* *(No, he is not coming tonight.)*		
Elle	Elle arrive demain	Arrive-t-elle demain?
Il On	Il part ce soir On mange bien en France	Part-il ce soir? Mange-t-on bien en France?
		Oui, elle arrive demain **Non**, il **ne** part **plus** ce soir
(Is she arriving tomorrow?) *(Yes, she arrives tomorrow.)* *(No, he is not leaving tonight anymore.)*		
Nous	Nous sommes déjà arrivés	Sommes-nous déjà arrivés?
		Oui, nous sommes déjà arrivés **Non**, nous **ne** sommes **pas encore** arrivés
(Are we there yet?) *(Yes, we have arrived.)* *(No, we have not arrived yet.)*		
Vous	Vous avez eu de la chance	Avez-vous eu de la chance?
		Oui, nous avons eu de la chance **Non**, nous **n'**avons **jamais** eu de chance
(Did you have any luck?) *(Yes, we were lucky.)* *(No, we never had any luck.)*		

Ils Elles	Ils auront un joyeux Noël Elles seront venues les voir	Auront-ils un joyeux Noël? Seront-elles venues les voir?
		Oui, ils auront un joyeux Noël **Non**, elles **ne** seront **pas** venues
(Will they have a Merry Christmas?) *(Yes, they will have a Merry Christmas.)* *(No, they will not have come.)*		

Inversion of a Subject Noun

Because a noun is longer, simply inverting it would make the sentence sound awkward; so when the subject is not a pronoun, you can still ask a question with an inversion but you must use a little trick.

The point is to invert a pronoun so just repeat the subject in the form of its corresponding pronoun after the verb. This way, you can recreate the verb-personal pronoun subject structure that was explained above.

DUPLICATION OF SUBJECT AND INVERSION PRONOUN AND VERB		
Jean (= il)	Jean vient ce soir	Jean vient-il ce soir?
		Oui, Jean vient ce soir **Non**, Jean **ne** vient **pas** ce soir
(Is Jean coming tonight?) *(Yes, Jean is coming tonight.)* *(No, he is not coming tonight.)*		
Sylvia (elle)	Sylvia arrive demain	Sylvia arrive-t-elle demain?
		Oui, Sylvia arrive demain **Non**, Sylvia **n'**arrive **plus** demain
(Is Sylvia arriving tomorrow?) *(Yes, Sylvia arrives tomorrow.)* *(No, she no longer arrives tomorrow.)*		
Les enfants (ils)	Les enfants sont partis	Les enfants sont-ils partis?
		Oui, Les enfants sont partis **Non**, ils **ne** sont **pas encore** partis
(Are the children gone?) *(Yes, the children have left.)* *(No, they have not left yet.)*		

- This is done only with the 3rd person singular or plural pronouns that replace all regular nouns.
- This construction is literary and rarely used in everyday or conversational French.

Negative Questions

Questions can be asked in a negative form, generally to seek reassurance or confirmation.

- Negative questions are generally formed by using the inversion of a negative sentence or **est-ce que** and the negative sentence:

> (Vous n'êtes plus marié.) **N'êtes-vous plus** marié? *(Aren't you married anymore?)*

> (Marc n'est pas marié.) Marc **n'est-il pas** marié? *(Isn't Marc married?)*

> (Vous n'avez pas de voiture.) **Est-ce que** vous **n'avez pas** de voiture? *(Don't you have a car?)*

- When negative questions are answered in an affirmative way, the positive adverb is not oui but **SI**:

> **N'**êtes-vous **plus** marié? **Si**, je suis marié. *(Yes, I am.)*

> **Est-ce que** vous **n'avez pas** de voiture? Non, je n'en ai pas. *(No, I don't.)*

Specific Questions

There is a lot of information that you can seek about who performs the action or the circumstances in which it is performed.

Interrogative Pronouns

To ask a question about the subject (who) or the object (what) of the action, the sentence must start with one of the interrogative pronouns.

INTERROGATIVE PRONOUNS		
Simple and Compound Pronoun with Inversion Subject-Verb		
Qui (Person)	Subject Direct Object Indirect Object	Qui vient ce soir? Qui veux-tu inviter ce soir? À qui écris- tu cette lettre?
Who is coming tonight? *Whom do you want to invite tonight?* *To whom are you writing this letter?*		
Que (Thing)	Direct Object	Que veut-elle pour son anniversaire? Que veut ton voisin?
What does she want for her birthday? *What does your neighbor want?*		
Quoi (Thing)	Indirect Object	À quoi penses-tu Vers quoi se dirige le *Titanic?* En quoi est fait le Parthénon?
What are you thinking about? *What is the Titanic heading toward?* *What is the Parthenon made of?*		
Lequel Auquel Duquel	Choice—Direct Choice—À Choice—De	J'ai 2 stylos. Lequel est le plus beau? À quelle université vas-tu? De quel professeur parlent ces étudiants?
I have 2 pens: which one is the most beautiful? *To which university are you going?* *Which prof are these students talking about?*		
Reinforced Oral Form with Est-ce que + Qui / Que and no inversion		
Qui est-ce qui Qui est-ce que	Person Subject Person Object	Qui est-ce qui vient ce soir? Qui est-ce que tu as invité?
Who is it that is coming tonight? *Who is it you invited tonight?*		
Qu'est ce qui Qu'est-ce que	Thing Subject Thing Object	Qu(e)' est-ce qui se passe ici? Qu(e)' est-ce que vous voulez?
What is going on here? *What is it you want?*		

Refer to Chapter 9 for
Interrogative Pronouns

Interrogative Adverbs

Questions asking for all other types of information require the corresponding interrogative adverb.

- Both the inversion and the **est-ce que** constructions are possible with all these adverbs. Your choice between them is the same as for regular **Oui** or **Non** questions.
- The duplication of the subject by its corresponding pronoun to recreate an inversion is also possible.

INTERROGATIVE ADVERBS AND POSSIBLE INTERROGATIVE STRUCTURES		
Quand—Où—Comment—Pourquoi—Combien		
Inversion—Est-ce Que . . . —Duplication of Subject + Inversion		
Circumstance	ADVERB	Interrogative Sentences
Time Temps	QUAND?	Quand **voulez-vous** diner? Quand **est-ce que** vous voulez diner? Quand **tes parents veulent-ils** diner?
		Nous voulons diner vers 20 heures.
(When do you want to eat? We want to eat around 8 o'clock.)		
Location Lieu	OÙ?	Où **êtes-vous** allés pendant vos vacances? Où **est-ce que** vous êtes allés cet été? Où **William est-il allé** cette-fois-ci?
		William n'est pas allé en vacances.
(Where did William go on vacation? William did not leave for his vacation.)		
Manner Manière	COMMENT?	Comment **va-t-elle** aujourd'hui? Comment **est-ce que** va Viviane aujourd'hui? Comment **Viviane va-t-elle** aujourd'hui?
		Viviane va beaucoup mieux, merci.
(How is Viviane today? Viviane is feeling much better, thanks.)		
Cause Cause	POURQUOI?	Pourquoi **allons-nous** voir ce film? Pourquoi **est-ce que** nous allons voir ce film? Pourquoi **tes amis vont-ils** voir ce film?
		Parce qu'il a une bonne critique.
(Why are your friends going to see this movie? Because the reviews are good.)		
Quantity Quantité	COMBIEN?	Combien **as-tu** de frères et soeurs? Combien **est-ce que** tu as de frères et soeurs? Combien **Florent a-t-il** de frères?
		Je n'ai ni frère ni soeur. Florent a six frères!
(How many brothers does Florent have? Florent has six brothers. I have neither brother nor sister.)		

Intermediate—Advanced Topic

Indirect Questions

Use

An indirect question is a question that is not directly posed or heard in a conversation, but reported.

- Indirect questions are generally introduced by a series of verbs that signify some form of request in themselves: demander—se demander, dire, expliquer, raconter *(to ask, to wonder, to say, to explain, to tell)*
- Never use the complex ~~Qui est-ce qui/que~~ or ~~Qu'est-ce qui/que~~ forms in indirect questions. They are replaced by **CE qui** and **CE que**.

 NOTE Be aware of the following ways of constructing indirect questions when you encounter them in written texts. They do require more advanced expertise in the language, so refer to the following examples below when you need to form one yourself.

Formation

- Indirect questions are located in the subordinate clause and they do not take a question mark.
- The construction of indirect questions depends on the interrogative elements you need to use. These can be
  - Interrogative Pronouns

    Qui, Ce qui-que, À quoi, De quoi, Lequel . . . , Auquel . . . , Duquel . . .

  - Interrogative Adverbs

    Quand, où, comment, pourquoi, combien

- The word order also varies according to the interrogative element.

INDIRECT QUESTION STRUCTURES WITH INTERROGATIVE **PRONOUNS** AND ADVERBS		
Indirect Question Referring to:	**PRONOUNS**	
People	**QUI** Subject Object After a preposition	Je me demande **qui** vient ce soir. Dis-moi **qui** tu as invité. Elle ne sait pas **à qui** elle parle!
		I wonder who is coming tonight. *Tell me who(m) you have invited.* *She does not know to whom she is speaking!*
Things	**CE QUI** Subject	Je me demande **ce qui** se passe ici.
		I wonder what is going on here.
	CE QUE Direct Object	Elle m'explique **ce que** le philosophe a écrit.
		She is explaining to me what the philosopher wrote.
	Prep + QUOI	Valentin ne sait pas **à quoi** Léa pense. Léa ne sait pas **de quoi** Valentin a besoin.
		Valentin does not know what Léa thinks about. *Léa does not know what Valentin needs.*
Choices	**LEQUEL . . .** **AUQUEL . . .** **DUQUEL . . .**	J'ai deux robes vertes. Je ne sais pas **laquelle** je préfère. Paul est au cinéma. Je me demande **auquel** il est allé. Tu me parles de tes frères, mais je ne sais pas **desquels** il s'agit.
		I do not know which one I prefer. *I wonder to which one he went.* *I have no idea which ones it is about.*
Indirect Question Asking about:	**ADVERBS**	
Time—Temps	**QUAND**	Je ne me rappelle plus **quand** tu es né.
		I do not remember when you were born.
Location—Lieu	**OÙ**	Paul se demande toujours **où** il a mis ses clés.
		Paul always wonders where he put his keys.

Manner—Manière	**COMMENT**	Dis-moi **comment** tu as réussi cet examen.
		Tell me how you passed this exam.
Cause—Cause	**POURQUOI**	Elle raconte **pourquoi** ses parents ont immigré.
		She is telling why her parents immigrated.
Quantity—Quantité	**COMBIEN**	Je sais **combien** ton abonnement Internet vaut.
		I know how much your Internet subscription is.

TIP BOX

Although indirect questions may not be easily recognizable, the best way of verifying if a <u>clause</u> is one is to try to transform it into a direct question:

Je me demande <u>qui vient ce soir</u>. **"Qui vient ce soir?"** *(I wonder who is coming tonight. "Who is coming tonight?")*

Elle m'explique <u>ce que le philosophe a écrit</u>. **"Qu'est-ce que le philosophe a écrit?"** *(She explains to me what the philosopher wrote. "What did the philosopher write?")*

Dis-moi <u>comment tu as réussi cet examen</u>. **"Comment as-tu réussi cet examen?"** *(Tell me how you passed this exam. "How did you pass this exam?")*

Je sais <u>combien ton abonnement Internet vaut</u>. **"Combien ton abonnement Internet vaut-il?"** *(I know how much your Internet subscription costs. "How much does your Internet subscription cost?")*

AFFIRMATION—NEGATION—INTERROGATION BASIC STRUCTURES			
Forme Affirmative	Sujet + **Verbe Conjugué** = **VC** (+ COD) (+ COI) (+ CC)		
	Cette phrase **est** affirmative.		
	Peut-être, À peine, Sans doute, Encore, Tout au plus, À plus forte raison, Du moins, Aussi, Ainsi . . . ▼ + **VC** + Sujet + COD + COI + CC		
	Sans doute **est**-elle **affirmative**.		
Forme Négative	NE	*(P.P. Comp)* **Verbe Conj** Temps Simple *(P.P. Comp = Pronom Personnel Complément)*	Que, Pas, Jamais, Personne, Guère, Nulle Part, Plus, Ni . . . ni, Aucun-e, Rien, Nul-le, Nullement
	Cette phrase **n'est nullement** affirmative.		

NE	*(PP. Comp)* **Aux. Conj.** VC Temps Composé Aux. Conj = Auxiliaire Conjugué	Pas, Plus, Guère, Rien Jamais, Nullement	**PARTICIPE PASSÉ**

Cette phrase **n'a jamais éte** affirmative!

NE	*(PP. Comp)* **Aux. Conj.** VC Temps Composé	**PARTICIPE PASSÉ**	Personne, Que, Ni . . . ni, Nulle Part, Nul-le, Aucun-e

Cette phrase **n' a EU aucun** élément affirmatif.

NE	Pas, Plus, Guère, Rien Jamais, Nullement	*(PP. Comp)* **V. INFINITIF**

Cette phrase est faite pour **ne pas être** affirmative.

NE	*(PP. Comp)* **V. INFINITIF**	Personne, Que, Nulle Part, Ni . . . ni, Nul-le, Aucun-e

Cette phrase est faite pour **n' AVOIR** aucun élément affirmatif.

Personne Rien Aucun-e Nul-le Ni . . . Ni	NE	*(PP. Comp)* **Verbe Conjugué** Temps Simple/Composé

Aucune phrase **n' est** complètement négative.

Forme Interrogative	Est-ce que + Sujet + **Verb Conjugué** . . . ? Est-ce que cette phrase **est** affirmative?	Oui / Non
	Verbe Conjugué + Pronom Sujet (sauf Je) . . . ?	
	Est-elle négative ou interrogative?	
	Sujet + **Verbe Conjugué** + Pronom . . . ?	
	Cette phrase **est**-elle interrogative?	
	Qui, Que, Quoi, Lequel, Auquel, Duquel · Est-ce qui/Est-ce que + S + **VC** Pronom Sujet + **VC**	

Qu'est-ce qui **est** interrogatif? Laquelle **est** négative?	
Quand, Où, Comment, Pourquoi, Combien	Est-ce qui/Est-ce que + S + **VC** **VC** + Pronom Sujet + Sujet + **VC** + Pronom
Pourquoi est-ce que cette phrase **est** interrogative? **Est**-elle négative? Ces phrases **sont**-elles affirmatives?	

Practice What You Learned

Exercises are rated according to four levels of difficulty:

- Beginner easy [*]
- Beginner challenging [**]
- Intermediate [***]
- Advanced [****]

1. Rewrite or complete the affirmative sentences with the appropriate modification. [**]

    A. Une belle princesse est née dans un pays fort lointain
       Dans un pays fort lointain _____

    B. Tu serais peut-être venu si tu avais su
       Peut-être _____

    C. Elle répondit en rougissant: "Je vous aime."
       "Je vous aime," _____

2. Rewrite the sentences with verbs in simple tenses in the negative form using the (negative element provided). [**]

Example:

Franz est allemand et gentil (ne / ni . . . ni)—Franz n'est ni allemand ni gentil

    A. Vous êtes au troisième étage (ne / pas encore).

    _____

    B. Il y avait beaucoup de biscuits au chocolat (ne / pas).

    _____

    C. Je suis déçue par mes étudiants (ne / jamais).

    _____

    D. Cet exercice paraît difficile (ne / pas vraiment).

    _____

E. Paul te donnera cinq Euros (ne / que).

_____

F. Christian a foi en Dieu (ne / aucun).

_____

G. Madame Lefour les leur confie (ne / nullement).

_____

3. Rewrite the sentences with verbs in compound tenses in the negative form using the (negative element provided). [***]

A. Carla a mangé hier (ne / rien).

_____

B. Cédric les a rencontrées (ne / nulle part).

_____

C. Le chanteur a reçu l'Oscar (ne / aucun).

_____

D. Tes cousins auront été contents de leur séjour (ne / guère).

_____

E. Fab a aimé le beurre de cacahuètes et le Dr. Pepper (ne / ni . . . ni . . .).

_____

F. Les étudiants d'À la Riviera y avaient participé avant (ne / jamais).

_____

4. Transform the affirmative sentences into a question using all the possible different interrogative structures: **est-ce que**, inversion verb—subject pronoun, or noun—inversion verb—subject pronoun. [**]

A. J'ai toujours raison

_____

_____

B. Marianne est mariée à Marc

_____

_____

C. Les caribous ne vivent pas aux Caraïbes

_____

_____

D. Vous parlez français très bien

_____

_____

5. Transform the affirmative sentence into a question using **est-ce que** or the inversion with a pronoun. Respond to it negatively, using the most logical negative elements in the following list: Ne . . . que — Ne . . . plus — Ne . . . aucun-e — Ne . . . jamais — Ne . . . nullement — Ne . . . pas encore. [***]

Examples:

> Edouard a une Ferrari et une Porsche.
>
> Est-ce qu'Edouard a une Ferrari et une Porsche?
>
> Non, Edouard n'a ni une Ferrari ni une Porsche!

A. Un astronaute a marché sur la planète Mars.

_____

_____

B. Vous croyez au Père Noël.

_____

_____

C. Nous sommes au 22ème siècle.

_____

_____

D. Francis accepte la responsabilité.

_____

_____

E. Il y a des conséquences à ses actes irresponsables.

_____

_____

F. Elle aime le chocolat au lait et noir.

_____

_____

6. Complete the following paragraph with the missing negative element(s): [**]

ne . . . guère — jamais — personne — ne . . . ni . . . ni — que — pas — rien

_____ n'est immortel. La plupart des gens oublient souvent que la vie et courte et ils n'en profitent _____ assez. Ils perdent du temps à se disputer et à ne _____ voir les choses vraiment importantes: la paix, la générosité, l'amitié. À part les biens matériels, _____ ne les intéresse. Pourtant, nous _____ avons _____ de temps devant nous, la moyenne de vie n'est _____ 72 années. Ce _____ est _____ long _____ suffisant pour apprendre la sagesse!

Chapter 15

SENTENCES, CLAUSES, AND CONJUNCTIVE SUBORDINATE CLAUSES

Introduction

Think of your sentence as a railroad on which to assemble a train. Words are like railroad cars that line up, one after another, in a certain order. The cars themselves can be replaced but their position in the sequence remains the same.

$$\boxed{\text{Subject}} + \boxed{\text{Verb} + \text{(Conjunction)}} + \boxed{\text{(Subject)}} + \boxed{\text{Verb}}$$

What gets the train going is its engine: the verb. To form a sentence, you must have an engine turned on, namely a conjugated verb—CV.

Sentences

Simple Sentences

Formation

A group of words that contains a conjugated verb and forms a meaningful unit is called a *clause*.

Minimal Word Needed to Form an Independent Clause

- The minimal clause is constituted solely of a conjugated verb. Such clauses are made of a verb in the imperative mood:

> Sors! *(Get out!)*
>
> Étudions! *(Let's study!)*
>
> Entrez! *(Come in!)*

> Refer to Chapter 11 on
> **Imperative Moods**

- The clause can also consist of other words—a subject and/or complements—but they are not mandatory. What constitutes the clause is the conjugated verb:

> **Venez** nous voir ce soir. *(Come and see us tonight.)*
>
> Nous vous **attendons** pour l'apéritif. *(We are expecting you over for a drink.)*

NOTE One conjugated verb forms one clause.

Minimal Clause Needed to Form a Simple Sentence

One clause constitutes a simple sentence. The minimum requirement for a clause is a conjugated verb, but there can be many other words in a clause. It remains a simple sentence as long as there is no other conjugated verbs:

> **Entrez**! *(Come in!)*
>
> **Asseyez**-vous. *(Sit down!)*
>
> Comment **allez**-vous? *(How are you doing?)*
>
> Votre visite **est** une surprise. *(Your visit is a surprise.)*
>
> Je ne m'**attendais** pas à cet agréable moment avec vous. *(I was not expecting this nice moment spent in your company.)*
>
> Nous ne nous **sommes** pas **vues** depuis le déjeuner pendant la réception en l'honneur de la Femme de l'Année sur le campus de l'Université de Cal Poly. *(We haven't seen each other since the lunch at the reception for the Woman of the Year Award ceremony, on the Cal Poly campus.)*

NOTE One clause forms one simple sentence.

Independent Clause

The clause that constitutes a simple sentence is called **independent**. As its name indicates, it is self-sufficient because it does not need any other group of words to form a meaningful unit on its own.

An independent clause contains only one conjugated verb and makes sense by itself. When it starts with a capital letter and ends with a period, it forms a *simple sentence*.

NOTE The clause that forms a simple sentence is independent.

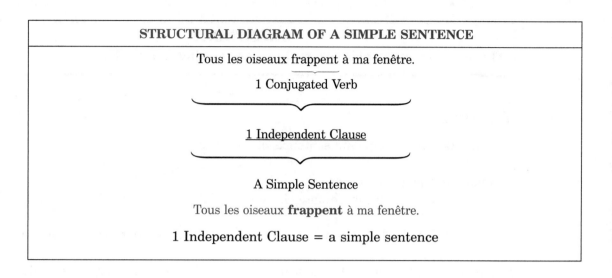

Compound Sentences

Formation

Compound sentences consist of two or more clauses; that is, they contain two or more conjugated verbs.

In the French sentence, the various clauses must be linked together by a specific work of junction. French clauses cannot simply be juxtaposed as they are in English:

The man (whom) I see is seven feet tall = L'homme **QUE** je vois fait 2 m.

I am telling you (that) he is a famous actor = Je te dis **QUE** c'est un acteur célèbre.

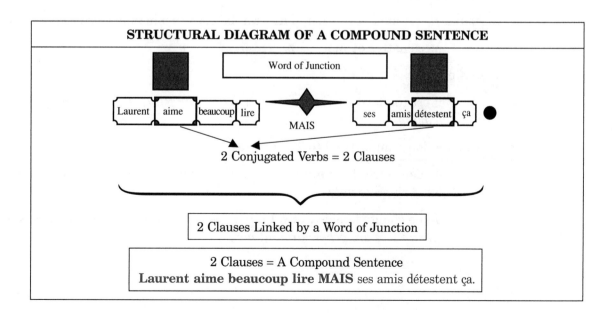

> ### IMPORTANT!
> **There are as many clauses as there are conjugated verbs.**

Types of Clauses

Once inserted in a compound sentence, clauses can

- remain independent clauses
- become principal or subordinate clauses.

The kind of clauses they become in the compound sentence depends on two factors:

1. The type of junction words that is used to bring the two previously independent clauses together into the compound sentence
2. The fact that the clause could stand on its own and remain a meaningful unit or not.

Linking Words

There are two kinds of linking words.

Conjunctions

Conjunctions can be:

1. of coordination
2. of subordination

- Certain conjunctions—**et, ou,** and **ni**—can be used to join nouns or pronouns together:

    mes chattes **et** moi . . . (*my cats and I . . .*)

as well as phrases:

    il est tombé en arrivant **ou** en partant (*he fell as he was coming or leaving*)

- All conjunctions can be used to join clauses:

    Je danse très bien **mais** je chante horriblement mal. (*I dance very well but I sing horribly.*)

    Je ne chante jamais **quand** il y a des gens autour de moi. (*I never sing when there are people around me.*)

Conjunctions of Coordination

Mais, ou, et, donc, or, ni, car *(Seven Conjunctions of Coordination)*

As their name indicates, these conjunctions organize each clause in the sentence on an equal basis. Coordinated clauses in the compound sentence are like coworkers in an office, on the same hierarchical level.

There are seven principal conjunctions of coordination.

mais, ou, et, donc, or, ni, car

CONJUNCTIONS OF COORDINATION		
		If the relation between clauses is one of:
Mais	*But*	Opposition
Ou	*Or*	Alternative
Et	*And*	Addition
Donc	*Therefore*	Consequence
Or	*In fact*	Precision
Ni	*Neither*	Negation
Car	*For* *(meaning because)*	Cause

Equality

All clauses joined by a conjunction of coordination are equal because they can be separated from each other and still form a meaningful sentence on their own.

Neither clause needs the other one to make sense.

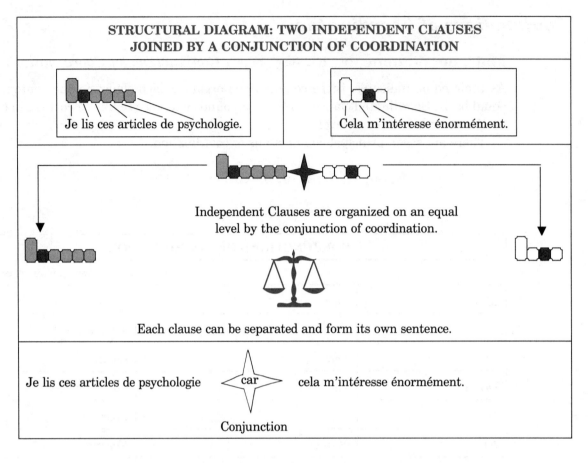

Il y a du vent **mais** il fait très bon.
Il y a du vent.
Mais il fait très bon.
(There is a little wind but it is very nice.)

Veux-tu sortir **ou** préfères-tu dormir?
Veux-tu sortir?
Ou préfères-tu dormir?
(Would you like to go out or would you rather sleep?)

Patrick veut réussir **et** je vais l'aider.
Patrick veut réussir.
Et je vais l'aider.
(Patrick wants to succeed and I will help him.)

Je pense **donc** je suis. (**Descartes**)
Je pense.
Donc je suis.
(Cogito ergo sum: I think, therefore I am.)

Il est accusé **or** il a un alibi.
Il est accusé.
Or il a un alibi.
(He is accused and yet he has an alibi.)

Je ne sais pas la date **ni** quelle heure il est.
Je ne sais pas la date.
Ni quelle heure il est.
(I do not know what day or what time it is.)

Je l'aime bien **car** elle est gentille.
Je l'aime bien.
Car elle est gentille.
(I like her for she is nice.)

TIP BOX

French children remember their conjunctions of coordination from the sentence:

"Mais où est donc Ornicar?" *(But where can Ornicar be?)*
Mais—Ou—Et—Donc—Or—Ni—Car

Remember: Coordination is Co-order. You are ORDERing your independent clauses as CO-lleagues in the compound sentence. But they can fight and split at any time to be by themselves since they are independent!

Conjunctions of Subordination

Use with Declarative Verbs

- Conjunctions of subordination are found with verbs that belong to certain categories.

Declaration	déclarer, dire, expliquer, raconter, répéter, assurer, confier, suggérer
(To declare, to say, to explain, to tell, to repeat, to assure, to confide, to suggest)	
Opinion	penser, croire, supposer, assumer, juger, estimer, conclure, signifier, savoir
(To think, to believe, to suppose, to assume, to judge, to estimate, to conclude, to signify, to know)	
Wish	espérer, souhaiter, rêver, désirer, inventer
(To hope, to wish, to dream, to desire, to invent)	
Command	ordonner, exiger, décréter, décider, imposer, trancher, statuer
(To command, to demand, to decree, to decide, to impose, to opt, to decide on)	
Request	demander, prier, implorer, revendiquer, supplier
(To ask, to pray, to implore, to claim, to beg)	

Il a déclaré **que** Dieu est mort. *(He declared that God is dead.)*

Vous pensez **qu'**il existe. *(You think he exists.)*

Nous demandons **que** vous y réfléchissiez. *(We ask you to think about it.)*

- Conjunctions of subordination are followed by a clause that starts with a subject.

Function

Conjunctions of subordination connect clauses that are not equal to each other:

  o   one clause is "superior,"

It is called the **principal clause: la proposition principale**.

  o   the other one(s) is put under the principal's orders,

It is called the **subordinate clause: la proposition subordonnée**.

Principal clause

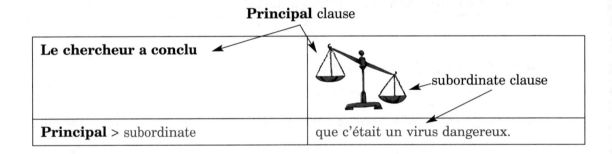

Le chercheur a conclu	
Principal > subordinate	que c'était un virus dangereux.

subordinate clause

Main Conjonction of Subordination-Inequality

The most common conjunction of subordination is **QUE**.

- **Que,** as a conjunction of subordination, is found directly after the verb of the **principal clause** or at the very beginning of the sentence if the subordinate starts it. This shows that the conjunction of subordination is actually part of the subordinate clause and not the principal:

    J'ai toujours dit que la grammaire française peut être facile. (*I have always said that French grammar can be easy.*)

    Que tu le croies ou non, **il y a un opossum dans notre jardin.** (*Whether you believe it or not, there is a possum in our garden.*)

- **Que** is often used in combination with an adverb or a preposition.

NOTE **Que** is a word with multiple natures. Que can be

- an adverb

in negative or comparative structures
(ne . . . **que**—plus/moins/aussi . . . **que**),

- a relative pronoun

replacing a direct object complement

- a conjunction

You can tell it is a conjunction, when **que** directly follows a verb whose meaning is linked to the categories of declaration, opinion, wish, command, and request. **Que** as a conjunction is also found in compound sentences at the beginning of the subordinate clause.

Always analyze the structure of your sentence to make sure that **que** is a conjunction.

In most cases, the **principal clause** comes first and is followed by the subordinate clause(s). But it is not mandatory and certain subordinate clauses can also start the sentence if one wishes to emphasize them. The conjunction of subordination is then the very first word of the sentence. The possibility of starting your sentence with the subordinate clause depends upon the verb of the principal clause.

> Qu'il pleuve ou qu'il vente, **ils se marieront sur les falaises de La Jolla.** (*Rain or wind, they will get married on the La Jolla cliffs.*)

TIP BOX
It is safer, at a beginner or intermediate level in French, to keep the order:

Principal clause + **Conjunction of Subordination** + Subordinate Clause

But if you want to invert the order, make sure to verify your sentence by translating the groups of words, as you want them to appear. If it sounds strange in English, it is most likely incorrect in French as well:

> Dès qu'il entrera, nous crierons "Surprise!" (*As soon as he comes in, we will shout "Surprise!"*)

> Wrong: ~~Que tu as raison, je dis.~~ (*That you are right I say.*)

> *Refer to Chapter 17 on*
> **Subjunctive Mood**

CONJUNCTIONS OF SUBORDINATION		
[possible word] **que***		
***<u>Conjunctions</u>** and **<u>Verbs</u>** underlined denote the subjunctive mood.		
Compound		**Simple**
Alors que While (opposition)	**Charlotte écoute de la musique alors qu'**elle devrait étudier.	**Comme**
(Charlotte is listening to music although she should be studying.)		As (comparison)
Afin que In order to	**Mes parents ont travaillé dur <u>afin que</u> je <u>puisse</u> faire des études.**	
(My parents worked hard so I could study at the university.)		
Avant que Before	**Rentrons les chaises du jardin <u>avant qu'</u> il ne se <u>mette</u> à pleuvoir.**	
(Let's bring the garden chairs in before it starts to rain.)		
Après que After	**Paul est parti tout de suite après que** tu lui as téléphoné.	
(Paul left right after you called him.)		
Aussitôt que Dès que As soon as	**Aussitôt que/Dès que** vous reviendrez **nous pourrons déjeuner.**	**Quand** When (time)
(As soon as you come back, we will be able to have lunch.)		
Bien que Although	**Elle porte un long manteau noir <u>bien qu'</u> il <u>fasse</u> très chaud!**	
(She is wearing a long black coat although it is very hot!)		
Depuis que Since (origin)	**Depuis que** Philip apprend le français, **son anglais s'est amélioré.**	
(Since Philip has been learning French, his English is improving.)		

Jusqu'à ce que Until	**Mes chattes jouent avec moi** <u>jusqu'à ce que</u> je <u>sois</u> fatiguée.	**Que** That (generic)
(*My cats play with me until I am tired.*)		
Pendant que While (duration)	**Pendant que** tu finis ce logiciel, **je vais écrire le guide de l'utilisateur.**	
(*While you finish this software code, I am going to write the User's Guide.*)		
Parce que Because	**Sylvie part en vacances aux Caraïbes** **parce qu'** elle fait de la plongée.	
(*Sylvie is going on vacation in the Caribbean islands because she scuba dives.*)		
Puisque Since (cause)	**Puisque** tu vas faire des courses, **achète le pain et une tarte tatin.**	
(*Since you are going shopping, buy the bread and an apple pie.*)		
Pour que So that	**Il faut faire des compromis** <u>pour que</u> tout le monde <u>soit</u> content.	**Si** If (condition)
(*One must compromise so that everyone is happy.*)		
Quoique Even though	**La vie est belle** <u>quoiqu'</u> elle ne <u>paraisse</u> pas facile	
(*Life is beautiful even though it may not seem easy.*)		
Selon que Depending upon	**Selon que** la neige tombe ou pas, **nous ferons du ski ou la sieste.**	
(*Depending upon it snowing or not, we will go skiing or take a nap.*)		
Vu que Considering that	**Marc ne sait pas quoi offrir pour son anniversaire** **vu que** Nicole n'aime jamais rien.	
(*Marc does not know what to buy for her birthday considering Nicole never likes anything.*)		

Comme tu l'avais prédit, **il fait un temps magnifique aujourd'hui.** (*As you had predicted, the weather is gorgeous today.*)

Thérèse sera heureuse quand elle entendra cette bonne nouvelle. (*Thérèse will be happy when she hears such good news.*)

Nous avons demandé que la maison soit peinte en gris et bleu. (*We asked that the house be painted in gray and blue.*)

Je ne sais pas si elle s'appelle Anne ou Anna. (*I do not know if her name is Anne or Anna.*)

Proposition Principale	Conjonction de **SUB**ordination	Proposition subordonnée
Il faut faire des compromis **Nous lui avons demandé** **Je ne sais pas**	**pour que** **que** **si**	
		tout le monde soit content. la maison soit peinte en bleu. elle s'appelle Anne ou Anna.
Il faut faire des compromis. **Nous lui avons demandé.** **Je ne sais pas.**	*Wrong*: ~~Pour que tout le monde soit content.~~ *Wrong*: ~~Que la maison soit peinte en bleu.~~ *Wrong*: ~~Si elle s'appelle Anne ou Anna.~~	
The principal clauses can become independent clauses to form a meaningful simple sentence.	The conjunctive subordinate clauses do not make sense without being attached to their principal clauses.	

IMPORTANT!

Many conjunctions of subordination are one of the signals of the subjunctive mood. The subjunctive mood conveys a highly subjective context.

Conjunctions demanding the subjunctive mood appear underlined in the overview on pages 302–303. Always make sure to verify if the conjunction of subordination you want to use in your sentence is a subjunctive mood trigger.

As a general rule:

As soon as you hear, read, or think QUE,
- **ask yourself: "subjective—subjunctive?"**
- **remember:**
  ConjunCtion // ConjonQUEtion: the main conjunction is QUE
  Conjunctions of SUBordination are found in clauses after a principal that may be SUBjective and thus require the SUBjunctive mood in the SUBordinate.

Refer to Chapter 17 on
Subjunctive Mood

Relative Pronouns

Relative pronouns are the second type of linking words. They join independent clauses that have a noun in common.

Refer to Chapter 16 on **Relative Clauses**

Function

The relative pronoun replaces the common noun in the relative clause so as to avoid a repetition in the compound sentence.

Once joined in the compound sentence by the relative pronoun, the originally independent clauses become principal and subordinate, in the same way as with conjunctions of subordination.

Structure

The relative compound sentence is formed of

- a **principal clause**, proposition principale,
- and a subordinate clause, proposition subordonnée relative.

The subordinate clause is called *relative* since it is introduced in the sentence by the relative pronoun.

TIP BOX

It is also called a relative clause because it is a parent of the principal clause. Like you and your relatives, they both share something in common: not blood or the bond of marriage, but a noun. It is this noun that is being replaced by the relative pronoun:

J'adore **ce livre**. *(I love this book.)*

Ce livre est de Gilles Deleuze. *(This book is by Gilles Deleuze.)*

J'adore ce livre **qui** est de Gilles Deleuze. *(I love this book that is by Gilles Deleuze.)*

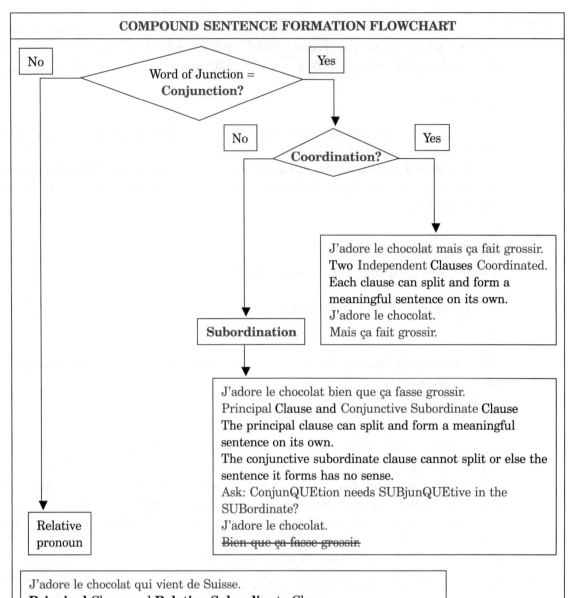

COMPOUND SENTENCE FORMATION FLOWCHART

No

Word of Junction =
Conjunction?

Yes

No

Coordination?

Yes

J'adore le chocolat mais ça fait grossir.
Two Independent Clauses Coordinated.
Each clause can split and form a
meaningful sentence on its own.
J'adore le chocolat.
Mais ça fait grossir.

Subordination

J'adore le chocolat bien que ça fasse grossir.
Principal **Clause** and Conjunctive Subordinate **Clause**
The principal clause can split and form a meaningful
sentence on its own.
The conjunctive subordinate clause cannot split or else the
sentence it forms has no sense.
Ask: ConjunQUEtion needs SUBjunQUEtive in the
SUBordinate?
J'adore le chocolat.
~~Bien que ça fasse grossir.~~

Relative
pronoun

J'adore le chocolat qui vient de Suisse.
Principal Clause and **Relative Subordinate** Clause
The principal clause can split and form a meaningful sentence on its own.
The relative subordinate clause cannot split or else the sentence it forms
has no sense.
J'adore le chocolat.
~~Qui vient de Suisse.~~

Practice What You Learned

Exercises are rated according to four levels of difficulty:

- Beginner easy [*]
- Beginner challenging [**]
- Intermediate [***]
- Advanced [****]

1. Rewrite the following text separating each sentence; indicate the number of clauses for each sentence and if they are independent, principal, or subordinate conjunctives. Specify the number of conjugated verbs and the conjunction if applicable. [**]

La Déclaration des Droits de l'Homme et du Citoyen

Inspirée de la déclaration de l'indépendance américaine de 1776 et de l'esprit philosophique du XVIIIème siècle, la Déclaration des Droits de l'Homme et du Citoyen de 1789 marque la fin de l'Ancien Régime et le début d'une ère nouvelle. Expressément visée par la Constitution de la Vème République, elle fait aujourd'hui partie de nos textes de référence.

L'histoire

La Déclaration des Droits de l'Homme et du Citoyen est, avec les décrets des 4 et 11 août 1789 sur la suppression des droits féodaux, un des textes fondamentaux votés par l'Assemblée nationale constituante formée à la suite de la réunion des Etats Généraux.

Adoptée dans son principe avant le 14 juillet 1789, elle donne lieu à l'élaboration de nombreux projets. Après de longs débats, les députés votent le texte final le 26 août 1789.

Elle comporte un préambule et 17 articles qui mêlent des dispositions concernant l'individu et la Nation. Elle définit des droits "naturels et imprescriptibles" comme la liberté, la propriété, la sûreté, la résistance à l'oppression. La Déclaration reconnaît également l'égalité, notamment devant la loi et la justice. Elle affirme enfin le principe de la séparation des pouvoirs.

http://www.elysee.fr/instit/text1.htm

Example:

Inspirée de la déclaration de l'indépendance américaine de 1776 et de l'esprit philosophique du XVIIIème siècle, la Déclaration des Droits de l'Homme et du Citoyen de 1789 *marque* la fin de l'Ancien Régime et le début d'une ère nouvelle.

One *conjugated verb* (marque): 1 clause, independent clause, simple sentence

A. _____

_____

B. _____

_____

C. _____

_____

D. _____

_____

E. _____

_____

F. _____

_____

G. _____

_____

H. _____

_____

2. Identify the conjugated verb(s) and specify if the sentence is simple or compound. [*]

Example:

Franz est allemand et gentil. 1 verb: est—simple.

A. Viens manger tes pâtes aux champignons des bois.

_____

B. Je me demande si tu comprends.

_____

C. Il n'y a rien à voir à la télé.

_____

D. François parle comme s'il était bébé.

_____

E. Ton frère est fort et il est bronzé.

_____

3. Combine the following independent clauses in compound sentences with the conjunction of coordination that makes the most sense in the context. [**]

Example:

> Franz parle allemand—Il est espagnol.
>
> Franz parle allemand **mais** il est espagnol.

A. Arthur parle japonais. Il est chinois. _____

B. Paul ne vient pas. Il déteste le football. _____

C. Il pleuvra. Il fera beau demain. _____

D. Il pleuvra. Il ne fera pas beau. _____

E. Je l'aime bien. Il m'énerve souvent. _____

F. Patricia part. Elle emmène Marc. _____

4. Identify the linking word (if any) in the following sentences and the types of clauses. [**]

Example:

> La durée de vie moyenne <u>est</u> plus longue que pendant le Moyen-Âge.
>
> Only one conjugated verb, no word of junction in this simple sentence. (**Que** here is not a conjunction of subordination; it does not follow a verb that belongs to one of the special categories. **Que** is part of the adverb used to form the comparative degree of the adjective longue.)

A. Je <u>partirai</u> dès que vous <u>arriverez</u>.

_____

B. Vous <u>êtes</u> en retard mais cela ne me <u>dérange</u> pas.

_____

C. Quand le Professeur Derrida <u>parle</u>, ses yeux <u>brillent</u> d'intelligence et il <u>a</u> beaucoup de charme.

_____

D. D'ici un siècle ou deux, l'humanité <u>pourra</u> se reproduire par clônage: quelle horreur!

_____

E. Bertrand lui <u>répète</u> qu'il l'<u>aime</u> mais Sybille ne le <u>croit</u> pas car c'<u>est</u> un menteur et elle le <u>sait</u>, ou bien elle <u>l'a deviné</u>.

_____

5. Divide the following sentences into clauses and specify which ones they are. [***]

Example: Je partirai dès que vous arriverez.	• Je partirai: principal • dès que vous arriverez: conjunctive subordinate
Vous êtes en retard mais cela ne me dérange pas.	
Quand le Professeur Derrida parle, ses yeux brillent d'intelligence et il a beaucoup de charme.	
D'ici un siècle ou deux, l'humanité pourra se reproduire par clônage: quelle horreur!	
Bertrand lui répète qu'il l'aime mais Sybille ne le croit pas car c'est un menteur et elle le sait, ou bien elle l'a deviné.	
Ton patron exige que tu lui fasses un rapport hebdomadaire.	
Ne sois pas en retard car c'est une surprise party.	
Une fois que les enfants seront couchés, Papa Noël descendra dans la cheminée.	

Chapter 16

RELATIVE CLAUSES

 Intermediate—Advanced Topic

Introduction

What is a relative?

Think about your relatives: who are they? A cousin, a sister, your mom, etc. They are your relatives because they are related to you, but what does that mean? It means that your cousin and sister and mom and you all have something in common: a little bit of the same family blood.

> Marc and Bérénice, Marc's sister-in-law, also have something in common: Maurice, who is Marc's brother and Bérénice's husband. They are all relatives.
>
> François and Xavier, who are stepbrothers, also have something in common: Claire, their mother. François and Xavier are each other's relative.

Because of this linking element, common blood or a person, individual people are related together in the same family.

Similarly, simple clauses can have something in common: a noun. When that is the case they are related. They can therefore be brought together in the same sentence thanks to a linking element: the relative pronoun.

Le relatif est un pronom qui relie les propositions

A *relative pronoun* is a pronoun that replaces a "relative" noun, namely a noun that is common between two sentences.

The relative pronoun brings together the clauses that had a noun in common to form a compound sentence.

When linking the two clauses together, the first common noun remains. It is called the *antecedent* in the compound sentence because it must always be located directly *before* the relative pronoun (ante = before).

Use of Simple Relative Pronouns
Common Noun

Reason for Relative Clauses

Most of the time, we do not write or speak in simple sentences:

> "Sylvia a un frère. Son frère s'appelle Florent. Florent travaille à l'Opéra de Paris. Tu as visité l'opéra. Florent est Directeur des Programmes. Tu parles de ces programmes. L'opéra est un édifice magnifique. Le *Fantôme de l'Opéra* se passe dans cet édifice." *(Sylvia has a brother. Her brother is called Florent. Florent works at the Paris Opera. You have visited the Opera. Florent is Program Director. You are talking about these programs. The Opera is a splendid edifice. The* Phantom of the Opera *takes place in that edifice.)*

This would sound silly so we form compound sentences in order to not talk like a four-year-old and to avoid repetitions. When nouns are repeated, they can be replaced by pronouns. These pronouns are called *relative* because they relate the clauses that had a common noun, thus are part of the same "family."

In this example, it is easy to see that the independent clauses have a *noun in common:*

> Sylvia a <u>un frère</u>. Son <u>frère</u> s'appelle Florent.
>
> Florent travaille à <u>l'Opéra de Paris</u>. Tu as visité <u>l'opéra</u>.
>
> Florent est Directeur <u>des Programmes</u>. Tu parles de <u>ces programmes</u>.
>
> L'opéra est <u>un édifice</u> magnifique. Le *Fantôme de l'Opéra* se passe dans <u>cet édifice</u>.

Because of their common noun, all these simple clauses are related. They can therefore be brought together in one family/sentence by a relative pronoun.

The relative pronoun

- replaces the noun appearing a second time,
- links the two previously independent clauses together,
- avoids a repetition in the final compound sentence.

Components of the Compound Sentence with a Relative Clause

Clauses

When bringing two clauses with a common noun together, the result is a compound sentence with a relative pronoun linking the originally independent clauses.

1. Let us consider a simple sentence #1: 1 conjugated verb = Independent clause:
_____ CV _____ <u>Noun#1</u> _____ _____ _____ _____.

2. Let us consider also simple sentence #2: 1 conjugated verb = Independent clause:
_____ <u>Noun #2</u> _____ _____ CV _____.

The nouns #1 and #2 are the same, so noun #2 does not need to be repeated.
Noun #1 = Noun #2 ➜ ~~Noun#2~~ can be replaced by a Relative Pronoun (RP)

3. A compound sentence can be formed by combining both clauses and the two Conjugated Verbs:
_____ CV#1 _____ <u>Noun #1</u> + RP _____ CV#2 _____ _____.

Antecedent: Common Noun #1 before the Relative Pronoun

> **NOTE** Because we do not want to forget what we are talking about when we combine two sentences and suppress a common noun, the relative pronoun replacing the Common Noun #2 stays very close to Common Noun #1. This way, we know what the pronoun refers to: the noun just before it.
>
> _____ Common Noun #1 Relative Pronoun _____
>
> Common Noun #1 is therefore placed *before* the relative pronoun. Because it is always written before, Common Noun #1 is called the ante**cedent** (in Latin: "before located") of the relative pronoun in the compound sentence.
>
> _____ Antécédent + Pronom relatif _____
>
> Each original clause now forms a unit of meaning in the compound sentence. The antecedent belongs to the unit #1 and the relative pronoun starts unit #2.
>
> | Meaningful Unit #1 | Meaningful Unit #2 |
> |---|---|
>
> __ ___ CV #1 ___ ___ Antecedent   RP ___ CV#2 ___ ___ ___.
>
> What results is a compound sentence with a relative pronoun.

Principal vs. Subordinate

The concept of subordinate is the same for relative clauses as for conjunctive clauses:

- If the unit can be written as a sentence and it still makes sense by itself, it is the **principal** clause—**la proposition principale**.
- If the unit cannot form a sentence on its own (start with a capital letter, end with a period, and make sense outside of any context), it is the subordinate relative clause—**la proposition subordonnée relative**.
- The relative clause can be linked to the principal with
  - a simple relative pronoun (**qui, que, dont, où**)
  - a compound relative pronoun (**lequel . . . , auquel . . . , duquel . . .**).

Formation of a Typical Relative Clause

Common Noun Changed to Relative Pronoun

Typical relative clauses are originally independent clauses that are linked to a previous sentence because they share a noun with it.

In the process, they lose this noun, but they gain a pronoun that takes on its characteristics (function, gender, and number when the pronoun allows it).

As the French eighteenth-century chemist Lavoisier said:

> "Rien ne se perd, rien ne se crée, tout se transforme." *(Nothing is lost, nothing is created, everything is transformed.)*

Here is an example of the *relative metamorphosis*:

Chaque soir, je retrouve <u>mes chattes</u>.

<u>Mes chattes</u> m'attendent derrière la porte.

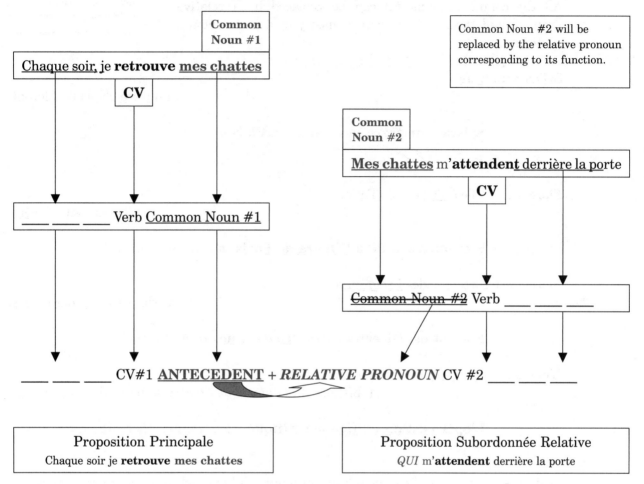

CV = **Conjugated Verb** + A = **Antecedent** + RP = **Relative Pronoun**

Analysis of the example:

- Two conjugated verbs—retrouve, attendent—therefore two clauses in a compound sentence
- Two clauses linked by a relative pronoun that replaces the common Noun #2 "mes chattes"—function of CN #2 = subject: qui
- First clause—Chaque soir, je retrouve mes chattes.—it makes sense by itself, therefore it is the principal clause = la proposition principale
- Second clause—Qui m'attendent derrière la porte.—it cannot constitute a sentence in itself; therefore it is subordinate. Because the linking word is a relative pronoun, it is a relative clause = une proposition subordonnée relative.

Let us look again at the paragraph about Sylvia and Florent. All the common nouns #2 can be replaced by a relative pronoun and these independent clauses joined in compound sentences.

> *Refer to Chapter 15 on* **Sentences and Clauses**

Sylvia a <u>un frère</u>.

Son <u>frère</u> s'appelle Florent.

Sylvia a <u>un frère</u> *qui* **s'appelle Florent.**

Florent travaille à <u>l'Opéra de Paris</u>.

Tu as visité <u>l'opéra</u>.

Florent travaille à <u>l'Opéra de Paris</u> *que* **tu as visité.**

Florent est Directeur des <u>Programmes</u>.

Tu parles de ces <u>programmes</u>.

Florent est Directeur des <u>Programmes</u> *dont* **tu parles.**

L'opéra est <u>un édifice</u> magnifique.

L'histoire du *Fantôme de l'Opéra* se passe dans <u>cet édifice</u>.

L'opéra est <u>un édifice</u> magnifique dans *lequel* **l'histoire du** *Fantôme de l'Opéra* **se passe.**

Qui, que, dont, lequel are the relative pronouns linking each subordinate relative clause to its principal clause.
    Qui, que, dont are simple relative pronouns.
    Lequel is a compound relative pronoun.

Simple Relative Pronouns as Hinge

Qui, que, dont, où (Who, Whom, Whose, Where)

The simple relative pronouns are very commonly used in French. Understanding how they work is easy, and it is so mechanical that you will find a flowchart on how to select and use them at the end of this chapter (page 343).

    They nevertheless create problems for students of French because, although their English equivalents exist, they often disappear in daily language.

TIP BOX

When dealing with French relative clauses, always think in the most academic English style. Reintroduce all the relative pronouns that have disappeared in everyday English and make your French sentences match this formal English.

> I need the book you borrowed from me = **I need the book** THAT **you borrowed from me.**
>
> I know the singer you talked about = **I know the singer** ABOUT WHOM **you talked.**
>
> It's the airline I flew to France on = **It is the airline** ON WHICH I **flew to France.**

There are four simple relative pronouns:

1. **Qui**—who, that
2. **Que**—whom, that
3. **Dont**—whose, of whom, of which
4. **Où**—where, when

Function of the Relative Pronoun

Each relative pronoun corresponds to the specific function of the noun it replaces.

FUNCTION OF QUI, QUE, DONT, OÙ	
Function of CN #2 =	**Relative Pronoun =**
Sujet (Subject)	**QUI**
Complément d'objet direct (Direct Object Complement)	**QUE**
Introduit par la préposition **DE** (Following the preposition DE)	**DONT**
Complément circonstanciel de **TEMPS** ou de **LIEU** (Location or Time Complement)	**OÙ**

A relative pronoun cannot be omitted in French. It must be present to link the two clauses and it must follow directly its antecedent—namely Common Noun #1.

Since it replaces it and you never want to lose any information when using a pronoun, choose the relative pronoun according to the function of Common Noun #2.

Que Conjunction or Relative Pronoun

The word **que** has two natures; it can be

- conjunction of subordination
- relative pronoun.

Que as Conjunction

When it follows a <u>verb</u> (of declaration, hope, wish, opinion, will, etc.), or when it is part of a comparative structure (plus . . . que, moins . . . que, autant . . . que), it is a conjunction:

> J'<u>espère que</u> vous aimerez ce livre. (*I <u>hope that</u> you will like this book.*)

> Je <u>pense que</u> la grammaire est comme un jeu. (*I <u>think that</u> grammar is like a game.*)

Que as Relative Pronoun

- As a relative pronoun, **que** must always be preceded by its antecedent, so when **que** follows a **noun**, it is most likely a relative pronoun:

> Vous aimerez **ce livre que** vous lisez. (You will like this **book that** you are reading.)

> **Le jeu que** je préfère est le Tarot. (The **game that** I prefer is Tarot.)

Placement of Pronouns

Qui (Before the Verb)

Since **qui** replaces the subject of Unit #2, it is located directly in front of Conjugated Verb #2: **Antecedent** + *qui* + **CV #2**:

> Les étudiants aiment **les exemples** *qui* **sont** faciles. (*Students like examples that are easy.*)

Que, Dont, Où (Before a Subject)

On the contrary, **que**, **dont**, **où** will be followed by a subject and the verb: Antecedent + *que/dont/où* + <u>Subject</u> + **CV #2**:

> Les étudiants aiment les exemples *que* <u>tu</u> **utilises**. (*Students like the examples that you use.*)

> Les étudiants aiment les exemples *dont* <u>le sens</u> **paraît** évident. (*Students like the examples whose meaning seems obvious.*)

> Les étudiants aiment les exemples *où* <u>tout</u> **est** logique. (*Students like the examples where everything is logical.*)

Think of the relative pronoun as the hinge holding the door and the wall together. The hinge is part of both the door and the wall; they have it in common. Without hinges, the door would fall and the wall would have a big hole. Without the relative pronoun in French, a compound sentence collapses.

Principal   Relative   Relative Subordinate Clause
                   Pronoun

Typical Structures of Compound Sentences

The structure of compound sentences depends on the type and place of the articulation between each clause. When this articulation (hinge) is a relative pronoun, its place varies according to the pronouns' function.

Function of Common Noun #2

Subject

When the function of Common Noun #2 is subject, the pronoun

- follows its antecedent (Common Noun #1)
- precedes the conjugated verb of the relative subordinate clause

Clauses		Verb #1	CN #1
Independent #1	Je	connais	**Cannes**.
Independent #2	CN #2 Subject	Verb #2	
	Cannes	est	une ville célèbre.
CN #2 = SUJET // RP = QUI Je connais **Cannes** QUI est une ville célèbre. (*I know Cannes, which is a famous town.*)			

CORRESPONDANCE FUNCTION OF CN #2 // RP			
Sujet	COD	DE + CN #2	Lieu—Temps
QUI	QUE	DONT	OÙ

Direct Object Complement

When the function of Common Noun #2 is direct object complement, the pronoun

- follows its antecedent (Common Noun #1)
- precedes the subject of the conjugated verb in the relative subordinate clause

Clauses		Verb #1	CN #1
Independent #1	Je	connais	**Cannes.**
Independent #2	Subject	Verb #2	Common Noun #2 Direct Object Complement
	Tu	aimes	beaucoup **Cannes.**
CN #2 = Complément d'objet direct // RP = QUE Je connais **Cannes** QUE tu aimes beaucoup. *(I know Cannes, which you like a lot.)*			

CORRESPONDANCE FUNCTION OF CN #2 // RP			
Sujet	**COD**	DE + CN #2	Lieu—Temps
QUI	**QUE**	DONT	OÙ

IMPORTANT!

Because que **replaces the direct object complement and is written before the Common Verb #2 that it complements, be careful when CV #2 is conjugated in a compound tense. Make sure that the past participle agrees with the gender and number of Common Noun #2 that que replaces.**

By the time you write your past participle, you have the gender and number information; they are not visible but they are implied. Even if que **always looks the same, as a pronoun it still carries all the attributes of the noun it replaces:**

J'adore les pommes QUE **tu as achetées.** (que = les pommes: feminine/plural)

Following *DE*

When Common Noun #2 follows the preposition **DE**, the pronoun

> *Refer to Chapter 12 on*
> **Past Indicative Tenses—**
> **Agreement of Past Participle**

- follows its antecedent (Common Noun #1)
- precedes the subject of the conjugated verb in the relative subordinate clause

Clauses		Verb #1	CN #1
Independent #1	Je	connais	**Cannes**.
Independent #2	Subject	Verb #2	Common Noun #2 follows DE
	Mes amis américains	parlent	de **Cannes**.

CN #2 = after preposition DE / RP = DONT
Je connais **Cannes** DONT mes amis américains parlent. (*I know Cannes, about which my American friends talk.*)

CORRESPONDANCE FUNCTION OF CN #2 // RP			
Sujet	COD	**DE – CN #2**	Lieu—Temps
QUI	QUE	**DONT**	OÙ

Circumstantial Complement of Place or Time

When the function of Common Noun #2 is circumstantial complement of place or of time, the pronoun

- follows its antecedent (Common Noun #1)
- precedes the subject of the conjugated verb in the relative subordinate clause

Clauses		Verb #1	CN #1
Independent #1	Je	connais	**Cannes**.
Independent #2	Subject	Verb #2	Common Noun #2 Circumstantial Complement of Location
	Il y	a	le célèbre Festival du Cinéma **à Cannes**.

CN #2 = Location/RP = OÙ
Je connais **Cannes** OÙ il y a le célèbre Festival du Cinéma. (*I know Cannes, where the famous Festival takes place.*)

Clauses	CN #1	Verb #1	
Independent #1	**L'été**	était	fabuleux.
Independent #2	Subject	Verb #2	Common Noun #2 Circumstantial Complement of Time
	J'	ai fait des études à Cannes	**cet été-là**.

CN #2 = Time // RP = OÙ
L'été OÙ j'ai fait des études à Cannes était fabuleux. (*The summer when I studied in Cannes was fabulous.*)

CORRESPONDANCE FUNCTION OF CN #2/RP			
Sujet	COD	DE + CN #2	**Lieu—Temps**
QUI	QUE	DONT	OÙ

IMPORTANT!

The Common Word #2 does not always appear under the form of a noun that repeats exactly Common Noun #1. It can also be a pronoun, a possessive adjective, or any expression referring to Common Noun #1.

> J'ai vu <u>Amélie</u>. **Elle** travaille à l'aéroport de Nice. (= Amélie travaille . . .)
>
> J'ai vu Amélie qui travaille à l'aéroport de Nice. *(I saw Amélie who works at the Nice airport.)*
>
> J'ai vu <u>cette jeune fille</u>. Tu <u>l'</u>aimes beaucoup. (= Tu aimes beaucoup cette jeune fille)
>
> J'ai vu cette jeune fille que tu aimes beaucoup. *(I saw this young lady that you like a lot.)*
>
> J'ai vu <u>Amélie</u>.—<u>Son</u> père est pilote. (= le père <u>de Amélie</u>)
>
> J'ai vu Amélie dont le père est pilote. *(I saw Amélie, whose father is a pilot.)*

Step-by-Step Method to Form of Compound Sentences with Relative Clauses

Because French grammar is so logical, once you have realized that there is a common noun, it is very easy to form compound sentences with a relative clause. If you follow the systematic step-by-step method indicated below, your compound sentences will be correct every time. Think:

R-E-L-A-T-I-V-E! (8 Steps)

1. Recognize the common nouns in each clause.

2. Entitle them <u>CN #1</u> (Common Noun #1) and <u>CN #2</u> (Common Noun #1). (Remember that Common Noun #1 belongs to Unit #1 and Common Noun #2 belongs to Unit #2.)

3. Learn the function of Common Noun #2:
   <u>CN #2</u> = Subject?
   > Direct object complement?
   > Introduced by the preposition **DE**?
   > Circumstantial complement of location or time?

4. Alter Unit #2: replace ~~Common Noun#2~~ by the relative pronoun corresponding to the function of CN #2

Sujet	COD	DE + CN #2	Lieu—Temps
QUI	QUE	DONT	OÙ

5. Turn your new sentence around the relative pronoun as you write it down first, in the middle of the line.
6. Insert Common Noun #1 just **before** this relative pronoun. CN #1 has now become the **ante**cedent of your relative pronoun.
7. Verify that all words remaining in each unit are organized around this axis of Antecedent—Relative Pronoun. They must remain in the same order in which they originally appeared in their independent clause.
8. Examine the structure of your sentence and translate it word for word. If it does not make sense in English, go back to Step 1 and make sure that:
   ○ the relative pronoun follows the common Noun #1:
   ○ the relative pronoun has the same function in Unit #2 as common Noun #2 did.

Memorize and follow these steps systematically every time you need to use a relative pronoun and you will no longer make mistakes.

COMPOUND SENTENCE WITH RELATIVE CLAUSE AND 8 STEP MAGIC METHOD			
1	R	**ECOGNIZE**	common nouns
2	E	**NTITLE**	common nouns CN #1 and CN #2
3	L	**EARN**	function of CN #2
4	A	**LTER**	unit #2: replace ~~CN #2~~ by its corresponding Relative Pronoun (RP)
5	T	**URN**	new sentence around RP
6	I	**NSERT**	CN #1 before RP
7	V	**ERIFY**	order of words around CN #1 + RP axis
8	E	**XAMINE**	sentence structure and translate verbatim

Examples: Step-by-Step-Formation

Example 1

Je connais Jean-François Berthault.

Il travaille au Ministère de l'Éducation.

1. **Recognize the common nouns.**

   Je connais <u>Jean-François Berthault. Il</u> travaille au Ministère de l'Éducation.

2. **Entitle them Common Nouns #1 and #2.**

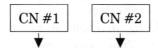

   Je connais <u>Jean-François Berthault. Il</u> travaille au Ministère de l'Éducation.

3. **Learn function of CN #2 =?**

   Il is the subject of the verb   CN #2 = Sujet

4. **Alter Unit #2: ~~CN #2~~ Relative Pronoun: Sujet—QUI.**

   (~~Il~~) . . . qui travaille au Ministère de l'Éducation

5. **Turn the compound sentence around the relative pronoun:**
   _____ qui _____

6. **Insert CN #1 = the antecedent right before the relative pronoun.**
   _____ Jean-François Berthault qui _____

7. **Verify the order of the words remaining in each unit:**

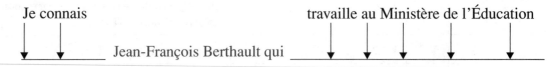

Je connais Jean-François Berthault qui travaille au Ministère de l'Éducation.

8. **Examine the structure and translate word for word:**
   - **Qui** follows CN #1: ✓
   - **Qui** is the relative pronoun subject and it replaces **Il**, which was also the subject in Unit #1: ✓

Je connais Jean-François Berthault qui travaille au Ministère de l'Éducation.
(_I know Jean-François Berthault who works at the Department of Education._)

Example 2

Jean-François est sympa.

Sa mère est professeur de philosophie.

1. Recognize **the common nouns:**

Jean-François est sympa. Sa mère est professeur de philosophie. (Sa
mère = la mère de Jean-François)

2. Entitle **them Common Nouns #1 and #2:**

Jean-François est sympa. (Sa mère) La mère DE Jean-François est
professeur de philosophie.

3. Learn **function of CN #2 =?**

CN #2 is introduced by the preposition DE
CN #2 = DE + CN #2

4. Alter **Unit #2: DE + ~~CN#2~~—Relative Pronoun:—DONT**

La mère ~~de Jean-François~~ Dont est professeur de philosophie.

5. Turn **the compound sentence around the relative pronoun:**

_____ dont _____

6. Insert **CN #1 = the antecedent right before the relative pronoun:**

_____ Jean-François dont _____

7. Verify **the order of words remaining in each unit.**

In this sentence, the antecedent begins Unit #1. It is still placed exactly where it was
originally, then followed by the relative pronoun. Since the relative pronoun started
Unit #2, all the words that belonged to that unit are written as they were originally.
The words remaining from Unit #1 are also written in their original order. The relative clause is inserted into the principal instead of following it.

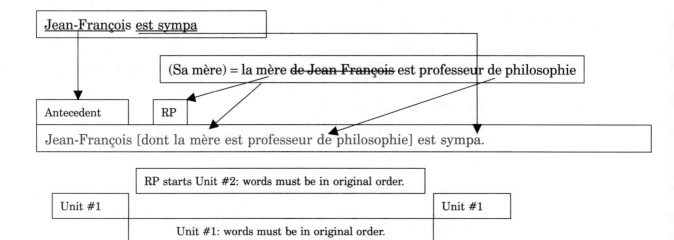

Jean-François est sympa

(Sa mère) = la mère ~~de Jean-François~~ est professeur de philosophie

Antecedent   RP

Jean-François [dont la mère est professeur de philosophie] est sympa.

RP starts Unit #2: words must be in original order.

Unit #1   Unit #1

Unit #1: words must be in original order.

Jean-François [dont la mère est professeur de philosophie] est sympa.

8. Examine the structure and translate word for word:
- **Dont** follows CN #1:
- **Dont** is the relative pronoun used when CN #2 came after the preposition DE— CN #2 = DE Jean-François:

    Jean-François dont la mère est professeur de philosophie est sympa.
    (Jean-François, whose mother is a philosophy professor, is cool.)

NOTE Relative clauses can either follow the principal clause or be inserted into it. But they cannot precede the principal clause since the relative pronoun must always follow its antecedent.

There can be more than one relative clause in a compound sentence.

Example 3

Marie va à Nice.

Il y a un marché aux fleurs splendide à Nice.

1. Recognize the common nouns:

    Marie va à Nice. Il y a un marché aux fleurs splendide à Nice.

2. Entitle them Common Nouns #1 and #2:

CN #1   CN #2

Marie va à Nice. Il y a un marché aux fleurs splendide à Nice.

3. Learn the function of CN #2 =?

CN #2 is a circumstantial complement of location.

4. Alter Unit #2: ~~CN #2~~—Relative Pronoun: OÙ

Il y a un marché aux fleurs splendide ~~à Nice~~ où . . .

5. Turn the compound sentence around the relative pronoun:

_____ où _____

6. Insert CN #1 = the antecedent right before the relative pronoun:

_____ Nice où _____

7. Verify the order of words remaining in each unit:

Marie va à Nice = Unit #1.

Il y a un marché aux fleurs splendide à Nice = Unit #2

Marie va à Nice où il y a un marché aux fleurs splendide.	
Proposition Principale	Proposition Subordonnée Relative
Unit #1	Unit #2

8. Translate word for word:

Marie va à Nice où il y a un marché aux fleurs splendide.

(Marie goes to Nice where there is a splendid open air flower market.)

IMPORTANT!

Pay attention to the common nouns. Identifying the right ones can be tricky.

Marie travaille à l'aéroport de Nice. Son père est pilote.

Without paying sufficient attention, airport and pilot could be associated and these sentences combined as:

> Marie travaille à l'aéroport où son père est pilote. *(Marie works at the airport where her father is a pilot.)*

The sentence is grammatically correct but it assumes that CN #2 is l'aéroport.
Since **l'aéroport** is a location, the noun must be replaced by **où**, which is not necessarily true.

(In fact, Marie works at the Nice airport, but her father is a pilot for American Airlines and works out of LAX, in Los Angeles.)

In **Marie travaille à l'aéroport où son père est pilote** the two original independent clauses are

Marie travaille à l'aéroport de Nice.

Son père est pilote.

and the common element #2 is **son**—le père de **Marie.**

In these sentences, Marie is in common, not the airport that appears only in the first clause.

Marie travaille à l'aéroport de Nice.

Son père = Le père DE Marie est pilote: DONT

Marie, dont le père est pilote, travaille à l'aéroport de Nice. *(Marie, whose father is a pilot, works at the Nice airport.)*

 Intermediate—Advanced Topic

Use of Compound Relative Pronouns

Compound relative pronouns are often necessary when Common Element #2 is preceded by a preposition in Unit #2.

Although they may seem to be more difficult to use, they articulate the sentence in the exact same way as the simple relative pronouns.

TIP BOX

The R-E-L-A-T-I-V-E step-by-step method indicated above is also applicable to compound relative pronouns.

Lequel, Auquel, Duquel: Compound Relative Pronoun Formation

Le-la-les + quel (Definite Article and Interrogative Adjective)

There is actually one set of compound relative pronouns but it has two variations. This basic set is the same as the interrogative pronouns lequel—laquelle—lesquels—lesquelles.

These combine a **definite article** and the interrogative adjective **Quel**.

Article défini	Adjectif interrogatif
Le—la—les	Quel—quelle—quels—quelles

- Because they combine an article and an adjective, compound relative pronouns convey the gender and number markers twice; both the article and the adjective change according to the gender and the number of the noun they replace.

FORMATION OF LEQUEL: ARTICLE + QUEL						
Articles Définis				**Adjectifs Interrogatifs**		
	Masculin	Féminin			Masculin	Féminin
Singulier	Le	La		Singulier	Quel	Quelle
Pluriel	Les	Les		Pluriel	Quels	Quelles

- Compound relative pronouns take on the gender and number of the noun they replace.
- Although it is sometimes possible to use a simple relative pronoun with certain prepositions, compound relative pronouns can always be used when Common Noun #2 is preceded in Unit #2 by a preposition.
- The use of a compound relative pronoun, when a simple one can also be used, raises the level of language.

> ### IMPORTANT!
> Since compound relative pronouns are formed with an article and an adjective, both parts of the word must have the same gender and number.
>
> ### PRONOMS RELATIFS COMPOSÉS
>
> | CN #2 is | Masculin | Féminin |
> |---|---|---|
> | **Singulier** | Lequel | Laquelle |
> | **Pluriel** | Lesquels | Lesquelles |
>
> Always check that **CN #2**, the first part (**le . . .**) and the second part (**quel . . .**) of the compound relative pronoun **match in gender and number**.

À/De + lequel = Auquel—Duquel Variations

Structure of the Compound Sentence

A compound relative pronoun is used when Common Noun #2 comes after a **preposition** in the independent clause that will become the relative subordinate clause:

> J'habite une maison jumelée. *(I live in a condominium.)*
>
> Il y a un parc **devant** ma <u>maison</u>. *(There is a park in front of my condo.)*

Unit #1 _____ CN #1 _____.
Unit #2 _____ [**Preposition** + <u>CN #2</u>] _____.

The preposition must remain before the relative pronoun that replaces CN #2 in the compound sentence.

_____ Antecedent + [**Preposition** + *RP*] _____.

> J'habite une maison jumelée **devant** *laquelle* il y a un parc.
>
> *(I live in a condominium in front of which there is a park.)*

There are three series of compound relative pronouns. The choice between series depends upon the preposition that precedes CN #2.

À + Lequel = Auquel

FORMATION OF AUQUEL: À + ARTICLE + QUEL					
Contraction	**Article Défini**		Contraction	**Pronom Relatif**	
Preposition	**Masculin**	**Féminin**	Preposition	**Masculin**	**Féminin**
À +	~~Le~~ AU	La À LA	**À +**	~~Le~~quel Auquel	La<u>quel</u>le À laquelle
	~~Les~~ AUX	~~Les~~ AUX		~~Les~~que<u>ls</u> Auxquels	~~Les~~que<u>lles</u> Auxquelles

Serge connaît <u>le professeur</u>. Tu parles à <u>ce professeur</u>.

Apply the R-E-L-A-T-I-V-E method.

1. Recognize: ce professeur
2. Entitle: le professeur = CN #1-Antecedent—ce professeur = CN #2
3. Learn: **À** + CN #2
4. Alter: ~~à ce professeur~~ = auquel
5. Turn: _____ Compound Relative Pronoun AUQUEL _____.
6. Insert: _____ Antecedent + CRP _____ _____ le professeur auquel
   _____.
7. Verify:

Serge connaît	Tu parles
_____ le professeur auquel _____.	

8. Examine: **Serge connaît le professeur** auquel tu parles =
   Serge knows the professor (principal) to whom you speak (relative subordinate).

To make sure you did not make a mistake choosing or inserting the right pronoun, use the following checklist:

- I am using a compound relative pronoun, therefore there must be a preposition before or integrated into this pronoun? ✓
- Common Noun #1 is directly before the compound relative pronoun? ✓
- Common Noun #2 is masculine singular and so is the compound relative pronoun auquel. ✓
- The English sentence is correct: ✓

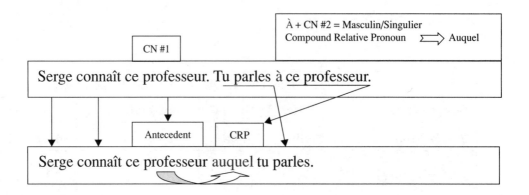

DE + Lequel = Duquel

FORMATION OF DUQUEL: DE + ARTICLE + QUEL					
Contraction	**Article Défini**		**Contraction**	**Pronom Relatif**	
Preposition	**Masculin**	**Féminin**	**Preposition**	**Masculin**	**Féminin**
DE +	~~Le~~ DU	La DE LA	DE +	~~Le~~quel Duquel	L~~a~~quelle De laquelle
	~~Les~~ DES	~~Les~~ DES		~~Les~~quels Desquels	~~Les~~quelles Desquelles

C'est la célèbre tour. On voit tout Paris de cette tour.
Apply the R-E-L-A-T-I-V-E method.

1. **R**ecognize: la tour
2. **E**ntitle: la tour = CN#1/Antecedent—cette tour = CN #2
3. **L**earn: **DE** + CN#2
4. **A**lter: ~~de cette tour~~ = de laquelle
5. **T**urn: _____ Compound Relative Pronoun DE LAQUELLE _____ .
6. **I**nsert: _____ Antecedent + CRP _____ _____ cette tour de laquelle

_____ .

7. **V**erify:

C'est   On voit tout Paris
_____ la célèbre tour **de laquelle** _____ .

8. **E**xamine: **C'est la célèbre tour de laquelle** on voit tout Paris. (*This is the famous tower from which one can see all of Paris.*)

Check your list:

- I am using a compound relative pronoun; therefore there must be a preposition before or integrated into this pronoun? ✓
- Common Noun #1 is directly before the compound relative pronoun? ✓
- Common Noun #2 is feminine singular and so is the compound relative pronoun **de laquelle**? ✓
- The English sentence is correct. ✓

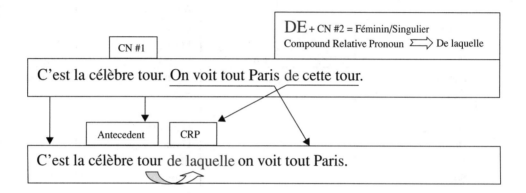

Lequel with ANY Preposition Except *à* or *de*

FORMATION OF LEQUEL WITH ANY PREPOSITION EXCEPT À OR DE					
Pas de Contraction	**Article Défini**		**Pas de Contraction**	**Pronom Relatif**	
Préposition	**Masculin**	**Féminin**	**Préposition**	**Masculin**	**Féminin**
Avec Chez Pour Parmi Devant Sans Derrière Dans Sur Sous	LE LES	LA	Avec Chez Pour Parmi Devant Sans Derrière Dans Sur Sous	Lequel Lesquels	Laquelle Lesquelles

J'adore les hôtels de Cannes. La Croisette serait triste sans ces hôtels.

Apply the R-E-L-A-T-I-V-E method.

1. Recognize: les hôtels.
2. Entitle: les hôtels de Cannes = CN #1—ces hôtels = CN #2
3. Learn: SANS + CN #2
4. Alter: ~~sans ces hôtels~~ = sans lesquels
5. Turn: _____ Compound Relative Pronoun SANS LESQUELS _____ .
6. Insert: _____ CN #1 + CRP _____
   _____ les hôtels de Cannes sans lesquels _____ .
7. Verify:

J'adore	La Croisette serait triste

_____ les hôtels de Cannes **sans** lesquels _____

8. Examine: **J'adore les hôtels de Cannes sans** lesquels la Croisette serait triste.

(I love the hotels in Cannes without which the Croisette avenue would look sad.)

Check your list:

- I am using a compound relative pronoun; therefore there must be a preposition before or integrated into this pronoun? ✓
- Common Noun #1 is directly before the compound relative pronoun? ✓
- Common Noun #2 is masculine/plural and so is the compound relative pronoun **sans lesquels**. ✓
- The English sentence is correct. ✓

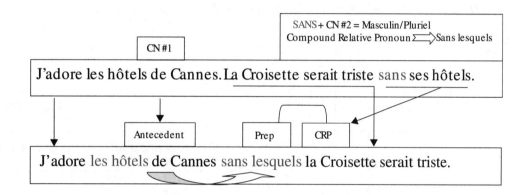

Use of Simple vs. Compound Relative Pronoun after a Preposition

Qui vs. Lequel as Subject

The pronoun **qui** can also be used after a preposition instead of **lequel, laquelle, lesquels, lesquelles**.

- **Qui** can replace Common Noun #2 if it designates animate beings (persons or animals), after any preposition

    except parmi and **entre**.

- **Lequel, laquelle, lesquels, lesquelles** can replace either animate or inanimate Common Nouns #2.

    Parmi and **entre** are **always** followed by **lequel, laquelle, lesquels, lesquelles**.

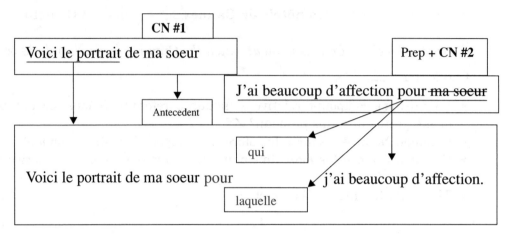

(*Here is the portrait of my sister for whom I have a lot of affection.*)

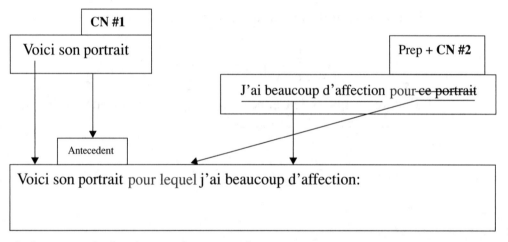

(*Here is her portrait that is very dear to me.*)

Dont vs. Duquel

The pronoun **dont** can sometimes be used instead of **duquel, de laquelle, desquels, desquelles** to replace either animate or inanimate Common Noun #2.

- **Dont** and **duquel, de laquelle, desquels, desquelles** are interchangeable with the preposition **de**, but **dont** is generally preferred.

    Le professeur **dont** tu parles vient du Cameroun.

    Le professeur **duquel** tu parles vient du Cameroun. (*The professor about whom you speak comes from Cameroon.*)

- Only **duquel, de laquelle, desquels, desquelles** can be used if the preposition is made of two elements:
  ○ [word] + **de**
  (**à côté** de, **à propos** de, **en face** de, **à partir** de, etc.):

> L'immeuble **à côté** duquel tu habites est un chef-d'oeuvre d'Art Déco.
> *(The building next to which you live is an Art Déco masterpiece.)*

> Tous ces gens, **en face** desquels tu te tiens, écoutent ta conférence religieusement. *(All these people, in front of whom you are standing, listen to your conference religiously.)*

- Dont cannot be used instead of De qui or Duquel-De laquelle-Desquels-Desquelles when the relative pronoun is complement of a **noun** that is preceded by a preposition.

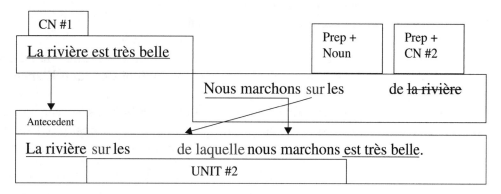

(The river along the sides of which we walk is very beautiful.)

Où vs. Lequel

- The pronoun Où can often replace Lequel-Laquelle-Lesquels-Lesquelles after a preposition of location, when the meaning of the sentence allows it:

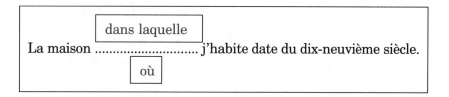

(The house in which / where I live was built in the nineteenth century.)

TIP BOX

When they can, French speakers tend to use simple relative pronouns because they are shorter and more casual. However, simple relative pronouns cannot always be used.

On the other hand, the compound relative pronouns are always correct after a preposition. It is therefore safer for you to systematically use compound relative pronouns when CN #2 is preceded by a preposition, until you are familiar with their possible alternatives. You may sound formal, but your sentence will be correct.

Use of Demonstrative Pronoun *CE* in Front of Simple Relative Pronouns

Reason for Using CE

Most of the time, a relative pronoun is used to replace a noun. However, it can also replace a common element that is not a precise noun like an undefined concept, a global reference, or an entire sentence.

When this common element is not a specific noun, the whole group cannot serve as a direct antecedent, yet the relative pronoun still demands its antecedent.

To replace larger or undefined entities, the demonstrative pronoun **CE** is used as the ultimate generic antecedent.

- **Ce**
  - replaces the entire Common Element #1
  - inserts itself before the relative pronoun
  - acts as a concrete antecedent to the relative pronoun.
- In the compound sentence, **ce** comes between Common Element #1 and the relative pronoun corresponding, as always, to the function of Common Element #2.

In the example below, the entire phrase "to play the bagpipe" is the element common to both sentences. Because it is not a simple noun, it is encapsulated in the generic and neutral **CE** pronoun, in order for the relative pronoun to have its antecedent.

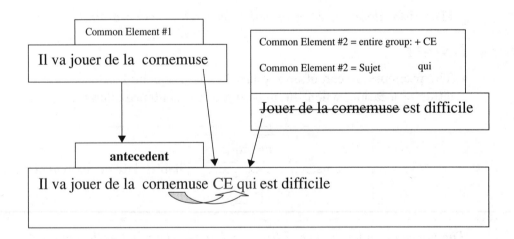

(He is going to play the bagpipe, which is difficult.)

Once you have determined that the generic antecedent **ce** is needed, choosing the relative pronoun follows the same rules as described throughout this chapter.

In this example, in Unit #2, **jouer de la cornemuse** is the subject of the auxiliary verb **être** (to play the bagpipe IS difficult). The relative pronoun that replaces it is consequently **qui**.

Applying the Relative Magic Method

Apply the R-E-L-A-T-I-V-E 8 step magic method:

Refer to the
**Pronoun Selection Process
flowchart** *on page 343*

Example:

Tu dessines une Porsche, un chat Birman, une maison grise et bleue, un tableau de Magritte et quatre petits cochons roses.

J'ai rêvé <u>**d**'une Porsche, d'un chat</u> Birman, <u>d'une maison grise et bleue, d'un tableau de Magritte et de quatre petits cochons roses</u> hier soir.

1. Recognize:

   Common Elements are all the words in the entire list: Porsche, cat, house, painting, pigs.

2. Entitle:

   une Porsche, un chat Birman, une maison grise et bleue, un tableau de Magritte et quatre petits cochons roses = Non specific Common Element #1: Antecedent + CE

   <u>une Porsche, un chat Birman, une maison grise et bleue, un tableau de Magritte et quatre petits cochons roses = Common Element #2</u>

3. Learn:

   <u>Common Element #2</u> follows the preposition **DE (d')**

4. Alter:

   Replace **de** + Common Element #2 by **DONT**

5. Turn:

   Rewrite your sentence with the relative pronoun in the middle:

   _____ **dont** _____

6. Insert:

   The **antecedent** before the relative pronoun + **CE** as generic pronoun recapitulating: _____ **[une Porsche, un chat Birman, une maison grise et bleue, un tableau de Magritte et quatre petits cochons roses]** **CE** dont _____

7. Verify:

   Tu dessines . . .
   _____ une Porsche, un chat Birman, une maison grise et bleue, un tableau de Magritte et quatre petits cochons roses, **CE** dont _____
   j'ai rêvé hier soir!

8. Examine:

Tu dessines une Porsche, un chat Birman, une maison grise et bleue, un tableau de Magritte et quatre petits cochons roses, **ce** dont j'ai rêvé hier soir! *(You are drawing a Porsche, a Sacred Birman cat, a blue and gray house, a painting by Magritte, and four little pink pigs, all the stuff about which I dreamed last night!)*

TIP BOX

Remember, **ce** replaces anything that is not contained in a single noun. Use **ce** when the antecedent is not specific but elusive and could be summarized by "that" or *the stuff.*

Quand on n'a pas **ce** *que* l'on aime, il faut aimer **ce** *que* l'on a. (Proverb) *When one does not have what one likes, one should like what one has. (If you don't have the stuff you like, you better like the stuff you have!)*

IMPORTANT!

Ce is a very convenient antecedent; it replaces any undefined reference.

However, because it is so generic, it generally follows the Common Element #1 it summarizes, and it always precedes the relative pronoun replacing Common Element #2.

Structure with CE:

_____ Common Element#1 + **CE** + Relative Pronoun _____

BASIC STRUCTURES WITH THE GENERIC ANTECEDENT *CE*		
Élément Commun #1 = proposition / concept	**Fonction de l'élément Commun #2**	**Most common structure**
CE	Sujet = **Qui**	**Concept #1** + CE + **qui** . . . Je me demande **ce** qui te dérange. (*I wonder what bothers you.*)
	Complément d'Objet Direct = **Que**	**Concept #1** + CE = **que** . . . Je me demande **ce** que tu veux. (*I wonder what you want.*)
	After Preposition DE = **Dont**	**Concept #1** + CE + **dont** . . . Je me demande **ce** dont tu parles. (*I wonder what you are talking about.*)
	Indéfini = **Quoi** Complément d'Objet Indirect After ALL prepositions except de	**Concept #1** + CE + *Prép.* + **Quoi** . . . Je me demande **ce** *à* quoi tu penses. Je me demande **ce** *pour* quoi tu travailles. Je me demande **ce** *avec* quoi tu survis. (*I wonder what you are thinking of.*) (*I wonder what you work for.*) (*I wonder what you survive with.*)

Marc adore <u>inventer des histoires compliquées</u>.

<u>Inventer des histoires compliquées</u> est parfois irritant.
Common Element #2 Subject: Qui

Marc adore <u>inventer des histoires compliquées</u>, **CE qui** est parfois irritant. (*Marc loves to invent complicated stories, which is annoying at times.*)

Marc insiste que ses aventures bizarres sont vraies.

Je ne supporte pas que <u>Marc insiste que ses aventures bizarres sont vraies.</u>
Common Element #2 Complement of Direct Object: Que

Marc <u>insiste que ses aventures bizarres sont vraies</u>, **CE que** je ne supporte pas. (*Marc maintains that his strange adventures are true, which I cannot stand.*)

Je lui ai dit: "C'est une maladie."

Il a ri <u>de moi quand je lui ai dit que c'est une maladie.</u>
Common Element #2—Follows the preposition **De**

<u>Je lui ai dit que c'était une maladie</u>, **CE dont** il a ri. *(I told him it was a disease, which made him laugh.)*

Il continue à <u>raconter des absurdités</u>.

Tout le monde le connaît <u>pour raconter des absurdités.</u>
Common Element #2 Indefinite—Follows the preposition **pour**: **Quoi**

Il continue à <u>raconter des absurdités</u>, **CE** *pour* **quoi** tout le monde connaît. *(He keeps telling absurd things, which is what he is known for by everyone.)*

IMPORTANT!

Although it seems there are many different relative pronouns to choose from, the decision process is always the same for all of them. You can choose the correct pronoun every time by asking yourself a series of yes or no questions that will lead you along the different paths you will find summarized in the following flowchart.

SIMPLE AND COMPOUND RELATIVE PRONOUNS SELECTION PROCESS

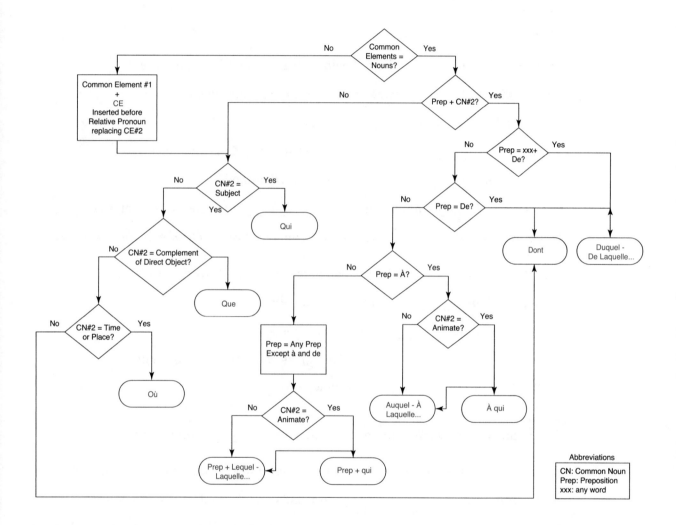

Practice What You Learned

Exercises are rated according to four levels of difficulty:

- Beginner easy [*]
- Beginner challenging [**]
- Intermediate [***]
- Advanced [****]

1. Complete the sentences in the following paragraph with **qui** or **que**. [*]

A. L'étudiant _____ travaille devant moi est américain.

B. Il parle avec un accent _____ j'adore.

C. Son livre _____ est sur la table est un livre de grammaire.

D. C'est celui _____ son professeur a recommandé.

E. Il rend facile la grammaire française _____ a la réputation d'être compliquée.

F. Ce livre génial _____ tu connais s'appelle *French Grammar the Easy Way*.

2. Complete the sentences in the following paragraph with **que** or **dont**. [*]

A. Cet étudiant _____ je te parle s'appelle Loy.

B. C'est un prénom _____ je trouve très joli.

C. Son nom de famille, _____ j'ai appris ce matin, est Newman.

D. Ça s'écrit comme l'acteur Paul Newman _____ les films sont si célèbres en France.

E. En fait, Loy ressemble un peu à cet acteur _____ j'aime tant.

3. Complete the sentences in the following paragraph with **qui**, **que**, **dont**, or **où**. [**]

A. Je connais un peu Loy _____ est dans ma classe de mathématiques.

B. Dans notre université _____ il y a beaucoup d'étudiants étrangers, Loy est différent.

C. C'est le seul _____ adore étudier la grammaire.

D. C'est un sujet _____ il parle tout le temps avec ses amis français.

E. Il pose des questions _____ je trouve intelligentes.

F. Il connaît les exceptions _____ on discute. Il rend des devoirs _____ il y a très peu d'erreurs.

4. Form a compound sentence with the following sets of clauses. Always use the bold clause as your first unit and the sentence that becomes the principal clause. [***]

A. **Vanessa Paradis est une actrice française.**
　　Elle est mariée avec Johnny Depp.
　　Les journaux parlent d'elle souvent.
　　Le public américain ne la connaît pas.

_____

_____

_____

B. **La politique est un sujet difficile.**
　　On parle beaucoup de politique en France.
　　Les Américains évitent ce sujet en famille.
　　Il n'y a pas de solution évidente dans ce sujet.

_____

_____

_____

5. Identify the relative pronoun and Common Element #1 to deconstruct the following sentences to make the original independent clauses and the preposition appear (reverse engineering). [***]

Example:

C'est le travail **dont** je rêve.
C'est le travail.
Je rêve **de** ce travail

A. La banquette sur laquelle vous êtes assis est confortable.

_____

_____

B. Montblanc est la marque du stylo avec lequel j'écris.

_____

_____

C. Muriel a deux collègues sans lesquels l'ambiance au bureau est triste.

_____

_____

D. Le proverbe auquel je crois est "Impossible n'est pas français."

_____

_____

E. Ce livre dont j'ai absolument besoin pour mes recherches est introuvable!

_____

_____

6. Complete the sentences with the appropriate relative pronouns and add the preposition if necessary. [***]

   A. Les hamburgers _____ mes amis mangent sont mauvais pour mon régime.

   B. Paul m'envoie des messages électroniques _____ je réponds toujours.

   C. Je suis contente de la solution _____ je suis arrivée.

   D. C'est une chanson _____ le texte est très poétique.

   E. Au moment _____ cette actrice est arrivée, la foule a applaudi.

   F. J'adore ce parc _____ il y a une collection de bonsaïs japonais.

7. Complete the paragraph with **ce qui, ce que, ce dont, ce à quoi**, depending on the function of the replaced Common Element #2. [****]

_____ est agréable, c'est de se promener sur la plage. Voilà _____ tout le monde doit faire après son travail: Marcher sous des palmiers, _____ relaxe les muscles. _____ nous avons tous besoin aussi, c'est de regarder l'eau bleue scintiller. Je ne sais pas _____ tu penses de ma solution pour diminuer ton stress. Il y a la Méditerranée et beaucoup de palmiers, _____ je pense toujours.

Chapter 17

CONDITIONAL AND SUBJUNCTIVE: THE "HIGHER" MOODS

 Intermediate—Advanced Topic

"J'écris sans voir. Je suis venu. Je voulais vous baiser la main et m'en retourner. Je m'en retournerai sans cette récompense. Mais ne serai-je pas assez récompensé <u>si je vous ai montré</u> combien je vous aime? Il est neuf heures. Je vous écris <u>que je vous aime</u>; je veux du moins vous l'écrire; mais je ne sais <u>si la plume se prête</u> à mon désir. Ne viendrez-vous point **pour que je vous le dise**, et **que je m'enfuie**?

Adieu, ma Sophie, bonsoir. Votre coeur ne vous dit-il pas <u>que je suis ici</u>? Voilà la première fois <u>que j'écris</u> dans les ténèbres. Cette situation *devrait* m'inspirer des choses bien tendres. Je n'en éprouve qu'une, c'est que je ne *saurais* sortir d'ici. L'espoir de vous voir un moment m'y retient, et je continue de vous parler, sans savoir <u>si je forme des caractères</u>. Partout où il n'y aura rien, lisez <u>que je vous aime</u>."

Denis Diderot, Lettre à Sophie Volland, 10 Juin 1759

(The translation is in the Appendix (page 419), along with an analysis of the use of the *Conditional* and **Subjunctive** vs. the <u>Indicative</u> Moods in this beautiful love letter. As you read the chapter, refer back to this text and try to understand why each mood is used or not.)

The Conditional Mood

Introduction

The mood is the third attribute of an action:

1. La personne (who does the action)
2. Le temps (when the action performed is on the time line)
3. Le mode (how real the action is)

One needs to determine all these attributes before choosing the correct conjugation for the verb that expresses each action.

As its name indicates, the *conditional mood* is connected with the concept of a condition. Shifting to this mood is necessary when the performance of an action is dependent upon the realization of another action, namely its *condition*.

Use of the Conditional

Cause and Consequence

The conditional expresses a **cause—consequence** relationship between two actions:

1. a real cause, C1
2. a potential result, R2.

- If C1 is or has been performed, then a potential R2 may become real.
- If C1 has not happened, then R2 can never be real.

> Si j'avais un million de dollars, j'achèterais une maison sur le Cap d'Antibes.
>
> C1 = Having a million dollars
>
> R2 = buying a house

(I will first need to have a million dollars to think about buying the house.)

The cause C1 is therefore the condition of existence of R2. Without C1 being realized, we cannot even contemplate the possibility of performance of R2.

> *(Without having a million dollars, it is useless to even think about the house. Having a million dollars conditions the buying.)*

Once C1 is realized, R2 may or may not be performed; the possibility of realization exists. On the contrary, R2 has no chance of being realized if C1 has not been performed.

> *(Once I have a million dollars, I may buy the house or change my mind, so the purchase is still not guaranteed. But it is surely not going to happen if I never manage to get the million dollars.)*

Suspension over Reality

All this uncertainty explains why the conditional mood is not anchored at the ground level of reality.

Level of Reality of Resulting Action

Conditional actions that might result or not from their cause are floating above the indicative level because there are no guarantees in life that certain conditions will be met. But the conditional is not the furthest away from reality because, although there cannot be any certainty, there is a possibility with certain conditions.

The conditional R2 action may always happen, at least until we know for sure that the cause C1 has not happened.

LEVEL OF REALITY OF THE CONDITIONAL MOOD				
Subjonctif		Least real		
Conditionnel			Conditional	Action is dependent upon the realization of another action first— various degrees of dependency
Impératif				
Indicatif		Most real	Indicative	Action has been, is, or will be, Real
Infinitif				

Feasibility of the Condition

The possibility of obtaining the result, R2, is directly linked to the feasibility of the condition, C1.

Conditions can be more or less realistic. The various possible ways of conjugating the verb that expresses this cause/condition—consequence/result relationship convey the corresponding levels of realism of the condition. There are three levels:

1. **Probability:**
   There are good chances that the condition C1 will be realized; consequently, the resulting action **R2** is probable.

2. Possibility:
   There are as many chances in favor of the condition C1 being realized as against it; consequently, the resulting action R2 is possible.

3. Regret:
   There is no chance that the condition C1 will be realized: we know that because we are looking back in time and seeing what happened; consequently, we can only regret the action R2. It has not resulted since the condition did not materialize.

Conditions are more or less realistic, depending on each context, not by themselves. A condition that is likely to be realized for me may be completely unrealistic for you, and vice versa. So the conditional levels are not built in certain verbs or actions; they have to be evaluated within each situation.

For instance, it is highly, if not completely, unlikely that I will ever have a million dollars and therefore the house of my dreams. But I may be able to borrow $15,000 and change my old car. Both the million and the loan are conditions, but the latter is more realistic than the former for me. Someone else, an actor or a football player, may have no problem getting 15 million dollars for their house: one million would be pocket money, not a condition!

Formation of the Conditional Mood

Condition/Cause—Result/Consequence Relation Components

Rationale

IMPORTANT!

Within the cause/condition—consequence/result relationship, the condition <u>C1</u> must in any case be real or else there is no point wondering about the result R2.

Therefore, the <u>condition C1</u> itself must be in the <u>indicative</u>.

It is the conditioned action or Result R2 that can be in the *conditional*.

Si-Signals the Condition

Although the condition can be more or less realistic, it is always indicated by the same marker. When stated, the condition C1 is easily recognizable. It is introduced by the conjunction **SI**.

But conditions may not always be in the same sentence as their resulting action R2. They can be implied or generic:

> Si tu **pouvais**, tu **passerais** ta vie à lire. (*If you could, you would spend your life reading.*)

> J'**aimerais** bien passer ma vie à lire. (*I would like to spend my life reading.*)

Condition/Cause—Result/Consequence Relation Tenses

Tense of Condition C1

Depending on the degree of realism of the condition, the **conditioning action C1** will be conjugated in a different tense of the **indicative mood**. The further away from the Present Indicative, the least likely the condition is to happen.

REMOVAL OF CAUSE FROM INDICATIVE PRESENT TENSE		
Indicatif Plus-que-Parfait	Indicatif Imparfait	**Indicatif Présent**

The condition can be conjugated in three tenses:

1. **Indicatif Présent**

> Si tu **fais** des courses, tu achèteras deux éclairs au chocolat comme d'habitude. *(If you go shopping, you will buy two chocolate eclairs as usual.)*

> Si tu **fais** des courses, achète deux éclairs au chocolat. *(If you go shopping, buy two chocolate eclairs.)*

2. **Indicatif Imparfait**

> Si tu **faisais** des courses, tu achèterais un dessert. *(If you went shopping, you would buy some dessert.)*

3. **Indicatif Plus-que-Parfait**

> Si tu **avais fait** des courses, tu aurais eu un dessert. *(If you had gone shopping, you would have had a dessert.)*

Tense of Result R2

Similar degrees of realism are consequently attributed to the conditioned result R2 by using different tenses and moods as well. The further away from the indicative, the least likely the result is to be realized.

REMOVAL OF RESULT FROM PRESENT INDICATIVE TENSE		
Conditionnel Passé	Conditionnel Présent	
	Impératif	
	Indicatif Présent	**Indicatif Futur**

1. Indicatif Futur

> Si tu **fais** des courses, tu **achèteras** deux éclairs au chocolat comme d'habitude. *(If you go shopping, you will buy two chocolate eclairs as usual.)*

or **Impératif**

> Si tu **fais** des courses, **achète** deux éclairs au chocolat. *(If you go shopping, buy two chocolate eclairs.)*

2. Conditionnel Présent

> Si tu **faisais** des courses, tu **achèterais** un dessert. *(If you went shopping, you would buy some dessert.)*

3. Conditionnel Passé

> Si tu **avais fait** des courses, tu **aurais** eu un dessert pour ce soir. *(If you had gone shopping, you would have had dessert tonight.)*

Tense / Feasibility Correspondance

On a percentage scale, the conditions can be:

- Very likely to be realized: [51%, 99%]
- Just as likely to be as not to be realized: 50%–50%
- ~~Not realized~~ at all—0%

It is this degree of realism of the condition that dictates your choice in the conjugation of the cause verb.

It is the conjugation of the *cause* verb that dictates your choice of conjugation of the *consequence* verb.

Conditional Structures

Cause: Probability, Hypothesis, Regret

For the purpose of clarity let us call:

- **Probability: the most likely condition**,
- Hypothesis: the possible condition,
- ~~Regret~~: *the condition that never was.*

Both **probability** and hypothesis are looking ahead at a still possible result. *Regret* implies looking back at the situation and realizing that the condition did not materialize.

In all cases, the cause/condition—consequence/result relationship has two components whose degree of reality varies.

- Because it is the *reality* of the condition that is in question, all conditioning actions start by **SI** and are put in the **indicative mood**.
- Yet, depending on how likely it is to happen, the **condition verb** is conjugated in the:
  - **Indicatif présent for probable conditions,**
  - **Indicatif imparfait** for hypothetical conditions,
  - *Indicatif plus-que-parfait for regretful ~~conditions~~.*

THREE TYPES OF CONDITIONS: PROBABILITY, HYPOTHESIS, REGRET		
SI + Condition	Proposition Principale: Action Conditionnelle	
	Result R2	
SI: PROBABILITY	Almost sure to become real	
SI: HYPOTHESIS	May or may not become real	
~~SI~~: Not a chance to be real	~~REGRET~~	

Probable, Possible, Nonexistent Results

The various combinations of moods and tenses convey the likelihood of the result. Each one matches how realistic the condition is or how feasible the cause is.

Likely Result

The **result—consequence R2** verb is conjugated in the **indicatif futur** or imperatif if it results from probable conditions.

NOTE The condition action (cause) is never **conjugated in the conditional mood.**
A conditional action (consequence) is not always **conjugated in the conditional mood.**
There is no need to use the conditional mood after a probable condition-cause, because the consequence resulting from it is very likely to become real. The future tense of the indicative mood is sufficient to express the probably upcoming result. Similarly, the imperative mood also conveys the likely materialization of the result while still letting us know that this result is not guaranteed; it is not anchored in the indicative line.

Si José **vient** en classe, je **serai** contente.

Si tu **viens** en classe, rapporte mon livre.

(José rarely misses class so I am pretty sure he's going to get here and I'll be happy. You rarely miss class, so I can order you to bring my book because I am almost sure you will.)

Refer to Chapter 11 on
**Imperative Moods—
Principal and Subordinates**

Feasible Result

The result-consequence R2 verb is conjugated in the *conditionnel présent* if it results from *hypothetical* conditions.

There is a much stronger doubt that the action dependent on a hypothesis will materialize; therefore, it is expressed in the conditional mood, to show that it is floating above the situation with only partial chances of coming down to reality:

Si Marc **venait** en classe, je *serais* très étonnée. *(Marc is well known for missing classes, so his coming would surprise me.)*

Nonexistent Result, Past Conditional

The **result verb** is conjugated in the ~~Conditionnel Passé~~ if it did not materialize.

There has been no resulting action because the condition never happened. Now that we look back into the past, we can only regret what could have been *if only . . .*

Si Marc **était venu** en classe, j'~~aurais été~~ vraiment surprise. *(The class is now over and Marc was indeed not there. Had he come, I would have been very surprised considering his being famous for missing classes. But he did not come, which ~~did not surprise me~~.)*

THREE DEGREES OF REALISM OF THE CAUSE AND LIKELIHOOD OF THE RESULT	
NOTE The conditional structures are absolutely equivalent in English and in French.	
PROBABILITÉ—PROBABILITY	
Probable Cause SI + Indicatif Présent	**Very Likely Result** **Indicatif Futur** **Imperative**
Si tu lis ce livre	tu **comprendras** mieux la grammaire. **fais** tous les exercices!
If you read this book, you **will understand** grammar better. If you read this book, do all the exercises.	
Hypothèse—Hypothesis	
Possible Cause SI + **Indicatif Imparfait**	*Feasible Result* *Conditionnel Présent*
Si tu allais en France	*tu améliorerais aussi ta prononciation.*
(If you went to France, you would improve your pronunciation too.)	
Regret—Regret	
Non-realized Cause **SI** + *Plus-que-Parfait*	~~*Nonexistent Result*~~ **Si + *Conditionnel Passé***
Si tu étais né en France	**tu** ~~*aurais étudié*~~ **la grammaire pendant ton enfance.**
*(**If you had been born in France**, you* ~~would have~~ studied grammar ~~as a child~~.)	

Conditional Conjugations

Tense Components

Union of Past and Future

> **TIP**
>
> As usual, if you forget how to conjugate the conditional, think about the logic and the implications of the concept and it might help you remember the mechanics.
>
> The way to conjugate the verb in the conditional is, in itself, a sign of the ambiguous status of actions that depend upon one another.
>
> The conditional is formed by uniting two opposites:
>
> the **future** and the **past**.
>
> The attempt to join these mutually exclusive temporal frames therefore physically suspends the conditional action above time.
>
> **FutuRe** Stem + Endings in **ImparfAIT** = CONDITIONAL

Structure of the Conditional Sentence

In a conditional sentence, the focus is on the potential action. The conditional mood is therefore found in the principal clause.

The word **SI** that introduces the condition is a conjunction. The condition is therefore expressed in a conjunctive subordinate clause.

Depending on how much emphasis one wishes to put on the condition, it can be placed before or after the principal clause.

The condition can also be omitted from the sentence if it has been stated earlier or if it is implied.

Proposition Subordonnée	Proposition Principale
Si j'étais Présidente *(If I was the president,)*	je rendrais les études gratuites. *(I would make education free.)*
Proposition Principale	**Proposition Subordonnée**
Les étudiants ne s'endetteraient pas pour leur diplôme, *(The students would not go into debt to get their diploma)*	si j'étais Présidente. *(if I was the president.)*
Proposition Indépendante	Implied context
Et il n'y aurait plus de guerre. *(And there would be no more war.)*	[si j'étais présidente] *([if I was the president])*

Conditional Stem and Endings

The conditional results from the unlikely marriage of two opposites:

- The FutuRe:
  The stem of the conditional is the same as the one used to form the indicative futuRe. So it must include an R.

- The Past:
  The endings of the conditional are the same as the ones used to form the **indicative imparfAIT**. So the set of endings must include an AIT ending.

The fruit of this unlikely marriage is a strange creature: neither real nor unreal, but a potential action.

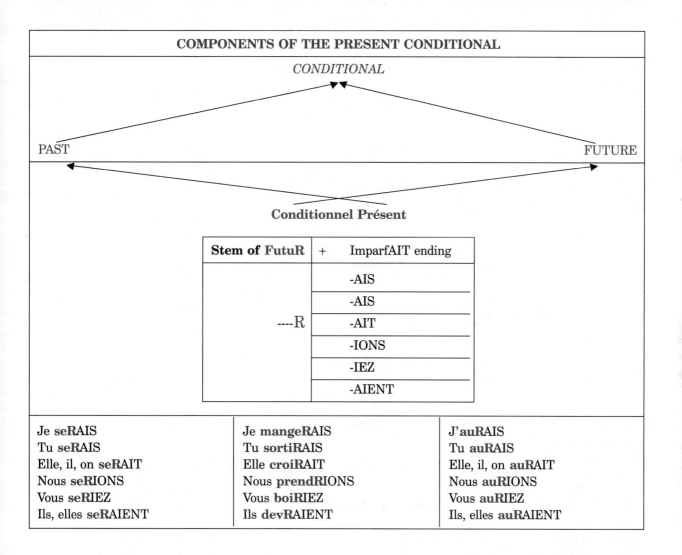

COMPONENTS OF THE PRESENT CONDITIONAL

CONDITIONAL

PAST   FUTURE

Conditionnel Présent

Stem of FutuR	+	ImparfAIT ending
		-AIS
		-AIS
----R		-AIT
		-IONS
		-IEZ
		-AIENT

Je se**RAIS**	Je mange**RAIS**	J'au**RAIS**
Tu se**RAIS**	Tu sorti**RAIS**	Tu au**RAIS**
Elle, il, on se**RAIT**	Elle croi**RAIT**	Elle, il, on au**RAIT**
Nous se**RIONS**	Nous prend**RIONS**	Nous au**RIONS**
Vous se**RIEZ**	Vous boi**RIEZ**	Vous au**RIEZ**
Ils, elles se**RAIENT**	Ils dev**RAIENT**	Ils, elles au**RAIENT**

Refer to Chapter 13 on
FutuRe
to review the futuRe stems of both
regular and irregular verbs

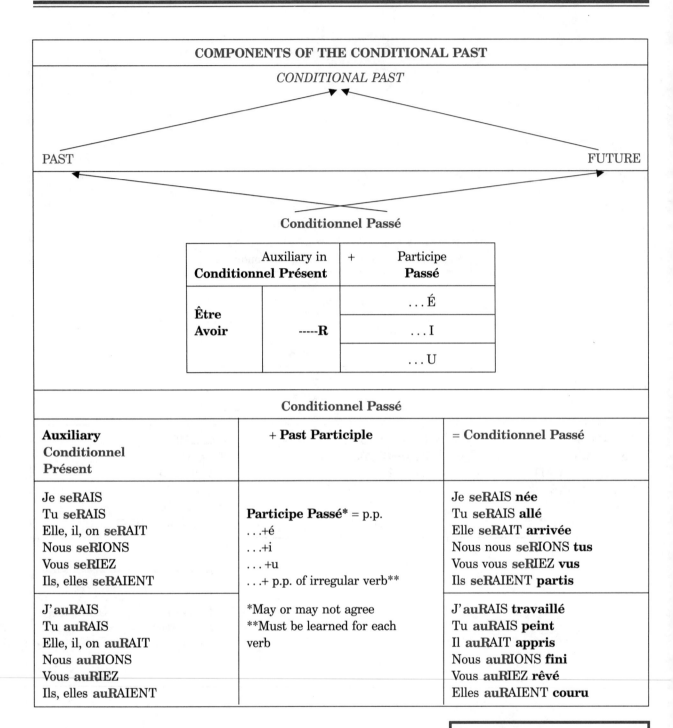

COMPONENTS OF THE CONDITIONAL PAST		

CONDITIONAL PAST

PAST   FUTURE

Conditionnel Passé

Auxiliary in **Conditionnel Présent**	+	Participe **Passé**
Être **Avoir**	-----**R**	. . . É
		. . . I
		. . . U

Conditionnel Passé

Auxiliary **Conditionnel** **Présent**	**+ Past Participle**	**= Conditionnel Passé**
Je se**RAIS** Tu se**RAIS** Elle, il, on se**RAIT** Nous se**RIONS** Vous se**RIEZ** Ils, elles se**RAIENT**	**Participe Passé*** = p.p. . . .+é . . .+i . . .+u . . .+ p.p. of irregular verb**	Je se**RAIS née** Tu se**RAIS allé** Elle se**RAIT arrivée** Nous nous se**RIONS tus** Vous vous se**RIEZ vus** Ils se**RAIENT partis**
J'au**RAIS** Tu au**RAIS** Elle, il, on au**RAIT** Nous au**RIONS** Vous au**RIEZ** Ils, elles au**RAIENT**	*May or may not agree **Must be learned for each verb	J'au**RAIS travaillé** Tu au**RAIS peint** Il au**RAIT appris** Nous au**RIONS fini** Vous au**RIEZ rêvé** Elles au**RAIENT couru**

Refer to Chapter 12 on
Passé Composé and Agreement
of Past Participle

- Condition C1, Cause:
  Depending on how strongly you feel about the realization of the condition, you will conjugate the verb of the condition (cause) in the **présent**, the **imparfait**, or the *Plus-que-Parfait* of the **indicative**.

  This is your choice because all actions can be at times more or less real.

- Result R2, Consequence:
  On the other hand, you cannot decide the conjugation of the action that is conditioned. The consequence has to be expressed in the tense that corresponds to the one you chose for the condition. You are not free to choose between **indicatif futur**, **impératif**, *conditionnel présent*, or ~~conditionnel passé~~. These tenses must follow the previous correspondence charts.

La Mode Conditionnelle

Going back to our analogy between mood and mode, **le mode et la mode**, how would you dress the verbs-actions resulting from each type of condition?

REVIEW TABLE: ALL CONDITIONAL STRUCTURES	
As in English, the condition can either precede or follow the result. Whichever clause (principal or subordinate) comes first in the sentence is naturally emphasized.	
Condition: Subordinate Clause	Result: Principal Clause

TIP BOX			
The conditional is a balanced structure:			
1 verbal component in the subordinate Stem + Ending		1 in the principal Stem + Ending	
2 verbal components in the subordinate		**2 in the subordinate**	
Auxiliary	**+ Past Participle**	**Auxiliary**	**+ P. P.**
Three Degrees of Realism—Feasibility			
Probability: 1 verbal component			
SI + **Indicatif Présent**		**Indicatif Futur** Impératif	
Si tu **veux** Si tu **arrives** tôt		nous **travaillerons**. fais la vaisselle.	

If you want, we will work.	
If you arrive early, do the dishes.	
Hypothesis: 1 verbal component	
SI + Indicatif Imparfait	*Conditionnel Présent*
Si j'avais plus de temps	*j'écrirais* un roman.
If I had more time, *I would write a novel.*	
Regret: 2 verbal components	
SI + Indicatif *Plus-que-Parfait*	*Conditionnel ~~Passé~~*
Si Victor **était venu**	*tu l'~~aurais revu~~.*
(If Victor had come, you ~~would have seen~~ him again.)	

Special Uses of the Conditional

Future of the Past

When narrating a series of events in the past, the conditional is used to indicate something that *was* scheduled to happen after a past action.

The conditional action is in the future of a past action. Its English equivalent is "would":

Viviane m'a promis qu'elle **viendrait** ce soir. *(Viviane promised me she **would come** tonight.)*

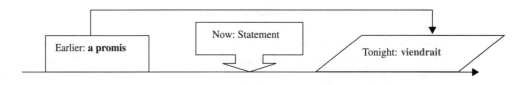

Suggestion, Advice, Recommendation, Politeness, Caution

Both **conditionnel présent** and **conditionnel passé** can be used by themselves, without the implication of a condition, to suggest, advise, or recommend something. They can also be used to ask a question or state a criticism very carefully. Such uses convey a sense of precaution and hesitation on the part of the "advisor." These contexts have various equivalents in English.

Suggestion—Advice—Recommendation:

Vous **devriez** peut-être faire un peu d'exercice si vous voulez mincir. *(You should perhaps do a little exercise if you want to lose weight.)*

Cautious Statement:

> Il se **pourrait** qu'il pleuve demain. *(There might be a possibility of rain tomorrow.)*

Politeness:

> **Pourriez**-vous m'accorder un entretien, Monsieur le Président? *(Would you consider granting me an interview, Mr. President?)*

Cautious Criticism:

> Vous **auriez pu** me prévenir; cela m'**aurait facilité** la tâche. *(You could have warned me; it would have made my task easier.)*

Warning for Possible Inaccuracy

Both **conditionnel présent** and **conditionnel passé** are also used by themselves to signify that a statement may not be accurate. This use is common in news reporting, when events have not yet been confirmed:

> L'attentat **aurait fait** quinze morts et plusieurs blessés. Il **serait** revendiqué par le groupe . . . *(The terrorist attack **would have killed** fifteen people and injured many others. It **would be claimed** by the group . . .)*

Supposition—In case . . .

In case of a milder condition, namely a supposition, the conditional mood is used after the expression **au cas où** —*in the case of*—that:

> **Au cas où** vous **auriez** le temps, passez-me voir ce soir. *(In case you have the time, come by and see me this evening.)*

This phrase is also used if the resulting action is not very important:

> *(Should you have the time, come by and see me.)*

The Subjunctive Mood

THINK!

> **La Mode Subjonctive**
> Going back to our analogy between mood and mode, **le mode et la mode**, how would you "dress" highly subjective actions?
>   List them below or find suggestions when you get to the Practice Exercises section.

Introduction

The conditional and subjunctive moods are comparable for two main reasons:

1. Both moods are not anchored in reality.
2. Both moods express a strong connection between two actions.

- In the conditional one action is dependent upon another.
- In the subjunctive one subject is dependent upon another.

Characteristics of the Subjunctive

Meaning of Subjective

The subjunctive is the mood that is the most detached from reality. Using the subjunctive basically means entering the "twilight" zone of subjectivity: everyone is free to decide what to do no matter what other people say/tell them to do.

    There is no black or white in the subjunctive; everything is gray.

LEVEL OF REALITY OF THE SUBJUNCTIVE MOOD				
Subjonctif	▲	Least real	Subjunctive	Action is dependent on each individual's decision: its realization is out of my control
Conditionnel				
Impératif				
Indicatif		Most real	Indicative	Action has been, is, or will be, Real
Infinitif	◆			

Personal Preferences

The *subjunctive* mood is used to render the subjective quality of actions that result from very individual factors:

- personal emotions
- wishes
- desires
- needs
- preferences
- tastes
- judgments
- opinions

The subjunctive is necessary when the performance of an action does not have an objective value but is due to a subjective decision.

Example of objectivity: The following word is BLUE.

Provided we are not color-blind, we can all agree on that. **It is an objective reality.**

Example of subjectivity: The most beautiful color is blue.

That is a subjective opinion, because you are free to disagree, and find red more beautiful. There is no way that I can prove I am right to think blue is the most beautiful color.

Loss of Control

There is even less possibility for me to force you to agree with me. What the subjunctive mood also indicates is an *absence of control* over another person's actions or feelings; even if I had you put in jail, I could not make you stop preferring red. In the below illustration of the sergeant's absence of control, no matter how many stripes he has or how loud he orders the reporter to stop taking photos, the journalist can still disobey.

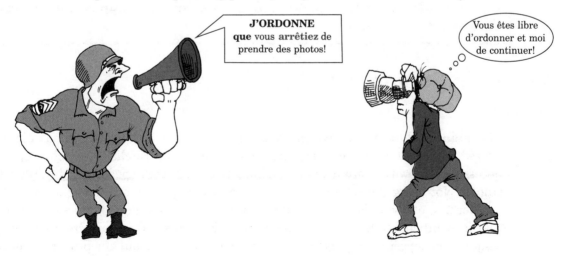

(I command you to stop taking photos.)

(You are free to give orders and I am free to continue taking photos.)

Rationale

Two Distinct Subjects

For a statement to be considered subjective, there must be another person who can contest it. If I was alone in the world, the most beautiful color would be whichever one I said!

Because there must two persons for subjectivity to appear, there must be *two* subjects and *two* actions in the sentence.

Two Different Actions

Think of your partner and yourself: When two people are together, one of them always wants the other one to do something. This desire is objective; what is much less concrete is the other person's fulfilling it. The verbs in the sentence convey this gap:

- **One action will be real**: the desire, wish, command, etc., and the verb are therefore in the mood of reality: the **indicative**
- The other action is virtual: what is entailed in this desire or command is left to another person's subjective decision to perform it or not. The subjective action is conveyed by a verb in the subjunctive.

Two Separate Clauses

The sentence itself embodies the difference between one person's expectation and the other person's compliance. Each action has it own clause:

- The principal clause expresses the real expectation.
- The subordinate clause contains the virtual response that is expected.

> **NOTE** The subjunctive mood is therefore found in compound sentences. The separation between the clauses indicates a potential opposition or clash between the two subjects.

Use of the Subjunctive

Context

The **mode subjonctif** is extremely common in French; however, it has almost disappeared, or is no longer recognized as such, in American English. French people may not necessarily know they are using the subjunctive when they speak daily but they do it constantly. Not using the subjunctive is proof of a very poor education or a complete lack of care for how one sounds. Although it is expected from foreigners because everyone is aware that it is difficult to learn, in the mouth of a French speaker, the absence of subjunctive conjugation is particularly irritating for people who care about the proper use of their language. The wrong indicative sounds like fingernails on a blackboard. Not using it may also be a form of provocation by famous music stars, for instance, or celebrities who criticize what is known as bourgeois values. But as an American, you will impress everyone when you use it correctly!

Everyday Situations

Overall, the subjunctive is used very often, since situations involving a possible conflict between two people are very common.

Will

You must use the subjunctive every time two different people are involved and A would like B to do, think, or feel something.

A's desire is real so it is conjugated in the **indicative mood**,

but A has no control over what B will eventually do, so B's response is conjugated in the subjunctive mood:

> Je **veux que** vous fassiez tous les exercices dans ce livre. *(I want you to do all the exercises in this book; it is very true that I want it very strongly, but that is not going to make you do the exercises—you will decide to do them or not; however much I want you to do them does not influence you.)*

Opinion

You must use the subjunctive when one person expresses a judgment, an opinion, or an emotion over another person.

A's opinion about B is real so it is conjugated in the **indicative mood**,

but B's action is judged through the eyes of A, so B's action is conjugated in the subjunctive mood.

The subjunctive here shows that two persons can have a completely different opinion or emotional reaction to a similar fact:

> Roger est républicain. **Il est content que** G. W. Bush ait été élu.
> Danièle est démocrate. **Elle est horrifiée que** G. W. Bush ait été élu.
> *(The same fact (that Bush was elected president) is provoking radically different feelings: contentment and horror. His election, although it is a fact, can be viewed completely differently; it has a very subjective dimension to it.)*

Doubt

You must use the subjunctive when the action itself is questionable:

> J'**aurai** la maison de mes rêves **pourvu qu'**on me la donne. *(There is serious doubt that someone will give me my dream house, yet you never know—there might be a philanthropist out there who likes dedicated teachers or my grammar book so much that she or he would want to be generous!)*

> Nous **verrons** le feu d'artifice à Cannes le 14 juillet, **à moins qu'**il ne pleuve. *(It is unlikely yet always possible that it rained on the Riviera in the middle of the summer; one never knows. The raining is in the subjunctive because we have no control over it.)*

Subjunctive Sentence Structure

Content and Form

Subjective Elements

The three central aspects that define subjectivity are:

1. Two distinct persons
2. Two related actions
3. Two separate clauses

These also explain the three characteristics of the structure of the subjunctive mood.

Subjunctive Components

The subjunctive sentence represents faithfully the subjective elements:

1. Two different subjects
2. Two connected verbs
3. Two hierarchical levels

The possible conflict between two personalities is made visible by this construction.

CONTENT AND FORM CORRESPONDENCE		
SUBJunCTivE	SUBJECTive	2 different SUBJECTs in the sentence
subjunCtive	subjunQUEtive	2 connected verbs linked by conjunction [. . .] QUE
SUBjunctive	SUBordinate	2 hierarchical levels: a principal and a SUBordinate clause for the SUBjunctive

Viviane **veut** que Patrick parte. *(Viviane wants Patrick to leave.)*

1. Two distinct persons—Two different subjects: Viviane—Patrick
2. Two related actions—Two connected verbs: veut—que—parte
3. Two separate clauses—Two hierarchical levels:

Proposition Principale **Viviane veut**		
	que	Proposition Subordonnée Patrick parte.

Compound Sentence

> *Refer to Chapter 15 on*
> **Sentences and Clauses**
> **Conjunctive Subordinate Clauses**

Since there must be two different subjects and two verbs, the subjunctive is found in compound sentences.

Principal Clause

The type of action that leads into the subjective realm (désirer, préférer, ordonner, recommander . . .) precedes and generates a subjective reaction from a different person.

The expression of such desire, command, opinion, advice, wish, etc. can be expressed by four different types of words (verbs, impersonal expressions, conjunctions, adjectives) but it is always found before the subordinate clause. It triggers the subjunctive mood that will be encountered later, in the subordinate itself.

SUBJUNCTIVE EXAMPLES—COMPOUND SENTENCE AND SUBJUNCTIVE TRIGGERS		
Principal Clause **Will**	CONJUNCTION of Subordination	Subordinate Clause Subjective **response**
Paul **veut**	QUE	Marie **vienne** à sa soirée.
Subjunctive Trigger = verb of will: vouloir *(Paul wants Marie to come to his party.)*		
Pour Paul, il est crucial	QUE	Marie **vienne** à sa soirée.
Subjunctive Trigger = impersonal expression: il est crucial *(For Paul, it is crucial that Marie came to his party.)*		
Paul **a** tout **organisé**	**pour QUE** conjunction	Marie **vienne** à sa soirée.
Subjunctive Trigger = conjunction: pour que *(Paul had organized everything so that Marie will come to his party.)*		
Paul **est** heureux	QUE	Marie **soit venue** à sa soirée.
Subjunctive Trigger = adjective of emotion: heureux *(Paul is happy that Marie came to his party.)*		

Conjunctive Subordinate Clause

Consequently, the subjunctive is always found in the subordinate clause; it is a response to the principal desire, dream, wish, advice ... The subordinate clause generally follows the principal one.

It can, however, also start the sentence if you wish to particularly emphasize its action:

> Je la **vérifie** dans ce manuel de grammaire pour que nous **soyons** sûrs de cette règle. (*I verify it in this grammar book for us to be sure about this rule.*)

> Pour que nous **soyons** sûrs de cette règle, je la **vérifie** dans ce manuel de grammaire. (*In order for us to be sure about this rule, I verify it in this grammar book.*)

SUBJUNCTIVE SENTENCES: CORRESPONDANCE CONTENT AND STRUCTURE		
SUBJunCTive	SUBJeCTive 2 <u>Subjects</u> S1 ≠ S2	<u>**S1**</u> + CV1 + ... que + <u>**S2**</u> + CV2 + ... Principal Subordinate
subjunCtive	subjunQUEtive <u>Conjunction</u> que or xxx que	S1 + CV1 + **QUE** + S2 + CV2 + ... Principal Subordinate
<u>SUBjunctive</u>	SUBordinate 2 Conjugated Verbs CV1—<u>CV2</u>	S1 + **CV1** + ... que + S2 + **CV2** + ... Principal Subordinate

Subjunctive Triggers

Various elements in a situation can solicit a person's response to someone else's expectations. In the language, four elements in the principal clause can signal that whatever happens in the subordinate will be up to someone else's subjective decision. These four elements open onto the twilight zone of subjectivity and trigger the subjunctive.

Verbs in the Principal Clause

These verbs express different actions; however, all imply that Subject S1 is interested in having Subject S2 do something but has no control over it.

Verbs of Will and Command

VOULOIR que	TENIR À ce que	ATTENDRE que	DEMANDER que
(To want)	*(To be adamant)*	*(To wait)*	*(To ask)*
PRÉFÉRER que	EXIGER que	ORDONNER que	IMPOSER que
(To prefer)	*(To demand)*	*(To command)*	*(To impose)*

Verbs of Desire and Wish

DÉSIRER que	AVOIR ENVIE que	SOUHAITER que
(To desire)	*(To feel like)*	*(To wish)*
ASPIRER à ce que	RÊVER que	IMAGINER que
(To aspire)	*(To dream)*	*(To imagine)*

Verbs of Interdiction and Fear

INTERDIRE que	DÉFENDRE que	EXCLURE que	S'OPPOSER à ce que
(To prohibit)	*(To forbid)*	*(To exclude)*	*(To oppose)*
AVOIR PEUR que	CRAINDRE que	REDOUTER que	S'ALARMER de ce que
(To fear)	*(To be worried)*	*(To dread)*	*(To be scared)*

NOTE After **craindre que** and **avoir peur que** one can find the negative adverb **ne** (it is called ne pléonastique). Since it is alone, it does not give a negative meaning to the sentence. This is a remnant of an archaic rule and this use of **ne** has almost disappeared in contemporary everyday language.

Verbs of Advice or Suggestion

CONSEILLER que	RECOMMANDER que	SOUS-ENTENDRE que
(To advise)	*(To recommend)*	*(To imply)*
SUGGÉRER que	PROPOSER que	RAPPELER que
(To suggest)	*(To propose)*	*(To remind)*

In all these cases,

- it is **true** and **real** that S1 wants, desires, recommends, reminds, advises, fears, proposes, prefers ... that S2 do something. **So the wanting, desire, fear ... are conjugated in the indicative.**
- But S1 has no control over S2's freedom, and S2's decision to comply or not is completely subjective. Therefore, S2's contemplated action is put in the subjunctive.

IMPORTANT!

If you do not have two different subjects, you cannot use the subjunctive.

If the subjects are the same (I wish that I did something) there is no need to use a subjunctive, since there is no reason for me *not* to do what I wish!

The subjunctive is replaced by an infinitive. The same subject is distributed over both actions. There is no need to conjugate both verbs since they would have the same person and tense markers.

The sentence remains simple:

Je veux **que** TU partes = I want, You leave: 2 subjects = subjunctive

Je veux *partir*. = I want, I leave: 1 subject = infinitive

Je lis beaucoup **pour que** mon cerveau soit content. = I read, my brain is happy: 2 subjects = subjunctive

Je lis beaucoup pour *être* contente. = I read, I am happy: 1 subject = infinitive

---

REVIEW TABLE: VERBAL TRIGGERS		
NOTE how varied the English translations are, even though the French structures are systematically the same.		
Clauses	Principal: **Indicative or Conditional**	Subordinate: **Subjunctive**
Will **Command**	Les étudiants **voudraient** Le professeur **exige**	QUE la grammaire **soit** facile. QUE les étudiants **travaillent**.
	(The students would like the grammar to be easy.) *(The professor demands that the students work.)*	
Desire **Wish**	Mon petit-ami **a envie** Je **souhaiterais**	QUE je **fasse** une ratatouille. QU'il **nettoie** la cuisine d'abord.
	(My boyfriend would like me to cook a vegetable stew.) *(I wish he'd clean the kitchen first.)*	
Interdiction **Fear**	Ce panneau **interdit** Elle **craint**	QU'on **marche** sur la pelouse. QU'il **pleuve** pour son mariage.
	(This sign forbids walking on the lawn.) *(She is afraid it might rain on her wedding day.)*	
Advice **Suggestion**	Nous **recommandons** Vous **suggérez**	QUE vous **arriviez** en avance. QUE nous **prenions** l'autoroute.
	(We recommend you come early.) *(You suggest we take the freeway.)*	

IMPORTANT!

There is an exception to the previously stated rule.

CROIRE que—ESPÉRER que—PENSER que—TROUVER que

are followed by:

- the indicative mood in affirmative sentences:

Je crois **que Paul** vient **de Nice.** (I think Paul is coming from Nice.)

J'espère **qu'il m'a acheté un souvenir.** (I hope he bought me a souvenir.)

Je pense **qu'il sera fatigué.** (I think he will be tired.)

Je trouve **qu'il a beaucoup de courage.** (I find him to have a lot of courage.)

- **the subjunctive mood in negative and interrogative sentences:**

Je ne crois pas **que Paul VIENNE de Nice mais de Paris.** (I do not think that Paul is coming from Nice but from Paris.)

Espères-tu **qu'il t'AIT ACHETÉ un souvenir?** (Do you hope that he has bought a souvenir for you?)

Je ne pense pas **qu'il SOIT fatigué après un vol en première classe.**
(I do not think he will be tired after flying in first class.)

Je ne trouve pas **qu'il AIT CHANGÉ.** (He does not seem to me to have changed.)

The reason for this exception makes a lot of sense if one keeps in mind that French grammar always tries to depict the situation as accurately as possible. The logic of each situation supercedes the universality of the rule.

When people use: *I believe that, I (sure) hope that, I think that, it seems to me that,* most of them mean that they know so in reality. People may be polite but they are quite sure of what they state. So the indicative is a more precise representation of the true meaning of the affirmative verbs and the rule bends.

But when they are negated or questioned, these beliefs, hopes, or thoughts are destabilized again, hence the reappearance of the subjunctive since there is no certainty at all, implied or not.

ImpersonaL Verbal Expressions: *IL . . .*

- These expressions are called *impersonal* because their subject is the neutral pronoun **IL** or **CE** (in front of the auxiliary verb **Être**)—**ÇA** (in front of **avoir** and any verb except the auxiliary verb **Être**). **Il**, **ce**, or **ça** replaces a general concept or a subject that does not actually exist. There are numerous impersonal expressions such as:

  Il y a, il pleut, il est tard, il était une fois, il reste . . . *(There is, it is raining, it's late, once upon a time, there remains.)*

  C'est gentil; Ça arrive. *(It is nice; It happens.)*

- All impersonal expressions consist of a neuter pronoun as subject and a verb, or the auxiliary verb **Être** and an adjective.
- Many of these expressions are used to also express will, command, desire, wish, advice, emotion, etc. They offer a second way of stating the need, necessity, or importance of something subjective. When it is the case, some impersonal expressions are therefore followed by the subjunctive.

REVIEW TABLE: IMPERSONAL EXPRESSIONS TRIGGERS			
NOTE how varied the English translations are, even though the French structures are systematically the same.			
Clauses	Principal: Impersonal Expression **Indicative**		Subordinate: **Subjunctive**
Will **Necessity** **Command**	**Il faut** **Il est nécessaire** **Il est important** **Il est impératif**	QUE	les étudiants **fassent** tous leurs exercices de grammaire.
	(It is mandatory, necessary, important, crucial that the students do all their grammar exercises.)		
Desire **Wish** **Possibility**	**Il est souhaitable** **Il se peut** **Il est possible** **Il est peu probable** **Il est incroyable**	QUE	nous **ayons déjà** couvert toute la grammaire française de base.
	(It is desirable, possible, unlikely, incredible that we had already covered the entire basic French grammar.)		

Clauses	Principal: Impersonal Expression **Indicative**		Subordinate: **Subjunctive**
Interdiction Fear	**Il ne faut pas** **Il est impensable** **Il est à craindre** **C'est effrayant** **C'est horrible**	QUE	cette guerre **soit** déclarée. cette guerre **ait été** déclarée.
	(This war must not be declared.) *(It is unthinkable that this war will be declared.)* *(I am afraid this war will be declared.)* *(It is scary, horrible that this war has been declared.)*		
Advice Suggestion Judgment	**Il serait bien** **Il semble** **Il est préférable** **C'est intéressant** **Il est étonnant**	QUE	vous **ayez lu** tout le livre avant d'étudier ce chapitre.
	(It would be good, it seems, it is better, it is interesting, it is surprising that you had read the whole book before studying this chapter.)		

Adjectives of Emotion, Opinion, Judgment

Many of the adjectives that are used in the verbal expressions with an impersonal subject can also be used with a subject representing an actual person. These adjectives express the same type of subjective emotion, undecided opinion, judgment, and assessment that is implied in both the verbs and the impersonal expressions above. In other words, adjectives can also depict the twilight zone of human subjectivity.

REVIEW TABLE: ADJECTIVE TRIGGERS			
NOTE how varied the English translations are, even though the French structures are systematically the same.			
Clauses	Principal: **Indicative or Conditional**		Subordinate: **Subjunctive**
Emotion Opinion Judgment	Je suis **contente** Tu n'es **pas sûr** Elle est **surprise** Nous sommes **enchantés** Vous êtes **désolés** Ils sont **impatients**	QUE	les étudiants **fassent** tous leurs exercices de grammaire.
	(I am happy, You are not sure, she is surprised, we are pleased, you are sorry that the students did all their grammar exercises. *They are impatient for the students to do their grammar exercises.)*		

Such adjectives are followed by a conjunctive subordinate clause whose subject is naturally different from that of the principal clause:

Mariane est **triste** QUE Bush **soit** président.

Tex est **content** QU'il **ait été** élu.

Sadness or happiness about a president being elected is a subjective reaction that leads into the subjunctive.

Certaines personnes sont **outrées** QUE l'avortement **soit** légal.

D'autres sont **effarées** QUE le droit à l'avortement **soit** en danger.

Being appalled that abortion is legal, or stunned that its legality would be jeopardized reflects a very subjective viewpoint on a sensitive question that is therefore put in the subjunctive.

Je ne suis pas **certaine** QUE tu **aies** raison.

Because I am not sure about it, your being right cannot be in the indicative; it must be in the subjunctive.

IMPORTANT!

In both impersonal verbal expressions and with subjects representing actual persons, certain adjectives may be followed by either the indicative or the subjunctive, depending on their meaning. They will be followed by the indicative if they imply something solid, sure, or verified. They will be followed by the subjunctive when they convey doubt, uncertainty, vagueness:

Je suis certaine **que tu** as **raison.** (*I am sure that you are right*: indicative **because I am sure of it.**)

Je ne **suis** pas certaine **que tu aies** raison. (*I am not so sure you're right*: **subjunctive due to my uncertainty.**)

Il n'est pas douteux **qu'Inès** est **intelligente.** (*There is no doubt that Ines is intelligent*: indicative **because there is no doubt; therefore it is a sure fact.**)

Il est douteux **qu'Inès sorte** de son enfer. (*It is doubtful that Inès will leave her hell*: **subjunctive because there is little chance that this Sartre character will change.**)

Conjunctions of Subordination formed with *QUE*

All the triggers of the subjunctive have an element in common: the conjunction **que**. This conjunction can also be used in combination with other numerous conjunctions: **parce que**, **avant que**, **pour que**, **dès que** . . .

A certain number of these conjunctions introduce a sense of doubt, opposition, fear, potentiality, goal, or dreaming that is similar to the verbs, expressions, or adjectives. They are the fourth way of entering the subjective zone, and should be identified as flags to use the subjunctive.

	REVIEW TABLE: CONJUNCTIONS OF SUBORDINATION TRIGGERS		
	Principal: **Indicative or Conditional**		Subordinate: **Subjunctive**
Postponement	Je **range** la cuisine	AVANT que EN attendant que JUSQU'À CE que	mes amis [ne] **viennent**. tu **finisses** de travailler. le film **commence**.
	(I am cleaning the kitchen before my friends arrive, while waiting for you to stop working, until the movie starts.)		
Opposition	Elle **va** démissioner	BIEN qu' QUOI que À MOINS que SANS que	il y **ait** peu d'offres d'emploi. son travail **soit** tolérable. son patron l'**augmente**. ses collègues **soient avertis**.
	(She is going to quit even though there are few job offers, although her job is acceptable, unless her boss gives her a raise, without her colleagues being warned.)		
Goal	Mes parents **ont** beaucoup **travaillé**	POUR que AFIN que DANS le but que DE sorte que DE manière que DE façon que	je **puisse** aller à l'université. ma vie **soit** confortable. j'**aie** plus de possibilités qu'eux. nous **ayons** une jolie maison. notre famille **soit** à l'abri. leur patron les **respecte**.
	(My parents worked a lot so that I could go to the university, for my life to be comfortable, in order for me to have more possibilities than they had, so that we had a pretty house, so our family could be united, so their boss respected them.)		
Potentiality	Fab **sera** satisfaite	POURVU que À CONDITION que	vous **aimiez** ce livre. ses explications vous **aident**.
	(Fab will be satisfied provided you like this book, her explanations are helpful to you.)		
Generality	Ce livre vous **aidera**	SI . . . que QUI que QUOI que	si difficile que la grammaire **paraisse**. vous **soyez**: étudiant ou non. vous **sachiez** déjà.
	(This book will help you as difficult as grammar seems to be, whoever you are: a student or not, whatever you may already know.)		

Formation of the Subjunctive Tenses

Although there are actually four different forms of the subjunctive, two are very literary and hardly ever used any more. On the other hand, both the **Subjonctif Présent** and the **Subjonctif Passé** are common in everyday language.

Present Subjunctive

As all simple tenses, the Subjunctive Present is formed by adding the appropriate set of endings to a stem.

Stem

Regular Stem

For most verbs, the stem is found by removing the -ent ending from the Indicative Present of the third person plural:

IDENTIFICATION OF THE SUBJUNCTIVE STEM		
ILS-ELLES FORM OF INDICATIVE PRESENT MINUS -ENT ENDING		
Devoir	Elles doiv~~ent~~	**doiv-**
Écrire	Elles écriv~~ent~~	**écriv-**
Finir	Ils finiss~~ent~~	**finiss-**
Manger	Elles mang~~ent~~	**mang-**
Partir	Ils part~~ent~~	**part-**
Vendre	Ils vend~~ent~~	**vend-**

Irregular Stems

Many common verbs have a specific stem that is unique and does not follow the above pattern. Others can also have two stems, which are both regular and irregular. In this case the first and second persons plural are always formed on the regular stem.

MOST COMMON VERBS WITH IRREGULAR SUBJUNCTIVE STEMS		
	1st, 2nd, 3rd Persons Singular 3rd Persons Plural	**1st, 2nd Persons Plural**
Aller	**aill-**	**all-**
Valoir	**vaill-**	**val-**
Falloir	**faill-**	
Vouloir	**veuill-**	**voul-**
Prendre	**prenn-**	**pren-**
Venir	**vienn-**	**ven-**
Savoir	**sach-**	
Faire	**fass-**	
Pouvoir	**puiss-**	
Recevoir	**reçoiv-**	**recev-**
Concevoir	**conçoiv-**	**concev-**
Boire	**boiv-**	**buv-**
Emouvoir	**émeuv-**	**émouv-**
Mourir	**meur-**	**mour-**

Boire: boiv- / buv-

> Sa religion défend **qu**'il **boiv**e de l'alcool.
>
> La loi interdit **que** nous **buv**ions de l'alcool avant vingt-et-un ans.
>
> *(His religion forbids him to drink alcohol.)*
>
> *(The law forbids us to drink alcohol before being twenty-one.)*

Concevoir: conçoiv- / concev-

> Il est crucial **que** tu **conçoiv**es ton projet de construction.
>
> Je ne crois pas **que** vous **concev**iez ce projet avant la date limite.
>
> *(It is crucial that you design your construction project.)*
>
> *(I do not think you will design your project before the deadline.)*

Émouvoir: émeuv- / émouv-

> Incroyable **que** ces films t'**émeuv**ent aux larmes!
>
> Il critique le fait **que** vous vous **émouv**iez pour si peu.
>
> *(It is incredible that these movies move you to tears!)*
>
> *(He criticizes the fact that you are moved for so little reason.)*

Mourir: meur- / mour-

> Tu n'arrives pas à croire **que** ce héros **meur**e à la fin du film.
>
> Il est fort peu probable **que** vous **mour**iez de peur au cinéma.
>
> *(You cannot believe that this hero dies at the end of the movie.)*
>
> *(It is very unlikely that you will die of fear at the movies.)*

Vouloir: veuill- / voul-

> Philippe est heureux **que** Brigitte **veuill**e partir en vacances avec lui.
>
> Il n'y a aucune chance **que** nous **voul**ions déménager cette année.
>
> *(Philippe is happy that Brigitte wants to go on vacation with him.)*
>
> *(There is no chance that we will want to move this year.)*

Endings

The subjunctive endings are borrowed from both the **Présent** and the **Imparfait** of the **Indicative** mood:

SUBJUNCTIVE ENDINGS		
	Indicatif **Présent**	Indicatif **Imparfait**
JE	**-e**	
TU	**-es**	
ELLE-IL	**e**	
NOUS		**-ions**
VOUS		**-iez**
ILS-ELLES	**-ent**	

Paul **ne pense pas** que je doi**ve** de l'argent. *(Paul does not think I owe money.)*

J'**ordonne** que tu aill**es** au supermarché. *(I order you to go to the supermarket.)*

Ses parents **souhaitent** qu'elle écri**ve** un roman. *(Her parents wish she would write a novel.)*

Il est possible que nous fass**ions** une croisière. *(It is possible we will go on a cruise.)*

Nous **voulions** que vous ven**iez** demain. *(We wanted you to come tomorrow.)*

Leurs amis sont **tristes** qu'ils veuill**ent** divorcer. *(Their friends are sad that they want to divorce.)*

TABLE OF PRINCIPAL IRREGULAR VERBS IN THE SUBJONCTIF PRÉSENT						
Infinitive	*QUE JE*	*QUE TU*	*QU'IL*	*QUE NOUS*	*QUE VOUS*	*QU'ELLES*
Aller	aille	ailles	aille	allions	alliez	aillent
Avoir	aie	aies	ait	ayons	ayez	aient
Connaître	connaisse	connaisses	connaisse	connaissions	connaissiez	connaissent
Croire	crois	crois	croit	croyions	croyiez	croient
Devoir	doive	doives	doive	devions	deviez	doivent
Dire	dise	dises	dise	disions	disiez	disent
Écrire	écrive	écrives	écrive	écrivions	écriviez	écrivent
Être	sois	sois	soit	soyons	soyez	soient
Faire	fasse	fasses	fasse	fassions	fassiez	fassent
Lire	lise	lises	lise	lisions	lisiez	lisent
Mettre	mette	mettes	mette	mettions	mettiez	mettent
Partir	parte	partes	parte	partions	partiez	partent
Pouvoir	puisse	puisses	puisse	puissions	puissiez	puissent
Prendre	prenne	prennes	prenne	prenions	preniez	prennent
Savoir	sache	saches	sache	sachions	sachiez	sachent
Tenir	tienne	tiennes	tienne	tenions	teniez	tiennent
Venir	vienne	viennes	vienne	venions	veniez	viennent
Vouloir	veuille	veuilles	veuille	voulions	vouliez	veuillent

Past Subjunctive

Components

As most past tenses, the **Subjonctif Passé** is a compound tense. It is formed by using the two standard components:

- the auxiliary verb conjugated in the subjunctive
- the past participle.

The choice between **Être** or **Avoir** follows the rule that is standard for all compound tenses. The agreement of the past participle follows the rule that is standard for all compound tenses. Both Être and Avoir auxiliary verbs have a specific series of forms in the subjunctive present.

CONJUGATIONS OF THE SUBJUNCTIVE OF ÊTRE AND AVOIR	
Subjonctif Présent	
ÊTRE	**AVOIR**
que je SOIS	que j'AIE
que tu SOIS	que tu AIES
qu'elle SOIT	qu'il AIT
que nous SOYONS	que nous AYONS
que vous SOYEZ	que vous AYEZ
qu'ils SOIENT	qu'ils AIENT

Subjonctif Passé

Auxiliary Subjonctif Présent	+ Participe Passé	= Subjonctif Passé
. . . que je sois . . . que tu sois . . . qu'il soit . . . que nous soyons . . . que vous soyez . . . qu'elles soient	**Participe Passe*** = p.p. . . . +é . . . +i . . . +u . . . + p.p. of irregular verb**	que je **sois née** que tu **sois allé** qu'elle **soit arrivée** que nous nous **soyons lavés** que vous vous **soyez vus** qu'ils **soient partis**
. . . que j'aie . . . que tu aies . . . qu'il ait . . . que nous ayons . . . que vous ayez . . . qu'elles aient	*May or may not agree **Must be learned for each verb	. . . que j'**aie travaillé** . . . que tu **aies peint** . . . qu'il **ait appris** . . . que nous **ayons fini** . . . que vous **ayez rêvé** . . . qu'elles **aient couru**

Paul ne pensait pas que Didier **ait** tant de dettes.

Paul ne pensait pas que Didier **ait dépensé** tant d'argent.

(Paul did not think that Didier had so much debt, had spent so much money.)

J'aurais voulu que Suzanne **soit** disponible.

J'aurais voulu que Suzanne **soit allée** au supermarché.

(I would have liked Suzanne to be available, to have gone to the supermarket.)

Ses parents souhaitent qu'elle **ait** du succès.

Ses parents souhaiteraient qu'elle **ait publié** son roman.

(Her parents would like her to be successful, to have published her novel.)

Il est possible que nous **ayons** des vacances.

Il est possible que nous **ayons fait** une croisière aux Caraïbes.

(It is possible that we have some vacation, that we will have gone on a cruise in the Caribbean.)

Nous aurions voulu que vous **soyez** libres de venir.

Nous aurions voulu que vous **soyez venus** mais c'est trop tard.

(We would have liked you to be free, to have come but it's too late.)

Leurs amis étaient tristes qu'ils **aient** tous ses problèmes.

Leurs amis étaient tristes qu'ils **aient divorcé**.

(Their friends were sad they had so many problems, that they had divorced.)

Use

The past subjunctive is used mostly to mark the precedence of the subjective action in respect to what is stated in the principal clause.

Il est possible qu'elle **parte** aujourd'hui.

(Her departure is possible and can happen anytime today or later.)

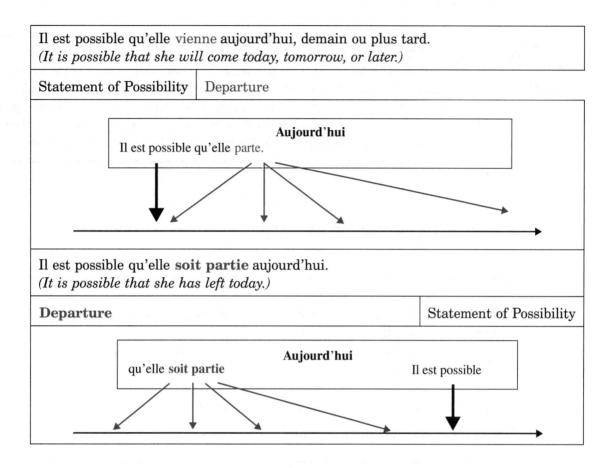

Il est possible qu'elle vienne aujourd'hui, demain ou plus tard.
(It is possible that she will come today, tomorrow, or later.)

Statement of Possibility	Departure

Aujourd'hui
Il est possible qu'elle parte.

Il est possible qu'elle **soit partie** aujourd'hui.
(It is possible that she has left today.)

Departure	Statement of Possibility

Aujourd'hui
qu'elle **soit partie**   Il est possible

Il est possible qu'elle **soit partie** aujourd'hui. (We do not know if she left, but if she did, it would already have happened. Her departure precedes our stating it is possible.)

Je suis contente que vous **finissiez** ce livre. (I am happy that you finish this book either now as we speak, or anytime in the future.)

Je suis contente que vous **ayez fini** ce livre. (I am happy that you have finished this book.)

Je suis contente	que vous finissiez ce livre
Statement of Satisfaction	Completion of the book
NOW	Any time on, including now

Je suis contente	que vous **ayez fini** ce livre	
Completion of the book		Statement of Satisfaction
Anytime before Now, excluding now		**NOW**

> **NOTE** Choosing the present subjunctive or past subjunctive does not depend on the tense in the principal clause. **All combinations are possible.** What matters is when the subjunctive action was scheduled in regard to the trigger in the principal clause. **If the subjective action happened after the principal action, it must be a present subjunctive. If it was scheduled to happen before, it must be a past subjunctive.**

Possible Uses of the Subjunctive

TIP BOX

Always draw a time line to verify the order of actions, and use the subordinate tense according to when the principal action is scheduled.

Indicative Present / Subjunctive Present

Stéphane **est** si triste que Sophie ne **l'appelle** pas.

Stéphane est si triste que Sophie ne l'appelle pas.			
Past	**Present**	Future	
	Sadness		
	Sophie not calling	Sophie not calling	Sophie not calling

Sadness and absence happen together now. Sophie not calling may go on in the future. *(Stephane is so sad that Sophie is not calling.)*

Indicative Present / Subjunctive Past

Stéphane **est** si triste que Sophie ne **l'ait** pas **appelé**.

Stéphane est si triste que Sophie ne l'**ait** pas **appelé**.			
Past	**Present**	Future	Future
	Sadness		
Sophie not calling			

Sadness happens now as result of the absence of a call before. *(Stephane is so sad that Sophie did not call.)*

Indicative Past / Subjunctive Past

Stéphane **était** si triste que Sophie ne l'**ait** pas **appelé**.

Stéphane était si triste que Sophie ne l'**ai** pas **appelé**.			
	Past	**Present**	Future
	Sadness		
Sophie not calling			

Sadness resulted in the past from an anterior absence of a call. *(Stephane was so sad that Sophie had not called.)*

Indicative Future / Subjunctive Present

Stéphane **sera** si triste que Sophie ne l'**appelle** pas.

Stéphane sera triste que Sophie ne l'**appelle** pas.			
Past	**Present**	Future	Future
		Sadness	
		Sophie not calling	Sophie not calling

Sadness will happen as the absence is noticed in the future. The absence of a call may continue in the future. *(Stephane will be so sad if Sophie does not call.)*

Indicative Future / Subjunctive Past

Stéphane **sera** si triste que Sophie ne **l'ait** pas **appelé**.

Stéphane sera si triste que Sophie ne l'**ait pas appelé**.			
Past	**Present**	Future	Future
		Sadness	
Sophie not calling	Sophie not calling		

Sadness will happen after the prior absence of a phone call has been noted.
(Stephane will be so sad that Sophie did not call.)

Conditional Present / Subjunctive Present

Stéphane **serait** si triste que Sophie ne l'appelle pas.

Stéphane serait si triste que Sophie ne l'**appelle** pas.			
		Sadness	
		Sophie not calling	
Past	**Present**	Future	Future

Sadness would happen if the absence happened too.
(Stephane would be so sad if Sophie was not calling.)

Conditional Past / Subjunctive Past

Stéphane **aurait été** si triste que Sophie ne l'**ait** pas **appelé**.

Stéphane aurait été si triste que Sophie ne l'**ait** pas appelé.			
	Sadness		
Sophie not calling			
Past	Past	**Present**	Future

Sadness would have happened if Sophie had not called prior to that.
(Stephane would have been so sad if Sophie had not called.)

IMPORTANT!

The variety of English translations demonstrates that you should not rely on the English sentences to decide to use a subjunctive or not.

Every time you have to write a compound sentence, pay attention to the French Principal Clause and always look in it for one of the four flags:

- verbs
- expressions
- conjunctions
- adjectives

of will, desire, wish, opinion, doubt, judgment, emotion, etc., that may signal a shift to subjectivity and trigger the subjunctive.

TIP

As a general rule, do not ask yourself "What is the French word for . . ." but "How do the French people express this situation?" If you have read this book, the answer coming to your mind should now be a logical rule to rely on, instead of vocabulary.

Example:

I want my boyfriend to wash the dishes.

Incorrect Question: ~~"What is the word for want?"~~
Correct Reaction: *"Want? That rings a bell . . . To want is a verb of will. I want someone to do something for me, but I am not sure that he will do it. That depends upon him. I have no control over him because he is a free individual. And my thinking that he has to do the dishes is very subjective; he always thinks he has already done his share of the chores today. Subjective! I know . . . the* **subjunctive***!*

Want = **vouloir** *in the principal (me!) +* **QUE** *to introduce the subordinate (him, I wish!)*

Je veux que mon petit ami . . .

What is **faire** in the subjunctive? Better check in my recapitulation table.

fass-

Je veux que mon petit ami fasse la vaisselle. That's it, perfect French! I will write a note and put it on the fridge with the French magnets he gave me. Now let's hope he has already read the subjunctive chapter . . .

Le Mode Subjonctif	**La Mode** Subjective

To conclude with the mood and fashion analogy—**le mode et la mode**—how would you dress your verbs in the subjunctive? I see them as ambiguous as possible, such as outfits worn to cross genders or disguise yourself undercover. The "look" would reflect that which other people want you to do or how you would like them to respond to your desires, which is highly unpredictable: **insaisissable**. As the French existentialist and humanist philosopher Jean-Paul Sartre said: "L'enfer. c'est les autres." (*Hell is other people.*) But others can also turn our life into a paradise, if they want to!

MYSTIC METHOD: ENTERING THE SUBJECTIVE ZONE—USING THE SUBJUNCTIVE MOOD

Principal Clause: Subject S1 + Flag Verb or Trigger + QUE + Subject S2 + Verb in Subjunctive: Subordinate Clause

Subject S1 of the Principal Clause	Flag and Triggers Gate to *the Subjective Zone*	Subordinate Subject S2 + Subjunctive
Will Desire Wish Command Judgment Opinion Advice Doubt Emotion Goal Dream Opposition Expectation Uncertainty Condition Provision Requirement Disagreement Prerequisite	Verbs Impersonal Expressions Adjectives Conjunctions	LACK OF CONTROL

Ted ordonne que

Guy attend bien que

Simon est triste que

Il est nécessaire que

REVIEW TABLE: ALL MOODS AND TENSES CHARACTERISTICS AND FORMATION	
Subjunctive	*Action is completely up to someone else's decision—out of my control*

Stem + Présent or Imparfait endings	Auxiliary verb **Être** or **Avoir**	+ Past Participle
-e, -es, -e -ions, -iez, -ent	sois, sois, soit, soyons, soyez, soient aie, aies, ait, ayons, ayez, aient	**Subjonctif Passé** **je sois venu . . .** **j'aie fait . . .**

4 triggers:
Verbs of will, desire, wish, judgment . . .
Impersonal expressions with same meaning
Adjectives of opinion, emotion, judgment
Conjunctions of subordination: pour que, bien que . . .

Conditional	*Action is dependent upon the realization of another action first—various degrees of dependency*

Stem of FutuRe Imparfait Endings	Auxiliary verbs **être** or **avoir**	+ Past Participle
-Rais, -Rais, -Rait -Rions, -Riez, -Raient	seRais, seRais, seRait seRions, seRiez, seRaient auRais, auRais, auRait, auRions, auRiez, auraient	**Conditionnel Passé** **je serais venu . . .** **j'aurai fait . . .**

SI + Indicative = Condition in the subordinate clause, conditional verb in the principal clause to indicate possible result

IMPERATIVE!			**ACTION IS NOT YET REALIZED BUT STRONGLY RECOMMENDED**

	Auxiliary verbs **être** or **avoir**	Présent Indicatif
2nd person singular - s 1st person plural	Sois! Soyons! Soyez! Aie! Ayons! Ayez!	_____e! _____ons!
2nd Person plural		_____ez!

Indicative

Simple Tenses		Imparfait	Présent		Futur
Compound Tenses	Plus-Que-Parfait	Passé Composé		Futur Antérieur	
Action Order	#1	#2		#1	#2

Action is Real in the past, the present, or will be real in the future

Temps Simples	**Auxiliary verbs être and avoir**	**+ Past Participle**
Présent -e, -es, -e, -ons, -ez, -ent	suis, es, est, sommes, êtes, sont ai, as, a, avons, avez, ont	**Passé Composé** je **suis venu** . . . j'**ai fait** . . .
Imparfait -ais, -ais, -ait -ions, -iez, -aient	étais, étais, était, étions, étiez, étaient avais, avais, avait, avions, aviez, avaient	**Plus-que-Parfait** j'**étais venu** . . . j'**avais fait**
Futur -rai, -ras, -ra -rons, -rez, -ront	serai, seras, sera, serons, serez, seront aurai, auras, aura, aurons, aurez, auront	**Futur Antérieur** je **serai venu** . . . j'**aurai fait** . . .

Infinitive
3 groups: -ER / -IR / -RE

Action is only potential but completely feasible.

Practice What You Learned

Exercises are rated according to four levels of difficulty:

- Beginner easy [*]
- Beginner challenging [**]
- Intermediate [***]
- Advanced [****]

1. Rewrite the text in the **conditional**. [**]

Si c'était un monde idéal . . .

A. On **habite** dans de jolies maisons et nous **connaissons** tous nos voisins.

B. Chacun **a** un grand jardin et vous **êtes** heureux avec votre famille.

_____

C. Le lundi, les magasins **livrent** les courses à domicile pour la semaine.

_____

D. Le mardi, une équipe spéciale **vient** nettoyer les maisons gratuitement.

_____

E. Les gens **travaillent**, mais ils **choisissent** leurs horaires et **peuvent** rester chez eux.

_____

F. Les enfants **se réunissent** le mercredi et **font** une promenade ou **prennent** un bain dans la piscine.

_____

G. Le jeudi et le vendredi **sont** les jours de marché.

_____

H. Les artisans et les commerçants locaux **viennent** sur la place commune et **apportent** leurs produits.

_____

I. Le week-end, les adultes **reçoivent** leurs amis, les enfants **chantent** et tu **danses** et les animaux familiers **jouent** dans le jardin que tout le monde **cultive** . . .

_____

2. Rewrite the sentences transforming the probability into supposition with **au cas où** and the **conditionnel présent**. [**]

Example:

Appelle-moi si tu as un problème. Appelle-moi **au cas où** tu **aurais** un problème.

A. Dis-lui de venir si tu en as envie. _____

B. Je te raconterai une histoire si tu es sage. _____

C. Prévenez la concierge si vous déménagez. _____

D. Frank viendra te voir si vous le voulez. _____

E. Prends un livre s'il est en retard. _____

3. Identify the type of condition and the tense in which to conjugate the result verb accordingly. [**]

A. Si tu viens cet été, nous [aller] _____ danser à Monte Carlo.

_____

B. Si les hommes avaient été moins fous, il n'y [avoir] _____ pas cette horrible guerre.

_____

C. [Prendre] _____ une veste, si tu sors ce soir.

_____

D. Si tu étais gentil, tu [faire] _____ la vaisselle.

_____

E. Si Ed était encore plus gentil, il [passer] _____ aussi l'aspirateur.

_____

F. Nous [nettoyer] _____ toute la maison, si nous avions eu moins de travail à faire.

_____

4. Complete the following probable conditions with an appropriate result. [**]

ne pas manger à MacDonald—aller visiter St. Tropez—prendre un bateau—ramener des pâtes—venir au bal du 14 juillet

A. Si tu viens ce week-end, _____

B. Si vous allez en Italie comme d'habitude, _____

C. Si tu pars en Grèce, _____

D. Si je peux danser, _____

E. Si vous visitez la France, _____

5. Complete the following hypothetical conditions with an appropriate result. [***]

être très fiers de toi—gagner le prix Nobel—voir des gens célèbres—être heureuse—vivre en paix

A. Si vous trouviez la cure du SIDA, vous _____

B. Si le Président était une Présidente, nous _____

C. Si tu faisais des études de philosophie, tes parents _____

D. Si je pouvais gagner ma vie en écrivant, je _____

E. Si Bill allait à Beverly Hills, il _____

6. Complete the following regretful conditions with an appropriate missed result. [***]

> rencontrer le maire—peut-être aimer ce film—ne pas venir—
> s'intéresser à son cas—téléphoner

A. Si elle avait eu un portable, elle _____

B. Si vous étiez venus à la cérémonie, vous _____

C. Si je l'avais vu au cinéma, j' _____

D. Si tu avais su qu'elle était là, tu _____

E. Si nous étions avocats, nous _____

7. Complete the sentence with either the condition or the result of your choice in the appropriate tense. Keep the same subject and the same auxiliary verb in both clauses, so as to use a different one in each sentence. Pay attention to the agreement of the past participle. [****]

Offrir des cyclamens
Se consulter
Bien s'entendre
Acheter une grande maison pour ma mère, mes chattes, mon partenaire et moi
Mettre deux réveils
Devoir recommander un livre de grammaire

A. Si j'avais un million de dollars, _____.

B. Tu serais arrivé en retard, _____.

C. Si Cécile vient la voir, _____.

D. _____, nous ne nous serions pas trompés.

E. _____, vous diriez *French Grammar the Easy Way*!

F. _____, s'ils s'étaient parlé en classe de philo.

8. Conjugate the subordinate verb in the present subjunctive or not, depending on the verb in the principal clause. Note and justify your choice of mood. [***]

A. Ton frère pense que tu [avoir] _____ une petite-amie.

_____

B. Je ne dis pas que Marie-Hélène [aller] _____ se marier.

_____

C. Nous doutons que vous [obtenir] _____ un délai supplémentaire.

_____

D. Tu t'imaginais qu'elle [avoir] _____ tant d'argent?

_____

E. Il m'assure que nous [être] _____ sur la bonne route.

_____

F. Vous avez ordonné qu'ils [venir] _____ vous voir immédiatement.

_____

9. Complete the sentences with the appropriate impersonal expression and conjugate the subordinate verb in the subjunctive present. [**]

Il faut que—Il est interdit que—Il est impensable que—C'est un hasard que—Ça arrive que

A. _____ les enfants [conduire] _____

B. _____ tu [être] _____ Lion aussi.

C. _____ cet ordinateur [faire] _____ du bruit.

D. _____ nous [aller] _____ faire des courses.

E. _____ que vous [pouvoir] _____ voler.

10. Complete the sentences with the indicative or the **subjunctive**. [**]

A. Je crois que François et Francis (avoir) _____ l'intention d'emménager ensemble.

B. Tu es triste que nous (partir) _____ demain.

C. Elle est sûre que vous (savoir) _____ la vérité.

D. Nous pensons que ces enfants (grandir) _____ comme des asperges.

E. Vous n'espérez plus que votre client (vouloir) _____ signer le contrat.

F. Ils sont désolés que ce film (ne pas sortir) _____ en version originale.

11. Complete the text with the indicative or the subjunctive present and insert the subjunctive (triggers) in parenthesis. [****]

Example:

Les médecins préfèrent que ce patient [être] **soit** (préférer) isolé pour l'instant.

A. Ils exigent qu'une infirmière [faire] _____ (_____) une permanence auprès de lui et que personne ne [venir] _____ (_____) le voir pendant une semaine.

B. Ils pensent que cette maladie [pouvoir] _____ être contagieuse et sont désolés que tu ne pas [avoir] _____ (_____) pas l'autorisation de rester avec lui.

C. Mais il faut que tu [comprendre] _____ (_____) que ça [aller] _____ mieux déjà.

D. Ils savent que sa famille aussi [se sentir] _____ désemparée et regrettent que tes parents [devoir] _____ (_____) repartir demain.

E. Mais ils ne croient pas qu'il y [avoir] _____ (_____) un véritable danger.

F. Ils veulent que tu leur [dire] _____ (_____) tout pour qu'ils [partir] _____ (_____) tranquilles.

G. Il n'y a aucun doute que tout [finir] _____ bien d'ici la fin de la semaine, sans que ton frère [subir] ne _____ (_____) d'opérations.

H. Ils espèrent que tu [être] _____ content d'apprendre tout ça et désirent que tu [être] _____ (_____) rassuré.

12. Conjugate the verb in the present subjunctive or past subjunctive according to the chronology of the actions. Organize the actions on a time line if it helps. [***]

A. Je doute que l'avion (atterrir) _____ déjà.

B. Elle n'était pas sûre que tu (venir) _____ d'Allemagne ou d'Autriche.

C. Tu avais préparé le diner avant que je te (dire) _____ le nombre d'invités!

D. C'est un scandale que ce criminel de guerre (être) _____ libéré hier.

E. Il n'est pas impossible que vous [téléphoner] _____: il y a 16 messages sur le répondeur.

F. Pour que cela (finir) _____ bien, je prendrai toutes les précautions possibles.

13. Explain why the underlined verbs are in the indicative, the *italicized verbs* are in the *conditional*, and the **bold** verbs are in the **subjunctive**. [***]

"J'écris sans voir. Je suis venu. Je voulais vous baiser la main et m'en retourner. Je m'en retournerai sans cette récompense. Mais ne serai-je pas assez récompensé si je vous ai montré combien je vous aime? Il est neuf heures. Je vous écris que je vous aime; je veux du moins vous l'écrire; mais je ne sais si la plume se prête à mon désir. Ne viendrez-vous point pour que je vous le **dise**, et que je m'**enfuie**? Adieu, ma Sophie, bonsoir. Votre coeur ne vous dit-il pas que je suis ici? Voilà la première fois que j'écris dans les ténèbres. Cette situation *devrait* m'inspirer des choses bien tendres. Je n'en éprouve qu'une, c'est que je ne *saurais* sortir d'ici. L'espoir de vous voir un moment m'y retient, et je continue de vous parler, sans savoir si je forme des caractères. Partout où il n'y aura rien, lisez que je vous aime."

Note: You will find my translation in the Appendix, but you should also do your own.

si je vous ai montré: _____

_____

_____

que je vous aime: _____

_____

_____

si la plume se prête: _____

_____

_____

que je suis ici: _____

_____

_____

que j'écris: _____

_____

_____

dise: _____

_____

_____

m'enfuie: _____

_____

_____

devrait: _____

_____

_____

saurais: _____

_____

_____

si je forme des caractères: _____

_____

_____

que je vous aime: _____

_____

_____

APPENDIX

Solutions to Practice Exercises

Chapter 2
Nouns

1. La mayonnaise, Aïoli: une mayonnaise, 2 jaunes, d'oeufs, moutarde, sel, huile, d'olive, gousses, d'ail, Cocktail: soupe, ketchup, trait, cognac, traits, **Worcestershire**, sauce, gouttes, **Tabasco**, Verdurette: 2 cuillérées, soupe, herbes, persil, cerfeuil, estragon, ciboulette. (Proper nouns are in **bold**.)

2. Un garçon, une dame, un garage, un homme, une lionne, une pharmacienne, une étudiante, un musicienne, une assiette, une fourchette, une chienne, un monsieur, un téléphone, une bicyclette, un fromage, une télévision, une sculpture, un téléscope, un nuage, une baguette, une image, une balance, un bâtiment, une voiture, un bateau, une aventure.

3. A. Un cheveu blond—des cheveux blonds
   B. Un caillou bleu—des cailloux bleus
   C. Un bureau spacieux—des bureaux spacieux
   D. Un monsieur polis—des messieurs polis
   E. Un noyau très dur—des noyaux très durs
   F. Un cours intéressant—des cours intéressants

4. A. L'homme est un animal spécial.—Les hommes sont des animaux spéciaux.
   B. Le saphir est un bijou merveilleux.—Les saphirs sont des bijoux merveilleux.
   C. Le chien est un animal amical.—Les chiens sont des animaux amicaux.
   D. Le chou est un légume indigeste.—Les choux sont des légumes indigestes.
   E. Le zèbre est un cheval sauvage.—Les zèbres sont des chevaux sauvages.
   F. J'ai un marteau et un clou.—J'ai des marteaux et des clous.

5. Pour le confort de nos clients, dans tous les modèles Renault:
   (vitre) les vitres
   (chauffage) le chauffage
   (carrosserie) la carrosserie
   (pneu) les pneus
   (siège) les sièges
   (transmission) la transmission
   (frein) les freins
   sont de qualité exceptionnelle.
   Dans (modèle) *les modèles* de haut de gamme, comme (cabriolet) *les cabriolets* C3 Pluriel, (contrôle) *le contrôle* de (vitesse) *la vitesse* est électronique et (frein) *les freins* anti-dérapants. Ne craignez plus (pluie) *la pluie*, (neige) *la neige* ou (orages) *les orages* et en Citroën appréciez (paysage) *le paysage*!

Chapter 3
Articles

1. Les gousses, les oignons, les légumes, les extrémités, les poivrons, l'huile, les légumes, les tomates, l'assaisonnement, le bouquet, les gousses, la préparation, le basilic

2. A. D'après le portrait robot de la police: specified portrait
    B. le suspect aurait les yeux bleus: body part
    C. et un pantalon vert: generic, article could be **des** since **pantalon** can also be used in the plural, but here the adjective indicates **it is** in the singular.
    D. Il est sorti de la bagarre avec un oeil au beurre noir: here **un** is one of two eyes
    E. et le menton tuméfié: body part.
    F. Le pistolet lui a échappé des mains: the gun belongs to the suspect, it is specific, **des** is the contraction of the preposition **de** (after the verb **échapper**) and the article **les** for the body part.
    G. Le policier a réagi sans violence: no article after **sans** when it is generic
    H. et avec **le calme de tout professionnel**: definite article since it has a complement.

3. A. L'appartement de Samira est un appartement superbe.
    B. L'éclairage du séjour est vert et celui de la chambre bleuté.
    C. Au milieu du salon, il y a un podium avec des coussins de toutes les couleurs.
    D. Le plafond de la salle de bains est peint avec des étoiles argentées comme un ciel d'hiver.
    E. Le lit où dorment les invités est couvert d'un tissu en soie grise sans motif, mais il y a des palmiers verts et gris sur la tapisserie derrière le lit.
    F. C'est une chambre marocaine très exotique!

4. A. J'adore les gâteaux au chocolat: contraction of the preposition **à** and **le**
    B. Veux-tu du gâteau au chocolat: partitive article
    C. Elle ne lit jamais de magazines: preposition **de** after a quantity adverb
    D. Céline ne veut pas de la crème que tu utilises: partitive article because cream is specific, it is not about quantity, it is not wanting this very cream
    E. C'est une spécialité du chef: contraction of the preposition **de** and **le**
    F. La pâte de la tarte est légère mais croustillante: preposition **de** and **la**, which does not get contracted
    G. Donne-moi un morceau de la tarte: partitive article

Chapter 4
Prepositions

1. A. Le chat est dans la cuisine ou sur le balcon?
    B. Charles est assis dans un fauteuil devant la télé, son journal est sur la chaise à côté de lui.
    C. J'ai vu *Urgence* avec le Dr. Carter à la télévision mais I.A. de Spielberg au cinéma.
    D. Veux-tu faire un pique-nique dehors, sur l'herbe mais sous les arbres à l'ombre?

2. A. Marilyn Monroe (1/6–siècle)—le 1er, en juin, au vingtième siècle.
    B. Albert Einstein (14/03/1879/siècle)—le 14, en mars, en 1879, au dix-neuvième siècle.

C. Le prochain jour de l'an sera le mercredi 1er janvier 2003.

D. Quel jour êtes-vous né-e? Je suis né-e le.............................

3. La France,   le Japon,   la Chine,
le Texas,   le Chili,   la Russie,
le Pakistan,   la Hongrie,   le Pérou,
les États-Unis,   la Suède,   le Mexique,
le Portugal,   le Canada,   la Virginie,
le Mississippi,   le Tibet,   le Brésil.

4. A. Caracas est au Vénézuela.

B. Athènes est en Grèce.

C. Copenhague est au Danemark.

D. Munich est en Allemagne.

E. Tel Aviv est en Israël.

F. Osaka est au Japon.

G. Bagdad est en Irak.

H. Amsterdam est aux Pays-Bas—en Hollande.

5. A. Je suis hôtesse d'accueil à Roissy, à l'aéroport, au premier étage.

B. Je commence à 15 heures précises.

C. Je suis en meeting environ une heure, une heure et quart.

D. Parfois je travaille sans interruption de 19 heures le lundi à 3 heures le mardi. Je n'ai pas de voiture et vais au travail en car, ça prend environ une heure s'il n'y a pas d'encombrement.

6. A. Choisissez au hasard parmi ces cartes.

B. Des bateaux circulent entre Marseille et les pays d'Afrique du Nord.

C. Entre la ville et la campagne, je préfère la campagne.

D. À Paris il n'y a plus de métro entre 1h et 5h 30 du matin.

E. Parmi tous les moyens de transport à Paris, je préfère la marche à pied!

7. A. Nous reviendrons dans dix jours.

B. Vous avez loué une villa en Provence pendant deux mois.

C. Elle a improvisé un excellent repas en moins d'une heure.

D. Philippe doit présenter sa thèse de Doctorat dans quinze jours; j'ai soutenu la mienne il y a sept ans.

E. Les enfants dorment depuis plus de deux heures: quel calme!

F. Olivier va travailler pendant tout l'été.

Chapter 5
Functions of Nouns

1. A. Mlle Pervenche a tué le **Professeur Violet** dans la **bibliothèque**, avec la **corde**, en **secret**, **aujourd'hui**, à cause de sa **couleur** violette et pour **l'harmonie** du décor.

B. Docteur Olive a tué **Mme Leblanc** dans la **cuisine**, avec un **couteau**, en toute **sérénité**, la **semaine dernière**, à cause de sa **préférence** pour le vin rouge ou de sa **psychose**.

C. Madame Leblanc avait tué le **Colonel Moutarde** ainsi que **Mlle Rose** sur la **véranda**, avec le **chandelier**, à **Noël**, par **folie** et pour son **amusement**.

2. A. Nous sommes arrivés au café.
   B. Il y avait beaucoup de monde sur la terrasse.
   C. Je me suis assise sous un parasol et mon amie.
   D. Emmanuelle a regardé les choix de desserts.
   E. Ils étaient nombreux.
   F. Elle a choisi une glace.
   G. Une glace au chocolat a été apportée par le garçon.
   H. Ma crème brulée était délicieuse.

3. A. Votre petit ami achète **des fleurs**: direct—*des* is indefinite article
   B. Je me sers de **mon ordinateur** tous les jours: indirect—se servir *de*
   C. Veux-tu **mes clés**?—direct
   D. Cette robe va bien **à Marie**: indirect—aller *à*
   E. Il ne prend pas **de sucre** dans son café: direct—*de* is partitive article

4. A. Elle se déplace ✂<en limousine: avec quoi? complément circonstanciel de moyen
   B. Valérie adore ✂<la vanille: quoi? complément d'objet direct
   C. Blanche parle ✂<de ses vacances: de quoi? complément d'objet indirect
   D. Barbara part ✂<à Bali: où? complément circonstanciel de lieu
   E. Florentin ressemble ✂<à Séverin: à qui? complément d'objet indirect
   F. Les yaourts de Yolande sont ✂<pour son régime: pour quoi? complément circonstanciel de cause
   G. Donne-moi ✂<du chocolat: quoi? complément d'objet direct
   H. Elisabeth peut lire ✂<à toute vitesse: comment? complément circonstanciel de manière
   I. Thierry t'envoie ✂<des tartes tatin: quoi? complément d'objet direct
   J. Étienne étudie ✂<en vue de ses examens: dans quel but? complément circonstanciel de but

5.

Complement	List each noun you think corresponds to the category
Direct Object 18 complements	emplois, monde, 3000 personnes, commandes, anniversaires, l'esprit, du tonus, la courtoisie, BTS, l'enseigne, les échelons, le sens, des aptitudes, les connaissances, 1 200 euros, 1 500 euros, 2 500 euros, 3 000 euros
Indirect Object 13 complements	jeunes, 30 ans, profil, compétences, équipiers, hôtesses, accueil, comptabilité, gestion, aux clients, au management, une formation, un McDonald
CC Location 10 complements	comptoir, le terrain, au restaurant, au siège, au niveau, des restaurants, des ANPE, dans le secteur, sur le site, rubrique
CC Time 2 complements	chaque année, par mois
CC Manner 5 complements	en majorité, comme équipier, en hygiène et sécurité, au Smic, en cas d'ouverture
CC Means 1 complement	avec un niveau
CC Purpose 1 complement	pour les fonctions

Chapter 6
Qualifying Adjectives

1. A. **Alexandra** est **jeune** et **timide**.
   B. **L'infirmière** est **aimable** et **compétente**.
   C. **La boulangère** est **mignonne** et **drôle**.
   D. **Cette leçon** est **simple** mais **idiote**.
   E. **Ta soeur** est **forte** et **bronzée**.
   F. **Cette étoffe** est **blanche** et **douce**.
   G. **Barbie** est **canadienne** et **sportive**.
   H. **Érica** est **menteuse** et **manipulatrice**.

2. A. **Arthur et Jean** sont **petits**.
   B. **Ses parents** sont **roux**.
   C. **Charles et Paul** sont **originaux**.
   D. **Charles et Marie** sont **originaux**.
   E. **Françoise et Marie** sont **originales**.
   F. **Ces costumes** sont **marron**.
   G. **Ken et Frank** sont beaux mais **banals**.
   H. **La voiture et le camion** sont **bleus**.

3. A. La durée de vie moyenne est **plus** longue **que** pendant le Moyen-Âge.
   B. La nourriture est **moins** naturelle aujourd'hui **qu'**avant.

C. Les femmes sont **plus** indépendantes dans les grandes villes **que** dans les campagnes.

D. Les garçons sont **aussi** intelligents **que** les filles.

4. A. la soie / le lin—léger—le tissu
La soie est **plus légère que** le lin; le coton est **le plus léger des** tissus.

B. Le charbon / le pétrole—rare—la ressource
Le charbon est **moins rare que** le pétrole; l'uranium est **la plus rare des** ressources.

C. les pommes / les poires—cher—les fruits
Les pommes sont **aussi chères que** les poires; les papayes sont **les plus chers des** fruits.

D. le train / l'avion—rapide—les moyens de transport
Le train est **moins rapide que** l'avion; la fusée est **la plus rapide** des moyens de transports.

Chapter 7
Determinative Adjectives

1. quatre mille
trente-cinq
zéro huit, zéro zéro, quatre-vingt-dix, onze, quatre-vingt-quatorze
deux mille trois
cinquante mille
cent
soixante-quinze mille deux cent soixante-deux
zéro six
zéro un, quarante-quatre, trente-deux, dix-neuf, zéro zéro

2. A. 400 = quatre cents
B. 200 000 = deux cent mille
C. 92 = quatre-vingt-douze
D. 17 361 = dix-sept mille trois cent soixante et un
E. 5 948 203,29 = cinq millions neuf cent quarante-huit mille deux cent trois virgule vingt-neuf

3. A. Bernard et Bernadette partent pour <u>leur</u> voyage de noces.
B. <u>Leurs</u> valises sont prêtes.
C. Bernadette appelle <u>son</u> frère qui leur a prété <u>sa</u> voiture Jeep pour <u>leur</u> voyage.
D. Ils partent en Afrique, Bernard va voir <u>ses</u> parents qui y habitent et présenter <u>sa</u> femme.

4. A. Marc et toi—la maison: votre maison
B. Fabienne et Sophie—le prénom: mes prénoms
C. Karine—les livres: ses livres
D. Amélie—le film: son film
E. Éliane et Caroline—le script: leur script

5. A. Ces poires sont jaunes.

    B. Ce roman est passionnant.

    C. Cet hôpital a une bonne réputation.

    D. Cette histoire est si triste.

    E. Ces bâtiments sont très laids.

6. A. homme gentil—méchant

      Cet homme-ci est gentil; cet homme-là est méchant.

    B. tableau beau—cher

      Ce tableau-ci est beau; ce tableau-là est cher.

    C. Éclair au café—au chocolat

      Cet éclair-ci est au café; cet éclair-là est au chocolat.

7. A. Chaque être humain est unique mais nul individu n'est parfait.

    B. Certains hommes sont banals mais tous ont différentes qualités.

    C. Toutes les femmes ne sont pas originales non plus, mais c'est une autre histoire!

8. Hervé, <u>jeune</u> écrivain, était un garçon très <u>sensible</u>, particulièrement <u>doué</u> pour la littérature et <u>cette</u> forme de romans que <u>différents</u> critiques appellent intimistes. <u>Ses premiers</u> mois à Paris ont été <u>difficiles</u>, mais il a vite rencontré d'<u>importantes</u> personnalités de la société <u>parisienne</u> des années <u>quatre-vingt</u>. Il prenait de <u>superbes</u> photos de <u>chaque</u> personne <u>célèbre</u> qui devenait <u>son</u> ami: Michel, Isabelle et <u>autres</u> intellectuels ou artistes. Il mentionne <u>sept</u> ou <u>huit</u> de <u>ces</u> connaissances dans <u>son</u> roman le plus <u>célèbre</u> *À l'ami qui...* <u>Quels</u> hommes ou femmes se cachent sous <u>chaque</u> pseudonyme? <u>Quelques</u> noms sont transformés, <u>plusieurs</u> personnages restent plus <u>mystérieux</u>. Mais <u>tous</u> les acteurs de <u>ce</u> livre <u>autobiographique</u>, <u>vivants</u> ou <u>disparus</u>, restent <u>gravés</u> dans la mémoire de <u>ses</u> lecteurs. Hervé est <u>mort</u> trop tôt, de <u>cette</u> maladie <u>atroce</u> <u>appelée</u> le SIDA. <u>Quelle</u> perte pour la scène <u>culturelle</u> d'une <u>telle</u> époque.

En hommage à Hervé Guibert et Michel Foucault.

<u>jeune</u> qual. apposed	<u>sensible</u> qual. attributive	<u>doué</u> qual. attr. superlative	<u>cette</u> dem.	<u>différents</u> indef.	<u>intimistes</u> qual. attributive	<u>Ses</u> poss.	<u>premiers</u> numeral ordinal
<u>difficiles</u> qual. attribute	d'<u>importantes</u> qual. epithetical	<u>parisienne</u> qual. epithetical	<u>quatre-vingt</u> numeral cardinal	<u>superbes</u> qual. epithetical	<u>chaque</u> indef.	<u>célèbre</u> qual. epithetical	<u>son</u> poss.
<u>autre</u> indef.	<u>sept</u> numeral cardinal	<u>huit</u> numeral cardinal	<u>ces</u> dem.	<u>son</u> poss.	<u>célèbre</u> qual. epithetical superlative	<u>Quels</u> interrog.	<u>chaque</u> indef.
<u>Quelques</u> indef.	<u>plusieurs</u> indef.	<u>mystérieux</u> qual. attr. comparative	<u>tous</u> indef.	<u>ce</u> dem.	<u>autobiographique</u> qual. epithetical	<u>vivants</u> qual. apposed	<u>morts</u> qual. apposed
<u>gravés</u> qual. attributive	<u>ses</u> poss.	<u>cette</u> dem.	<u>atroce</u> qual. epithetical	<u>appelée</u> qual. epithetical	<u>Quelle</u> exclam.	<u>culturelle</u> qual. epithetical	<u>telle</u> indef.

Chapter 8
Personal Pronouns

1. A. Allô, Marc? Bonjour, **c'**est Marie.
   B. **Je** suis à Nice avec mon mari François.
   C. **Il** est ingénieur et veut travailler à Sophia-Antipolis. Nos enfants Charles et Julien sont ici aussi.
   D. **Ils** veulent te voir.
   E. **Nous** pouvons aller à Grasse chez toi cet après-midi.
   F. Est-ce que **tu** es libre?
   G. Si **vous** voulez, ta femme et toi, **nous** pourrions tous aller visiter les grandes parfumeries.
   H. **Elles** sont si célèbres!

2. A. *Ed et moi* arrosons les fleurs le samedi. Nous les arrosons le samedi.
   B. *Philippe* garde sa petite nièce. Il la garde.
   C. *Guy et toi* n'aimez pas les sandwiches au beurre de cacahuète. Vous ne les aimez pas.

3. A. *Sylvie et Sophie* téléphonent <u>à leur mère.</u> **Elles lui téléphonent.**
   B. *Ton frère et ta soeur* répondent <u>au professeur.</u> **Ils lui répondent.**
   C. *Leur ami* n'écrit pas <u>à ton frère et ta soeur.</u> **Il ne leur écrit pas.**
   D. *Ken et toi* envoyez des fleurs <u>à Barbie et moi.</u> **Vous nous envoyez des fleurs.**

4. A. Oui, **je vous l'envoie.**
   B. Oui, **je les lui laisse**.
   C. Non, **il ne nous la vend pas**.
   D. Oui, **elle me les prête**.

5. A. **Il m'en offre.**
   B. **Elle m'en apporte à Noël.**
   C. **Vous en empruntez.**
   D. **Ils en donnent.**

6. A. **Non, je ne les leur laisse pas.**
   B. **Non, je ne vous les donne pas.**
   C. **Non, nous ne leur en achetons pas.**
   D. **Non je ne lui en donne pas.**

7. A. **Vous y allez maintenant?**
   B. **Nous y sommes pour une semaine.**
   C. **Elle s'y intéresse.**
   D. **J'y pense souvent.**

8. A. Oui, je les utilise.
   B. Non, je n'y vais pas.
   C. Non, il ne lui parle pas.
   D. Oui, ils en veulent.
   E. Non, elle ne lui va pas bien.
   F. Oui, j'en fais.
   G. Non, je ne leur ai pas téléphoné.

9. A. **Bernard et Bernadette s'aiment.**
   B. **Tu te lèves tôt.**
   C. **Ils s'habillent.**
   D. **Je me pose beaucoup de questions.**
   E. **Nous nous écrivons souvent.**
   F. **Ils s'habillent.**

10. A. Roger est mon ami. **C'est** un homme bon et admirable.
    B. **Il** est médecin cancérologue.
    C. **C'est** une profession difficile.
    D. **Ça** demande beaucoup de gentillesse pour les patients.
    E. Être cancérologue, **ce** n'est pas comme les autres spécialités.
    F. **Ça** confronte à tant de souffrances.
    G. Et **ça** exige du courage et de l'abnégation.

Chapter 9
Demonstrative, Possessive, Interrogative, Indefinite Pronouns

1. A. Ta maison est très belle, mais je préfère celle de Mathieu.
   B. Ce garçon-ci est roux; celui-là est blond.
   C. Je voudrais ces boucles d'oreilles argentées et aussi celles en or.
   D. Tous ceux que Kévin portent sont des costumes Armani; ceux de Monsieur Alex Trebek viennent de Perry Ellis, je crois.

2. A. Tatiana—la tante: sa tante—la sienne
   B. Nicolas et Ninon—l'anniversaire: leur anniversaire—le leur
   C. Toi et moi—les livres: nos livres—les nôtres
   D. Vous et moi—les libertés: nos libertés—les nôtres
   E. Toi et ton ami—l'appartement: votre appartement—le vôtre

3. A. Cette ceinture est à Saturnin? Non, ce n'est pas la sienne.
   B. Ces livres sont aux étudiants? Oui, ce sont les leurs.
   C. Cet ordinateur est à vous, Odette? Non, ce n'est pas le mien.
   D. Cet ordinateur est à vous, Odile et Didier? Oui, c'est le nôtre.

4. A. Les enfants d'Annie sont adorables; les siens sont des démons (Valérie).
   B. Vos chattes sont mignonnes mais les miennes sont splendides (moi).
   C. La valise de Viviane est légère; la leur pèse une tonne (Aline et Aude).
   D. Ton bureau est loin; le nôtre est tout à côté (Luc et moi).

5. A. J'ai un Mac et un PC. Lequel veux-tu utiliser?
   B. À quoi penses-tu en ce moment?
   C. Qui est-ce qui va venir ce soir?
   D. Je vais acheter des piles, tu as besoin desquelles?
   E. Qu'est-ce que Léa veut pour son anniversaire?
   F. Elle ressemble à une actrice, mais à laquelle?

6. A. Gaëtan est un enfant très gaté. Il veut toujours tout.

   B. Ses parents lui ont offert beaucoup de jouets, et il en a cassé plusieurs.

   C. Dès qu'il voit quelque chose à la télé, un jeu, un ours, un ballon, n'importe quoi, il pleure pour qu'on lui achète.

   D. Il a tous les jeux électroniques, certains même en double bien que tous valent très cher!

   E. Quelqu'un dans sa famille devrait refuser ses caprices, mais dans les magasins, il crie très fort et rien ne l'arrête.

   F. Alors personne ne lui résiste.

Chapter 10
Simple Tenses—*Être* and *Avoir* Auxiliary Verbs

1. A. Je [aller] futur irai à la banque demain.

   B. Marc fait la vaisselle tous les jours pendant que Marie [préparer] présent prépare le diner.

   C. Quand elle [être] imparfait était jeune, Mère Thérésa [aider] aidait déjà les gens malheureux.

2. A. Charlotte et Serge sont en voyage.

   B. C'est le mois d'août et il y a beaucoup de gens en vacances.

   C. Ils ont trois filles: Christiane, Célestine et Sissy.

   D. Christiane a 9 ans.

   E. Céleste est plus jeune.

   F. Nous sommes leurs voisins à Antibes et nous avons trois garçons.

   G. Christiane, Célestine et Sissy disent toujours: "Vous avez nos maris."

   H. Et nos fils répondent "Nous sommes célibataires!"

3. A. Quand il avait 10 ans, Hector avait toujours faim.

   B. À dix heures du matin, il avait d'abord chaud, puis froid; il avait besoin de nourriture.

   C. Ses parents avaient peur pour lui.

   D. Il leur disait: "J'ai honte; quand je ne mange pas, j'ai très sommeil."

   E. Maintenant, Oscar sait qu'il avait tort d'avoir peur.

   F. Il mangera dès qu'il aura faim et il boira dès qu'il aura soif.

4. A. Hier j'<u>étais</u> au bureau.

   B. <u>Il y a trente-cinq ans</u> nous <u>étions</u> sur la lune.

   C. <u>Au siècle précédent</u>, les médecins n'<u>avaient</u> pas d'antibiotiques.

   D. <u>La semaine dernière</u>, vous <u>étiez</u> rousse!

   E. <u>Avant</u> tu <u>avais</u> souvent du chocolat mais tu es toujours au régime ces jours-ci.

5. Demain, je serai au Cap d'Antibes avec mes amis Vincent et Vladimir. Nous serons à l'Hôtel du Cap. Vincent n'aura pas de rendez-vous et Vladimir sera en vacances. Ils auront une partie de tennis prévue. Puis Vincent et moi aurons un grand diner à préparer. Vincent et Vladimir seront des chefs excellents. Il y aura un concours de cuisine à vingt heures. Les juges seront célèbres dans la région. Les invités auront déjà leur place à table et nous serons à leur service. Tout le monde sera en tenue de soirée. La soirée et les invitations seront intitulées: "Vous aurez faim? Bon Appétit!"

Chapter 11
Infinitive, Indicative, and Imperative Moods—
The Present Indicative

1. A. Je vais à la banque.
   B. Félicie arrive à huit heures tous les jours.
   C. Karine et toi finissez vos exercices.
   D. Tu acceptes sa proposition.
   E. Nous dînons au restaurant ce soir.
   F. Elle entend l'océan dans le coquillage.
   G. Jean-Paul et Jean-Jacques pendent un filet de tennis.
   H. Les gentils parents ne punissent jamais leurs enfants.
   I. Tu vends des olives sur le marché d'Antibes.
   J. Cette société fournit des ordinateurs gratuits aux écoles.
   K. Je ne crois plus ce garçon.
   L. Vous devez trois livres à la bibliothèque.

2. George <u>se lève</u> tôt pour <u>aller</u> tous les jours au gymnase. Il <u>met</u> un survêtement et <u>prend</u> son sac. Son ami Gérard et lui <u>sont</u> entraîneurs. Je les <u>connais</u> bien parce que nous nous <u>promenons</u> en vélo souvent. Je <u>m'entraîne</u> sur le tapis roulant avant de <u>partir</u> au bureau. Quand George et Gérard me <u>voient</u>, ils me <u>disent</u>: "Fab, tu <u>dois</u> aussi <u>faire</u> de la muscu mais sans <u>utiliser</u> des poids très lourds." Je leur <u>réponds</u>: "D'accord, mais vous, <u>venez</u> à mon cours d'aérobic alors!"

3. A. Ton petit frère est dans ta chambre, il joue et il crie. Tu dois étudier, tu lui dis: Sors!
   B. Tes parents vont rentrer de vacances et la maison est en désordre. Tu dis à ton frère et à ta soeur: Rangeons la maison!
   C. Ton ami joue du piano et cela te plaît, tu lui demandes: N'arrête pas s'il te plaît!
   D. La cigale a chanté tout l'été, la méchante fourmi, qui n'est pas son amie, lui dit: Eh bien, Dansez maintenant!
   E. Il y a trop de sel dans la soupe et ton patron invité à diner déteste le sel, tu lui recommandes: Ne mangez pas la soupe!
   F. Votre prof dit toujours aux étudiants: Étudiez!

4. A. Acheter le pain, 2nd p. pl.: Achetez-le! Ne l'achetez pas!
   B. Apporter de la glace, 1st p. pl.: Apportons-en! N'en apportons pas!
   C. Donner aux voisins, 2nd. p. sing.: Donne-leur! Ne leur donne pas!
   D. Écouter mon ami et moi, 2nd p. pl.: Écoutez-nous! Ne nous écoutez pas!
   E. Monter les livres au grenier, 2nd p. sing.: Monte-les-y! Ne les y monte pas!
   F. Rendre sa veste à Vladimir, 2nd p. sing.: Rends-la! Ne la lui rends pas!
   G. Avoir de la tolérance, 2nd p. pl.: Ayez-en! N'en ayez pas!
   H. Se cacher dans le garage, 1st p. pl.: Cachons-nous y! Ne nous y cachons pas!
   I. Prêter de l'argent à moi, 2nd p. sing.: Prête-m'en! Ne m'en prête pas!
   J. Être à la mode, 1st p. pl.: Soyons-y! N'y soyons pas!

5.

		s		a	i	e	
a	y	o	n	s			s
		y			n		
		e		o			
		z		y			
	s	i	o	s			
		s		z	e	y	a

- aie
- ayons
- ayez
- sois
- soyons
- soyez

Chapter 12
Past Indicative Passé Composé and Agreement of the Participe Passé

1. A. Ce matin j'ai retiré de l'argent au distributeur.
   B. Hier soir, tu as téléphoné à une copine de vacances.
   C. Cet après-midi, elle a mangé une tarte aux pommes.
   D. La semaine dernière, nous avons eu une panne de voiture.
   E. Vous avez fini vos exercices déjà!
   F. L'été passé, ils ont tourné un film à Cannes.

2. A. Hier, je suis arrivé(e) en retard.
   B. Ce matin je me suis levé(e) tôt.
   C. Hier soir, tu es allé(e) en boîte.
   D. Cet après-midi, elle est sortie à 16 heures.
   E. La semaine dernière, nous sommes devenus parents.
   F. Vous êtes déjà passé(e)(s)(es) devant cet immeuble trois fois!
   G. L'été passé, ils se sont mariés.

3. A. J'ai couru sous la pluie.
   B. Nous avons inventé un programme de fitness.
   C. Elles sont montées dans un taxi.—Displacement
   D. Tu t'es dépêché(e) de rentrer.—Reflexive
   E. Vous êtes entré(s) sur la scène.—Displacement
   F. Sissi a cassé le vase de Soisson.
   G. Cet homme est tombé amoureux fou.—Displacement
   H. Tu as attendu l'autobus.
   I. Isabelle et Nicolas se sont salués.—Reciprocal
   J. Ils ont pris un café au lait.
   K. Les touristes sont partis enfin.—Displacement

4. A. Vous vous êtes habillé(e)(s)(es) en tenue de soirée.
   B. Mes collegues se sont mis(es) au travail.
   C. Ta fille s'est amusée pour son anniversaire.
   D. Nous nous sommes promené(s)(es) sur le sable.
   E. Elles se sont perdues dans cette grande ville.

5. A. Les techniciens ont démonté la machine.
   B. Ils sont allés vérifier l'alimentation.
   C. Ils ont passé deux heures à la cave.
   D. J'ai posé beaucoup de questions.
   E. Un ingénieur a expliqué la panne.
   F. Nous avons écouté et nous sommes allés acheter la pièce de rechange.
   G. Ces gens sont enfin partis et le calme est revenu.

6. A. Karine (se lever) s'est levée <u>-s'</u> à huit heures.
   B. Elle (se faire) s'est fait <u>un café</u>.
   C. Elle (se dépêcher) <u>s</u>'est dépêchée de s'habiller.
   D. Elle (se maquiller) s'est maquillé <u>les yeux</u> en bleus et elle (se brosser) <u>s</u>'est brossée.
   E. Quand elle (se regarder) <u>s</u>'est regardée dans la glace, elle (se rendre) s'est rendu <u>compte</u> qu'elle ne (se plaire) pas s'est pas plu (plaire **à**: s' is an Indirect Object) dans cette couleur de Tee-shirt.
   F. Elle (se changer) <u>s</u>'est changée et (s'ajouter) s'est ajouté <u>du rouge à lèvres</u>.

7. La semaine dernière, mes amies et moi, nous (aller) sommes allées faire un pique-nique et nous (apporter) avons apporté des sandwichs. Nous les (manger) <u>les</u> avons mangés rapidement parce que les fourmis nous (trouver) <u>nous</u> ont trouvées et elles (partir) sont parties à l'attaque de nos paniers. Felicia (jouer) a joué de la guitare et (chanter) a chanté les chansons qu'elle (apprendre) <u>qu'</u>elle a apprises en Espagne. Nous (rencontrer) avons rencontré un groupe de garçons qui (passer) sont passés près de nous. Ils (se promener) se sont promenés dans la forêt et (ramasser) ont ramassé des champignons. Mais ceux qu'ils (trouver) <u>qu'</u>ils ont trouvés étaient vénéneux alors nous les (jeter) <u>les</u> avons jetés. Deux mecs sympas (rester) sont restés pour nous aider à tout ranger. Ils nous (proposer) ont proposé de les revoir. Nous (prendre) avons pris rendez-vous pour la semaine prochaine. On (se séparer) s'est séparé sur le parking et je (penser) ai pensé qu'on (passer) a passé une excellente journée. Nous (s'amuser) <u>nous</u> sommes amusés tous et toutes comme des fous!

8.

Example: **a tué**: **passé composé**, single event, rapid action that is over now and not ongoing in the present, interrupts the normal life.	

	adorait: **imparfait**, long lasting, emotion, action can still be going on in the present

❝ Malade, ma nièce a tué son fils qu'elle adorait ❞

Ma nièce est dans une situation épouvantable. Elle est en prison pour avoir tué son fils. Un enfant qu'elle adorait. Ma nièce était en instance de divorce, accablée par les dettes et sa maladie, une sclérose en plaques. Le jour où le drame a eu lieu, elle n'était pas elle-même. Elle avait mélangé médicaments et alcool et son cerveau a disjoncté. Elle s'était enfermée dans sa maison avec ses enfants, sa fille a pu s'échapper pour demander de l'aide, car elle voyait que sa mère n'était pas comme d'habitude. Quand elle s'est retrouvée en garde à vue, elle se demandait ce qu'elle faisait là. Les gendarmes lui ont expliqué les faits, et elle s'est effondrée. Si je vous écris, c'est parce que ma nièce se laisse mourir. La seule raison de se battre serait qu'elle puisse voir sa fille plus souvent, mais je ne sais pas comment faire. On ne peut pas s'imaginer ce que c'est la prison. On est coupé du monde. Alors, si des personnes ont vécu une telle atrocité ou ont souffert d'avoir perdu un enfant, qu'ils lui écrivent pour la réconforter. Bien amicalement.

André, réf. 951.02

était en instance: **imparfait**, description, action was interrupted by the drama
a eu lieu: **passé composé**, single event, dramatic point in time that interrupts the normal ongoing life
n'était pas elle-même: **imparfait**, description, action was interrupted by the drama
a disjoncté: **passé composé**, single event, dramatic instant that launches the drama
a pu s'échapper: **passé composé**, single event, rapid action
voyait: **imparfait**, description, action of looking at the mother was taking a while before the girl realized it
n'était pas comme d'habitude: **imparfait**, description, action was ongoing for a while, considered in its extension
s'est retrouvée: **passé composé**, single event, action considered as a result: finally arrested
se demandait: **imparfait**, emotional state, action was ongoing for a while as the mother was trying to understand what had happened
faisait là: **imparfait**, description, action was ongoing while the mother was in custody
ont expliqué: **passé composé**, single event, action considered as one block: the explanation
s'est effondrée: **passé composé**, single event, rapid and brusk action
ont vécu: **passé composé**, single event, action is now over: this experience would be completed in the past of other people
ont souffert: **passé composé**, single event, action is now over: this experience would be completed in the past of other people

Chapter 13
Indicative Mood—Past and Future Tenses:
Imperfect—Pluperfect/Future—Future Perfect

1. A. Il (être) une fois une princesse. Narration: était
   B. Les enfants (attendre) Noël impatiemment. Regularity: attendaient
   C. Je (arriver) à mon bureau au moment de l'attentat. Interruption: arrivais
   D. Pascal (travailler) comme moniteur de ski de décembre à février. Extension: travaillait
   E. Il (diriger) les gentils organisateurs au Club Med tous les étés. Repetition: dirigeait
   F. Nous (s'amuser) dans la cabane construite par mon père. Narration: nous amusions
   G. Vous (sembler) triste et découragé. Emotion: sembliez

2. A. Mes chattes ont sorti les souris en peluche que j'<u>avais mises</u> dans leur panier de jouets.
   B. Tu <u>avais perdu</u> ce stylo mais je viens de le retrouver sous le canapé.
   C. J'ai revu ce célèbre philosophe que nous <u>avions rencontré</u> à Irvine.
   D. Fiona <u>s'était fiancée</u> avant d'avoir rencontré la famille de Florent.
   E. Vous ne vous rappelez plus ce que vous m'<u>avez écrit</u>.

3. A. Sylvia a fini la lessive qu'elle avait commencée hier.
   B. Marc avait rangé le garage que tu as nettoyé aujourd'hui.
   C. La voleuse était partie depuis longtemps quand les policiers sont arrivés.
   D. Je n'avais pas encore terminé mes études quand j'ai trouvé un travail.

4. Demain, j'irai à la plage. Il n'y aura pas de monde parce que ce sera le mois de septembre. Mais il fera toujours chaud et le soleil brillera. Le vent ne soufflera pas le matin et les vagues viendront doucement sur le sable. Je te téléphonerai pour te demander un matelas. Tu voudras me rejoindre avec tes enfants mais vous ne pourrez pas à cause de ton travail. Nous prendrons rendez-vous pour y retourner ensemble dimanche.

5. A. J'achèterai une voiture quand j'aurai passé le permis.
   B. Tu feras l'exercice #3 quand tu auras fait l'exercice #2.
   C. Il sera heureux quand il aura réussi.
   D. Nous plongerons dans la piscine quand nous nous serons mis en maillot.
   E. Vous débrancherez quand vous aurez enregistré les données.
   F. Ils protègeront tout le monde quand ils auront supprimé les véhicules tout terrain.

6. La semaine dernière. . . .
   A. . . . le spectacle (commencer) allait commencer sans moi.
   B. . . . je (laver la vaisselle) venais de laver et il fallait déjà préparer le repas.
   C. . . . vous aviez déjà oublié ce que vous (me dire) veniez de me dire.
   D. . . . tu étais encore en retard, mais nous (t'attendre) allions t'attendre.
   E. . . . ces idiots (répéter) allaient répéter la même propagande alors j'ai changé de table.

7. Quand Tofa (avoir) <u>a eu</u> deux ans, j' (chercher) <u>ai cherché</u> un futur mari pour elle. Je (vouloir) <u>voulais</u> des bébés chats et elle (se porter) <u>se portait</u> bien. Auparavant, elle (être) <u>avait été</u> souvent malade mais tout (aller) <u>allait</u> beaucoup mieux. Je (mettre) <u>ai mis</u> une annonce dans le journal de Ann Arbor qui (décrire) <u>décrivait</u> une jolie blonde aux yeux bleus. On (me recommander) <u>m'avait recommandé</u> de chercher un mari parmi les chats de sa race, mais j' (décider) <u>avais décidé</u> que la personnalité et la santé du futur papa (être) <u>étaient</u> plus importantes que le pedigree. Un couple de gens très gentils (m'appeler) <u>m'ont appelée</u>. Leur chat Mittens (avoir) <u>avait</u> d'immenses yeux bleus aussi et des pattes toute blanches. Si je le (désirer) <u>désirais</u>, ils (venir) <u>allaient venir</u> immédiatement le présenter à Tofa. Quand Mittens (arriver) <u>est arrivé</u>, il (venir) <u>est venu</u> tout de suite vers moi gentiment. Il (être) <u>était</u> encore plus adorable que ses "parents" le (décrire) <u>l'avait décrit</u>. Tofa ne pas (vouloir) <u>n'a pas voulu</u> l'approcher parce que c' (être) <u>était</u> leur premier rendez-vous. Mais elle lui (dire) <u>a dit</u>: "Quand vous (revenir) <u>serez revenu</u> une fois ou deux, je vous (laisser) <u>laisserai</u> jouer avec moi." Mittens (répondre) <u>a répondu</u>: "D'accord, quand je vous (revoir) <u>reverrai</u>, je vous (rappeler) <u>rappellerai</u> ce que vous me (promettre) <u>venez de me promettre</u>."

Tout (se terminer) <u>s'est terminé</u> bien, Tofa (avoir) <u>a eu</u> des bébés magnifiques dont une (ressembler) <u>ressemble</u> à son gentil papa comme une copie conforme. Elle (s'appeler) <u>s'appelle</u> Vanille parce que ces pattes (être) <u>sont</u> toute blanches aussi! Naturellement, je (garder) <u>garderai</u> toujours toute la famille avec moi!

Chapter 14
Structure—Affirmative, Negative, Interrogative Sentences and Clauses

1. A. Dans un pays fort lointain est née une belle princesse.
   B. Peut-être serais-tu venu si tu avais su.
   C. "Je vous aime," répondit-elle en rougissant.

2. A. Vous n'êtes pas encore au troisième étage.
   B. Il y n'avait pas beaucoup de biscuits au chocolat.
   C. Je ne suis jamais déçue par mes étudiants.
   D. Cet exercice ne paraît pas vraiment difficile.
   E. Paul ne te donnera que cinq Euros.
   F. Christian n'a aucune foi en Dieu.
   G. Madame Lefour ne les leur confie nullement.

3. A. Carla n'a rien mangé hier.
   B. Cédric ne les a rencontrées nulle part.
   C. Le chanteur n'a reçu aucun Oscar.
   D. Tes cousins n'auront guère été contents de leur séjour.
   E. Fab n'a aimé ni le beurre de cacahuètes ni le Dr. Pepper.
   F. Les étudiants d'À la Riviera n'y avaient jamais participé avant.

4. A. Est-ce que j'ai toujours raison?
      Ai-je toujours raison?
   B. Est-ce que Marianne est mariée à Marc?
      Marianne est-elle mariée à Marc?

    C. Est-ce que les caribous ne vivent pas aux Caraïbes?
       Les caribous ne vivent-ils pas aux Caraïbes?
    D. Est-ce que vous parlez français très bien?
       Parlez-vous français très bien?

5. A. Est-ce qu'un astronaute a marché sur la planète Mars?
       Non, un astronaute n'a jamais marché sur la planète Mars!
    B. Croyez- vous au Père Noël?
       Non, je ne crois plus au Père Noël!
    C. Sommes-nous au 22ème siècle?
       Non, nous ne sommes pas encore au 22ème siècle!
    D. Est-ce que Francis accepte la responsabilité?
       Non, Francis n'accepte aucune responsabilité!
    E. Y a-t-il des conséquences à ses actes irresponsables?
       Non, il n'y a nullement des conséquences à ses actes irresponsables!
    F. Aime-t-elle le chocolat au lait et noir?
       Non, elle n'aime que le chocolat au lait!

6. Personne n'est immortel. La plupart des gens oublient souvent que la vie et courte et ils **n'**en profitent **jamais** assez. Ils perdent du temps à se disputer et à **ne pas** voir les choses vraiment importantes: la paix, la générosité, l'amitié. À part les biens matériels, **rien ne** les intéresse. Pourtant, nous **n'**avons **guère** de temps devant nous, la moyenne de vie **n'**est **que** 72 années. Ce **n'**est **ni** long **ni** suffisant pour apprendre la sagesse!

Chapter 15
Sentences, Clauses, and Conjunctive Subordinates

1. A. Expressément visée par la Constitution de la Vème République, elle fait aujourd'hui partie de nos textes de référence.
      One conjugated verb (**fait**): 1 clause, independent clause, simple sentence
    B. La Déclaration des Droits de l'Homme et du Citoyen est, avec les décrets des 4 et 11 août 1789 sur la suppression des droits féodaux, un des textes fondamentaux votés par l'Assemblée nationale constituante formée à la suite de la réunion des Etats Généraux.
      One conjugated verb (**est**): 1 clause, independent clause, simple sentence
    C. Adoptée dans son principe avant le 14 juillet 1789, elle donne lieu à l'élaboration de nombreux projets.
      One conjugated verb (**donne lieu**): 1 clause, independent clause, simple sentence
    D. Après de longs débats, les députés votent le texte final le 26 août 1789.
      One conjugated verb (**votent**): 1 clause, independent clause, simple sentence
    E. Elle comporte un préambule et 17 articles qui mêlent des dispositions concernant l'individu et la Nation.
      Two conjugated verbs (**comporte, mêlent**): 2 clauses, principal clause: elle comporte . . . , subordinate clause: qui mêlent . . . , compound sentence

    F. Elle définit des droits "naturels et imprescriptibles" comme la liberté, la propriété, la sûreté, la résistance à l'oppression.
        One conjugated verb (**définit**): 1 clause, independent clause, simple sentence
    G. La Déclaration reconnaît également l'égalité, notamment devant la loi et la justice.
        One conjugated verb (**reconnaît**): 1 clause, independent clause, simple sentence
    H. Elle affirme enfin le principe de la séparation des pouvoirs.
        One conjugated verb (**affirme**): 1 clause, independent clause, simple sentence

2. A. Viens manger tes pâtes aux champignons des bois. 1 conjugated verb (**viens**)—Simple
    B. Je me demande si tu comprends. 2 verbs (**demande, comprends**)—Compound
    C. Il n'y a rien à voir à la télé. 1 conjugated verb (**a**)—Simple
    D. François parle comme s'il était bébé. 2 verbs (**parle, était**)—Compound
    E. Ton frère est fort et il est bronzé. 2 verbs (**est, est**)—Compound

3. A. Arthur parle japonais **or** il est chinois.
    B. Paul ne vient pas **car** il déteste le foot.
    C. Il pleuvra **ou** il fera beau demain.
    D. Il pleuvra **donc** il ne fera pas beau.
    E. Je l'aime bien **mais** il m'énerve souvent.
    F. Patricia part **et** elle emmène Marc.

4. A. Je <u>partirai</u> dès que vous <u>arriverez</u>.
        2 conjugated verbs (**partirai, arriverez**)—Compound sentence with **dès que**: conjunction of subordination
    B. Vous <u>êtes</u> en retard mais cela ne me <u>dérange</u> pas.
        2 conjugated verbs (**êtes, dérange**)—Compound sentence with **mais**: conjunction of coordination
    C. Quand le Professeur Derrida <u>parle</u>, ses yeux <u>brillent</u> d'intelligence et il <u>a</u> beaucoup de charme.
        3 conjugated verbs (**parle, brillent, a**)—Compound sentence with **quand**: conjunction of subordination and **et**: conjunction of coordination.
    D. D'ici un siècle ou deux, l'humanité <u>pourra</u> se reproduire par clônage: quelle horreur!
        1 conjugated verb (**pourra**)—Simple sentence.
    E. Bertrand lui <u>répète</u> qu'il l'<u>aime</u> mais Sybille ne le <u>croit</u> pas car c'<u>est</u> un menteur et elle le <u>sait</u>, ou bien elle <u>l'a deviné</u>.
        6 conjugated verbs (**répète, aime, croit, est, sait, a deviné**)—Compound sentence with **que**: conjunction of subordination and **mais, car, et** and **ou** conjunctions of coordination.

5.

Example: Je partirai dès que vous arriverez.	• Je partirai: principal • dès que vous arriverez: conjunctive subordinate
Vous êtes en retard mais cela ne me dérange pas.	• Vous êtes en retard: independent • mais cela ne me dérange pas: independent coordinated
Quand le Professeur Derrida parle, ses yeux brillent d'intelligence et il a beaucoup de charme.	• Quand le Professeur Derrida parle: conjunctive subordinate • ses yeux brillent d'intelligence: principal • et il a beaucoup de charme: independent coordinated
D'ici un siècle ou deux, l'humanité pourra se reproduire par clônage: quelle horreur!	Independent
Bertrand lui répète qu'il l'aime mais Sybille ne le croit pas car c'est un menteur et elle le sait, ou bien elle l'a deviné.	• Bertrand lui répète: principal • qu'il l'aime: conjunctive subordinate • mais Sybille ne le croit pas: independent coordinated • car c'est un menteur: independent coordinated • et elle le sait: independent coordinated • ou bien elle l'a deviné: independent coordinated
Ton patron exige que tu lui fasses un rapport hebdomadaire.	• Ton patron exige: principal • que tu lui fasses un rapport hebdomadaire: conjunctive subordinate
Ne sois pas en retard car c'est une surprise party.	• Ne sois pas en retard: independent coordinated • car c'est une surprise party: independent coordinated
Une fois que les enfants seront couchés, Papa Noël descendra dans la cheminée.	• Une fois que les enfants seront couchés: conjunctive subordinate • Papa Noël descendra dans la cheminée: principal

Chapter 16
Relative Clauses

1. A. L'étudiant **qui** travaille devant moi est américain.
B. Il parle avec un accent **que** j'adore.
C. Son livre **qui** est sur la table est un livre de grammaire.
D. C'est celui **que** son professeur a recommandé.
E. Il rend facile la grammaire française **qui** a la réputation d'être compliquée.
F. Ce livre génial **que** tu connais s'appelle *French Grammar the Easy Way*.

2. A. Cet étudiant **dont** je te parle s'appelle Loy.
   B. C'est un prénom **que** je trouve très joli.
   C. Son nom de famille, **que** j'ai appris ce matin, est Newman.
   D. Ça s'écrit comme l'acteur Paul Newman **dont** les films sont si célèbres en France.
   E. En fait, Loy ressemble un peu à cet acteur **que** j'aime tant.

3. A. Je connais un peu Loy **qui** est dans ma classe de mathématiques.
   B. Dans notre université **où** il y a beaucoup d'étudiants étrangers, Loy est différent.
   C. C'est le seul **qui** adore étudier la grammaire.
   D. C'est un sujet **dont** il parle tout le temps avec ses amis français.
   E. Il pose des questions **que** je trouve intelligentes.
   F. Il connaît les exceptions **dont** on discute. Il rend des devoirs **où** il y a très peu d'erreurs.

4. A. Vanessa Paradis est une actrice française qui est mariée avec Johnny Depp.
   Vanessa Paradis est une actrice française dont les journaux parlent souvent.
   Vanessa Paradis est une actrice française que le public américain ne connaît pas.
   B. La politique est un sujet difficile dont on parle beaucoup en France.
   La politique est un sujet difficile que les Américains évitent en famille.
   La politique est un sujet difficile où il n'y a pas de solution évidente.

5. A. La banquette sur laquelle vous êtes assis est confortable.
   La banquette est confortable.
   Vous êtes assis sur la banquette.
   B. Montblanc est la marque du stylo avec lequel j'écris.
   Montblanc est la marque du stylo.
   J'écris avec ce stylo.
   C. Muriel a deux collègues sans lesquels l'ambiance au bureau est triste.
   Muriel a deux collègues.
   L'ambiance au bureau est triste sans ces deux collègues.
   D. Le proverbe auquel je crois est "Impossible n'est pas français."
   Le proverbe est "Impossible n'est pas français."
   Je crois au proverbe "Impossible n'est pas français."
   E. Ce livre dont j'ai absolument besoin pour mes recherches est introuvable!
   Ce livre est introuvable!
   J'ai absolument besoin de ce livre pour mes recherches.

6. A. Les hamburgers **que** mes amis mangent sont mauvais pour mon régime.
   B. Paul m'envoie des messages électroniques **auxquels** je réponds toujours.
   C. Je suis contente de la solution à **laquelle** je suis arrivée.
   D. C'est une chanson **dont** le texte est très poétique.
   E. Au moment **où** cette actrice est arrivée, la foule a applaudi.
   F. J'adore ce parc **dans lequel** il y a une collection de bonsaïs japonais.

7. **Ce** qui est agréable, c'est de se promener sur la plage. Voilà **ce que** tout le monde doit faire après son travail: Marcher sous des palmiers, **ce qui** relaxe les muscles. **Ce dont** nous avons tous besoin aussi, c'est de regarder l'eau bleue scintiller. Je ne sais pas **ce que** tu penses de ma solution pour diminuer ton stress. Il y a la Méditerranée et beaucoup de palmiers, **ce à quoi** je pense toujours.

Chapter 17
Conditional and Subjunctive: The Higher Moods

1. A. On **habiterait** dans de jolies maisons et nous **connaîtrions** tous nos voisins.

    B. Chacun **aurait** un grand jardin et vous **seriez** heureux avec votre famille.

    C. Le lundi, les magasins **livreraient** les courses à domicile pour la semaine.

    D. Le mardi, une équipe spéciale **viendrait** nettoyer les maisons gratuitement.

    E. Les gens **travailleraient**, mais ils **choisiraient** leurs horaires et **pourraient** rester chez eux.

    F. Les enfants se **réuniraient** le mercredi et **feraient** une promenade ou **prendraient** un bain dans la piscine.

    G. Le jeudi et le vendredi **seraient** les jours de marché.

    H. Les artisans et les commerçants locaux **viendraient** sur la place commune et **apporteraient** leurs produits.

    I. Le week-end, les adultes **recevraient** leurs amis, les enfants **chanteraient** et tu **danserais** et les animaux familiers **joueraient** dans le jardin que tout le monde **cultiverait** . . .

2. A. Dis-lui de venir au cas où tu en **aurais** envie.

    B. Je te raconterai une histoire au cas où tu **serais** sage.

    C. Prévenez la concierge au cas où vous **déménageriez.**

    D. Frank viendra te voir au cas où vous le **voudriez**.

    E. Prends un livre au cas où il **serait** en retard.

3. A. Si tu viens cet été, nous [aller] irons danser à Monte Carlo. (probability: futur **irons**)

    B. Si les hommes avaient été moins fous, il n'y [avoir] aurait pas eu cette horrible guerre. (regret: conditionnel passé **aurait eu**)

    C. [Prendre] prends une veste, si tu sors ce soir. (probability: impératif **prends**)

    D. Si tu étais gentil, tu [faire] ferais la vaisselle. (hypothesis: conditionnel présent **ferais**)

    E. Si Ed était encore plus gentil, il [passer] passerait aussi l'aspirateur. (hypothesis: conditionnel présent **passerait**)

    F. Nous [nettoyer] aurions nettoyé toute la maison, si nous avions eu moins de travail à faire. (regret: conditionnel passé **aurions nettoyé**)

4. A. Si tu viens ce week-end, nous irons visiter St Tropez.

    B. Si vous allez en Italie comme d'habitude, ramenez des pâtes!

    C. Si tu pars en Grèce, tu prendras un bateau.

    D. Si je peux danser, je viendrai au bal du 14 juillet.

    E. Si vous visitez la France, ne mangez pas à MacDonald!

5. A. Si vous trouviez la cure du SIDA, vous gagneriez le Prix Nobel.

    B. Si le Président était une Présidente, nous vivrions en paix.

    C. Si tu faisais des études de philosophie, tes parents seraient très fiers de toi.

    D. Si je pouvais gagner ma vie en écrivant, je serais heureuse.

    E. Si Bill allait à Beverly Hills, il verrait des gens célèbres.

6. A. Si elle avait eu un portable, elle aurait téléphoné.

    B. Si vous étiez venus à la cérémonie, vous auriez rencontré le maire.

   C. Si je l'avais vu au cinéma, j'aurais peut-être aimé ce film.

   D. Si tu avais su qu'elle était là, tu ne serais pas venu.

   E. Si nous étions avocats, nous nous serions intéressés à son cas.

7. A. Si j'avais un million de dollars, j'achèterais une grande maison pour ma mère, mes chattes, mon partenaire et moi.

   B. Tu serais arrivé en retard, si tu n'avais pas mis deux réveils.

   C. Si Cécile vient la voir, Sylvia achètera des cyclamens.

   D. Si nous nous étions consultés, nous ne nous serions pas trompés.

   E. Si vous deviez recommander un livre de grammaire, vous diriez *French Grammar the Easy Way!*

   F. Trevor et Travis se seraient bien entendus, s'ils s'étaient parlé en classe de philo.

8. A. Ton frère pense que tu [avoir] **as** une petite-amie. **as**—indicative: **penser que** = exception

   B. Je ne dis pas que Marie-Hélène [aller] **va** se marier. **va**—indicative: **dire** = statement

   C. Nous doutons que vous [obtenir] **obteniez** un délai supplémentaire. **obteniez**—subjunctive: **douter** = doubt

   D. Tu t'imaginais qu'elle [avoir] **ait** tant d'argent? **ait**—subjunctive: **imaginer** = dream

   E. Il m'assure que nous [être] **sommes** sur la bonne route. **sommes**—indicative: **assurer** = certainty

   F. Vous avez ordonné qu'ils [venir] **viennent** vous voir immédiatement. **viennent**—subjunctive: **ordonner** = command

9. A. Il est interdit que les enfants [conduire] conduisent.

   B. C'est un hasard que tu [être] sois Lion aussi.

   C. Ça arrive que cet ordinateur [faire] fasse du bruit.

   D. Il faut que nous [aller] allions faire des courses.

   E. Il est impensable que vous [pouvoir] puissiez voler.

10. A. Je crois que François et Francis (avoir) ont l'intention d'emménager ensemble.

   B. Tu es triste que nous (partir) **partions** demain.

   C. Elle est sûre que vous (savoir) savez la vérité.

   D. Nous pensons que ces enfants (grandir) grandissent comme des asperges.

   E. Vous n'espérez plus que votre client (vouloir) **veuille** signer le contrat.

   F. Ils sont désolés que ce film (ne pas sortir) **ne sorte pas** en version originale.

11. A. Ils exigent qu'une infirmière [faire] **fasse** (exiger) une permanence auprès de lui et que personne ne [venir] **vienne** (exiger) le voir pendant une semaine.

   B. Ils pensent que cette maladie [pouvoir] peut être contagieuse et sont désolés que tu ne pas [avoir] **n'aies** (désolés) pas l'autorisation de rester avec lui.

   C. Mais il faut que tu [comprendre] **comprennes** (il faut que) que ça [aller] va mieux déjà.

   D. Ils savent que sa famille aussi [se sentir] se sent désemparée et regrettent que tes parents [devoir] **doivent** (regrettent) repartir demain.

   E. Mais ils ne croient pas qu'il y [avoir] **ait** (ne pas croire) un véritable danger.

   F. Ils veulent que tu leur [dire] **dises** (vouloir) tout pour qu'ils [partir] **partent** (pour que) tranquilles.

G. Il n'y a aucun doute que tout [finir] finira bien d'ici la fin de la semaine, sans que ton frère [subir] <u>(ne)</u> **subisse** <u>(sans que)</u> d'opérations.

H. Ils espèrent que tu [être] seras content d'apprendre tout ça et désirent que tu [être] **sois** <u>(désirer)</u> rassuré.

12. A. Je doute que l'avion (atterrir) ait déjà atterri.

B. Elle n'était pas sûre que tu (venir) viennes d'Allemagne ou d'Autriche.

C. Tu avais préparé le diner avant que je te (dire) dise le nombre d'invités!

D. C'est un scandale que ce criminel de guerre (être) ait été libéré hier.

E. Il n'est pas impossible que vous [téléphoner] ayez téléphoné: il y a 16 messages sur le répondeur.

F. Pour que cela (finir) finisse bien, je prendrai toutes les précautions possibles.

13. "J'écris sans voir. Je suis venu. Je voulais vous baiser la main et m'en retourner. Je m'en retournerai sans cette récompense. Mais ne serai-je pas assez récompensé <u>si je vous ai montré</u> combien je vous aime? Il est neuf heures. Je vous écris <u>que je vous aime</u>; je veux du moins vous l'écrire; mais je ne sais <u>si la plume se prête</u> à mon désir. Ne viendrez-vous point pour que je vous le **dise**, et que je m'**enfuie**?

Adieu, ma Sophie, bonsoir. Votre coeur ne vous dit-il pas <u>que je suis ici?</u> Voilà la première fois <u>que j'écris</u> dans les ténèbres. Cette situation *devrait* m'inspirer des choses bien tendres. Je n'en éprouve qu'une, c'est que je ne *saurais* sortir d'ici. L'espoir de vous voir un moment m'y retient, et je continue de vous parler, sans savoir <u>si je forme des caractères</u>. Partout où il n'y aura rien, lisez <u>que je vous aime</u>."

<u>si je vous ai montré</u>: **condition** is normally in the indicative, here in the present as it is likely his visit showed his love

<u>que je vous aime</u>: indicative and not subjunctive because there is no subjective trigger in the principal; **que** is followed by the subjunctive only if the verb or the impersonal expression belongs to the subjective "triggers" list; here the verb is **écrire**, which is an **objective** action.

<u>si la plume se prête</u>: **si** here does not express a condition but an indirect interrogation: a question the author asks himself: je ne sais si la plume se prête = "Est-ce que la plume se prête...?"

<u>que je suis ici</u>: indicative and not subjunctive because there is no subjective trigger in the principal; **que** is followed by the subjunctive only if the verb or the impersonal expression belongs to the subjective "triggers" list; here the verb is **dire**, which is an **objective** action.

<u>que j'écris</u>: indicative and not subjunctive because there is no subjective trigger in the principal; **que** is followed by the subjunctive only if the verb or the impersonal expression belongs to the subjective "triggers" list; here it is **the first time that**, which is an **objective** fact.

dise: subjunctive after the trigger conjunction "**pour que**," in order to, indicates a goal

m'enfuie: subjunctive after the trigger conjunction "**pour que**," in order to, indicates a goal

devrait: conditional because the situation is linked to the condition of her presence and it might be inspiring or not

saurais: conditional because he is careful and cautious not to leave in case she arrived si je forme des caractères: indicative because **si** here expresses an indirect interrogation: a question the author asks himself: je ne sais si la plume se prête = "Est-ce que je forme des caractères . . . ?"

que je vous aime: indicative and not subjunctive because there is no subjective trigger in the principal; **que** is followed by the subjunctive only if the verb or the impersonal expression belongs to the subjective "triggers" list: here the verb is **lisez in the imperative**, which is an **objective** request.

"I write without seeing. I came by. I wanted to kiss your hand and leave. I will leave without this reward. But won't I be rewarded enough if I showed you how much I love you? It is 9 in the evening. I am writing that I love you, at least, that is what I want to write you, but I do not know if the quill complies with my desire. Won't you arrive so I can tell you so before I flee? Farewell, my Sophie, good night. Didn't your heart tell you that I was here? This is the first time that I write in the darkness. This situation should inspire me very tender things. I only feel one, that I could not possibly go away from here. The hope to see you for but a moment holds me back, and I continue to talk to you, without knowing if I am forming letters. Everywhere there will be nothing, read that I love you."

INDEX

Page numbers followed by "t" refer to tables

NOTES

NOTES

NOTES

NOTES

Helpful Guides for Mastering a Foreign Language

 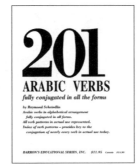 

2001 Idiom Series

Indispensable resources, these completely bilingual dictionaries in four major European languages present the most frequently used idiomatic words and phrases to help students avoid stilted expression when writing in their newly acquired language. Each book includes illustrative sentences. Each feature is easy to locate and designed with clarity in mind.

2001 French and English Idioms, 2nd
0-8120-9024-1 $16.95, Can $23.95

2001 German and English Idioms
0-8120-9009-8 $16.95, Can $23.50

2001 Italian and English Idioms
0-8120-9030-6 $16.95, Can $24.50

2001 Japanese and English Idioms
0-8120-9433-6 $16.95, Can $23.95

2001 Russian and English Idioms
0-8120-9532-4 $18.95, Can $26.50

2001 Spanish and English Idioms
0-8120-9028-4 $14.95, Can $21.00

201 Verb Series

The most commonly used verbs are presented alphabetically and in all their forms, one to a page, in each of the many foreign languages listed here. Features of this series include discussions of participles, punctuation guides, listings of compounds, the phrases and expressions often used with each verb, plus much more!

201 Arabic Verbs
0-8120-0547-3 $13.95, Can $17.95

201 Dutch Verbs
0-8120-0738-7 $13.95, Can $19.50

201 Modern Greek Verbs
0-8120-0475-2 $13.95, Can $19.95

301 Polish Verbs
0-7641-1029-9 $16.95, Can $24.50

201 Swedish Verbs
0-8120-0528-7 $15.95, Can $23.50

201 Turkish Verbs
0-8120-2034-0 $14.95, Can $21.00

501 Verb Series

Here is a series to help the foreign language student successfully approach verbs and all their details. Complete conjugations of the verbs are arranged one verb to a page in alphabetical order. Verb forms are printed in bold-face type in two columns, and common idioms using the applicable verbs are listed at the bottom of the page in each volume.

501 English Verbs
0-7641-0304-0 $14.95, Can $19.95

501 French Verbs, 4th
0-7641-2429-3 $14.95, Can $21.95

501 German Verbs, 3rd
0-7641-0284-2 $14.95, Can $19.95

501 Hebrew Verbs
0-8120-9468-9 $18.95, Can $27.50

501 Italian Verbs
0-7641-1348-8 $14.95, Can $21.00

501 Japanese Verbs, 2nd
0-7641-0285-0 $16.95, Can $23.95

501 Latin Verbs
0-8120-9050-9 $16.95, Can $23.95

501 Portuguese Verbs
0-8120-9034-9 $16.95, Can $23.95

501 Russian Verbs
0-7641-1349-6 $14.95, Can $21.00

501 Spanish Verbs, 4th
0-7641-2428-5 $14.95, Can $21.00

Books may be purchased at your bookstore, or by mail from Barron's. Enclose check or money order for total amount plus sales tax where applicable and add 18% for postage and handling (minimum charge $5.95). NY State and California residents add sales tax. All books are paperback editions. Prices subject to change without notice.

Visit our website at: www.barronseduc.com

Barron's Educational Series, Inc. · 250 Wireless Boulevard, Hauppauge, NY 11788
In Canada: Georgetown Book Warehouse, 34 Armstrong Avenue, Georgetown, Ont. L7G 4R9

(#33) R 2/04

NOTES

MOVE TO THE HEAD OF YOUR CLASS
THE EASY WAY!

Barron's presents THE EASY WAY SERIES—specially prepared by top educators, it maximizes effective learning while minimizing the time and effort it takes to raise your grades, brush up on the basics, and build your confidence. Comprehensive and full of clear review examples, **THE EASY WAY SERIES** is your best bet for better grades, quickly!

0-7641-1976-1	Accounting the Easy Way, 4th Ed.—$14.95, Can. $21.95
0-7641-1972-9	Algebra the Easy Way, 4th Ed.—$13.95, Can. $19.50
0-7641-1973-7	American History the Easy Way, 3rd Ed.—$14.95, Can. $21.00
0-7641-0299-0	American Sign Language the Easy Way—$14.95, Can. $21.00
0-7641-1979-6	Anatomy and Physiology the Easy Way—$14.95, Can. $21.95
0-8120-9410-7	Arithmetic the Easy Way, 3rd Ed.—$14.95, Can. $21.95
0-7641-1358-5	Biology the Easy Way, 3rd Ed.—$14.95, Can. $21.95
0-7641-1079-9	Bookkeeping the Easy Way, 3rd Ed.—$14.95, Can. $21.00
0-8120-4760-5	Business Law the Easy Way—$14.95, Can. $21.00
0-7641-0314-8	Business Letters the Easy Way, 3rd Ed.—$13.95, Can. $19.50
0-7641-1359-3	Business Math the Easy Way, 3rd Ed.—$14.95, Can. $21.00
0-8120-9141-8	Calculus the Easy Way, 3rd Ed.—$13.95, Can. $19.50
0-7641-1978-8	Chemistry the Easy Way, 4th Ed.—$14.95, Can. $21.95
0-7641-0659-7	Chinese the Easy Way—$14.95, Can. $21.00
0-7641-2579-6	Creative Writing the Easy Way—$12.95, Can. $18.95
0-7641-2146-4	Earth Science The Easy Way—$14.95, Can. $21.95
0-7641-1981-8	Electronics the Easy Way, 4th Ed.—$14.95, Can. $21.00
0-7641-1975-3	English the Easy Way, 4th Ed.—$13.95, Can. $19.50
0-8120-9505-7	French the Easy Way, 3rd Ed.—$14.95, Can. $21.00
0-7641-2435-8	French Grammar the Easy Way—$14.95, Can. $21.95
0-7641-0110-2	Geometry the Easy Way, 3rd Ed.—$14.95, Can. $21.00
0-8120-9145-0	German the Easy Way, 2nd Ed.—$14.95, Can. $21.00
0-7641-1989-3	Grammar the Easy Way—$14.95, Can. $21.00
0-8120-9146-9	Italian the Easy Way, 2nd Ed.—$14.95, Can. $21.95
0-8120-9627-4	Japanese the Easy Way—$14.95, Can. $21.00
0-7641-0752-6	Java™ Programming the Easy Way—$18.95, Can. $25.50
0-7641-2011-5	Math the Easy Way, 4th Ed.—$13.95, Can. $19.50
0-7641-1871-4	Math Word Problems the Easy Way—$14.95, Can. $21.00
0-8120-9601-0	Microeconomics the Easy Way—$14.95, Can. $21.00
0-7641-0236-2	Physics the Easy Way, 3rd Ed.—$14.95, Can. $21.00
0-7641-2393-9	Psychology the Easy Way—$14.95, Can. $21.95
0-7641-2263-0	Spanish Grammar—$14.95, Can. $21.00
0-7641-1974-5	Spanish the Easy Way, 3rd Ed.—$13.95, Can. $19.50
0-8120-9852-8	Speed Reading the Easy Way—$14.95, Can. $21.95
0-8120-9143-4	Spelling the Easy Way, 3rd Ed.—$13.95, Can. $19.50
0-8120-9392-5	Statistics the Easy Way, 3rd Ed.—$14.95, Can. $21.00
0-7641-1360-7	Trigonometry the Easy Way, 3rd Ed.—$14.95, Can. $21.00
0-8120-9147-7	Typing the Easy Way, 3rd Ed.—$19.95, Can. $28.95
0-8120-9765-3	World History the Easy Way, Vol. One—$16.95, Can. $24.50
0-8120-9766-1	World History the Easy Way, Vol. Two—$14.95, Can. $21.00
0-7641-1206-6	Writing the Easy Way, 3rd Ed.—$14.95, Can. $21.00

Barron's Educational Series, Inc.
250 Wireless Boulevard • Hauppauge, New York 11788
In Canada: Georgetown Book Warehouse • 34 Armstrong Avenue, Georgetown, Ontario L7G 4R9
www.barronseduc.com $ = U.S. Dollars   Can. $ = Canadian Dollars

Prices subject to change without notice. Books may be purchased at your local bookstore, or by mail from Barron's. Enclose check or money order for total amount plus sales tax where applicable and 18% for postage and handling (minimum charge $5.95 U.S. and Canada). NY State and California residents add sales tax. All books are paperback editions.   (#45) R 2/04

NOTES